Inclusion and Resilience

MENA DEVELOPMENT REPORT

Inclusion and Resilience

The Way Forward for Social Safety Nets in the Middle East and North Africa

Joana Silva
Victoria Levin
Matteo Morgandi

THE WORLD BANK
Washington, D.C.

Library of Congress Cataloging-in-Publication Data

Silva, Joana.
Inclusion and resilience : the way forward for social safety nets in the Middle East and North Africa / Joana Silva, Victoria Levin, and Matteo Morgandi.
    pages cm. — (MENA development report)

Includes bibliographical references.
ISBN 978-0-8213-9771-8 (alk. paper)—ISBN 978-0-8213-9772-5 (ebk.)

1. Middle East—Social policy—21st century. 2. Africa, North—Social policy—21st century. 3. Middle East—Economic policy—21st century. 4. Africa, North—Economic policy—21st century. I. Title.

HN656.A8S55 2013
306.0956—dc23   2012047958

Contents

Figures

Tables

Preface

Transitions are defining moments for social welfare systems. Most social safety net (SSN) programs around the world were introduced during such periods (such as independence after the collapse of the former Soviet Union, Nepal's transition to democracy, decentralization in Indonesia, and regime change in Brazil and Portugal), and they remained in place afterward. Transitions are forward-looking times, when crucial rethinking takes place. In fulfilling people's aspirations of greater social inclusion and better access to economic opportunities, SSN systems come under increased scrutiny when key questions such as these are discussed:

- How much redistribution is optimal and on what terms?

- What are the basic goals and priorities for safety nets?

- What should be the range and scope of welfare systems?

- How can existing systems be reformed to achieve these goals?

Before the Arab Spring, many governments in the Middle East and North Africa tended to rely on a redistribution system that protected against destitution through universal subsidies of basic consumption items, which guaranteed affordable access to food and fuel for all citizens, irrespective of their needs. This system's only available response to crises was to scale up these subsidies or to provide more and better-paid public employment for middle and upper classes. While popular, this system was not sustainable. Perhaps even more importantly, it did not empower citizens to prepare for better livelihoods.

Today, SSNs in the Middle East and North Africa are ripe for reform, for moving forward on a path that goes from existing systems to ones that incentivize investments in education and health among the poor, protect adults and children against destitution, and help poor and near-poor households navigate the effects of shocks.

To better capture the spirit of the post–Arab Spring Middle East and North Africa, and to help in meeting the expectations of its citizens, this report was developed in an inclusive and interactive way. Its development comprised a variety of activities, all designed to share information and to capture the region's knowledge, preferences, and ideas for present and future SSNs.

Specifically, the report reached more than 4,000 Middle East and North Africa citizens through the nationally representative MENA SPEAKS surveys (fielded in collaboration with Gallup in the Arab Republic of Egypt, Jordan, Lebanon, and Tunisia), which inquired about citizens' attitudes on, knowledge about, and support for reform of SSNs in the Middle East and North Africa. This was an innovative way to collect systematic information on these citizens' views and ideas on the topic of safety nets. Moreover, the report reached more than 400 Jordanian middle-class citizens through a behavioral game (Jordan Gives), which collected information on revealed preferences for redistribution using real trade-offs, in a nationally representative sample of the Jordanian middle class.

The report also reached more than 250 representatives of government; academia; civil society; nongovernmental organizations; community-based organizations from Algeria, Bahrain, Iraq, Jordan, Kuwait, Lebanon, Morocco, Oman, Saudi Arabia, Tunisia, the United Arab Emirates, and West Bank and Gaza; and multilateral and bilateral donors (including the International Labour Organization and the United Nations Economic and Social Commission for Western Asia). These representatives participated in the regional consultation workshops in Beirut (January 13–14, 2012), Tunis (January 16–17, 2012), and Muscat (April 16–17, 2012). The workshops were organized jointly with the World Bank MENA Social Protection Strategy team, which allowed for leveraging the dialogue beyond SSNs to encompass active labor market policies and social insurance systems. During the workshops, the report's team presented a showcase of global best practices on SSNs using posters and a quiz highlighting key results and features that make SSN programs work. The team also moderated expert cafes/roundtables where more than 20 experienced SSN practitioners from across the region discussed openly their views on the way forward for SSNs in the Middle East and North Africa and shared knowledge on their experience with various aspects of SSN reform. Following up on these initiatives, the team reached out to governments and workshop participants to develop the MENA SSN Inventory (see appendix C), featuring each country's major SSN programs and their key characteristics (including program objectives and design, as well as recent estimates of budgets and number of beneficiaries).

This report, as well as the new tools that it developed for policy makers—including the survey instruments, the game, the posters, and the SSN inventory—all aim at enhancing knowledge about the state of existing SSNs and at informing the debate about their largely unexploited potential. By mitigating the costs of the unforeseeable, by placing the least-endowed on a path of self-reliance, and by reducing the social and political cost of transformations, effective social safety nets represent the policy lever that MENA countries can least afford to overlook during this epoch of change.

Acknowledgments

This report is the product of the collaborative effort of a core team led by Joana Silva and comprising Victoria Levin and Matteo Morgandi (principal authors), Mohamad Alloush (data management and analysis), Facundo Cuevas, Tarsicio Castañeda, and Carole Abi Nahed Chartouni. In addition, Victoria Levin and Facundo Cuevas supported at different stages the coordination of the project; Facundo Cuevas also helped to raise funds for the realization of the MENA SPEAKS survey and the Jordan Gives experiment. Bénédicte de la Brière, Ruslan Yemtsov, Karla Hoff, and Hana Brixi provided guidance and useful inputs at different stages of this report. Amy Gautam and Mary Anderson edited the report.

Background papers were written for this report by Tarsicio Castañeda, Facundo Cuevas, Abhishek Gupta, Mohamad Alloush, Carole Abi Nahed Chartouni, Yohana Dukhan, Paul B. Siegel, and Quentin Wodon. Anne Hilger, Rania Atieh, Yohana Dukhan, Haneen Sayed, Samira Hillis, Sherine Al-Shawarby, Dorothee Chen, Ezequiel Molina, Lillian Frost, Maaouia Ben Nasr, Sebastian Trenner, Hala Ballout, Kristen Himelein, and Yasmeen Tabbaa provided very useful inputs.

The report benefited greatly from the feedback received during extended consultations. In particular, we are grateful to representatives of government, academia, civil society, NGOs, and CSOs from Algeria, Bahrain, Iraq, Jordan, Kuwait, Lebanon, Morocco, Oman, Saudi Arabia, Tunisia, the United Arab Emirates, and West Bank and Gaza as well as to the International Labour Organization and the United Nations Economic and Social Commission for Western Asia, who participated in the regional workshops (in Beirut, January 13–14, 2012; Tunis, January 16–17, 2012; and Muscat, April 16–17, 2012) and in national consultations in Jordan (January 10, 2012). We thank the team that developed the World Bank Social Protection Strategy for MENA, and in particular Rebekka Grun (task leader), Surat Nsour, Victoria Levin, Sebastian

Trenner, Rania Atieh, and Nicole La Borde for co-organizing these workshops with our team.

We are grateful to Gallup, and in particular to Krista Hoff, Cynthia English, and Joe Daly, for guidance and effective implementation of the MENA SPEAKS surveys. We thank the Center for Strategic Studies at the University of Jordan, and particularly Musa Shteiwi, Yasmina Suleyman, and Walid Alkhatib, for guidance and effective implementation of the Jordan Gives behavioral experiment.

We thank our peer reviewers Margaret Grosh, Harold Alderman, and Lynne D. Sherburne-Benz for their valuable guidance and Lire Ersado for his helpful comments. We are also grateful to Jehan Arulpragasam, Trina Haque, David Coady, Haneen Sayed, Samira Hills, Ghassan N. Alkhoja, Jeffrey Waite, Nadine Poupart, Alaa Mahmoud Hamed, Surat Nsour, Mira Hong, Rasmus Heltberg, Umar Serajuddin, Hassan Zaman, William Stebbins, May Wazzan, Phillippe Leite, Nidhal Ben Cheikh, Mehdi Barouniand, Patrick Canel, and Paolo Verme for insightful discussions and feedback. This work was supported by the Arab World Initiative and by the Trust Fund for Environmentally and Socially Sustainable Development (TFESSD)—Social Protection Window. We thank Steen Jorgensen, Caroline Freund, Yasser El-Gammal, and Roberta Gatti for their strategic guidance.

Executive Summary

Transitions are defining moments for social welfare systems. Most social safety net (SSN)[1] programs around the world were introduced during transition periods (such as independence after the collapse of the former Soviet Union, decentralization in Indonesia, and regime change in Brazil and Portugal), and they remained in place afterward. When SSN systems come under increased scrutiny regarding their ability to fulfill people's aspirations of greater social inclusion and better access to economic opportunities, key questions are discussed:

- How much redistribution is optimal and on what terms?

- What are the basic goals and priorities for safety nets?

- What should be the range and scope of welfare systems?

- How can existing systems be reformed to achieve these goals?

The Arab Spring brought the need for social inclusion and a new social contract to the forefront. Countries in the region have been relying on a redistribution system that protected against destitution through universal subsidies, which guaranteed affordable access to food and fuel for all citizens, irrespective of their needs. Governments could respond to crises only by scaling subsidies up or by increasing the size and generosity of public employment. While popular, this system proved hard to sustain. Perhaps even more important, it did not empower citizens to prepare for better livelihoods.

Continued growth and poverty reduction, as well as a growing middle class in the Middle East and North Africa, go often hand in hand with chronic poverty and high vulnerability. Children and rural residents face a high risk of poverty, translating into disappointing human development outcomes. More than a quarter of children in the bottom income quintile in the Arab Republic of Egypt, Morocco, and the Syrian Arab Republic are chronically malnourished. By the ages of 16–18, children in the poorest quintile in Egypt and Morocco are more likely to have dropped out of school than to have continued studying. Low levels of human capital accumulation carry a higher risk of either unemployment or precarious employment in jobs with limited chances of upward mobility. When well crafted, SSNs can contribute toward breaking the cycle of intergenerational poverty by helping families to keep children healthy and in school. SSNs along with increased social services can also help to tackle the problem of spatial pockets of poverty in slums and rural areas by promoting the demand for safety net services and building community assets. In addition to those in chronic poverty, a large share of the region's population hovers close to the poverty line and exhibits low resilience to shocks. As many as 15–17 percent of Egyptians, Iraqis, Syrians, and Yemenis, and 10 percent of Moroccans, have per capita consumption levels that are no more than US$0.50 per day above the US$2 per day poverty line (in purchasing power parity [PPP] terms). If SSNs that help in navigating the effects of shocks are not in place, vulnerable households face a high probability of an irreversible loss of human capital during shocks. In addition to the poor and vulnerable, some social groups (such as women and people with disabilities) face particular barriers in gaining access to social services and labor market opportunities. Together with improved service provision, SSNs can help to start addressing these barriers.

SSNs in the Middle East and North Africa are ripe for reform. Most of the region's spending on SSNs finances energy subsidies, crowding out more effective interventions. Middle Eastern and North African countries spend, on average, 6 percent of gross domestic product (GDP) on subsidies. Fuel subsidies alone represent an average of 4.6 percent of GDP. In sharp contrast, other SSNs in the region are underresourced—receiving less than 0.7 percent of GDP, on average, and being fragmented among many small programs with significant overlaps. Most of the poor and vulnerable fall through the cracks: two out of three people in the poorest quintile are not reached by nonsubsidy SSNs. In fact, existing coverage of the bottom quintile in the region is less than half of the world average. Moreover, inadequate targeting results in significant leakages of SSN benefits to the nonpoor, siphoning off resources that could be used to decrease poverty and improve the distribution of welfare. The average nonsubsidy SSN program in the region distributes only 23 percent of its total benefits to the bottom quintile, while the corresponding figure for the average comparator programs in Latin America and the Caribbean and in Eastern Europe and Central Asia is 59 percent. Although subsidies (and in particular, fuel subsidies) are inefficient and frequently ineffective relative to other SSN interventions, because of their sheer size, many people depend on them to stay out of poverty. Moving from the status

---

BOX ES.1

Listening to the Middle East and North Africa

The activities conducted in preparation for this report reached more than 4,000 Middle Eastern and North African citizens through the nationally representative MENA SPEAKS (Social Protection Evaluation of Attitudes, Knowledge, and Support) surveys, which were fielded in collaboration with Gallup in Egypt, Jordan, Lebanon, and Tunisia. Moreover, the report surveyed more than 400 Jordanian middle-class citizens through a behavioral game (Jordan Gives) that collected information on revealed preferences for redistribution, using real trade-offs, from a nationally representative sample of the Jordanian middle class.

Through consultation workshops across the region, the report also involved more than 250 representatives of government; academia; civil society; nongovernmental organizations (NGOs); community-based organizations from Algeria, Bahrain, Iraq, Jordan, Kuwait, Lebanon, Morocco, Oman, Saudi Arabia, Tunisia, the United Arab Emirates, and West Bank and Gaza; and multilateral and bilateral donors (including the International Labour Organization and the United Nations Economic and Social Commission for Western Asia).

---

quo toward more effective, reliable, and equitable social safety nets requires careful thinking not only about the technical aspects of reform but also, and perhaps more important, about the sensitive issues concerning the political economy of reform.

Political economy considerations have been a major reason why SSN reform has largely stalled or never began in some Middle Eastern and North African countries; new evidence suggests that better information, improved design, and increased transparency of SSNs can help the region move forward. The region's citizens are expecting their governments to be more effective providers of SSNs that target the poor. New opinion surveys conducted in Egypt, Jordan, Lebanon, and Tunisia as part of this study (see box ES.1) reveal that close to 90 percent of citizens see the government as the main provider of SSNs. However, in Egypt and Lebanon, less than a third found the current SSN policies and programs effective, while in Jordan and Tunisia the poor reported much more dissatisfaction than the rich. The surveys also showed the uneven coverage of SSNs and, to some extent, their regressive nature. In Egypt, 23 percent of all respondents—particularly the poor—did not know any of the main SSN programs in the country, while in Lebanon and Tunisia, the rich were more likely than the poor to know an SSN beneficiary. In spite of their large fiscal cost, awareness of fuel subsidies is below 50 percent in all four countries. The opposition to subsidy reform varies strongly across countries (higher in Egypt and lower in Lebanon) and in terms of priority, with gasoline in Egypt, tobacco in Lebanon, and diesel in Jordan and Tunisia being the subsidies most accepted for reform. In addition to the opinion surveys, this study conducted a behavioral experiment (Jordan Gives) among a nationally representative sample of the Jordanian middle class, collecting information on preferences for redistribution to the poor using valuable trade-offs. This experiment showed not only that middle-class individuals support redistribution to the poor, but also, more important, that this support varies according to the design of the assistance and the credibility of targeting. Altogether, these activities suggest that (a) much scope remains to increase support for reform by raising awareness on the existence and true cost of subsidies; and (b) customizing the design of renewed SSNs can help to shift public opinion in favor of SSN reform. For instance, in all countries but Lebanon, those who approved of subsidy reform opted for a cash transfer targeted to the poor rather than more broad-based measures; in general, citizens showed a clear preference for SSNs that focus on the poor (rather than on specific groups) and that deliver cash (rather than in-kind benefits).

Recent experience has demonstrated the feasibility of SSN reform in the Middle East and North Africa. There are several examples of successful reforms that have attained significant positive results:

- *West Bank and Gaza* created a unified registry across SSN programs that significantly improved targeting accuracy and crisis response capacity.

- *The Republic of Yemen* responded quickly during the global economic crisis with a workfare program to bridge a consumption gap of the poor and vulnerable while also creating community assets. Simultaneously, important reforms were implemented in the main cash transfer program, the Social Welfare Fund, such as improving poverty targeting with a proxy means-test formula, strengthening capacity for service delivery, and implementing a new legal and policy framework.

- *Morocco*'s Tayssir program—a pilot cash transfer program conditional on school attendance and targeting areas with high incidences of school dropouts and poverty—has had a significant positive impact in reducing dropouts in rural areas, especially among girls.

- *Djibouti* has adopted an innovative program design to make a workfare program work for children and women.

- *Lebanon* recently launched a central targeting database (National Poverty Targeting Program), laying the foundation for an effective SSN.

- *Jordan* has made important steps toward rebalancing SSNs away from subsidies and developing a targeting and poverty reduction strategy.

The remaining key human development challenges in the region and the disappointing performance of existing SSN systems call for more effective and innovative SSNs that promote inclusion and resilience. Although there is no single solution, better results can be achieved through action on the following four agenda items:

- **Improving the impact of SSN programs in the Middle East and North Africa,** including their effect on present and future poverty. Currently, most of the region's nonsubsidy SSN programs have a limited impact on poverty and inequality because of the combination of low coverage (with inefficient targeting) and inadequate or nonexistent monitoring and evaluation (M&E) systems. Hence, the way forward on this front could entail the following:

  - *Prioritizing interventions that promote investment in human capital.* SSN programs should be geared to addressing the observed human development challenges, such as child malnutrition and school dropouts. This can be achieved by (a) scaling up the region's existing successful conditional cash transfer (CCT) programs (such as the Tayssir program in Morocco) and workfare programs (such as the Republic of Yemen's Social Welfare Fund); (b) tweaking the design of existing programs to make them work better for children and women (such as Djibouti's workfare plus nutrition program); or (c) creating new interventions to fill the gaps based on best practices around the world but adjusting their design to empower the poor and vulnerable. Given the reluctance to condition SSN transfers, as observed in the MENA SPEAKS surveys, a well-developed information and communication strategy about the benefits of this approach should precede the implementation of CCT programs in the region.

  - *Enhancing targeting toward the poor and vulnerable.* Improved targeting can contain costs, ensure equity, allow SSNs to act as insurance, and increase effectiveness. Most of the programs in the region remain categorically or geographically targeted, even though these methods are effective only in environments of concentrated poverty. At the same time, in the MENA SPEAKS surveys, citizens indicated their strong preference for poverty-based targeting as opposed to categorical targeting. There is already substantial movement in the region (as in Iraq, Jordan, Lebanon, West Bank and

Gaza, and the Republic of Yemen) in the direction of poverty-based targeting. Results in these places have demonstrated the power of such reforms and outlined a clear path forward.

○ *Improving the focus on SSN program results through M&E and social accountability.* In the Middle East and North Africa, enhanced M&E for SSNs can help allocate budget resources among programs, monitor day-to-day operations, and track the results of interventions. M&E has been particularly effective when the evaluation results and empirical data are used to inform budgetary decisions and reshape programs. This was the case in West Bank and Gaza and the Republic of Yemen. Moreover, introducing well-functioning social accountability systems can improve efficiency and accountability and combat corruption.

○ *Reaching out to other stakeholders (citizens, NGOs, civil society organizations [CSOs], the private sector, and nonprofits).* Citizens' awareness about existing SSN programs is low and skewed toward the wealthy. On-demand registration requires awareness about the existence of programs, eligibility criteria, and application procedures. Comprehensive communication campaigns are needed to inform poor and vulnerable citizens of the safety nets that are available to them. Moreover, engaging a broader spectrum of stakeholders (such as NGOs, CSOs, the private sector, and nonprofits) in financing and implementing SSN programs could add leverage from their existing financial and human resources.

• Establishing a reliable yet flexible SSN infrastructure that can be used in normal times as well as during crises. An effective SSN system can help citizens navigate the effects of idiosyncratic and systemic shocks. The recent global economic crisis underscored the weak capacity of existing SSN systems in the Middle East and North Africa to serve this function. Promoting households' resilience to shocks through SSNs requires a strong administrative infrastructure. Having this infrastructure in place ahead of a crisis allows for quicker and more efficient development of remedial and mitigation actions, such as scaling up of benefits for the most vulnerable or expanding coverage, thus enhancing resilience. In particular, setting up an improved SSN infrastructure could entail the following:

○ *Creating unified registries of beneficiaries* that can be used to target multiple programs. In normal times, unified registries can reduce costs and facilitate coherence and convergence because all agents work with the same database. In times of crisis, unified registries can be used to quickly disburse additional benefits to the target population or to promptly expand coverage by adjusting eligibility criteria. In this regard, West Bank and Gaza provides an example of best practice in the region.

○ *Using effective service delivery mechanisms.* In normal times, modern benefit delivery systems are important to reduce administrative costs and leakages to nonbeneficiaries, avoid corruption, and make the transfer of payments to beneficiaries quick and flexible. Effective use of modern technologies such as smart cards, mobile payments, and over-the-counter payments in bank branches facilitates rapid response during crises.

- **Consolidating fragmented SSN programs.** In the Middle East and North Africa, direct transfer programs (cash-based or in-kind) are often small and highly fragmented. International experience suggests that having a few comprehensive programs, specifically designed to reach different segments of the poor and vulnerable, can address current vulnerabilities and social protection gaps by increasing both coverage (currently below 20 percent of the poor in most countries) and benefits (currently covering about 5–10 percent of consumption of the poor). A few parts of the region (for example, Morocco and West Bank and Gaza) have started reforming their SSNs in this direction. To achieve progress in this respect, governments can start by identifying gaps in SSN systems and creating an inventory of SSN programs with program objectives, eligibility criteria, and benefit types. Morocco recently undertook this type of analysis. Informed by such an analysis, governments can identify programs that can be expanded or consolidated and formulate a strategy for implementation of the reform.

- **Rebalancing the financing and priorities of safety net systems** by focusing on targeted programs rather than on subsidies. Middle Eastern and North African countries spend the lion's share of SSN expenditure, in terms of GDP, on energy subsidies and a small share on targeted safety nets. Reducing costly and regressive general fuel and food price subsidies would decrease fiscal imbalances and free up resources for other safety net instruments. In particular, this could entail

○ *Increasing spending and improving coverage of nonsubsidy SSNs to protect against destitution.* Successful subsidy reforms have demonstrated the importance of gaining citizens' trust in the government's capacity to deliver fair and reliable compensation. In light of the evidence provided by the MENA SPEAKS surveys and the Jordan Gives exercise, delivering effective and inclusive SSN programs would be an essential step toward comprehensive subsidy reform.

○ *Reforming price subsidies through wholesale or internal reforms.*
Sequencing of sensitive reforms such as that of universal price subsidies is crucial for their success. To gain credibility, governments
could start by

- *Improving targeting* (for example, through differentiated
marketing and packaging, which can lead to self-targeting, as in
Tunisia), narrowing subsidy coverage (such as through lifeline
tariffs in electricity), and reducing leakages in the distribution
chain.

- *Identifying the most sensitive subsidies and focusing instead on the most
regressive ones.* According to the MENA SPEAKS surveys, the
least-preferred products for subsidy reform were cooking oil in
Egypt, bread in Lebanon and Tunisia, and electricity in Jordan.
These subsidies could be subject to reform only when the governments demonstrate their success at reforming less-sensitive
subsidies. Given that spending on fuel subsidies is triple the
spending on food subsidies, nonfood subsidy reform is the
lower-hanging fruit. In the MENA SPEAKS surveys, citizens
indicated that if they had to pick one subsidized product for reform, this product would be tobacco in Lebanon, gasoline in
Egypt, and diesel in Jordan and Tunisia.

- Engaging citizens early on in the dialogue on compensation
packages and promoting awareness through information campaigns. Governments can use the findings from the MENA
SPEAKS surveys to initiate a dialogue on preferred compensation packages in their countries. The evidence so far shows that
people in the Middle East and North Africa prefer subsidy reform that targets cash-based compensation to the poor alone
(Egypt, Jordan, and Tunisia), perhaps combined with investment of savings in education and health (Lebanon).

The Middle Eastern and North African economies find themselves at
different stages of progress on human development outcomes and SSN
reforms. Notably, the two places that have advanced the most in SSN
reform are West Bank and Gaza and the Republic of Yemen, which have,
respectively, medium- and low-level human development outcomes (as
proxied by the United Nations Development Programme's human development index). They were able to implement successful SSN interventions (establishing a unified registry in West Bank and Gaza and reforming the Social Welfare Fund in the Republic of Yemen) that help to
address their specific needs. Bahrain, Djibouti, Jordan, Lebanon, and
Morocco have made important steps toward SSN reform, such as a work-

fare plus nutrition program in Djibouti, a pilot CCT in Morocco, reforms in the subsidy system in Bahrain and Jordan, and a targeting database in Lebanon. Other countries are currently considering new programs or reforms of their SSN systems.

In each country, the way forward would include short- and medium-run interventions with complementary and mutually reinforcing objectives. In the short run, Middle Eastern and North African countries can start demonstrating better results using existing SSN systems by tweaking the design of existing programs, building unified registries, or piloting new programs such as CCTs and "workfare plus." In the medium run, the focus can shift to reforms that require more preexisting capacity, such as refining the SSN infrastructure and comprehensive subsidy reform. Engaging a broad spectrum of stakeholders in an inclusive and open dialogue can facilitate the envisioned reforms and promote an empowering role for social safety nets in the region.

Note

1. Social safety nets (SSNs) are defined as noncontributory transfers targeted to the poor or vulnerable. They include income support, temporary employment programs (workfare), and services that build human capital and expand access to finance among the poor and vulnerable.

Overview

Introduction

There is currently an unparalleled opportunity for Middle Eastern and North African countries to improve their social safety nets (SSNs)[1] to better promote inclusion, livelihood, and resilience. There is a growing international consensus that effective SSN coverage can promote economic opportunity and help vulnerable populations to overcome poverty. Approximately 80 percent of developing countries currently plan to develop or strengthen their SSNs (World Bank 2012a), and those of the Middle East and North Africa are no exception. Historically, transitions and crises have often opened new space for SSN building. Around the world, 70 percent of SSN programs were introduced after a major transition (for example, independence after the collapse of the former Soviet Union; Nepal's transition to democracy; decentralization in Indonesia; and political changes in Brazil and Portugal). More recently, the global financial crisis spurred dozens of countries to create new SSN programs, expand old ones, and improve overall administrative systems to enhance governance and make programs more efficient (IEG 2011).

The Arab Spring has brought the need for social inclusion and a new contract between states and citizens to the forefront. Traditionally, many governments in the region tended to rely on a redistribution system that promoted (a) a minimum standard of living by providing universal subsidies of basic consumer goods, and (b) public employment in response to the demand for secure jobs by the middle and upper classes. In times of crisis, governments relied on the same narrow set of policy tools. The subsidy system, which does not require targeting, is popular but has not achieved the desired outcomes of SSNs in an effective and efficient way. During the Arab Spring, demands for increased social inclusion and better access to economic opportunities implied a turning point for the region as a whole and intense scrutiny of the role of SSNs.

1

The challenge in the Middle East and North Africa today is to invest in effective SSN systems that are fiscally, politically, and administratively sustainable. To be effective in promoting inclusion, livelihood, and resilience, SSNs should be carefully designed and implemented, ensuring that they reach the most vulnerable and help them to build human capital. To achieve *fiscal sustainability*, some countries around the world have consolidated fragmented programs and focused on efficient and lower-cost interventions, linking them to asset creation. To achieve *political sustainability*, some countries have designed programs in accordance with public opinions about poverty and redistribution; established a record of transparency, effectiveness, and impact; and considered both the poor's demand for inclusion and the middle class's demand for fairness. To achieve *administrative sustainability*, some countries have defined appropriate institutional responsibilities and incentives while developing efficient targeting and management systems as well as administrative budgets. Effective planning and design can ensure that sustainability objectives are met by new or reformed SSN programs.

Report Objectives

The report aims to meet two broad objectives: (a) enhance knowledge about the current state of existing SSNs and assess their effectiveness in responding to new and emerging challenges to the poor and vulnerable in the region by bringing together new evidence, data, and country-specific analysis; and (b) open up and inform a debate on feasible policy options to make SSNs in the Middle East and North Africa more effective and innovative. To those ends, this report seeks to answer the following four questions:

- What are the key challenges of the poor and vulnerable in the Middle East and North Africa that call for renewed SSNs?

- Are the region's SSNs achieving their goals of promoting social inclusion, livelihood, and resilience to crises?

- Which SSN reforms do the region's citizens want?

- What types of policies can be part of the agenda for SSN reform, and how could these policies be developed for maximum effectiveness?

Report Structure

Chapter 1, *A Framework for SSN Reform in the Middle East and North Africa*, describes and illustrates the reasons for the region's growing need for SSN reform and establishes the framework for renewed SSNs. It identifies key goals for SSNs (promoting social inclusion, livelihood, and resilience) and illustrates how these goals have been achieved in some parts of the region and elsewhere.

Chapter 2, *The Challenge: Poverty, Exclusion and Vulnerability to Shocks*, analyzes the challenges facing the region's poor and vulnerable households, which SSNs should focus on as a priority. Two large groups are at higher-than-average poverty risk: children and those who live in rural or lagging areas. The chapter examines factors—such as inequality of opportunities and lack of access to services—that can perpetuate the lower human development outcomes among the poor in these groups. It also describes the challenge of vulnerability (that is, the state of being close to the poverty line and thus at risk of falling into poverty as a consequence of a short-term shock). Finally, it identifies particular social groups that are at a higher risk of exclusion from access to services and employment.

Chapter 3, *The Current State of SSNs in the Middle East and North Africa*, analyzes SSN spending and assesses different aspects of the SSN systems' performance (including coverage, targeting, generosity, and the impact on poverty and inequality of both subsidy and nonsubsidy SSNs). It benchmarks such performance against that of other regions and countries and identifies the gaps in existing systems.

Chapter 4, *The Political Economy of SSN Reforms in the Middle East and North Africa: What Do Citizens Want?* presents new evidence on citizens' preferences concerning redistribution and SSN design, using newly collected data (MENA SPEAKS surveys and the Jordan Gives behavioral experiment). It also discusses how political economy considerations could be taken into account in designing renewed SSNs in the region.

Chapter 5, *The Way Forward: How to Make Safety Nets in the Middle East and North Africa More Effective and Innovative*, analyzes and proposes an agenda for reform and the path for moving forward, using global experience and the evidence presented in the preceding chapters.

A Framework for SSN Reform

Recent economic and social transitions in the Middle East and North Africa have refocused attention on the need for greater social inclusion, livelihood, and resilience. Although sustained growth in many of the region's countries has pulled people out of poverty and into the middle class, economic progress has yet to reach many who face persistent poverty and the risk of destitution because of unemployment, disability, or illness. Moreover, many more in the Middle East and North Africa are vulnerable to economic shocks, natural disasters, and political or other crises. Without a safety net, poor families who are systematically unable to afford their

FIGURE O.1

Citizens' Self-Reported Ability to Buy Sufficient Food in the Middle East and North Africa, Selected Countries, 2009–11

Have there been times in the past 12 months when you did not have enough money to buy food that you or your family needed?

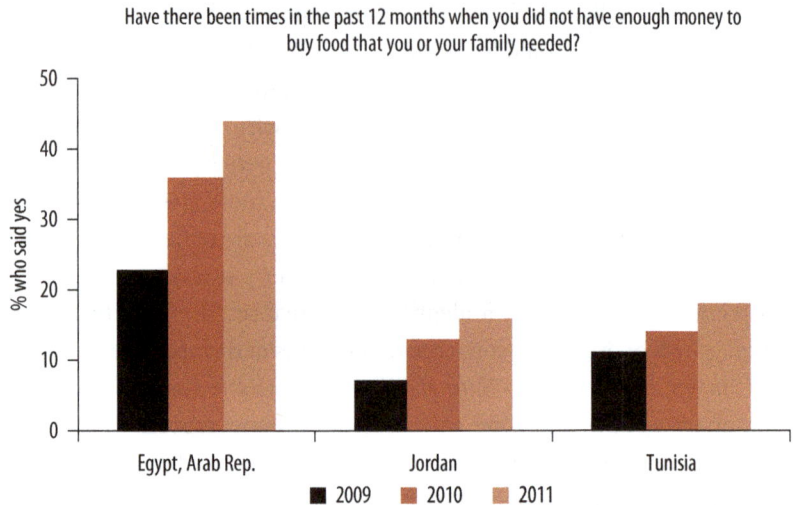

Source: Gallup Inc. 2011.

basic needs are likely to lose hope of escaping poverty; malnourished children are likely to grow up as poor adults; and, as a consequence of crises, vulnerable families are likely to face difficult choices between survival today and avoiding irreversible damage to their future welfare.

In fact, economic anxiety is on the rise in the Middle East and North Africa. According to a Gallup World Poll, in 2011, the share of the population who admitted having difficulties buying food in the Arab Republic of Egypt, Jordan, and Tunisia was significantly higher than in 2009 (see figure O.1). At the same time, citizens in some of the region's large countries expressed low levels of satisfaction with ongoing government efforts to help the poor, as shown in figure O.2. By providing assistance to the poor and vulnerable, SSNs can create a springboard to help citizens preserve their independence and be in a position to share in the benefits of economic progress.

SSNs can be crucial instruments of economic and social transitions in the Middle East and North Africa. Figure O.3 introduces a framework for effective and empowering SSNs in the region. As it illustrates, SSNs can promote three outcomes:

- *Social inclusion*, by enabling investment in human capital (such as supporting school attendance or better nutrition for children)

FIGURE O.2

Citizens' Satisfaction with Government Assistance to the Poor in the Middle East and North Africa, Selected Countries, 2011

In your country, are you satisfied or dissatisfied with efforts to deal with the poor?

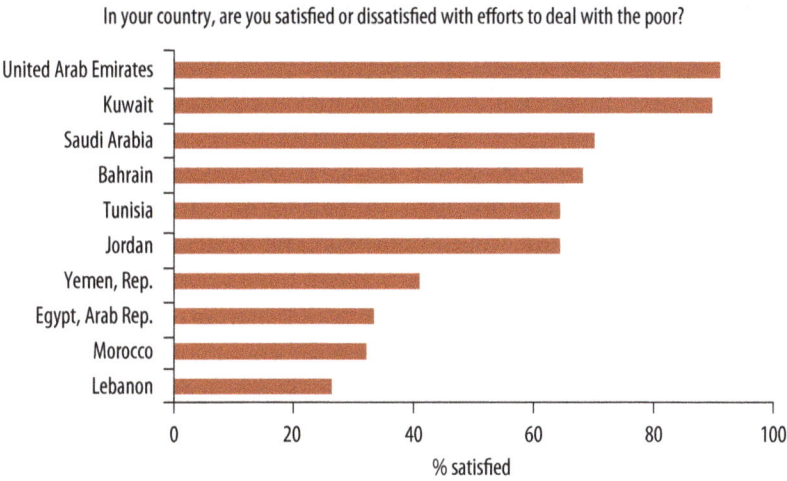

Source: Gallup Inc. 2011.

FIGURE O.3

Framework for Renewed Social Safety Nets in the Middle East and North Africa

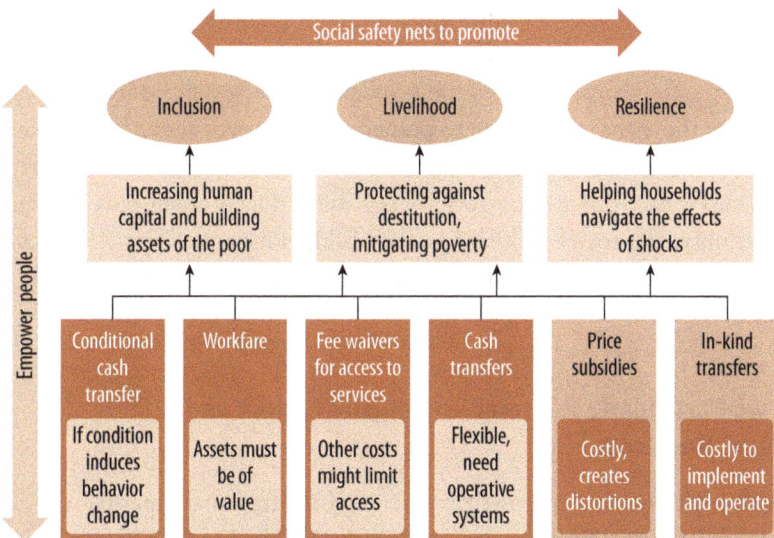

- *Livelihood*, by protecting against destitution

- *Resilience to crises*, by helping households to navigate the effects of shocks.

Experience in many countries, including some in the Middle East and North Africa, shows that several SSN instruments improve investments in human capital through multiple pathways. For example, conditional cash transfers (CCTs) and education fee waivers help to increase school enrollment and attendance. Similarly, CCTs and noncontributory health insurance increase health care use, especially for preventive care (such as mother and child health), while workfare programs can increase the assets of the poor and their communities. Some of these instruments also protect the poor from destitution, and their children from malnutrition and disease, by improving households' immediate consumption and income without being as expensive and distortionary as price subsidies. In case of shocks, cash transfers reach those in need more effectively than subsidies and in-kind transfers because of their greater flexibility.

Key Challenges that Call for Renewed SSNs

Understanding the specific challenges faced by the poor and vulnerable is a crucial precondition for effective design of SSN instruments in the Middle East and North Africa. SSN programs encompass a range of flexible instruments that can be tailored to the highest-priority needs of the target beneficiaries—advancing the SSNs' triple goals of promoting inclusion, livelihood, and resilience. Thus, SSN effectiveness depends on the accurate identification of the principal challenges faced by the poor, such as those that contribute to perpetuating poverty across generations and those that can lead the vulnerable into a quick descent into poverty. To this effect, this section reviews key stylized facts about poverty, vulnerability, and social exclusion in the Middle East and North Africa and the associated human development challenges faced by the people in need.

Two Particularly Vulnerable Groups: Children and Rural Residents

Although economic growth in the region lifted many people out of poverty, the decline in poverty rates in the Middle East and North Africa occurred at a slower pace than in other regions, such as Eastern Europe and Central Asia or East Asia and the Pacific. Two large groups of the population face a higher-than-average risk of poverty: children and rural

TABLE O.1

Child Poverty Rates in the Middle East and North Africa, Selected Countries, c. 2006–10

percent

Country	Child (0–14) poverty rate	Overall poverty rate
Egypt, Arab Rep. 2009	29	22
Iraq 2007	27	23
Jordan 2010	20	14
Morocco 2010[a]	25	20
Yemen, Rep. 2006	36	35

Source: Authors' calculations based on data from latest available household surveys.

Note: Poverty rates are based on national poverty lines for all countries except Morocco.

a. Poverty line defined as the bottom quintile cutoff.

residents. These groups suffer from inequality of opportunities, which is exacerbated by lack of access to services, all leading to lower human development outcomes. In the absence of SSNs that effectively promote human capital formation among the poor and protect against destitution, these outcomes may be perpetuated.

Some countries in the Middle East and North Africa—such as Egypt, Iraq, and the Republic of Yemen—have high levels of child poverty, with at least one in every four children living below the national poverty line (see table O.1). Even in Jordan and Morocco, where child poverty is not as high, children face a significantly higher poverty risk than other age groups.

Being born into a poor household puts a child at a significant disadvantage compared with his or her peers. The average parent of a poor child in the region has no formal education and has to provide for a family of five or more members. In Egypt and Morocco, 70 percent of the households in the poorest quintile have a head who has never attended school. Poor children often live in dwellings without a sewage connection or basic amenities. In Jordan, a 10-year-old girl in the poorest quintile is 40 percent less likely to drink treated water and 50 percent less likely to have a bed than a girl in the richest quintile. These inequalities are also reflected in the size and quality of dwellings and access to technology.

Progress on some human development outcomes in the Middle East and North Africa is still disappointing—and alarmingly low among the poor, with potentially life-long irreversible impacts. For example, early childhood malnutrition is strikingly high in the region's low-income countries and in some middle-income ones. The level of economic devel-

FIGURE O.4

Prevalence of Wasting Relative to GDP per Capita in the Middle East and North Africa, Selected Countries, c. 2009–12

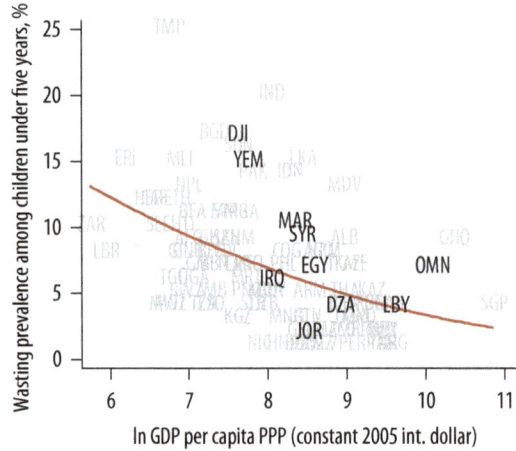

Sources: Authors' calculations based on malnutrition data from UNICEF 2009; GDP per capita data from World Bank 2012b.

Note: PPP = purchasing power parity.

opment contributes but does not completely explain the incidence of malnutrition, as shown in figure O.4: Djibouti, Morocco, and the Republic of Yemen have high malnutrition rates even relative to their development peers. Within countries, malnutrition rates are higher among children in poor households (see figure O.5). In terms of education, older children face higher school dropout rates and are more likely to enter the job market as low-skilled youth.

The region has important geographic disparities, with those born in lagging areas of even relatively rich countries at high risk of poverty. The rural poverty rates in Iraq and the Republic of Yemen are twice those of urban areas (see figure O.6). Even middle-income countries such as Egypt, Jordan, and Tunisia have spatial pockets (such as slums in urban areas and isolated rural areas) where extreme poverty is prevalent (figure O.6); access to basic services, such as antenatal care and clean water, is lacking (figure O.7); and human development indicators are considerably below the national average. For instance, a child in rural Upper Egypt is 3.4 times less likely than a child in urban Lower Egypt to attend primary school.

Inequality of opportunities, combined with lack of access to basic services, severely limits the prospects of people who grow up in poor

FIGURE O.5

Stunting, by Wealth Quintile, in the Middle East and North Africa, Selected Countries, 2006

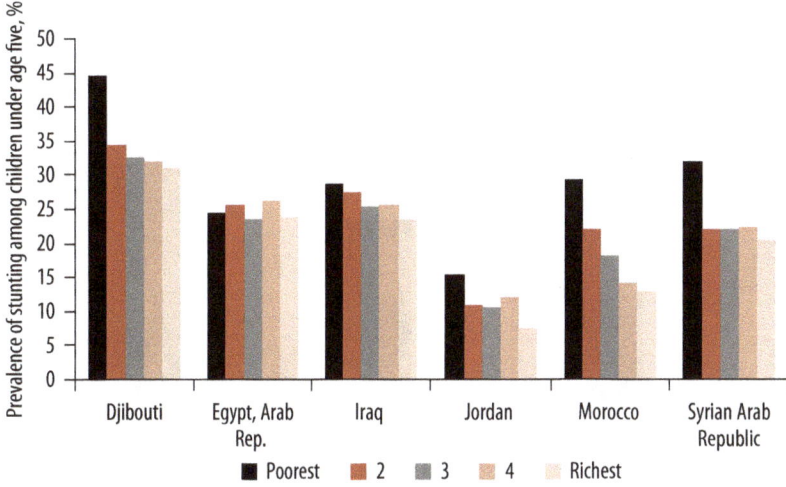

Source: Authors' calculations based on UNICEF's latest available Multiple Indicator Cluster Surveys, http://www.childinfo.org/mics.html.

FIGURE O.6

The Rural-Urban Divide: Poverty Rates in the Middle East and North Africa, Selected Countries, c. 2005–10

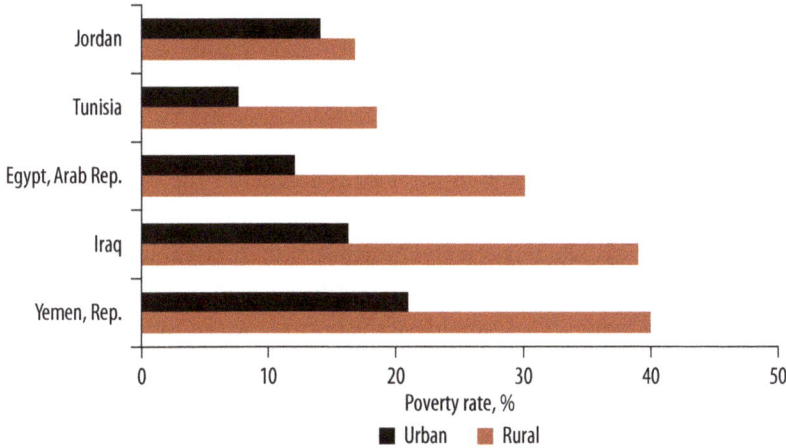

Source: Authors' calculations based on the following household surveys: HIECS, Egypt 2009; IHSES, Iraq 2007; HIES, Jordan 2010; HBS, Republic of Yemen 2006; and World Bank (Poverty Reduction and Economic Management Network) staff estimates using Tunisia HBS 2005. For full identification and descriptions of the surveys, see appendix A.

Note: Poverty rates are based on national poverty lines.

FIGURE O.7

Share of Young Urban Males out of School and out of Work, by Family Wealth, in the Arab Republic of Egypt, Jordan, and Morocco, c. 2009–10

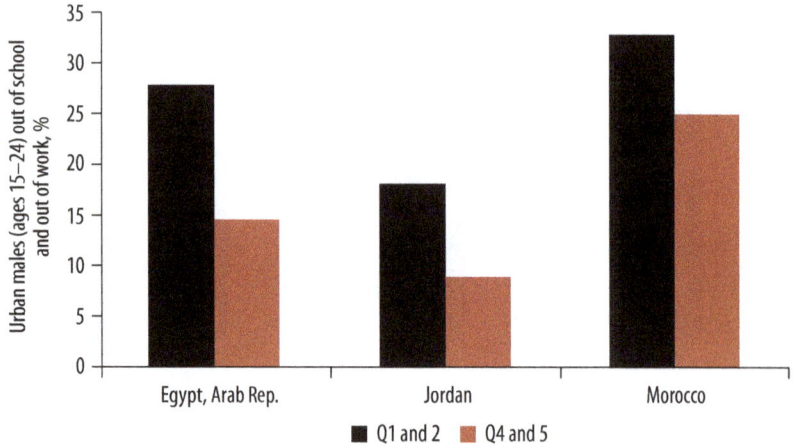

Source: Authors' calculations based on data from the following household surveys: SYPE, Egypt 2009; LMPS, Jordan 2010; and MHYS, Morocco 2010. For full descriptions, see appendix A.
Note: Q = income quintile (1 = lowest, 5 = highest).

households, locking them into a low-productivity path. The process by which children and young adults attain desirable education and health outcomes in the Middle East and North Africa depends, to a large extent, on circumstances beyond their control, such as their location at birth, their gender, and their parents' wealth and education. Wealth is a significant determinant of access to basic services across the region, such as antenatal care, immunizations, and high-quality child care as well as preschool education. Among the poor, the inability to cover health costs is significant and especially affects children and pregnant women. Growing up in a poor household and in rural areas also limits the opportunity to accumulate key human capital, including education and health. Most adults in poor Middle Eastern and North African households have either only primary or no formal education. For instance, in 2010, 70 percent of male workers living in households of the bottom consumption quintile in Egypt had primary education or no formal education, compared with only 16 percent of workers living in households at the top income quintile. Once in the labor market, individuals with low levels of human capital accumulation are at the highest risk of being unemployed or in poor-quality jobs because low educational achievement makes poor people less employable.

Figure O.7 shows that poor young men are more likely to be out of school and out of work than nonpoor young men. Even when they are employed, the poor are more likely to work in informal, low-paying jobs,

FIGURE O.8

Work Status of Urban Wage-Employed Men, by Wealth Quintile, in the Arab Republic of Egypt, Jordan, and Morocco, 2009–10

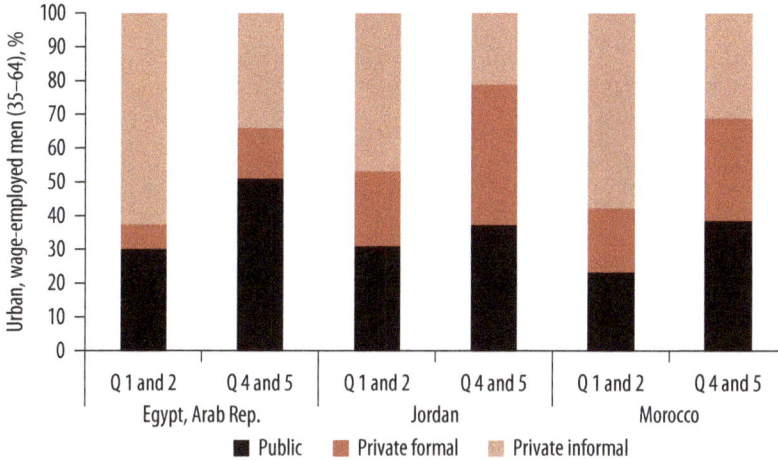

Sources: Authors' calculations based on data from the following household surveys: SYPE, Egypt 2009; LMPS, Jordan 2010; and MHYS, Morocco 2010. For full descriptions, see appendix A.

Note: Q = wealth quintile (1 = lowest, 5 = highest).

while those in higher-income households are more likely to be in formal jobs, as shown in figure O.8. Escaping this situation is difficult: figure O.9 shows that workers in the bottom quintile in Egypt are less likely to move from a "bad job" (a job that is neither protected nor well paid) to a good job, and they are more likely than wealthier workers to fall out of good-quality jobs into low-quality ones.

High Vulnerability to Poverty, without Effective Coping Strategies

Even those who rode the trajectory of economic growth into the middle class remain vulnerable to the risk of falling back into poverty if an economic contraction takes place. In fact, as many as 15–17 percent of Egyptians, Iraqis, Syrians, and Yemenis and 10 percent of Moroccans have consumption levels that are no more than US$0.50 per day above the US$2 poverty line, as shown in figure O.10. This large share of the population hovers around the poverty line and therefore has low resilience to shocks.

Vulnerable households have little disposable income and spend a high share of total expenditures on essentials. This implies that these households cannot easily scale down their expenditures during shocks, and thus they can easily move into poverty, as figure O.11 illustrates. For instance, between 2005 and 2008, 55 percent of Egyptians experienced at least one episode of poverty or near-poverty (Marotta et al. 2011).

FIGURE O.9

Probability of Transition to a Good or Bad Job in 2009, by Consumption Quintile and Employment Condition of Young Egyptian Males, 2008

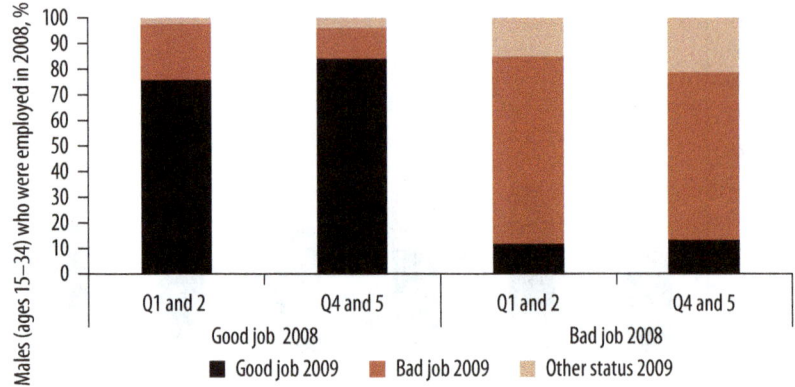

Source: Authors' calculations based on HIECS, Egypt 2008 and 2009. For a full description, see appendix A.
Note: "Good job" is defined as offering social security or with earnings above two-thirds of the median. "Bad job" is defined as informal and with earnings below two-thirds of the median. "Other status" is defined as being unemployed or out of the labor force. Q = consumption quintile (1 = lowest, 5 = highest).

FIGURE O.10

Share of Population Living on US$2–US$2.50 a Day in the Middle East and North Africa, Selected Countries

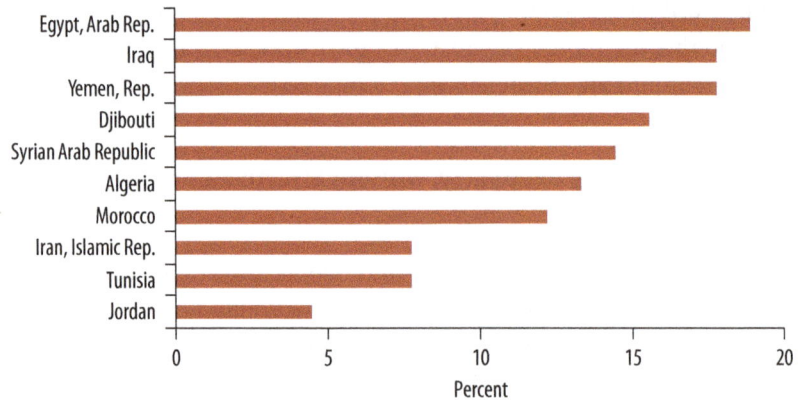

Source: Calculations from PovcalNet, http://iresearch.worldbank.org/povcalnet.

There is a high probability of an irreversible loss of human capital during shocks and crises if SSNs that help households navigate the effects of risk are not in place. In the face of a major shock, Middle Eastern and North African households rely on their own income, savings, and assets as well as on informal safety nets (such as private support from family and neighbors) because few have access to formal safety nets. As many as 15

FIGURE O.11

Expenditure Composition by Income Quintile in the Arab Republic of Egypt, 2009

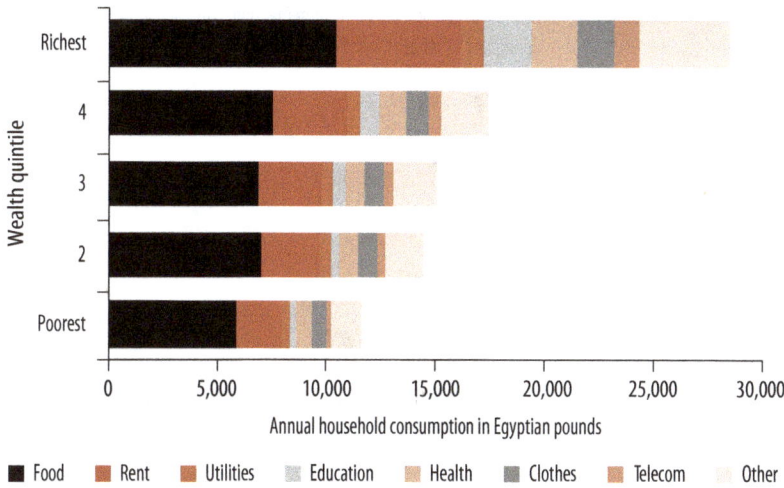

Source: Data from HIECS, Egypt 2009. For a full survey description, see appendix A.

percent of households in Iraq, Morocco, and the capital of the Republic of Yemen reported suffering at least one major shock during the previous 12 months. Formal safety nets do not reach the shock-affected households. As shown in figure O.12, only about 1 percent of all households experiencing a major shock in Iraq and Morocco reported receiving help from formal safety nets (that is, support from the government and nongovernmental organizations [NGOs]). In this context, poorer families, with their limited incomes, savings, and assets, are again at greater risk. Similarly, the region's workforce is vulnerable because of predominantly informal employment, precarious jobs, and the absence of income-support assistance for the unemployed. In addition, weather-related shocks have considerably increased vulnerability among rural agricultural households. For example, in Morocco, 22 percent of all households in 2010 reported having experienced a major weather shock (such as drought, flood, pest infestation, or crop and livestock diseases).

Inequitable Access to Social Services and Job Opportunities

In addition to the challenges particularly facing poor children, the rural poor, and the vulnerable, pockets of social exclusion impede women, people with disabilities, and displaced people from gaining access to needed social services and job opportunities. Therefore, SSNs that promote inclusion should be designed in ways that are sensitive to the specific needs of these groups and promote their participation in the safety net programs.

FIGURE O.12

Household Coping Mechanisms for Shocks in Iraq and Morocco, 2009–10

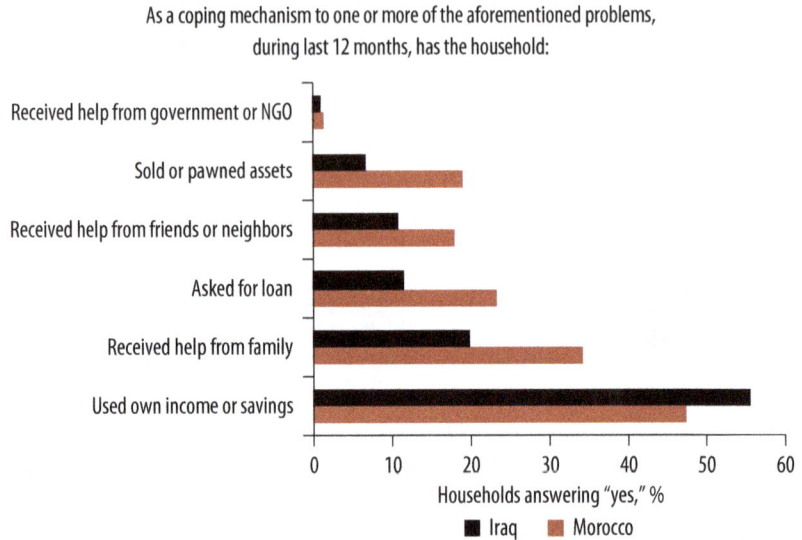

As a coping mechanism to one or more of the aforementioned problems, during last 12 months, has the household:

Sources: Data from IHSES, Iraq, 2009 and MHYS, Morocco 2010. For full survey descriptions, see appendix A.
Note: NGO = nongovernmental organization.

Some of the main factors hindering female labor force participation in the Middle East and North Africa are weak support systems (such as public transportation and child care services), lack of empowerment, educational disadvantages, and wage discrimination as well as gender segregation in various industries (UNDP 2005; World Bank 2004, 2012a). A comparative household survey conducted by the World Bank in Cairo, Egypt; Amman, Jordan; and Sana'a, the Republic of Yemen shows that fewer than 10 percent of women living in households with a member who opposes their work end up participating in the labor market (Chamlou, Muzi, and Ahmed 2008a, 2008b). This is particularly of concern because more than 30 percent of young men oppose female participation in the labor market. Furthermore, in several Middle Eastern and North African countries, tax- and employment-related benefits to families are channeled through men.

Countries in the Middle East and North Africa also face challenges, as do other regions, in effectively addressing the difficulties that persons with disabilities consistently face, including high unemployment rates; inaccessible and unaffordable health care; low educational attainment (only 20 percent of women and 40 percent of men with disabilities in the Syrian Arab Republic are literate); inaccessible transportation and infrastructure to reach jobs and services; and stigmatization resulting in social exclusion and marginalization (WHO and World Bank 2010). In 2006, a national survey of people with disabilities in Morocco revealed their high expressed need for improved access to a range of social services (Kingdom of Morocco 2006). In combination with better provision of services, unconditional cash transfers for people with disabilities can help to start addressing the additional barriers faced by this group in, for instance, accessing health care and rehabilitation, transportation, education, and employment.

In some countries of the Middle East and North Africa, externally displaced people can count on a reduced set of social benefits and services than the domestic population. According to the United Nations High Commissioner for Refugees (UNHCR) and the United Nations Relief and Works Agency for Palestine Refugees in the Near East (UNRWA), the region hosts almost half of all the registered externally displaced people in the world. UNHCR also estimates that the total number of internally displaced persons in the region is around 10 million. The integration of the displaced varies substantially from country to country, and often by particular group. In some countries, displaced people face higher education and health costs than the host country's population; restricted access to formal sector professions; and constrained mobility due to regulations on driver's licenses (Human Rights Watch 2010). In countries with ongoing conflicts or returning displaced persons, UNHCR and NGOs often step in to provide basic services to the displaced.

The Current State of SSNs in the Middle East and North Africa

Despite the needs described above, the Middle East and North Africa lags behind other regions in the efficient use of SSN resources. Most countries in the region adopt one of two approaches to SSNs: (a) relying primarily on inefficient and pro-rich universal subsidies or ration programs, effectively crowding out more-effective interventions; or (b) offering a multitude of small and fragmented programs that do not have a significant impact on poverty and inequality because of their low coverage, high leakage, and limited benefit levels.

Universal Subsidies at the Expense of More Effective Programs

Despite the needs described above, the Middle East and North Africa lags behind other regions in the efficient use of SSN resources. In particular, the region's countries spend, on average, 5.7 percent of GDP on subsidies, as opposed to 1.3 percent of GDP in the average benchmark devel-

FIGURE O.13

SSN Spending with and without Subsidies, Middle East and North Africa Relative to Other Developing Countries, c. 2008–11

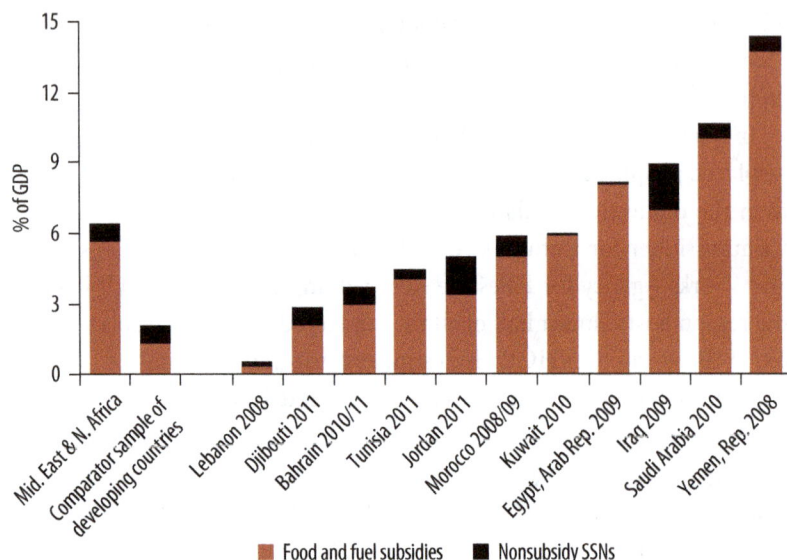

Sources: Authors' calculations based on Government of Jordan 2011b; World Bank 2009, 2010a, 2010b, 2010c, 2011a, 2011b; World Bank, FAO, and IFAD 2009; IMF Fiscal Affairs Department database.
Note: SSN = social safety net.

oping country, as figure O.13 shows. With the notable exception of Iraq, the region's countries spend much more on the more distortionary and pro-rich fuel subsidies (4.5 percent of GDP, on average) than on food subsidies and ration cards (1.1 percent of GDP, on average), as shown in figure O.14.

Subsidies capture substantial financial resources that could be spent on more efficient and effective SSN programs, as noted in figure O.15. Subsidies aside, administrative data collected as part of this study (Middle East and North Africa SSN Inventory, see appendix A for the description of the methodology) show that nonsubsidy SSNs in the Middle East and North Africa are fragmented among many small programs (see figure O.16); for example, in Morocco, 12 different programs all aim at increasing school enrollment.

Small Impact of Nonsubsidy SSNs on Poverty and Inequality

The Middle East and North Africa region has significant scope to improve the reach of its nonsubsidy safety nets to the poor and vulnerable population. Everywhere in the region except for West Bank and Gaza, two out

FIGURE O.14

Food and Fuel Subsidies as Percentage of GDP in the Middle East and North Africa, Selected Countries, c. 2008–11

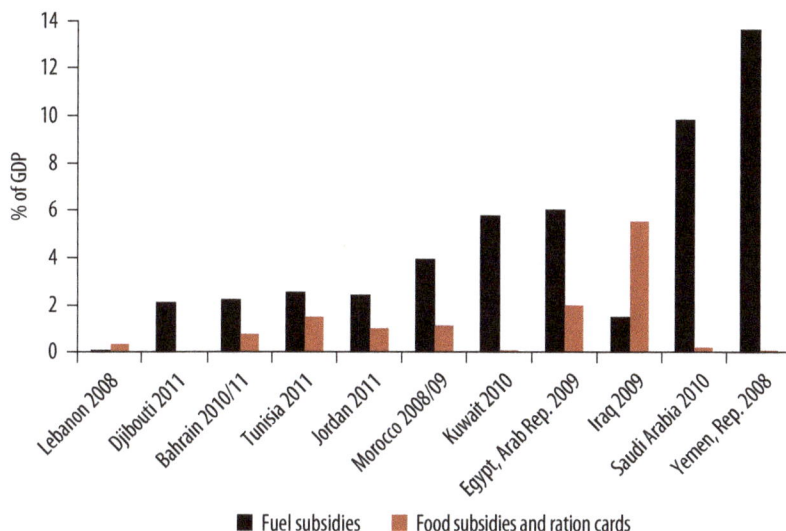

Sources: Authors' calculations based on Government of Jordan 2011b; World Bank 2009, 2010a, 2010b, 2010c, 2011a, 2011b; World Bank, FAO, and IFAD 2009; IMF Fiscal Affairs Department database.

FIGURE O.15

Comparison of Subsidy and Nonsubsidy SSN Expenditures for the Poor in the Middle East and North Africa, Selected Countries, c. 2008–11

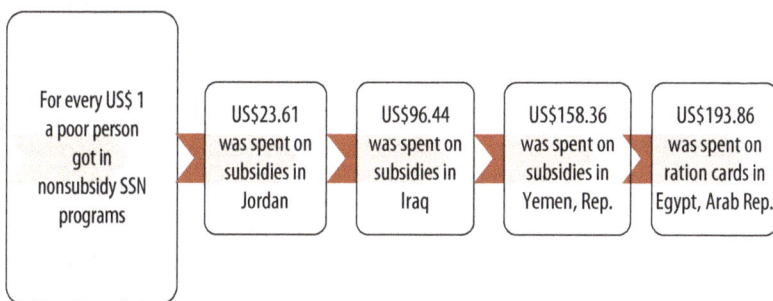

Sources: Authors' calculations based on latest household surveys and Government of Jordan 2011a; World Bank 2009, 2010a, 2010b, 2010c; IMF Fiscal Affairs Department database.
Note: SSN = social safety net.

of three people in the poorest quintile are not reached by (nonsubsidy) SSNs—less than half of the world average. The only area in the region with SSN coverage above the world average is West Bank and Gaza, where government, donor, and NGO programs cover more than half of

FIGURE O.16

Nonsubsidy SSN Program Mix by Type, Middle East and North Africa, c. 2008–11

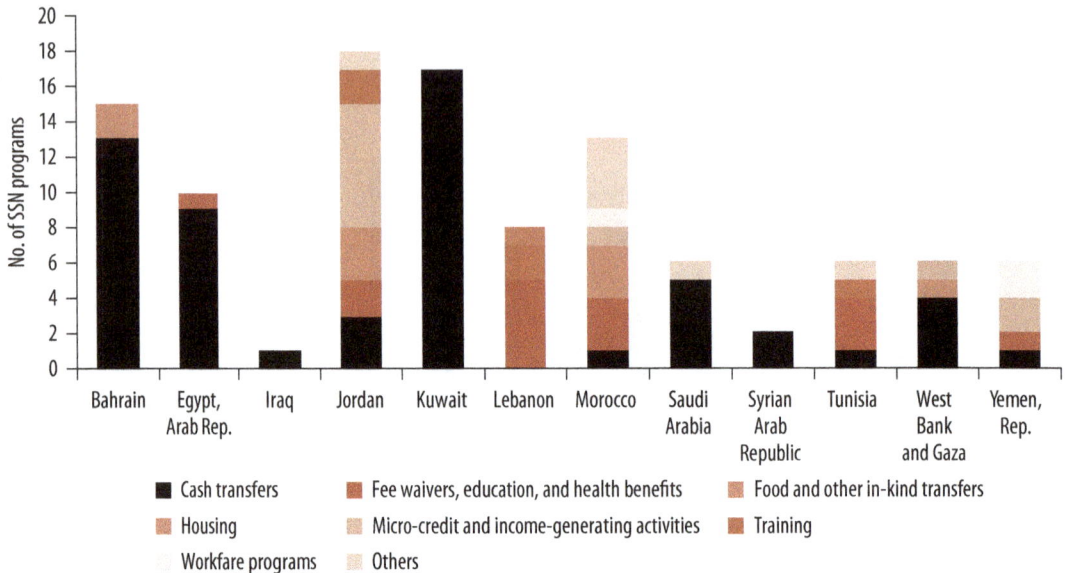

Legend:
- Cash transfers
- Fee waivers, education, and health benefits
- Food and other in-kind transfers
- Housing
- Micro-credit and income-generating activities
- Training
- Workfare programs
- Others

Source: Authors' calculations based on Middle East and North Africa SSN Inventory.

the poorest quintile, as shown in figure O.17. Overall, coverage of the bottom quintile by SSNs in the Middle East and North Africa is less than half the world average and less than a third of the SSN coverage in Europe and Central Asia or Latin America and the Caribbean (see figure O.17).

Different targeting methods are applicable in different contexts. In the Middle East and North Africa, SSN programs overwhelmingly use geographic and categorical targeting methods (see figure O.18), which work well in environments where poverty is concentrated, but not when poverty is multifaceted and spatially dispersed. In the latter case, methods that identify households or individuals based on their means or correlates of poverty (proxy means testing [PMT]) are preferable. Given the over-reliance on such targeting methods, leakages in the Middle East and North Africa are very high, with only a quarter of nonsubsidy SSN beneficiaries in the average country coming from the poorest quintile, while about 15 percent are from the richest quintile, as shown in figure O.19. A comparison with other regions confirms the underperformance of the Middle East and North African SSNs in terms of beneficiary incidence, since elsewhere the bottom quintile constitutes more than 30 percent of SSN beneficiaries, with Latin America and the Caribbean leading the world at 36 percent.

Still, some parts of the Middle East and North Africa region, such as Jordan, West Bank and Gaza, and the Republic of Yemen, have already

Coverage by Nonsubsidy SSN Programs, Middle East and North Africa Relative to Other Regions

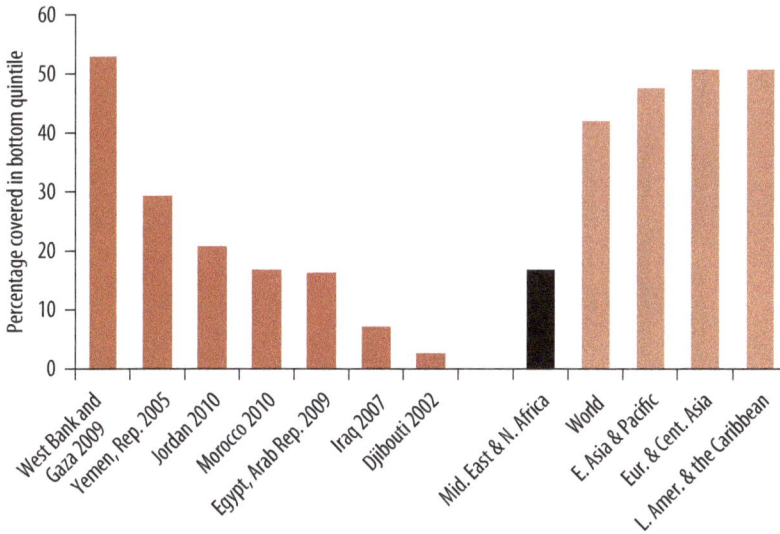

Sources: Middle East and North Africa: Authors' calculations based on national household surveys. Other regions: World Bank 2012a.

Note: SSN = social safety net. All regional averages are population-weighted.

Nonsubsidy SSN Program Mix by Targeting Type, Middle East and North Africa, Selected Countries, 2008–11

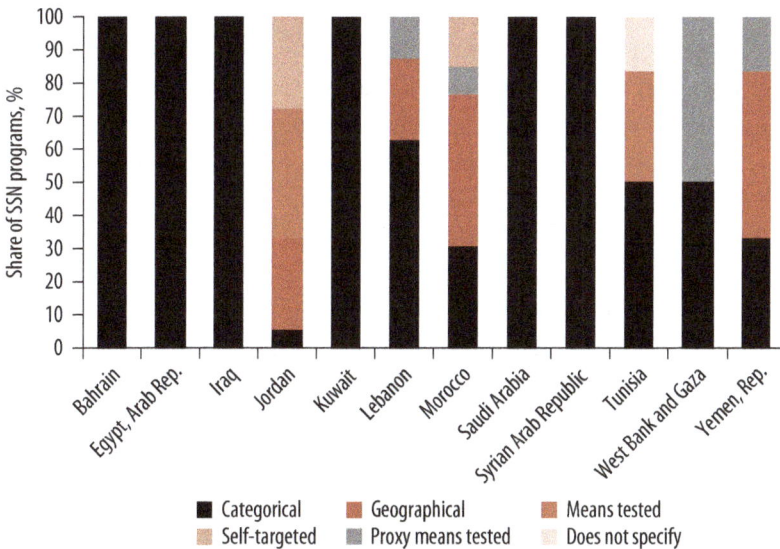

Source: Authors' calculations based on Middle East and North Africa SSN Inventory.

Note: SSN = social safety net.

FIGURE O.19

Benefit Incidence of Nonsubsidy SSNs, Middle East and North Africa, Relative to Other Regions

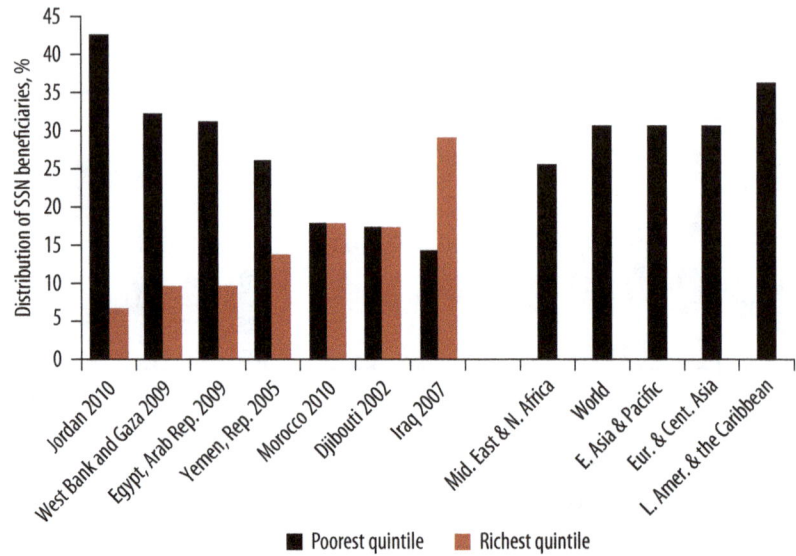

Sources: Middle East and North Africa: Authors' calculations based on national household surveys. Other regions: World Bank 2012a.

Note: SSN = social safety net. All regional averages are population-weighted.

begun to improve their targeting methods. For example, Jordan's National Aid Fund relies on a semiverified means test combined with categorical targeting, while West Bank and Gaza, the Republic of Yemen, and, most recently, Lebanon have introduced PMT-based targeting.

In terms of generosity, setting the benefit size for an SSN program is an important but difficult policy decision. On the one hand, a robust safety net should deliver adequate consumption protection for the most vulnerable members of a society, those who cannot provide for themselves due to age or disability and those who need temporary assistance to rebound from an economic or health shock. On the other hand, overly generous benefits may discourage working-age, able-bodied adults from participating in the labor force and instead encourage them to depend on the assistance provided by the government.

As shown in figure O.20, the generosity of SSN programs that reach the bottom quintile in the Middle East and North Africa is low, as these transfers constitute less than a quarter of the bottom quintile's welfare (as measured by consumption, expenditure, or assets). The greatest impact of SSN transfers on the welfare of the poorest quintile is in West Bank and Gaza, followed by Jordan. However, in countries such as the Republic of Yemen, the consumption levels of beneficiaries in the bottom quintile are barely affected.

FIGURE O.20

Benefit Generosity of Nonsubsidy SSNs, Middle East and North Africa Relative to Other Regions

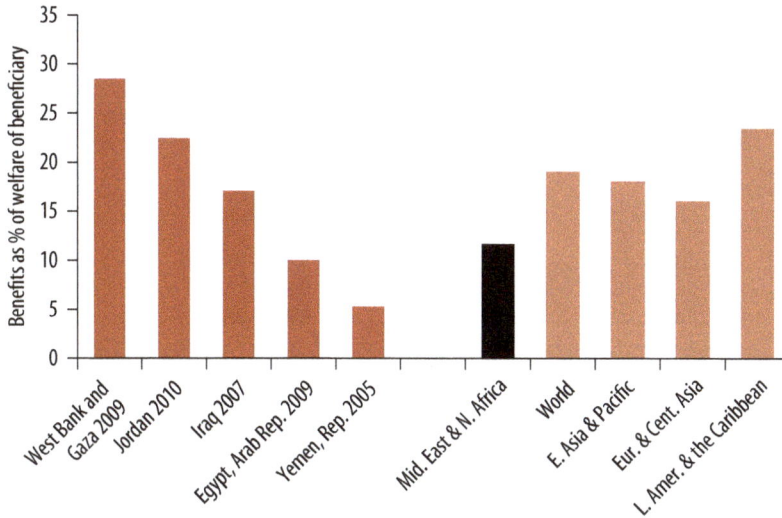

Sources: Middle East and North Africa: Authors' calculations based on national household surveys. Other regions: World Bank 2012a.

Note: SSN = social safety net. All regional averages are population-weighted.

Overall, whereas the average SSN system in the world provides transfers of almost 20 percent of the bottom quintile's welfare, in the Middle East and North Africa, this figure stands at only 12 percent, far below the other regions, as shown in figure O.20. This suggests that the benefit generosity of SSNs in the Middle East and North Africa can be increased without triggering work disincentives.

The most important indicator of SSN effectiveness is the impact on poverty and inequality. This indicator combines the separate forces of coverage, targeting, and generosity of SSN programs to assess the overall effect of the presence of SSNs on the welfare distribution of the country. With the exception of West Bank and Gaza and Jordan, SSNs in the region have little effect on poverty rates, as estimated through a simulation of poverty in the absence of SSNs (see figure O.21, panel a). SSN presence in Egypt, Iraq, and the Republic of Yemen reduces poverty rates in these countries by at most 3 percent. SSNs in the Middle East and North Africa perform better in terms of poverty impact than SSNs in East Asia, but much worse than the world average or in Europe and Central Asia and Latin America and the Caribbean. Notably, West Bank and Gaza's SSNs have a higher impact on poverty than the best-performing region (Europe and Central Asia).

The regional leader in terms of SSN impact on inequality is West Bank and Gaza, with its SSNs reducing the Gini coefficient by more than

FIGURE O.21

Poverty and Inequality Impact of Nonsubsidy SSNs in the Middle East and North Africa, Selected Economies, Compared with Other Regions

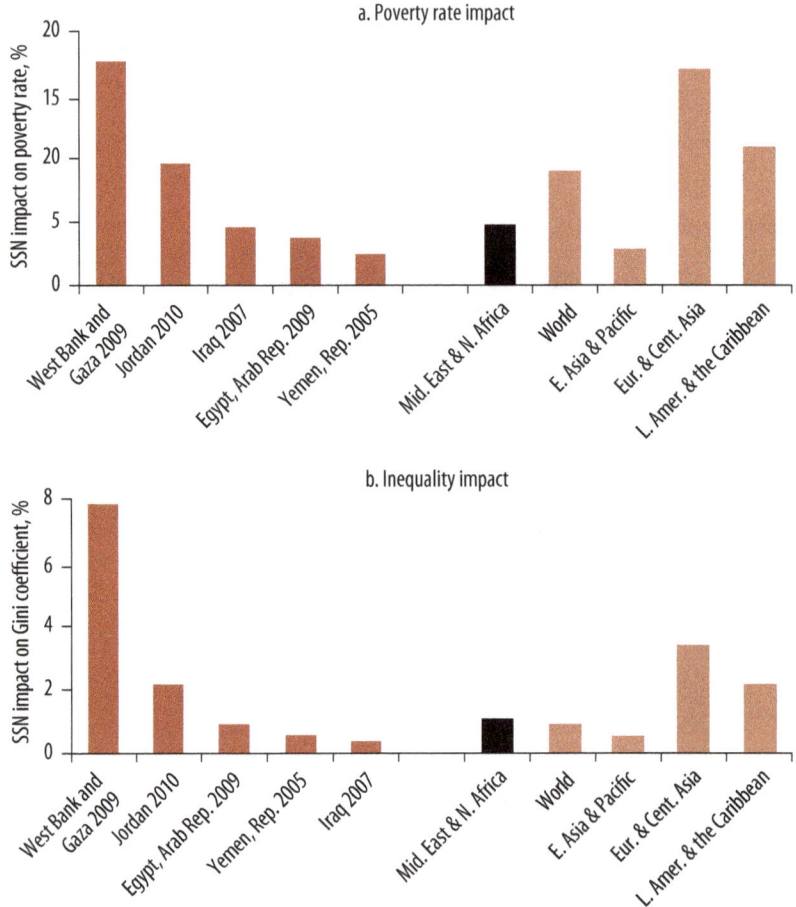

Sources: Middle East and North Africa: Authors' calculations based on national household surveys. Other regions: World Bank 2012a.

Note: SSN = social safety net. All regional averages are population-weighted.

7 percent (see figure O.21, panel b). On the other hand, in Egypt, Iraq, and the Republic of Yemen, SSNs have an imperceptible effect on welfare distribution, with the Gini coefficient declining by less than 1 percent. Comparisons with other regions demonstrate that in terms of reducing inequality, the region's performance is in the middle of the regional rankings, below Europe and Central Asia as well as Latin America and the Caribbean, but above East Asia.

Low coverage, poor targeting, and insufficient generosity of SSNs in the Middle East and North Africa account for these relatively small impacts on poverty and inequality. The impact on inequality measures the effect of SSNs on welfare distribution; as such, it is directly tied to targeting accuracy. Even excluding subsidies and ration cards, the region's SSNs are not adequately targeted to the poor and vulnerable, which explains the negligible effect on the Gini coefficient.

Universal Subsidies Are Inefficient and Pro-Rich—but Many People Depend on Them

The most frequently cited reason for reliance on subsidies is protection of the poor by guaranteeing access to food and other essential items at affordable prices. When used as SSNs, universal subsidies (in particular, fuel subsidies) suffer from significant deficiencies in targeting accuracy, as shown in figure O.22, panel a. Indeed, in Egypt, Jordan, and the Republic of Yemen, the richest quintile captures 40–60 percent of all fuel subsidy benefits because the rich consume more energy products than the poor. While the benefits of food subsidies are more equitably distributed, inefficiencies due to leakages of subsidies remain staggering: more than 70 percent of spending on food subsidies in Egypt and Iraq could be saved if such leakages were eliminated (World Bank 2010a, 2010b).

Still, due to their sheer magnitude as well as the high vulnerability in the Middle East and North Africa, subsidies have a significant impact on poverty, and any reform needs to take this fact into account. Despite their inefficiency, simple removal of subsidies would have significant impoverishing effects in many Middle Eastern and North African countries. Given their wider coverage and generosity (in terms of subsidization rates of essential goods in the consumption baskets), subsidies have major impacts on keeping people out of poverty (see figure O.22, panel b).

In Egypt and Iraq, food ration cards reduced poverty rates by more than 30 percent (or about 10 percentage points). Notably, fuel subsidies have lower impacts on poverty than food subsidies. Given the significant poverty-reducing impact of subsidies (especially, food subsidies) and the low impact of nonsubsidy SSNs, reform of subsidies has to be accompanied by significant expansion of other SSN instruments that promote livelihood and resilience.

The Political Economy of SSN Reforms in the Middle East and North Africa: What Do Citizens Want?

A large body of evidence about citizens' perceptions and aspirations concerning SSNs has been collected as part of this report, with the objective of understanding citizens' key preferences for the SSNs of the future.

FIGURE O.22

Inefficient but Poverty-Reducing Subsidies in the Middle East and North Africa, Selected Countries, c. 2004–10

a. Benefit incidence of subsidies

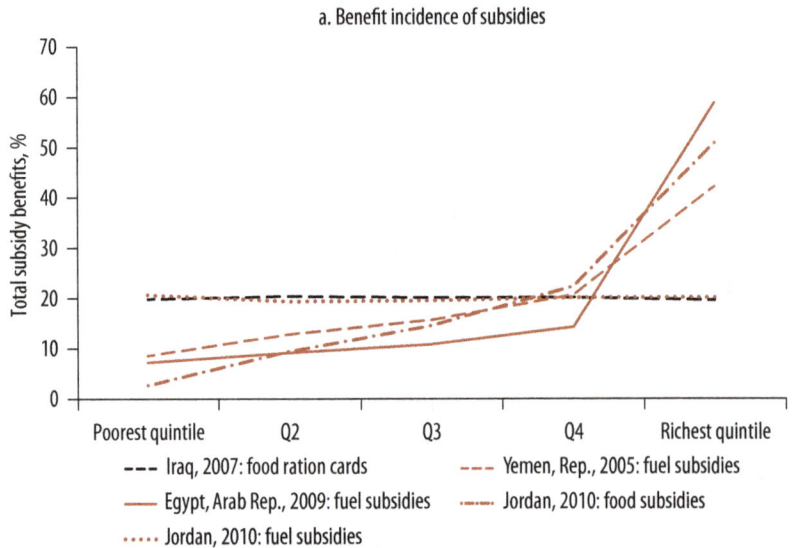

Legend:
- – – – Iraq, 2007: food ration cards
- ——— Egypt, Arab Rep., 2009: fuel subsidies
- ····· Jordan, 2010: fuel subsidies
- – – – Yemen, Rep., 2005: fuel subsidies
- ·–·–· Jordan, 2010: food subsidies

Source: Authors' calculations based on national household surveys.

b. Poverty impact of subsidies

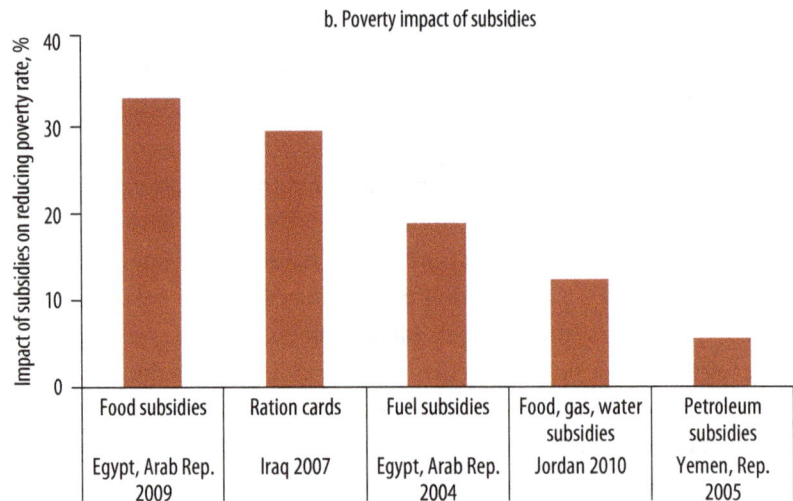

	Food subsidies	Ration cards	Fuel subsidies	Food, gas, water subsidies	Petroleum subsidies
	Egypt, Arab Rep. 2009	Iraq 2007	Egypt, Arab Rep. 2004	Jordan 2010	Yemen, Rep. 2005

Sources: Government of Jordan 2011a; Government of Yemen, World Bank, and UNDP 2007; World Bank 2005, 2010a, 2010b.

Although many of the technical shortcomings of SSNs have been highlighted in the past—and although governments have attempted to reform untargeted subsidies at different times—political economy considerations have been a major reason why SSN reforms have largely stalled or never began across the region. As part of this study, new cross-country data were collected using opinion surveys (MENA SPEAKS [Social Protec-

FIGURE O.23

Self-Reported Poverty and Perceived High Inequality, by Income Quintile, in the Middle East and North Africa, Selected Countries, 2012

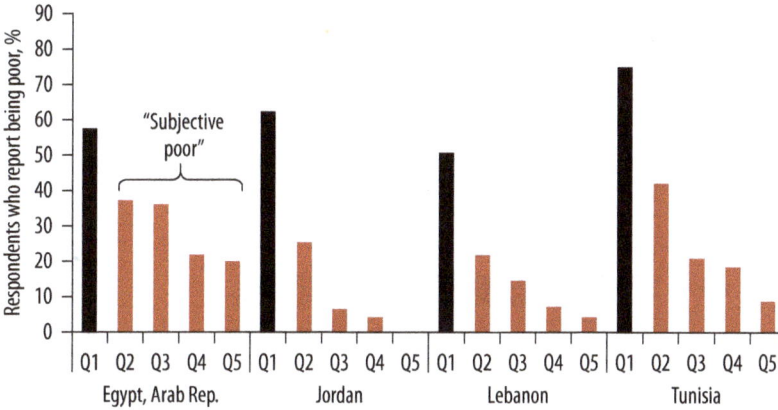

Source: Authors' calculations based on MENA SPEAKS survey.
Note: Q = income quintile (1 = lowest, 5 = highest).

tion Evaluation of Attitudes, Knowledge, and Support]) in partnership with Gallup in Egypt, Jordan, Lebanon, and Tunisia. In addition, this chapter presents the findings from an innovative behavioral experiment (Jordan Gives), which simulated the real trade-offs involved in SSNs by providing participants with fuel vouchers and giving them an option to donate these vouchers in exchange for different designs of SSNs for the poor in their communities. The new data provide evidence on possible entry points for SSNs' renewal and reform that the poor and middle classes are likely to support.

The self-reported poor are an important share of the region's population, and they include both a large majority of the poor and also the "subjective poor"—those who are not in the bottom income quintile and yet report themselves to be poor (see figure O.23). The subjective poor can constitute up to one-fifth of the population, as in the case of Tunisia, and stand out for being those more likely to say that "the rich own almost all of the wealth" in the country. In turn, those who believe that income inequality is high tend to demand more redistributive policies. The subjective poor is the group that perceives inequality more acutely. This group is also more likely to be dissatisfied with the government's effectiveness in providing SSNs.

The demand for redistribution also varies according to personal beliefs about poverty and social mobility. In the questionnaire used after the Jordan Gives experiment, middle-class participants expressed a general belief that hard work usually brings success. This belief was more preva-

FIGURE O.24

Opinions on Causes of Success among the Jordanian Middle Class, 2012

What is in your opinion the main cause of professional success?

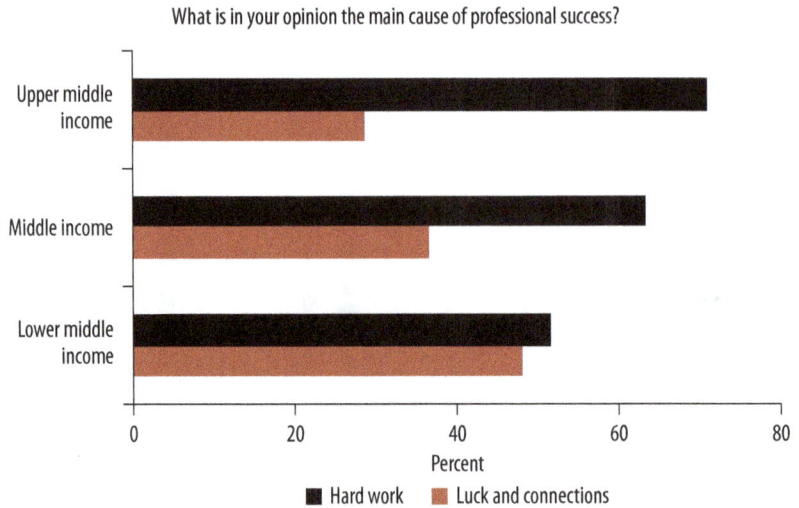

■ Hard work ■ Luck and connections

Source: Authors' calculations based on Jordan Gives 2012 data.

lent among those who define themselves as upper- and middle-income, while those who feel their income to be closer to the poor are more likely to say that success is due to luck and connections, as shown in figure O.24. These perceptions are in line with those in Latin America and Western Europe but less stark than in the United States, where individuals overwhelmingly believe that success is the result of individual effort.

Government Most Responsible for SSNs but Often Seen as Ineffective

When asked about who should bear the primary responsibility for aiding the poor, the vast majority of MENA SPEAKS respondents replied "the government," as shown in figure O.25, panel a. In Jordan and Tunisia, the poor had markedly the most critical evaluations of government effectiveness regarding SSNs, as shown in figure O.25, panel b.

In addition, regression analysis in MENA SPEAKS countries shows that in Egypt and Tunisia, but not in Lebanon, citizens who agreed with the statement that "government corruption is widespread" were much more likely to find the existing SSNs ineffective. Similarly, in the Jordan Gives experiment, those who had more doubts about the accuracy of targeting existing SSNs to the poor were less likely to donate their vouchers to the poor.

FIGURE O.25

Opinions about Responsibility for SSNs and Government Effectiveness in SSN Provision in the Middle East and Northern Africa, Selected Countries, 2012

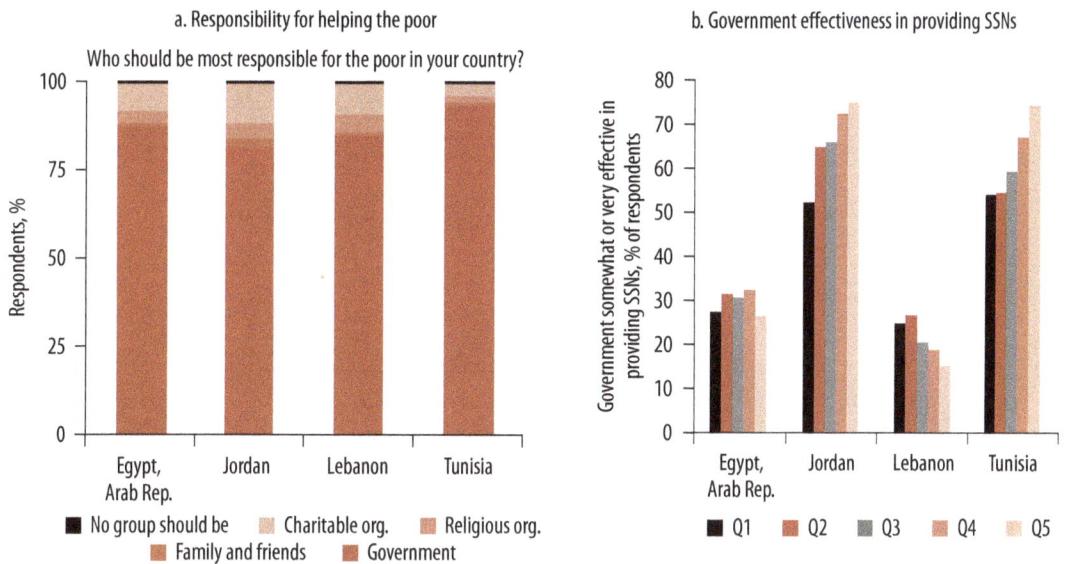

Source: Authors' calculations based on MENA SPEAKS survey.

Note: SSN = social safety net. Q = income quintile (1 = lowest, 5 = highest).

Awareness of available SSN programs varies strongly by country and is higher among the wealthy. Egyptians have low awareness about existing nonsubsidy SSN programs, while Tunisian and Lebanese SSN programs have high name recognition. For instance, 23 percent of respondents in Egypt had never heard about a single SSN program, even after being prompted with program names; this rate was far lower among the poor than among high-income respondents, as shown in figure O.26. In Lebanon, however, a quarter of the respondents knew about three out of five programs on the list.

In Tunisia (and, to a lesser extent, in Lebanon), the rich are much more likely than the poor to *personally* know someone who participates in an SSN program than are the poor, which could be an imperfect proxy for the level of leakage. In Tunisia, the probability of knowing a beneficiary of the National Program of Assistance to Needy Families (*Programme Nationale d'Aide aux Familles Nécessiteuses*) was twice as high among people in the top and middle-income quintiles than among the poor, as shown in figure O.27, panel a. In contrast, in Jordan, most of the programs are better known among the bottom two quintiles than among the top two quintiles, as shown in figure O.27, panel b.

FIGURE O.26

Awareness of SSNs, by Income Quintile, in the Middle East and North Africa, Selected Countries, 2012

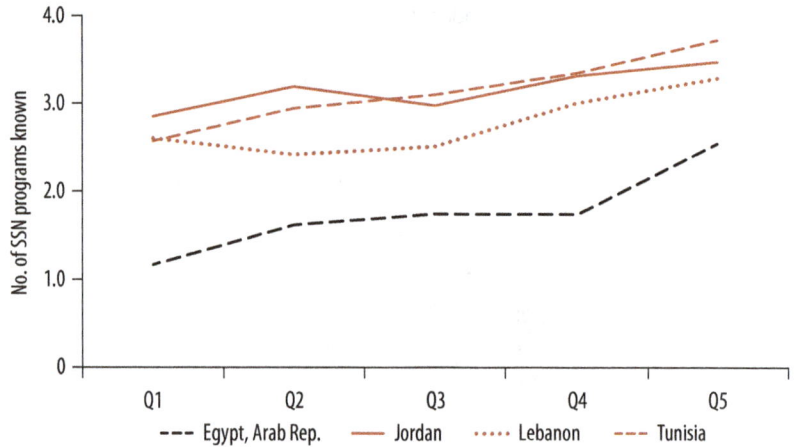

Source: Authors' calculations based on MENA SPEAKS survey.
Note: SSN = social safety net; Q = income quintile (1 = lowest, 5 = highest).

Public awareness of food subsidies in the Middle East and North Africa is much higher than awareness of fuel subsidies, and knowledge about subsidies improves with income, especially for fuel. The awareness that fuel was subsidized ranged from 25 percent in Jordan to 47 percent in Tunisia. However, the awareness of the bread subsidy ranged from 47 percent in Lebanon to 87 percent in Egypt. The higher awareness of food subsidies is particularly relevant considering that the fuel subsidies tend to be more regressive and consume more resources than food subsidies across the region's countries. For example, Egypt spends much more on fuel subsidies (6.9 percent of GDP in 2009) than on food subsidies (1.8 percent of GDP). Raising awareness of the costs incurred due to fuel subsidies could be the starting point for an honest dialogue on SSN reform.

Preferences for SSNs Targeting the Poor, with Cash Rather than In-Kind Benefits

More than 85 percent of people would prefer to have SSN programs targeted to the poor rather than to different categories of people, such as widows, orphans, and the disabled, as shown in figure O.28, panel a. This preference is stronger among the poor themselves, which is understandable because categorical targeting is more likely to exhibit leakage to the nonpoor or not to cover them if they do not belong to the targeted

FIGURE O.27

Knowledge of SSN Program Beneficiaries, by Income Quintile, in Tunisia and Jordan, 2012

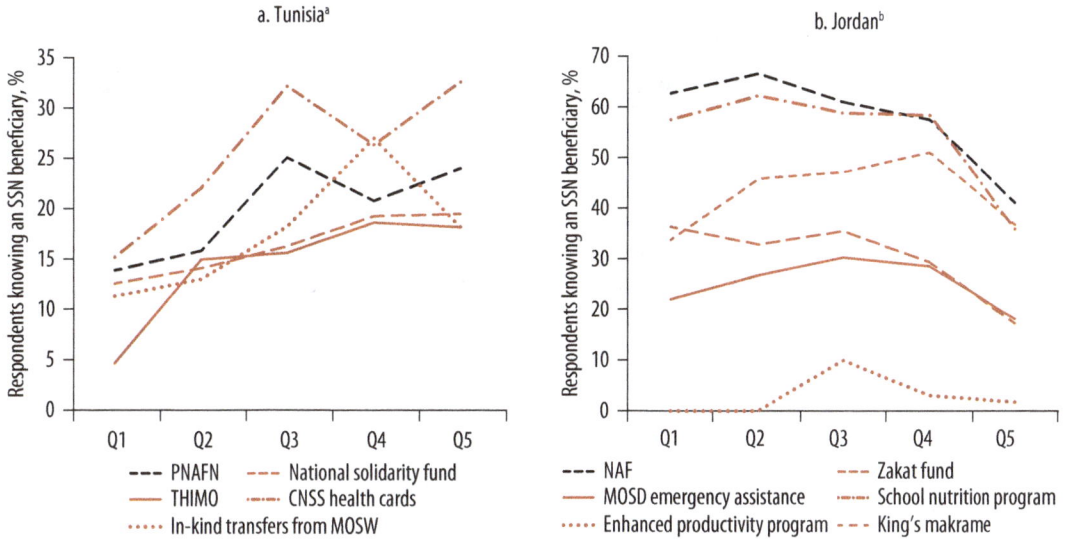

Source: Authors' calculations based on MENA SPEAKS survey.

Note: SSN = social safety net; Q = income quintile (1 = lowest, 5 = highest).

a. CNSS = Social Security Fund (*Caisse nationale de sécurité sociale*); MOSW = Ministry of Social Welfare; PNAFN = National Program of Assistance to Needy Families (*Programme national d'aide aux familles nécessiteuses*); THIMO = Labor intensive works (*Travaux à haute intensité de main d'œuvre*).

b. MOSD = Ministry of Social Development; NAF = National Aid Fund.

FIGURE O.28

SSN Design Preferences, in the Middle East and North Africa, Selected Countries, 2012

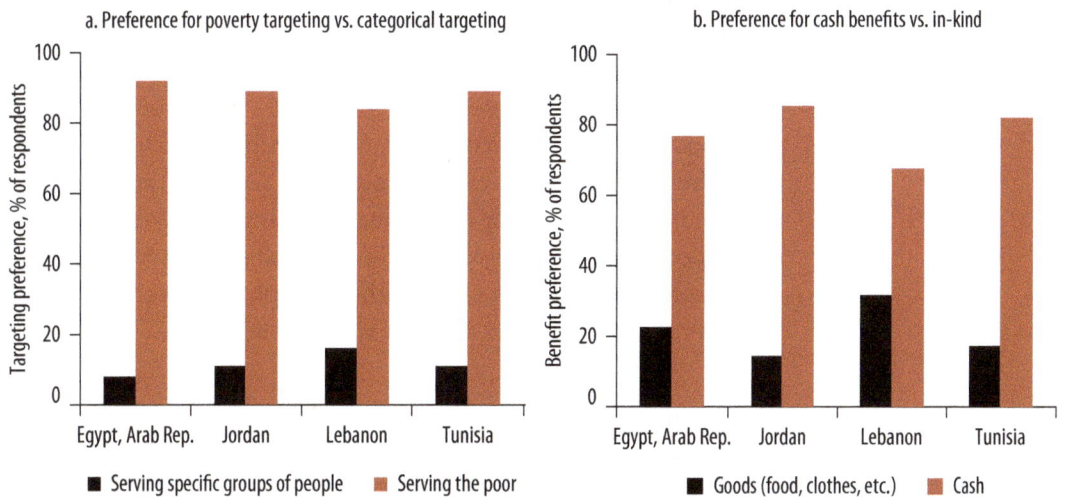

Source: Authors' calculations based on MENA SPEAKS survey.

Note: SSN = social safety net.

FIGURE O.29

Support for Conditionality of SSN Programs in the Middle East and North Africa, Selected Countries, 2012

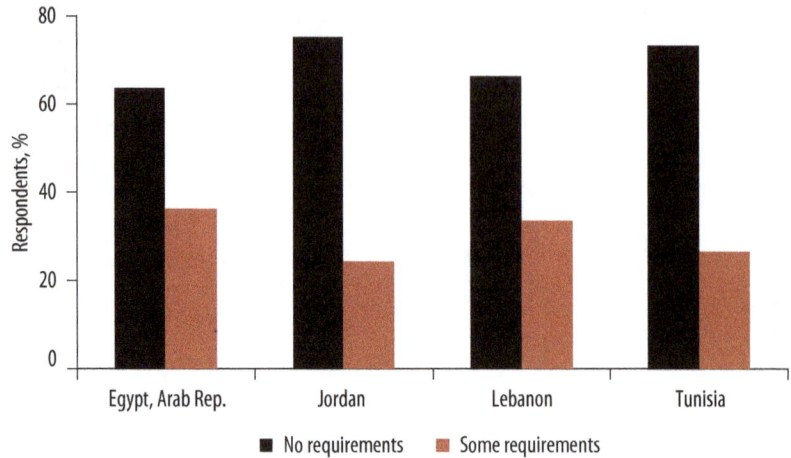

Source: Authors' calculations based on MENA SPEAKS survey.
Note: SSN = social safety net.

categories. Also, more than two-thirds of respondents in each of the four countries under study preferred cash-based SSNs—ranging from 68 percent in Lebanon to 85 percent in Jordan—although the rich were more likely than the poor to prefer in-kind transfers, as shown in figure O.28, panel b.

Unlike in Latin America, where conditionality of cash transfers increased support for SSNs, respondents in the Middle East and North Africa do not seem ready to impose requirements on safety net recipients. About two-thirds of the survey respondents in Egypt and Lebanon and three-quarters of the respondents in Jordan and Tunisia rejected the idea of conditioning SSN transfers (see figure O.29). For those who agreed with imposing some requirements on SSN beneficiaries, conditions tied to children's school attendance and active job search efforts were most preferred. Interestingly, in Egypt, the self-identified poor were much more open to the idea than the middle class and the wealthy. If governments were to establish programs with conditionality, an effective communication campaign on its rationale would be necessary.

Subsidy Reform Acceptance Varies, with Compensation Targeting the Poor Preferred

Acceptance of subsidy reform is very country-specific, ranging from a low in Egypt to a high in Lebanon. Figure O.30 illustrates the relative tolerance of subsidy reform concerning a list of subsidized products. In all

FIGURE O.30

Opposition to Subsidy Reform of Any Product, by Self-Reported Income Group, in the Middle East and North Africa, Selected Countries, 2012

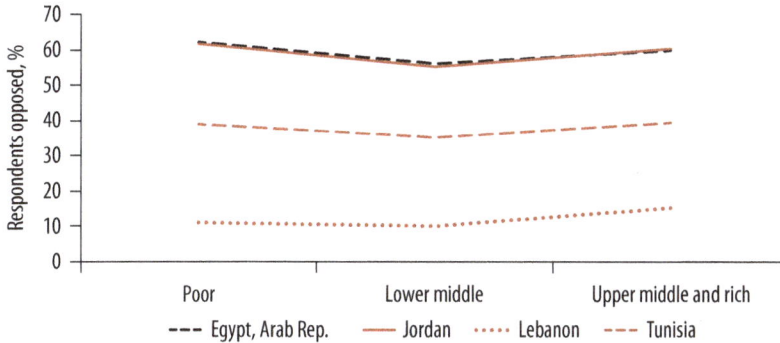

Source: Authors' calculations based on MENA SPEAKS survey.

countries, the lower-middle-income group is less likely to oppose subsidy reform than the upper-middle-income and wealthy groups. And in three out of four countries (all except Lebanon), the lower-middle-income group is more willing to consider subsidy reform than the self-identified poor. One hypothesis explaining this could be that those of lower-middle income do not depend on subsidies as much as the poor, but they also do not consume a lion's share of the subsidy benefits, as do those of upper-middle income and the rich.

In addition, citizens who were ready to consider the reform of at least one subsidy were more tolerant of reforming fuel subsidies than food subsidies. In Lebanon, an overwhelming majority of citizens appeared to support the removal of the relatively unknown tobacco subsidy (see figure O.31). Governments can use such information in building a pro-reform coalition.

The majority of citizens in the Middle East and North Africa prefer spending the savings from subsidy reform on cash-based transfers targeted to the poor, although in Egypt and Tunisia, support for this type of compensation package decreases among those who stand to lose the most. When asked how the savings from subsidy reform could be spent, most people in Egypt, Jordan, and Tunisia preferred targeted transfers only to the poor rather than increased spending on public goods, loosely targeted transfers, or universal compensation (see figure O.32). In Lebanon, the majority of respondents preferred to complement cash transfers to the poor with increased investment in education and health.

However, support for cash transfers narrowly targeted to the poor decreases with income. Respondents identifying themselves as lower-middle-income, upper-middle-income, or rich were less likely to prefer

FIGURE O.31

Preferred Product for Subsidy Removal (Assuming Necessity of Reform) in the Middle East and North Africa, Selected Countries, 2012

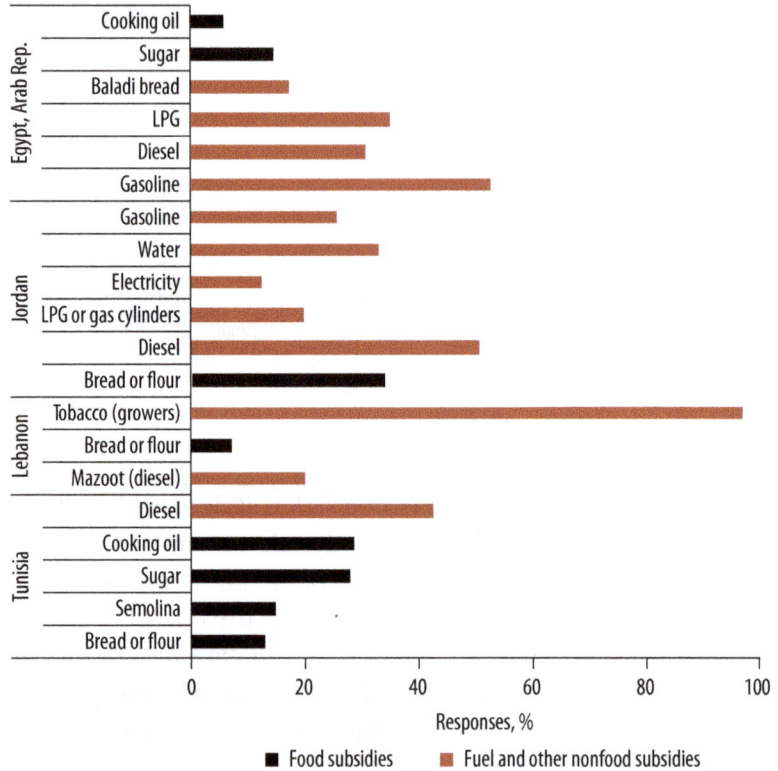

Source: Authors' calculations based on MENA SPEAKS survey.

Note: LPG = liquefied petroleum gas. Each bar displays the percent of respondents in each country who named the product as their first or second preferred for subsidy removal.

narrowly targeted cash transfers to the poor, with many opting instead either for more loosely targeted cash transfers or for expansion of health and education spending, so that they could benefit from this reform. It is important to read these results in light of the fact that a broader spectrum of the population defined themselves as poor than those who actually belong to the bottom income quintile. These individuals would likely consider themselves to be among the reform winners and could, in fact, be highly disappointed if they were among the losers.

"Jordan Gives" Experiment Tests Support for SSN Designs

The Jordan Gives behavioral experiment provides empirical evidence of some of the characteristics that drove preferences for particular methods of redistribution.

FIGURE O.32

Preferred Targeting of Compensation following Subsidy Reform, in the Middle East and North Africa, Selected Countries, 2012

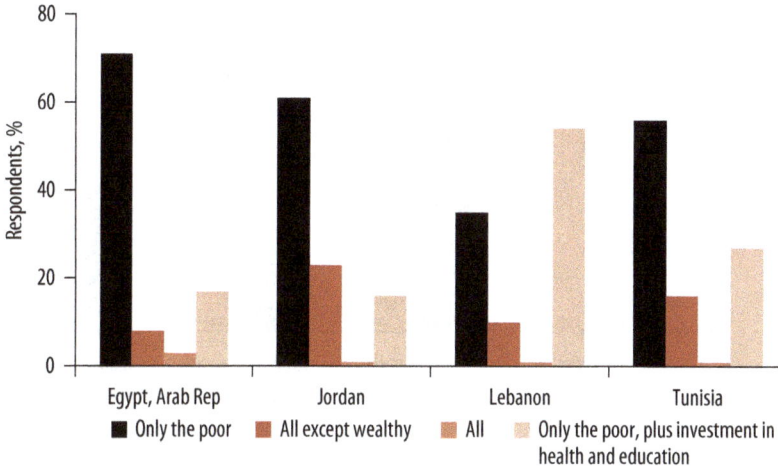

Source: Authors' calculations based on MENA SPEAKS survey.

Overall, about two-thirds of 420 participants in the Jordan Gives experiment decided to donate their fuel vouchers worth 10 Jordanian dinars (JD) of fuel at any gas station in exchange for helping the poor in their communities.

In addition, the experiment enabled the evaluation, through a randomized controlled trial, of the impact of introducing additional information meant to enhance the participants' confidence that the transfers would reach the intended target (see figure 33). Overall, individuals in the treatment group tended to donate visibly more than those in the control group (though this difference is not statistically significant).

The treatment, however, significantly increased donation rates among two large groups of participants: young people, and those who had low trust in the accuracy of the existing targeting of national SSN programs.

An important consequence of enhancing transparency was that while in the control group the SSN design that achieved the highest rate of fuel voucher donations was unconditional in-kind transfer, in the treatment group the most popular decision was unconditional cash transfers, which may be perceived as more prone to elite capture in spite of being more beneficial for the welfare of the poor.

The experiment suggests that there is scope for governments to improve individuals' support for effective SSNs, even from low levels of confidence, through transparency enhancing measures.

FIGURE O.33

Propensity to Donate Vouchers by SSN Design and Treatment Group in Jordan, 2012

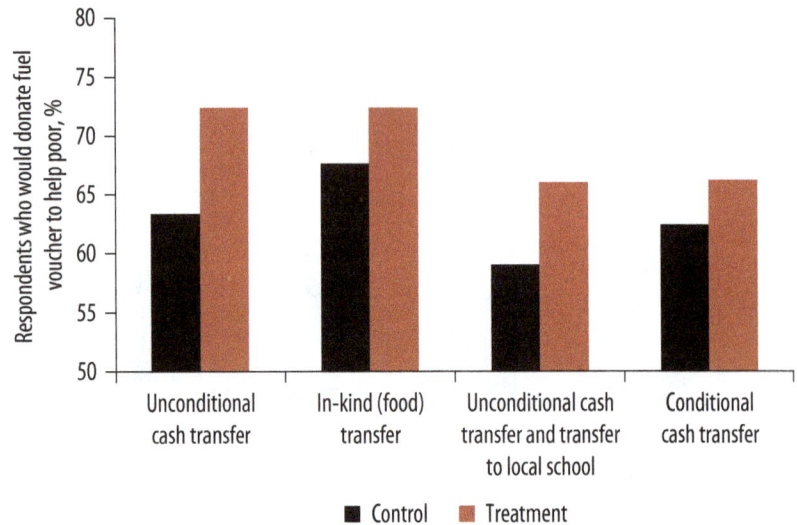

Source: Authors' calculations based on Jordan Gives 2012 data.
Note: SSN = social safety net.

Moreover, participants' characteristics were associated with specific donation patterns:

- Everything else equal, individuals who considered themselves as middle class (compared with individuals who reported to be either in lower-income or in upper-income households) were more likely to donate in all options except the conditional cash transfer (where income had no impact).

- Those who thought that the government-run social assistance was ineffective were less likely to donate their vouchers for options associated with government-provided services (school and training), compared to individuals who thought the government was effective in providing social assistance.

- Those who believed that poverty is caused by laziness rather than an unjust society or bad luck chose less often to donate to the school, while those who thought that career success comes from hard work (as opposed to luck and connections) were more likely to donate to the school.

- Interestingly, the education level of participants did not seem to play a role in the propensity to donate cash, food, or to the school; however, having higher education proved to be an important predictor of the support for the conditional cash transfer option.

- Compared with prime-age participants, young and elderly individuals were more likely to donate their fuel vouchers in exchange for food baskets to poor families in their communities.

The Way Forward: How to Make Safety Nets in the Middle East and North Africa More Effective and Innovative

SSNs can become a crucial instrument of economic and social transitions in the Middle East and North Africa. As previously described in the framework for SSN reform (figure O.3), the three outcomes that social safety nets can promote are (a) social inclusion, by enabling investment in human capital (such as supporting school attendance or better nutrition for children); (b) livelihood, by protecting against destitution; and (c) resilience to crises, by helping households navigate the effects of shocks.

Achieving these outcomes implies refocusing the goals of the region's SSNs. The predominant SSN instrument in the Middle East and North Africa—fuel and food subsidies—focuses on guaranteeing, at a high fiscal cost, affordable access to basic goods. This instrument meets only one of the SSN goals: supporting livelihood. Meanwhile, the region currently pays scant attention to promoting inclusion and resilience. Achieving all three outcomes will require reorienting SSNs toward the following goals:

- Enhance the focus on the poor and vulnerable

- Empower individuals with tools to improve their lives

- Ensure ready and rapid temporary support in response to crises

- Give citizens a greater voice to promote civic engagement and policy ownership.

SSNs in the Middle East and North Africa are ripe for reform. The region relies too heavily on untargeted price subsidies and ration cards, which waste the scarce resources of governments because of high leakage rates and a high propensity for waste, fraud, and corruption. Subsidies aside, SSNs in the Middle East and North Africa are underresourced and fragmented. Most of the poor and vulnerable fall through the cracks of the small, categorically or geographically targeted programs. Moreover, poor targeting methods result in significant leakages of SSN benefits to the nonpoor, siphoning off resources that could be used elsewhere to decrease poverty and improve the distribution of welfare in the region.

Although subsidies (and in particular, fuel subsidies) are inefficient and frequently ineffective relative to other SSN interventions, many of the poor and vulnerable depend on them to stay out of poverty. Moving from the status quo toward more effective, reliable, and equitable SSNs requires careful thinking not only about the technical aspects of reform but also, and perhaps more important, about the sensitive issues revolving around political economy of reform.

SSNs in the Middle East and North Africa can perform better in promoting inclusion, livelihood, and resilience, and the region's citizens are expecting them to do so. The MENA SPEAKS survey and Jordan Gives behavioral experiment have demonstrated that people hold the government responsible as the main provider of SSNs, and many are not satisfied with the effectiveness of current SSN policies and programs. In fact, the types of programs preferred by citizens in several of the region's countries are in line with best practices in SSN design. Thus, governments have an enabling environment that can be rallied behind SSN reform.

Moreover, successful reforms that have attained significant positive results have already been implemented in several parts of the region. For example, West Bank and Gaza created a unified registry across SSN programs that significantly improved targeting accuracy and crisis response capacity. During the last crisis, the Republic of Yemen responded quickly with a workfare program to bridge a consumption gap of the poor and vulnerable, while also creating community assets. Simultaneously, important reforms were implemented in the main cash transfer program (the Social Welfare Fund), such as (a) improving poverty targeting with a proxy means test formula, (b) strengthening capacity for service delivery, and (c) implementing a new legal and policy framework.

In light of the specific challenges faced by the poor and vulnerable in the Middle East and North Africa, and in light of the current state of SSNs, the path toward more effective and innovative SSNs calls for action on several fronts. While there is no single solution, better results can be achieved through action on the following four agenda items:

- *Improve the impact of SSN programs*, including their effect on present and future poverty

- *Establish a reliable yet flexible SSN infrastructure* that can be used in normal times as well as during crises

- *Consolidate fragmented SSN programs* and integrate these programs within social protection systems

- *Rebalance the financing and priorities* of SSN systems by focusing on targeted programs rather than on subsidies.

Engaging citizens and other stakeholders in this reform agenda can improve feasibility and facilitate success.

Improve the Impact of SSN Programs

Currently, most nonsubsidy SSN programs in the Middle East and North Africa have limited impact on poverty and inequality because of low coverage combined with inefficient targeting practices and inadequate or nonexistent M&E systems. Hence, the way forward could entail the following:

- *Prioritizing interventions that promote investment in human capital.* This can be achieved by (a) scaling up the region's existing successful CCTs (such as the Tayssir program in Morocco) and workfare programs (such as the Social Welfare Fund in the Republic of Yemen); (b) tweaking the design of existing programs to make them work better for children, youth, and women (such as Djibouti's workfare plus nutrition program); or (c) creating new interventions to fill the gaps based on best practices around the world but adjusting their design to empower the poor and vulnerable.

- *Enhancing targeting toward the poor and vulnerable.* Improved targeting can contain costs, ensure equity, allow SSNs to act as insurance, and increase effectiveness. Most of the programs in the region remain categorically or geographically targeted even though these methods are effective only in environments of concentrated poverty. At the same time, citizens in the MENA SPEAKS surveys indicated their strong preference for poverty-based targeting as opposed to categorical targeting. There is already substantial movement in the region (in Djibouti, Iraq, Jordan, Lebanon, West Bank and Gaza, and the Republic of Yemen) in the direction of poverty-based targeting. The results have demonstrated the power of such reforms and outlined a clear path forward.

- *Improving the focus on results in SSN programs through M&E and social accountability.* In the Middle East and North Africa, enhanced M&E for SSNs can help allocate budget resources between programs, monitor day-to-day operations, and track results of interventions. M&E has been particularly effective when the results of evaluation and the empirical data produced are used to inform budgetary decisions and reshape programs. This was the case in, for example, West Bank and Gaza and the Republic of Yemen. Moreover, introducing well-functioning social accountability systems can improve efficiency and accountability and combat corruption.

- *Reaching out to other stakeholders (citizens, NGOs, civil society organizations [CSOs], the private sector, and nonprofits)*. As revealed by the MENA SPEAKS survey, citizens' awareness about existing SSN programs is low and skewed toward the wealthy. On-demand registration requires awareness about the existence of the program, eligibility criteria, and application procedures. Comprehensive communication campaigns are needed to inform poor and vulnerable citizens of the safety nets that are available to them. Moreover, engaging a broader spectrum of stakeholders (such as NGOs, CSOs, the private sector, and nonprofits) in financing and implementing SSN programs could leverage their existing financial and human resources.

Establish a Reliable Yet Flexible SSN Infrastructure

An effective SSN system can help citizens navigate the effects of both idiosyncratic shocks during normal times and systemic shocks during times of crisis. The recent global economic crisis underscored the weak capacity of existing SSN systems in the Middle East and North Africa to serve this function.

Promoting households' resilience to shocks through SSNs requires a strong administrative infrastructure. Having this infrastructure in place *ahead* of a crisis allows for quicker and more efficient development of remedial and mitigative actions, such as scaling up of benefits for the most vulnerable or expanding coverage, thus enhancing resilience. In particular, setting up an improved SSN infrastructure could entail the following:

- *Creating unified registries of beneficiaries*. Such registries can be used to target multiple programs. In normal times, unified registries can reduce costs and facilitate coherence and convergence because all agents work with the same database. In times of crisis, unified registries can be used to quickly disburse additional benefits to the target population or to promptly expand coverage by adjusting eligibility criteria. West Bank and Gaza provides an example of best practice in this regard in the region.

- *Using effective service delivery mechanisms*. In normal times, modern benefit delivery systems are important to reduce administrative costs and leakage to nonbeneficiaries, to avoid corruption, and to make the transfer of payments to beneficiaries quick and flexible. Effective use of modern technologies such as smart cards, mobile payments, and over-the-counter payments in bank branches facilitates rapid response during crises.

Consolidate Fragmented SSN Programs

In the Middle East and North Africa, direct transfer programs (cash-based or in-kind) are often small and highly fragmented. International experience suggests that having a few comprehensive programs, specifically designed to reach different segments of the poor and vulnerable, can address current vulnerabilities and social protection gaps by increasing both coverage (currently below 20 percent of the poor in most countries) and benefits (currently at about 5–10 percent of consumption of the poor). A few parts of the region (for example, West Bank and Gaza and Morocco) have started reforming their SSNs in this direction.

To achieve progress in this respect, governments can start by identifying gaps in SSN systems and creating an inventory of SSN programs by program objective, eligibility criteria, and benefit type. For example, Morocco recently undertook this type of analysis. Informed by such analysis, governments can identify programs that can be expanded or consolidated, and formulate a strategy for implementation of the reform. Moreover, consolidation of SSNs has few prerequisites; thus, Middle Eastern and North African countries can move forward on this agenda item fairly quickly.

Rebalance Financing and Priorities of SSN Systems

Instead of focusing on targeted programs, Middle Eastern and North African countries spend the lion's share of SSN spending on energy subsidies and only a small share on targeted safety nets. Rebalancing the financing and priorities of SSN systems away from subsidies and toward more effective and efficient programs could be a major step for SSN renewal. In particular, this effort could entail the following:

- *Increasing spending and improving coverage of nonsubsidy SSNs to protect against destitution.* Around the world, successful subsidy reforms have demonstrated the importance of gaining citizens' trust in government's capacity to deliver fair and reliable compensation for the reduction or loss of those subsidies. In light of the evidence provided by MENA SPEAKS and Jordan Gives, demonstrating readiness to deliver effective and inclusive SSN programs would be an essential step on the path toward comprehensive subsidy reform. This could be achieved by creating new programs, scaling up effective programs, and reforming ineffective programs.

- *Reforming price subsidies through wholesale or internal reforms.* Sequencing of sensitive reforms—such as reform of universal price subsidies—is crucial for their success. To gain credibility, government could start by

○ *Improving subsidy targeting* (for example, through differentiated marketing and packaging, which can lead to self-targeting, as in Tunisia); narrowing subsidy coverage (for example, through lifeline tariffs in electricity); and reducing leakages in the distribution chain.

○ *Identifying the most sensitive subsidies and focusing instead on the most regressive ones.* According to the MENA SPEAKS survey, the least-preferred products for subsidy reform were cooking oil in Egypt, bread in Lebanon and Tunisia, and electricity in Jordan. These subsidies could be subject to reform only when governments have already demonstrated their success at reforming less-sensitive subsidies. Given that fuel subsidy spending is more than three times the spending on food subsidies, it appears that nonfood subsidy reform is the lower-hanging fruit. In MENA SPEAKS, citizens indicated that if they had to pick one subsidized product for reform, this product would be tobacco in Lebanon, gasoline in Egypt, and diesel in Jordan and Tunisia.

○ *Engaging citizens early on in a dialogue about compensation packages and promoting awareness through information campaigns.* Governments can use the findings from the MENA SPEAKS surveys to initiate a dialogue on preferred compensation packages in their countries. The evidence so far shows that people in the Middle East and North Africa prefer the government to either (a) target cash-based compensation for subsidy reform to the poor alone (Egypt, Jordan, and Tunisia) or (b) combine cash transfers to the poor with investment in savings in education and health (Lebanon).

Tailor Country-Specific SSN Reforms

The SSN reform path is different for every country in the region, given their varying stages of development and the main challenges of the existing SSN systems. Countries in the Middle East and North Africa find themselves at different stages of progress on human development outcomes and SSN reforms. Notably, the two parts of the region that have advanced the most in SSN reform are West Bank and Gaza and the Republic of Yemen, which have, respectively, medium and low levels of human development outcomes (as proxied by the United Nations Development Programme's Human Development Index). These countries were able to implement successful SSN interventions (establishing a unified registry in West Bank and Gaza and reforming the Social Welfare Fund in the Republic of Yemen) that help to address their specific needs. Bahrain, Djibouti, Jordan, Lebanon, and Morocco have made important steps toward SSN reform, such as workfare plus nutrition in Djibouti, a pilot CCT program in Morocco, reforms in the subsidy system in Jordan and Bahrain, and a targeting database in Lebanon. Other countries are currently considering new programs or reforms of their SSN systems.

In each country, the way forward would include short- and medium-run interventions with complementary and mutually reinforcing objectives. In the short run, Middle Eastern and North African countries can start demonstrating better results using existing SSN systems, tweaking the design of existing programs, building unified registries, or piloting new programs such as CCTs and "workfare plus." In the medium run, the focus can shift to reforms that require more preexisting capacity, such as refining the SSN infrastructure and comprehensive subsidy reform. Engaging a broad spectrum of stakeholders in an inclusive and open dialogue can facilitate the envisioned reforms and promote an empowering role for SSNs in the region.

Note

1. Social safety nets (SSNs) are defined as noncontributory transfers targeted to the poor or vulnerable. They include income support, temporary employment programs (workfare), and services that build human capital and expand access to finance among the poor and vulnerable.

References

Chamlou, N., S. Muzi, and H. Ahmed. 2008a. *MENA Home-Based Work: Evidence from Amman, Cairo, and Sana'a*. Unpublished report, World Bank, Washington, DC.

———. 2008b. *Women Labor Force Participation, Education and Non-Economic Factors: The Case of Middle East and North Africa Countries*. Unpublished report, World Bank, Washington, DC.

Gallup Inc. 2011. World Poll Survey.

Government of Jordan. 2011a. "An Analysis of Consumption Subsidies." Note prepared for the Hashemite Kingdom of Jordan, World Bank, Washington, DC, and Government of Jordan, Amman.

———. 2011b. *The Hashemite Kingdom of Jordan: Social Protection Review*. Unpublished report for the Hashemite Kingdom of Jordan, Amman.

Government of Yemen, World Bank, and UNDP (United Nations Development Programme). 2007. *Yemen Poverty Assessment*. World Bank, Washington, DC.

Human Rights Watch. 2010. *Stateless Again: Palestinian-Origin Jordanians Deprived of their Nationality*. Report 1-56432-575-X, New York. NY

IEG (Independent Evaluation Group). 2011. *Social Safety Nets: An Evaluation of the World Bank Support, 2010–2011*. Washington, DC: World Bank.

Kingdom of Morocco. 2006. *Childhood and Disabled Persons: The National Survey on Disability*. Data set, Kingdom of Morocco, Rabat.

Marotta, D. M., R. Yemtsov, H. El-Laithy, H. Abou-Ali, and S. Al-Shawarby. 2011. "Was Growth in Egypt between 2005 and 2008 Pro-Poor? From Static to Dynamic Poverty Profile." Policy Research Working Paper 5589, World Bank, Washington, DC.

PovcalNet (database). Online Poverty Analysis tool. World Bank, Washington, DC. http://iresearch.worldbank.org/povcalnet.

UNDP (United Nations Development Programme). 2005. *Arab Human Development Report 2005: Towards the Rise of Women in the Arab World*. New York, NY: UNDP.

UNICEF (United Nations Children's Fund). 2009. *State of the World's Children*. New York, NY: UNICEF.

———. n.d. Multiple Indicator Cluster Surveys (database). http://www.childinfo .org/mics.html.

WHO (World Health Organization) and World Bank. 2010. *World Report on Disability*. Geneva: WHO.

World Bank. 2004. *Gender and Development in the Middle East and North Africa: Women in the Public Sphere*. MENA development report. Washington, DC: World Bank.

———. 2005. *Egypt: Toward a More Effective Social Policy: Subsidies and Social Safety Net*. Report 33550-EG, World Bank, Washington, DC.

——— 2009. *Iraq: Poverty Assessment 2009*. Poverty Assessment report, World Bank, Washington, DC.

———. 2010a. *Arab Republic of Egypt. Egypt's Food Subsidies: Benefit Incidence and Leakages*. Report 57446, Washington, DC.

———. 2010b. *Iraq: First Programmatic Fiscal Sustainability DPL Program Document*. Report 51528–IQ, Washington, DC.

———. 2010c. *Yemen: Private Sector Growth and Social Protection Development Policy Grant Program Document*. Report 55649-YE, Washington, DC.

———. 2011a. *Poverty in Egypt 2008–9: Withstanding the Global Economic Crisis*. Report 60249-EG, Washington, DC.

———. 2011b. *Royaume du Maroc: Note Strategique sur le Ciblage et la Protection Sociale. Ciblage et protection sociale: Note d'orientation stratégique*. Report AAA65–MA, Washington, DC.

———. 2012a. (Online database). Atlas of Social Protection: Indicators of Resilience and Equity (ASPIRE). http://www.worldbank.org/spatlas.

———. 2012b. "Safety Nets Work: During Crisis and Prosperity." Staff Paper DC2012-0003, World Bank, Washington, DC.

———. 2012c. *2012 World Development Indicators*. Washington, DC: World Bank.

World Bank, FAO (Food and Agriculture Organization of the United Nations), and IFAD (International Fund for Agricultural Development). 2009. *Improving Food Security in Arab Countries*. Joint report, Washington, DC.

CHAPTER 1

The Framework for Social Safety Net Reform in the Middle East and North Africa

The Growing Need for Safety Nets

Recent economic and social transitions in the Middle East and North Africa have refocused attention on the need for greater social inclusion, livelihood, and resilience. Although sustained growth in many of the region's countries has pulled people out of poverty and into the middle class, economic progress has yet to reach many families who face persistent poverty, unemployment, disability, and illness. And many more families in the Middle East and North Africa are vulnerable to economic shocks, natural disasters, and political or other crises. Without a safety net, poor families who are systematically unable to afford their basic needs are likely to disengage socially; malnourished children are more likely to become poor adults; and near-poor families who lose their livelihoods as a consequence of shocks are likely to fall into poverty.

In fact, economic anxiety in the region is on the rise. Figure 1.1 depicts the share of people who report being in need for lack of means (Gallup and World Bank 2011). In particular, the following question was posed: "Were there times in the past 12 months when you did not have enough money to buy food that you or your family needed?" The share of the population who responded in the affirmative in the Arab Republic of Egypt, Jordan, and Tunisia in 2011 was significantly higher than in 2009, having increased from 23 to 44 percent in Egypt, from 7 to 16 percent in Jordan, and from 11 to 18 percent in Tunisia. By providing assistance to the poor and vulnerable, social safety nets (SSNs) can improve this situation, serving as a springboard to help citizens become more independent and share in the benefits of economic progress (see box 1.1 for the definition of SSNs).

Most Middle Eastern and North African countries responded to the 2008–09 food, fuel, and financial crisis and to the early Arab Spring unrest

FIGURE 1.1

Citizens' Self-Reported Ability to Buy Sufficient Food in the Middle East and North Africa, Selected Countries, 2009–11

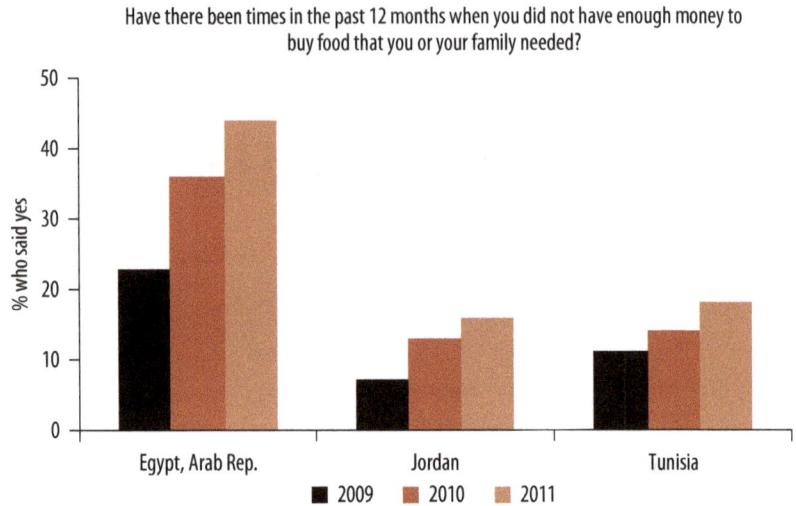

Have there been times in the past 12 months when you did not have enough money to buy food that you or your family needed?

Source: Gallup Inc. 2011.

by scaling up generalized price subsidies and increasing public sector wages, at enormous fiscal costs (see table 1.1). These solutions are costly and difficult to remove, and have significantly amplified fiscal pressures (for example, in Egypt and Jordan). Although some governments chose these solutions because subsidies and public sector wages continue to be their preferred instruments for redistribution, others chose them because no effective SSNs were in place that could have been scaled up. In fact, many countries in the region found that existing poverty-targeted SSNs were not flexible enough to expand quickly or that they lacked poverty data and systems to target and deliver other types of benefits. Safety nets are needed at all times, and having them in place before a crisis makes the response more effective.

Citizens in some Middle Eastern and North African countries reveal low levels of satisfaction with ongoing government efforts to assist the poor. For example, only about 30 percent of the population of Egypt and Morocco indicates that they are satisfied, as shown in figure 1.2. Yet a few parts of the region have started SSN reforms aimed at achieving better effectiveness and results. West Bank and Gaza and the Republic of Yemen enhanced targeting of their cash transfer programs. Morocco is implementing a conditional cash transfer (CCT) program requiring that families send their children to school regularly to receive the transfer. Djibouti and the Republic of Yemen are implementing integrated workfare programs that generate short-term employment opportunities for

BOX 1.1

Social Safety Nets (SSNs) Defined

Social safety nets, sometimes termed "welfare" or SSNs, are noncontributory transfer programs targeted at the poor or vulnerable and encompassing different program designs and objectives (Weigand and Grosh 2008):

- *Unconditional cash transfer programs (UCTs).* UCTs provide assistance in the form of cash. Some target the poor (poverty-based targeting), while others target specific regions (geographic targeting) or groups of people such as widows, orphans, the sick, and the elderly (categorical targeting). They are often linked to national registries and can be used to provide emergency assistance in response to a crisis by increasing assistance either through an existing program or as a stand-alone transfer.

- *Conditional cash transfer programs (CCTs).* CCTs are transfers of money to poor and vulnerable households under certain conditions, usually related to investment in human capital. In contrast with UCTs, CCT recipients are required to engage in an activity in exchange for the transfer. For example, beneficiaries' children can be required to attend school regularly; if they stop, the assistance is no longer provided. Other types of requirements might include primary health care appointments for children or expectant mothers, or job training for able-bodied beneficiaries.

- *Food or other in-kind transfer programs.* These provide SSNs in the form of goods, including food, school feeding, mother and child food supplements, take-home food rations, or school supplies.

- *Workfare programs.* These provide SSNs in the form of short-term employment opportunities in small-scale, labor-intensive public works, often at the community level. Beneficiaries must accept the work provided by the program in exchange for the assistance. The wage is set at a level at which less-poor households will not be interested in participation because they can command higher wages elsewhere (self-targeting).

- *Price subsidies (for example, for food or energy).* Some governments subsidize the prices of certain products by either keeping their prices fixed or preventing them from rising too quickly.

- *Fee waivers.* These are used to gain access to essential services such as health care, schooling, utilities, or transportation.

able-bodied members of poor and vulnerable households, providing income for families as well as building community assets as part of the safety net. Beyond these examples, a diverse suite of available SSN programs give governments many options for protecting citizens in incentive-compatible and fiscally sustainable ways.

TABLE 1.1

Social Policy Measures Implemented during the Arab Spring in the Middle East and North Africa, Selected Countries, 2011

	Special salary increases in public sector	Special financing in food subsidies or price controls	Special tax cuts	One-off transfers	Infrastructure investment	Bulk expansion of public sector hiring
Gulf Cooperation Council (GCC) oil exporters						
Bahrain	Yes	Yes	Yes	Yes	Yes	Yes
Kuwait	Yes	Yes	No	Yes	Yes	No
Oman	Yes	Yes	No	Yes	No	Yes
Qatar	Yes	No	No	No	No	No
Saudi Arabia	Yes	No	No	Yes	Yes	Yes
United Arab Emirates	No	Yes	No	No	No	No
Developing oil exporters						
Algeria	Yes	Yes	No	No	Yes	Yes
Iran, Islamic Rep.	No	No	No	Yes	No	No
Syrian Arab Republic	No	Yes	No	Yes	No	No
Yemen, Rep.	Yes	Yes	Yes	Yes	No	Yes
Oil importers						
Egypt, Arab Rep.	Yes	Yes	No	Yes	No	Yes
Jordan	Yes	Yes	Yes	Yes	Yes	No
Lebanon	No	No	No	Yes	No	No
Morocco	Yes	Yes	No	Yes	No	Yes
Tunisia	Yes	Yes	Yes	Yes	Yes	Yes

Source: World Bank 2011.

FIGURE 1.2

Citizens' Satisfaction with Government Assistance to the Poor in the Middle East and North Africa, Selected Countries, 2011

In your country, are you satisfied or dissatisfied with efforts to deal with the poor?

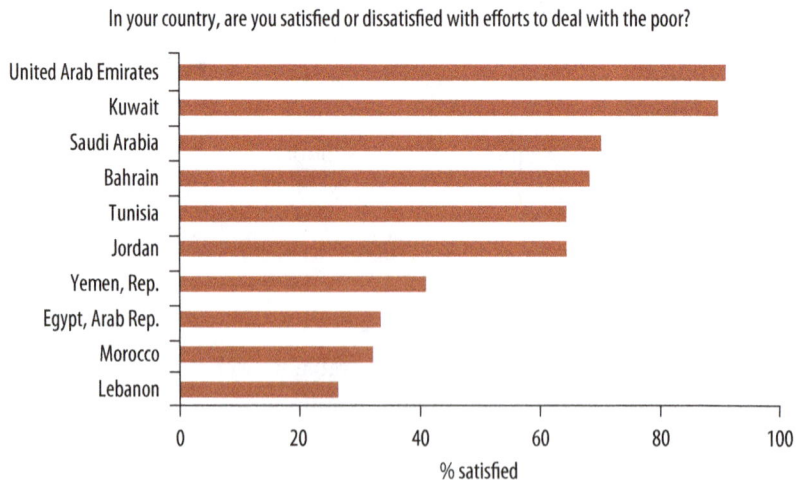

Source: Gallup Inc. 2011.

FIGURE 1.3

Where Social Safety Nets Fit in Larger Development Policy

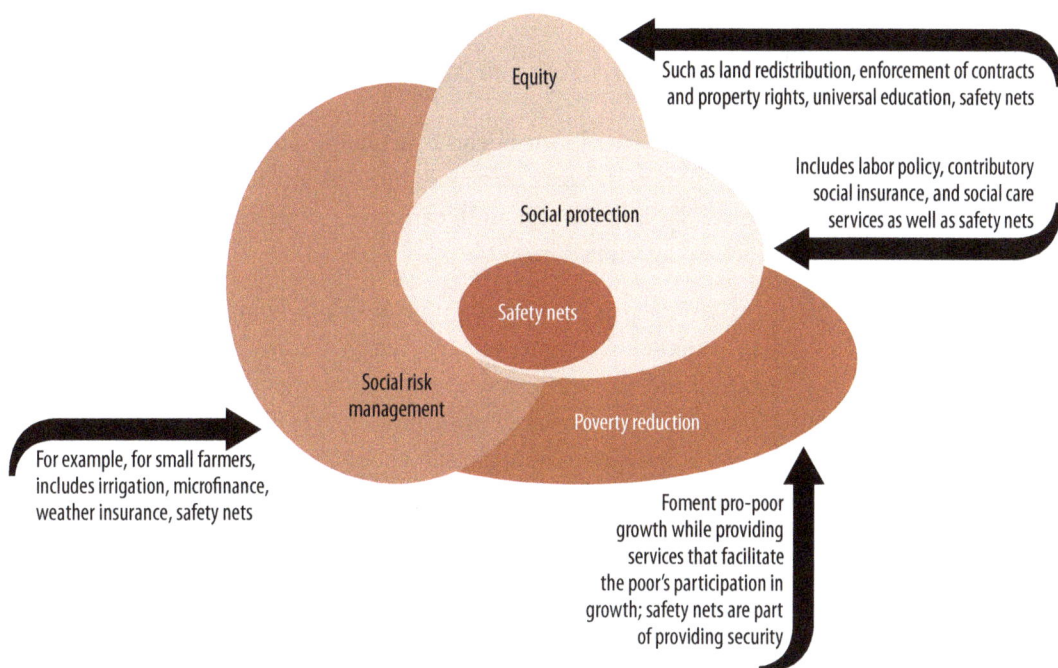

Equity

Such as land redistribution, enforcement of contracts and property rights, universal education, safety nets

Includes labor policy, contributory social insurance, and social care services as well as safety nets

Social protection

Safety nets

Social risk management

Poverty reduction

For example, for small farmers, includes irrigation, microfinance, weather insurance, safety nets

Foment pro-poor growth while providing services that facilitate the poor's participation in growth; safety nets are part of providing security

Source: Grosh et al. 2008.

SSNs are an integral part of the wider social protection system, which also includes social insurance (such as old-age and disability pensions, health insurance, and unemployment insurance) as well as labor market programs (such as skill-building, job search, and matching programs) (World Bank 2012a). Moreover, SSNs fit into the wider array of policies involved in poverty reduction, social risk management, and equity-enhancing programs, as figure 1.3 illustrates. However, in the Middle East and North Africa, formal social insurance systems are mostly nascent, consisting of mandatory pension and health insurance systems, which have low coverage. These systems tend to cover only about a third of the workforce, and tend to be focused on high-income and public sector workers in metropolitan and urban areas (Gatti et al., forthcoming). Thus, they often miss large shares of the rural population, particularly the poor, the elderly, and informal workers. Besides the coverage gap, demographic transition in the region poses additional challenges to the solvency of the social insurance systems and their adequacy for protecting against risks. To date, no country in the region offers genuine unemployment insurance, although the recent social insurance reforms in Jordan and Egypt should be noted. Such limited access to complementary instruments of the social protection systems implies an even greater need for effective and innovative SSNs.

Key Objectives and Results of Effective SSNs

SSNs can be crucial instruments of economic and social transitions in the Middle East and North Africa. Figure 1.4 introduces a framework for effective SSNs in the region. In particular, social safety nets can promote the following three outcomes:

- *Social inclusion*, by enabling investment in human capital. SSNs can help households build human capital by stimulating the demand for health and education services and by improving the gender balance in access to these services. For example, CCTs and education fee waivers help to promote school enrollment and attendance. Similarly, CCTs and noncontributory health insurance schemes can encourage health care utilization, especially for preventive care (such as mother and child health), while workfare programs can increase the assets of the poor and their communities. These opportunities can become catalysts for empowering citizens to become more productive and self-sufficient participants in the benefits of economic growth.

FIGURE 1.4

Framework for Renewed Social Safety Nets in the Middle East and North Africa

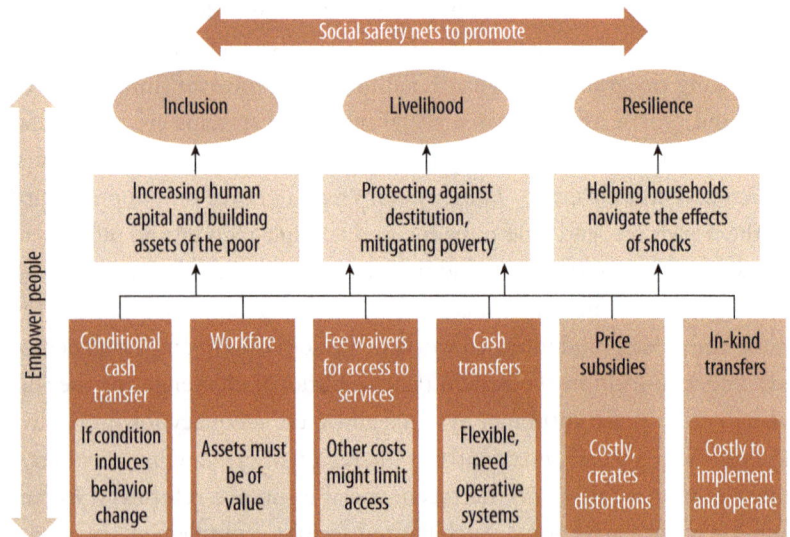

- *Livelihood,* by protecting against destitution. SSN instruments such as cash and in-kind transfers, workfare programs, fee waivers, and subsidies can help to protect the poor from deprivation and their children from malnutrition and disease by improving households' immediate income and consumption. These programs address the problem of chronic poverty, helping to protect poor families from catastrophic losses of human capital.

- *Resilience to crises,* by helping households navigate the effects of shocks. Cash and in-kind transfers as well as subsidies can cushion the effects of shocks on the poor and vulnerable. Although universal subsidies can guarantee affordable access to basic goods even during crises, this instrument comes at a very high fiscal cost. In contrast, cash transfers are sufficiently flexible to ensure rapid and ready support at a lower cost because of the possibility of targeting benefits to a subset of the total population. To be effective, cash transfers require well-functioning operational systems to be in place ahead of the crisis.

Promoting Social Inclusion

Beyond the direct effect of income support, SSNs have been proven to stimulate households' investment in assets and human capital (such as increases in school enrollment and attendance as well as health care utilization, and improvements in nutritional outcomes). In many countries around the world, SSNs have boosted the productive capacity of poor and vulnerable youth, thus enhancing their future earnings and contributing to breaking the vicious intergenerational cycle of poverty, as in the following examples:

- *CCTs have significantly decreased school dropouts* (for instance, by 57 percent in Morocco; see Benhassine et al., forthcoming); *enhanced the overall educational attainment of poor children* (for instance, by 10 percent in Mexico; see Skoufias 2005); and *increased school enrollment* (for instance, by 2.1 and 5.6 percentage points among children 8–13 and 14–17 years old, respectively, in Colombia [see Attanasio, Fitzsimmons, and Gómez 2005; Attanasio et al. 2006]). CCTs achieved similar results in Cambodia, Chile, Ecuador, Nicaragua, and Pakistan (Fiszbein et al. 2009). Besides increasing enrollment and attainment, CCTs were found to also have some impacts on learning performance (for example, on scores on mathematics or vocabulary tests), but the evidence so far has been mixed (in Cambodia, Colombia, Mexico, and Morocco; see World Bank 2009).

- *Health requirements in CCTs have had a positive effect on the prevalence of health care visits,* which increased by 23 and 33 percentage points among Colombian children aged, respectively, 0–24 and 24–48 months, with similar results attained in Honduras and Nicaragua (Fiszbein et al. 2009; IEG 2011a). Encouraging effects were also found on early childhood development, including a long-term impact on the development of cognitive and noncognitive skills among young children (see Macours, Schady, and Vakis 2012) and on nutritional status (as in Colombia, Ecuador, Mexico, and Nicaragua; Fiszbein et al. 2009; IEG 2011a). For example, the Mexican CCT reduced the prevalence of stunting (by 31 percent), anemia (10 percent), and the likelihood of illness among children (40 percent) while also reducing infant mortality (11 percent).

- *Workfare programs have augmented the assets of the poor.* For example, in Ethiopia, beneficiaries were more likely to borrow for productive purposes, use improved agricultural technology, and operate nonfarm business activities (see Gilligan, Hoddinott, and Taffesse 2008). They were also more likely to develop community assets and rural infrastructure, which have other positive socioeconomic impacts. These enhanced assets and infrastructure are likely to contribute to future human development outcomes, for example, by facilitating access to schools, clinics, and hospitals.

Protecting Livelihood

Unequal opportunities and structural factors can lock a child into a low-productivity path for life. By providing income support to poor and vulnerable families, SSNs protect the poor from destitution and their children from malnutrition and disease, promoting decent living. SSNs can ensure that every family has sufficient resources to meet its basic food and housing needs. Impact evaluations demonstrate that SSNs have reduced poverty, destitution, and food insecurity among beneficiaries, as in the following examples:

- *CCTs have led to a reduction in extreme poverty* (by 16 percent in Brazil); *the poverty rate* (by 3 percentage points in Colombia); *inequality* (by 20–25 percent in Brazil); and *decreased child labor* (by 10 percentage points in Cambodia). They have also increased the share of resources that families spend on food, leading to a more varied diet (in Ecuador and Nicaragua) (Fiszbein et al. 2009; IEG 2011a; Macours, Schady, and Vakis 2012 for Nicaragua; Schady and Rosero 2008 for Ecuador).

- *Workfare programs have provided income support to a large number of beneficiaries* (for instance, more than 1 million workers in Ethiopia). Despite drought and high food prices in the past few years, Ethiopian workfare beneficiaries were more likely to be food-secure than nonbeneficiaries (Gilligan, Hoddinott, and Taffesse 2008). Argentina's workfare program reduced moderate poverty (by 2 percentage points) and averted extreme poverty for 10 percent of participating households (Galasso and Ravallion 2003; Galasso, Ravallion, and Salvia 2001).

- *School feeding programs have avoided hunger and enhanced the cognitive ability of students, thereby increasing retention and attendance in schools.* Hunger and consequent poor health can diminish the ability of children to perform well in school; even short-term hunger, resulting from not having breakfast before school, can decrease the level of concentration on complex tasks (Bundy et al. 2009). School feeding interventions—such as those implemented in Bangladesh, Burkina Faso, India, Kenya, and Uganda—have been shown to increase school attendance by 6–20 percentage points (IEG 2011a).

- *Price subsidies also have shown positive results in preventing poverty but in a very inefficient way because of high fiscal costs and distortions created* (for instance, Government of Yemen, World Bank, and UNDP 2007 for Yemen; World Bank 2010a for Egypt; World Bank 2010b for Iraq).

Enhancing Resilience to Crises

SSNs enhance resilience by helping households navigate the effects of shocks or systemic crises, thereby preventing them from falling into persistent poverty. SSNs can protect the welfare of children and the consumption levels of households affected by adverse shocks to income, such as from job or crop loss or sickness. These income shocks can be individual or systemic, and each type requires different SSN responses. SSNs can serve *ex post* by helping vulnerable populations to cope with the aftermath of a shock or a crisis, and *ex ante* by providing families with increased security (that is, ensuring them against potential loss resulting from risk) so that they can undertake riskier but more productive activities (for example, using higher-yielding seed varieties or migrating in search of employment). SSNs fulfill this function by providing liquidity (such as through cash transfers), offering short-term employment (such as through workfare programs), or providing free or discounted access to essential services like health care (such as through fee waivers).

During the 2008–09 food, fuel, and financial price crisis, in economies *without* adequate SSNs, global progress in reducing child malnutrition (von Braun and Tadesse 2012), hunger (Tiwari and Zaman 2010), and poverty (de Hoyos and Medvedev 2009) was undermined. In coping with higher food prices or loss of income during the crisis, the main strategy of unprotected households was to reduce food quality (dietary diversity), which has been shown to lead to micronutrient deficiency, and then reduce food quantity (Compton, Wiggins, and Keats 2011; World Bank 2012b).

Instead, in economies *with* adequate SSNs, the effects of the crisis were less severe, and the recovery was faster, as in the following examples:

- *In Latin America*, CCTs in Honduras, Mexico, and Nicaragua protected consumption, helped keep children in school, and prevented children from engaging in child labor when families were faced with individual shocks (IEG 2011b). El Salvador's *Red Solidaria* CCT program contributed to maintaining consumption levels during the 2008–09 food, fuel, and financial crisis. The rate of stunting did not increase among children in poor areas of the country who participated in the program, as it did among children in the same area who did not participate (De Brauw and Murrugarra 2011). Similarly, Brazil, Colombia, and Jamaica were able to scale up programs and benefits quickly during the 2008–09 food, fuel, and financial crisis with good results (World Bank 2011).

- *In Africa*, Ethiopia's workfare program (Productive Safety Net Program [PSNP]), originally designed to protect the chronically poor, offered an effective response to the recent crisis. Specifically, the government increased the regular transfer amount for the 4.4 million beneficiaries who were adversely affected by the 2008 crisis and drought. In 2011, the program was quickly scaled up after the severe droughts in the Horn of Africa, thereby preventing destitution (World Bank 2012b).

- *In the Middle East and North Africa*, West Bank and Gaza and the Republic of Yemen also scaled up their SSN programs. In the Republic of Yemen, a labor-intensive public works program was created, offering support during the crisis and, in parallel, the cash transfer program was strengthened to serve as the main SSN for poverty reduction and crisis response in the future. A similar strategy was used by countries in other regions. For example, during the East Asian financial crisis of the late 1990s, both Indonesia and the Republic of Korea introduced large workfare programs, as did Mexico in the 1995 "peso crisis," Peru during its recession in 1998–2001, and Argentina in the 2002 financial crisis—all of which having simultaneously developed more permanent transfer programs. In West Bank and Gaza, because the cash transfer program was ready to expand its coverage quickly, assistance was provided using its single targeting system to over 25,000 people to help them cope with the 2008–09 global food and fuel crisis.

The wealth of global experience in SSN best practice, presented above, makes a clear case that SSNs can be effective in promoting inclusion, protecting livelihood, and enhancing resilience to crises. Box 1.2 tests the reader's knowledge of the global best practice in SSN through a short quiz.

BOX 1.2

Global Experience through an SSN Quiz

In the context of this report, global best practices in SSNs were compiled and summarized in a set of posters. In each case, they provide a brief description of the program; indicate its objectives; and highlight the approach, the costs, and the design features that make the program work. They cover places as diverse as Australia, Brazil, Chile, Colombia, Djibouti, Ethiopia, Georgia, Mexico, Morocco, Turkey, West Bank and Gaza, and the Republic of Yemen. The posters were presented at consultations in Lebanon, Oman, and Tunisia, accompanied by the quiz below.

SSN Quiz

Unconditional Cash Transfers

Q1) Which economy reached almost 25,000 additional people during the 2011 crisis with its SSN program?

Conditional Cash Transfers

Q2) Which countries provide social safety net programs that reach 30 percent of the population and cost 0.5 percent of GDP?

Q3) Which country has an SSN program that brought about a decrease in the poverty rate of 3 percentage points?

Q4) Which country provided a transfer to poor families, conditional on regular attendance of primary school by their children, that significantly decreased school dropouts?

Workfare

Q5) In which three countries did beneficiaries build productive assets at the community level as part of the SSN?

Health Insurance for the Poor

Q6) Which country has a program providing health insurance for 50 percent of its poor, at an estimated cost of 0.33 percent of GDP?

Answers

Q6) *Turkey.*

Q5) *Djibouti, Ethiopia, and the Republic of Yemen, with their productive safety net programs.*

Q4) *Morocco.*

Q3) *Colombia, with its CCT (Familias en Acción) program.*

Q2) *Mexico's (Progresa/Oportunidades) and Brazil's (Bolsa Família) CCT programs are reaching a large share of the population (30 percent), and do so at a low cost (0.5 percent of GDP).*

Q1) *West Bank and Gaza, with an SSN program that is flexible and can be scaled up in times of crisis.*

References

Attanasio, O., E. Fitzsimmons, and A. Gómez. 2005. *The Impact of a Conditional Education Subsidy on School Enrollment in Colombia*. Report summary: Familias 01, Institute for Fiscal Studies, London.

Attanasio, O., E. Fitzsimmons, A. Gómez, D. López, C. Meghir, and A. Mesnard. 2006. "Child Education and Work Choices in the Presence of a Conditional Cash Transfer Programme in Rural Colombia." Working Paper W06/01, Institute for Fiscal Studies, London.

Benhassine, N., F. Devoto, E. Duflo, P. Dupas, and V. Pouliquen. Forthcoming. "Unpacking the Effects of Conditional Cash Transfer Programs on Educational Investments: Experimental Evidence from Morocco on the Roles of Mothers and Conditions." World Bank, Washington, DC.

Bundy, D., C. Burbano, M. Grosh, A. Gelli, M. Jukes, and L. Drake. 2009. *Rethinking School Feeding: Social Safety Nets, Child Development, and the Education Sector*. Directions in Development Series. Washington, DC: World Bank.

Compton, J., S. Wiggins, and S. Keats. 2011. *Impact of the Global Food Crisis on the Poor: What Is the Evidence?* Research report, Overseas Development Institute, London.

De Brauw, A., and E. Murrugarra. 2011. "How CCTs Help Sustain Human Capital during Crises? Evidence from Red Solidaria in El Salvador during the Food Price Crisis." Paper presented at the World Bank Economists' Forum. World Bank, Washington, DC, April 27, 2009.

De Hoyos, R., and D. Medvedev. 2009. "Poverty Effects of Higher Food Prices: A Global Perspective." Policy Research Working Paper 4887, World Bank, Washington, DC.

Fiszbein, A., N. Schady, F. Ferreira, M. Grosh, N. Kelleher, P Olinto, and E. Skoufias. 2009. *Conditional Cash Transfers: Reducing Present and Future Poverty*. Washington, DC: World Bank.

Galasso, E., and M. Ravallion. 2003. "Social Protection in a Crisis: Argentina's Plan *Jefes y Jefas*." Policy Research Working Paper 3165, World Bank, Washington, DC.

Galasso, E., M. Ravallion, and A. Salvia. 2001. "Assisting the Transition from Workfare to Work: A Randomized Experiment." Policy Research Working Paper 2738, World Bank, Washington, DC.

Gallup and World Bank. 2011. World Poll Survey (database). The Gallup Organization and World Bank, Washington, DC. http://www.gallup.com/se/126845/Action.aspx.

Gatti, R., D. Angel-Urdinola, J. Silva, and A. Bodor. Forthcoming. *Striving for Better Jobs: The Challenge of Informality in the Middle East and North Africa Region*. Directions in Development Series. Washington, DC: World Bank.

Gilligan, D. O., J. Hoddinott, and A. S. Taffesse. 2008. "The Impact of Ethiopia's Productive Safety Net Programme and Its Linkages." Discussion Paper 839, International Food Policy Research Institute, Washington, DC.

Government of Yemen, World Bank, and UNDP (United Nations Development Programme). 2007. *Yemen Poverty Assessment*. Washington, DC: World Bank.

Grosh, M., C. Ninno, E. Tesliuc, and A. Ouerghi. 2008. *For Protection and Promotion: The Design and Implementation of Effective Safety Nets*. Washington, DC: World Bank.

IEG (Independent Evaluation Group). 2011a. *Evidence and Lessons Learned from Impact Evaluations on Social Safety Nets*. Washington, DC: World Bank.

———. 2011b. *Social Safety Nets: An Evaluation of World Bank Support, 2000–10*. Washington, DC: World Bank.

Macours, K., N. Schady, and R. Vakis. 2012. "Cash Transfers, Behavioral Changes, and Cognitive Development in Early Childhood: Evidence from a Randomized Experiment." *American Economic Journal: Applied Economics* 4 (2): 247–73.

Schady, Nobert and Rosero, José, 2008. Are cash transfers made to women spent like other sources of income? Economic Letters, Elsevier, vol. 101(3), pages 246–248, December.

Skoufias, E. 2005. *PROGRESA and Its Impacts on the Welfare of Rural Households in Mexico*. Research report 139, International Food Policy Research Institute, Washington, DC.

Tiwari, S., and H. Zaman. 2010. "The Impact of Economic Shocks on Global Undernourishment." Policy Research Working Paper 5215, World Bank, Washington, DC.

von Braun, J., and G. Tadesse. 2012. "Global Food Price Volatility and Spikes: An Overview of Costs, Causes, and Solutions." Discussion Paper on Development Policy 161, ZEF Center for Development Research, University of Bonn, Bonn.

Weigand, C., and M. Grosh. 2008. "Levels and Patterns of Safety Net Spending in Developing and Transition Countries." Social Protection Discussion Paper 0817, World Bank, Washington, DC.

World Bank 2009. "Building Resilient Communities: Risk Management and Response to Natural Disasters through Social Fund and Community-Driven Development Operations." Resource toolkit, World Bank, Washington, D.C.

World Bank. 2010a. "Arab Republic of Egypt. Egypt's Food Subsidies: Benefit Incidence and Leakages." Document 57446, Social and Economic Development Group, Middle East and North Africa Region, World Bank, Washington, DC.

———. 2010b. *Iraq: First Programmatic Fiscal Sustainability DPL Program Document*. Report 51528–IQ, World Bank, Washington, DC.

———. 2011. *Investing for Growth and Jobs*. Economic Development and Prospects report, Middle East and North Africa Region, World Bank, Washington, DC.

———. 2012a. *Resilience, Equity, and Opportunity: World Bank 2012–2022 Social Protection and Labor Strategy*. Washington, DC: World Bank.

———. 2012b. *Safety Nets Work: During Crisis and Prosperity*. Report prepared for the Development Committee Meeting of April 21, 2012, World Bank, Washington, DC.

CHAPTER 2

The Challenge: Poverty, Exclusion, and Vulnerability to Shocks

Introduction

Chapter 1 presented the evidence of the impact that social safety nets (SSNs) can have on a variety of human development and welfare outcomes of the poor and the vulnerable. However, different SSN instruments are appropriate to meet different goals. Thus, understanding the human development challenges that the poor and the vulnerable face in the Middle East and North Africa is a precondition to identifying the SSN design options that can best promote inclusion, livelihood, and resilience.

This chapter documents the key challenges facing the poor and vulnerable households, which SSNs should target as a priority. In particular, it first describes the situation of two large groups—children and inhabitants of rural or lagging areas—that exhibit high incidence of poverty and lack access to basic services. Then explores additional factors, including vulnerability to poverty and social exclusion, that deplete the human capital and productive potential of the region's households (see box 2.1 for definitions). By doing so, the chapter makes a case for the renewal of SSNs and highlights the main challenges that SSNs can help to address in the region.

The evidence brought to bear on the topics covered in this chapter draws mainly on data from the most recent household surveys, including budget-consumption surveys, demographic and health surveys, and labor force surveys in the region, described in detail in appendix A. The chapter is structured into the following sections and major subsections:

- "Poverty and Lack of Access to Service" starts with a snapshot of poverty in the Middle East and North Africa, presenting the poverty levels and trends as benchmarked against other regions.

BOX 2.1

Poverty, Vulnerability, and Social Exclusion Defined

Poverty, vulnerability, and social exclusion are three intertwined and complex concepts that describe different challenges for safety nets and have different implications for SSN design (such as targeting methods, flexibility of registries, and activities selected for workfare programs).

Poverty: The poor are defined here as those falling under a certain threshold level of welfare (poverty line), as measured by household per capita expenditure or consumption. This chapter uses national poverty lines, in addition to US$1.25 and US$2 a day poverty lines (when presenting international comparisons). Wealth quintiles used in the analysis are constructed using either consumption or expenditure data; where these are unavailable, a wealth index based on the state of household dwelling and assets is used instead. Although consumption measures in surveys are, to a certain extent, comprehensive, it should be noted that even the best consumption data do not adequately reflect all dimensions of well-being, such as access to public services and within-household inequality (Ackland, Dowrick, and Freyens 2006). To get a better understanding of the circumstances faced by poor households, the analysis in the chapter supplements poverty measures by looking at other factors, such as malnutrition and access to services (see Coudouel, Hentschel, and Wodon 2002; Ravallion 1996).

Vulnerability to poverty: Beyond the chronic poor, SSNs also target the vulnerable to

help them navigate the effects of shocks. Siegel, Alwang, and Jorgensen (2003) define vulnerable households as "those that have moved or are likely to move into a state of poverty or destitution as a result of the cumulative process of risk and response." In addition, Coudouel and Hentschel (2000) recognize the complicated nature of vulnerability by stating that "vulnerability is a broad concept, encompassing not only income vulnerability but also such risks as those related to health, those resulting from violence, and those resulting from social exclusion—all of which can have dramatic effects on households." For the purposes of this chapter, a household is defined as vulnerable to poverty if it is close to and can easily fall below a socially accepted minimum reference of welfare (such as a poverty line). We limit our analysis to vulnerability to consumption or expenditure changes, which is one of the many facets of vulnerability that is most intimately tied to SSN provision.

Social exclusion: Equitable access to social services is an important condition for equality of opportunities and thus social inclusion. Among the many existing definitions of social exclusion, it can be defined as a process that excludes individuals or groups from social, economic, and cultural networks or denies them resources associated with well-being because of a specific aspect of their identity (Bhalla and Lapeyre 1999; Burchardt, Le Grand, and Piachaud 2002; Gore and Figueiredo 1997). Social exclusion can also be seen from the lens of

---

BOX 2.1 *Continued*

Sen's (2000) capability approach, and in that sense is defined as a process leading to a state of functioning deprivation; as such, social exclusion is a process that has visible outcomes, such as deprivation and lack of access to decent living, and it is inherently correlated with poverty and vulnerability. In this chapter, an individual is considered socially excluded if he or she is unable (partially or fully) to participate in society due to factors beyond his or her control.

- "Child Poverty and Human Development Outcomes" focuses on children living in poor households, examining the structural factors that can lock individuals into a low-productivity path for life. These include the prevalence of inequality of opportunities in the accumulation of essential human capital, and service provision that is skewed toward the better off.

- "Poverty in Rural or Lagging Areas" puts a spotlight on the second group at high risk of poverty: those living in the rural areas of several middle-income countries that exhibit a stark rural-urban divide and where provision of basic services in rural areas lags far behind national averages.

- "The Poor in the Labor Market" discusses how the failed accumulation of essential human capital, combined with the limited access to opportunities at a young age, translates into high risk of joblessness, working poverty, and limited mobility, which in turn perpetuate poverty across generations.

- "Vulnerability to Poverty" assesses the high vulnerability of the Middle East and North Africa's middle class to both individual shocks ("crises at the micro level") and systemic crises ("crises at the macro level"), which can precipitate poverty and destitution and increase the likelihood of human capital depletion. Particular attention is given to the consequences of climate-related shocks on the poor and vulnerable.

- "Social Exclusion" covers the plight of socially excluded groups that often remain unnoticed by governments and discusses the barriers that women, people with disabilities, and displaced people face in the labor market and in obtaining basic services.

- The conclusion points toward the subsequent chapters in asking why the region has fallen so short in protecting the poor, promoting human capital formation, and ensuring the vulnerable against the long-term losses brought about by short-duration shocks.

Poverty and Lack of Access to Services

Poverty Levels and Trends

Although the incidence of absolute poverty has been declining in the Middle East and North Africa, the total number of poor people remains at its 1990s level. The absolute poverty rate (the percentage of people living below US$2 per day) declined by 26 percent in the region between 1990 and 2005. While a significant achievement, this decline in the absolute poverty rate occurred at a slower pace than the reduction experienced in other regions, such as Eastern Europe and Central Asia and East Asia and the Pacific. Furthermore, as shown in figure 2.1, the number of the poor in the Middle East and North Africa has remained stagnant: in 2005, 52.7 million people in the region lived on less than US$2 a day, a number similar to that in 1990 (Chen and Ravallion 2012).

Despite some progress against absolute poverty, relative poverty has been rising in the Middle East and North Africa. The average relative poverty lines increased from US$2.84 in purchasing power parity (PPP) terms per person per day in 1981 to US$3.02 PPP per person per day in 2005, reflecting the change in the region's living standards as a result of economic growth (Chen and Ravallion 2012).[1] Using these lines, the headcount index of relative poverty increased from 30 percent in 1990 to 36 percent in 2005, and the number of relative poor increased from 59 to

FIGURE 2.1

Little Change in the Absolute Poor but Rising Numbers of Relative Poor in the Middle East and North Africa, 1981–2005

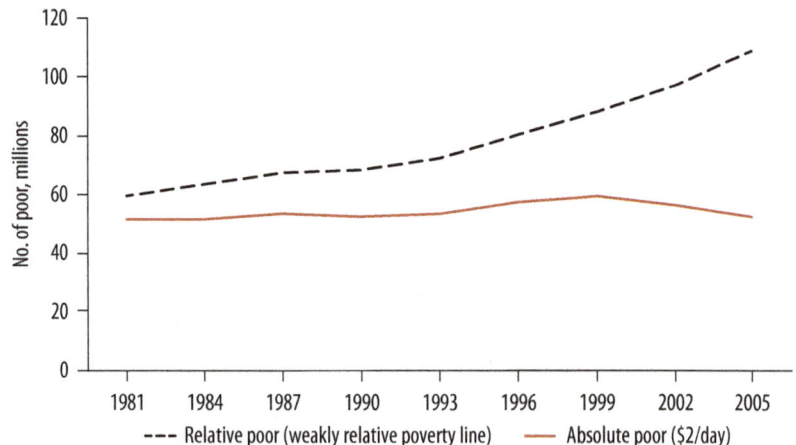

Source: Chen and Ravallion 2012.

Note: Absolute poor = individuals living on US$2 or less per capita per day in PPP terms; Relative poor = individuals living on incomes of US$2–3 per capita per day PPP; PPP = purchasing power parity.

109 million over the same period, as also shown in figure 2.1. The change in relative poverty rates emphasizes that, despite overall progress in living standards, the benefits of economic growth have not homogeneously accrued across the population.

Regional Heterogeneity in Poverty Reduction

Middle Eastern and Northern African countries face varying degrees of challenge in their fight to eradicate absolute poverty. In the region in 2005, 18 percent of the population lived on less than US$2 a day at PPP.[2] This poverty rate is higher than in Europe and Central Asia, similar to that of the Latin America and the Caribbean region, and significantly lower than the poverty rates in the Sub-Saharan Africa, South Asia, and East Asia and the Pacific regions. The regional average masks heterogeneity in absolute poverty between countries. In Djibouti, Iraq, and the Republic of Yemen, the share of the population living with less than US$2 a day was above 40 percent, while in West Bank and Gaza this share constituted less than 2 percent, as shown in figure 2.2.

Highest-Priority Challenges: Child Poverty and Rural Poverty

Although absolute poverty is not very prevalent in the region, some groups face a higher risk of poverty than others. Annex 2A, at the end of the chap-

FIGURE 2.2

Poverty Headcount at US$2 per Day in the Middle East and North Africa, Selected Economies

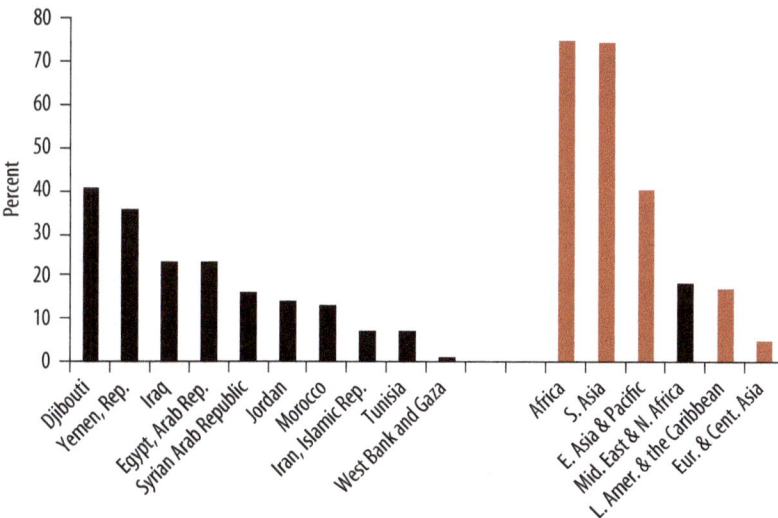

Source: PovcalNet, http://iresearch.worldbank.org/povcalnet.

Note: Headcount data are from the following years: Djibouti 2002; Egypt, Arab Rep. 2008; Iran, Islamic Rep. 2005; Iraq 2006; Jordan 2010; Morocco 2007; Syrian Arab Republic 2004; Tunisia 2005; West Bank and Gaza 2009; and Yemen, Rep. 2005.

ter, illustrates the incidence of poverty among different demographic groups. Among them, two groups call for priority focus: children living in poor households and people living in rural areas.[3] Besides being numerous, and at higher risk of poverty, these groups are particularly affected by the high inequality of opportunities in Middle Eastern and North African countries in terms of accumulating essential human capital (such as health and skills), and they tend to have very limited access to social services. To prevent perpetuation of poverty among children in poor households and rural residents, action is needed on both the supply side (through universal and effective provision of social services) and the demand side (through SSNs that motivate beneficiaries to use these services).

Child Poverty and Human Development Outcomes

This section examines key human development outcomes for children in poor households. In many Middle Eastern and North African countries, children are more likely to be poor than other age groups. Many key outcomes are largely determined during childhood. For instance, malnourished children are likely to become poor adults; and children who drop out of school and enter the labor market are likely to end up in low-paying, precarious jobs. Clearly, poverty during childhood can have irreversible impacts on human capital accumulation and future productivity. However, when well-crafted, SSNs can help to break the cycle of intergenerational poverty by helping families to keep children healthy and in school. In other regions, safety nets have been redesigned to compensate for the disadvantages faced by children in poor households—for example, by linking transfers to sensitization sessions on good nutrition and hygiene practices, use of preventive health care services, or enrollment and attendance of primary and secondary schooling.

Child Poverty Rates in the Region

Children in the Middle East and North Africa are at a particularly high risk of poverty. As in the rest of the world, childhood poverty is high both in low-income countries (for example, 36 percent in the Republic of Yemen) and in some middle-income countries (29 percent in the Arab Republic of Egypt, 27 percent in Iraq, and 20 percent in Jordan), as shown in table 2.1. In Jordan, based on the latest household survey data, more than 20 percent of all children are poor, in contrast to about 12 percent of youth and working-age adults and 7 percent of the elderly.

Implications of Childhood Poverty for Human Development

Being born into a poor household puts a child at a significant disadvantage compared with his or her peers in multiple aspects. The average head of a poor household in the Middle East and North Africa is uneducated,

TABLE 2.1

Child Poverty Rates in the Middle East and North Africa, Selected Countries, c. 2006–10

percent

Country	Child (0–14) poverty rate	Overall poverty rate
Egypt, Arab Rep. 2009	29	22
Iraq 2007	27	23
Jordan 2010	20	14
Morocco 2010[a]	25	20
Yemen, Rep. 2006	36	35

Source: Authors' calculations based on data from latest available household surveys.

Note: Poverty rates are based on national poverty lines for all countries except Morocco.

a. Poverty line defined as the bottom quintile cutoff.

between 45 and 50 years of age, and provides for a family of five or more members, as shown in table 2.2. In fact, 70 percent of the households in Egypt and Morocco in the poorest quintile have a head who has never attended school. The conditions contrast starkly with those of rich households in the same country. In Iraq, for example, poor households, on average, have almost twice as many members as rich households.

These inequalities are also reflected in the size and quality of dwellings where children grow up. Children in the poorest quintile are much less likely to live in a household with proper sanitation. For instance, poor households in Egypt, Jordan, and the Syrian Arab Republic are significantly less likely to be connected to a sewage system; and less than a third of households in the poorest quintile in Djibouti, Syria, and the Republic of Yemen have a functional bathroom in their dwelling. In Jordan, a 10-year-old girl in the poorest quintile is 40 percent less likely to drink treated water and 50 percent less likely to have a bed than a girl in the richest quintile. Similarly, access to technology is highly limited among the poor, with computer ownership hovering around 6 percent in Jordan and 1 percent in Iraq and Syria.

One early manifestation of poverty is childhood malnutrition, which is strikingly high in the Middle East and North Africa's low-income countries and even in some middle-income countries, particularly among the poor. Eight of the region's countries (Djibouti, Egypt, Iraq, Kuwait, Libya, Morocco, Syria, and the Republic of Yemen) face high rates of child malnutrition, as defined by a rate of stunting (low height for age) or underweight (by at least 20 percent). The stunting rate of children under five years in the Republic of Yemen is as high as 60 percent, as shown in figure 2.3. The rate of wasting (indicating acute malnutrition) among Djibouti's children is one of the world's highest (UNICEF 2009).

TABLE 2.2

Characteristics of Poorest and Richest Households in the Middle East and North Africa, Selected Countries, c. 2006–09

Country		HH size	Age of head	Female head of HH (%)	Head w/o formal education (%)	HH has fridge (%)	Rooms (no.)	Sewerage connected (%)	Has bath-room (%)	Owns computer (%)
Jordan	Poorest	5.0	45.2	14	23	87	2.8	17	—	6
	Richest	5.0	49.9	13	2	100	4.6	87	—	86
Morocco	Poorest	5.3	38.7	1	72	25	2.6	—	71.5	9
	Richest	5.5	43.1	2	36	98	4.1	—	100	59
Egypt, Arab Rep.	Poorest	4.4	47.2	24	72	—	3.1	23	80.4	—
	Richest	4.1	49.0	16	14	—	4.0	90	97.3	—
Iraq	Poorest	11.3	45.2	8	32	78	3.8	64	80.8	1
	Richest	6.0	46.7	13	20	94	4.0	80	98.2	21
Yemen, Rep.	Poorest	6.4	44.2	8	59	0	2.8	0	12.2	—
	Richest	7.7	46.4	9	23	97	4.1	49	97.8	—
Syrian Arab Republic	Poorest	6.1	48.1	9	42	89	3.1	17	31.1	1
	Richest	5.2	48.1	6	8	100	3.4	100	100	51
Djibouti	Poorest	5.8	47.6	16	62	33	—	2	18.2	—
	Richest	5.8	48.1	20	49	48	—	9	29.3	—

Sources: Authors' calculations based on data from the following surveys: Jordan DHS 2009; Morocco MHYS 2010; Egypt HIES 2009; Iraq HSES 2007; Republic of Yemen MICS 2006; Syria MICS 2006; and Djibouti MICS 2006. For full survey descriptions, see appendix A at the end of the volume.

Note: HH = household; poorest = bottom income quintile; richest = top income quintile; — = not available.

The level of economic development contributes to, but does not completely explain, the incidence of malnutrition: Djibouti, Morocco, and the Republic of Yemen have high malnutrition rates even when compared with their development peers, as shown in figure 2.4. As expected, wasting (acute malnutrition) rates are lower in countries with higher levels of gross domestic product (GDP) per capita. But some Middle Eastern and North African countries (Djibouti, Egypt, Iraq, Morocco, Syria, and the Republic of Yemen) are notable for having stunting rates high above what would be predicted given their levels of income. This might indicate that dimensions other than income are the cause of malnutrition in these countries—which might be the case in Djibouti, for example, where nutrition practices such as exclusive breastfeeding are rare.[4]

Malnutrition has potentially lifelong and irreversible impacts. It can increase the risk of morbidity and mortality, impair cognitive development, and reduce economic productivity later in life. The most sensitive period for influencing a person's subsequent human development outcomes comes very early in life: from conception to two years of age. If chronic malnutrition and cognitive stimulation are not adequately addressed in this period, they can lead to stunting, with irreversible losses in cognitive ability, lower learning outcomes, and lower income-earning potential as an adult (Horton et al. 2010).

FIGURE 2.3

Prevalence of Child Underweight, Wasting, and Stunting in the Middle East and North Africa, c. 2009–10

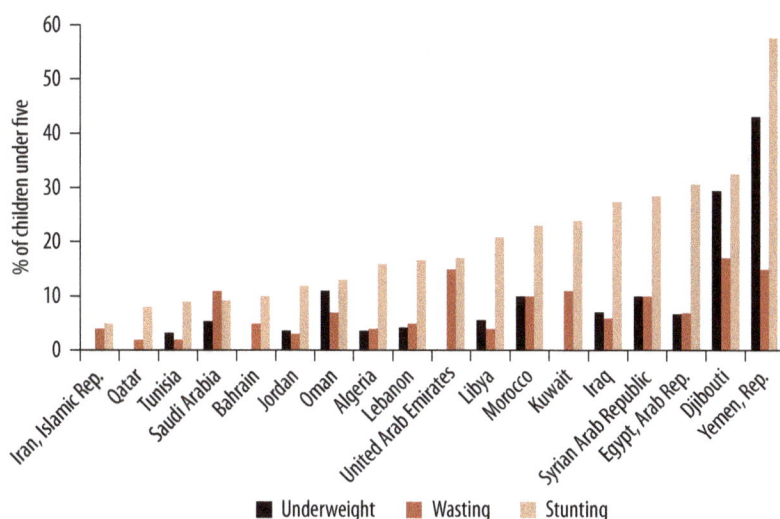

Sources: Adapted from World Bank 2010c. Stunting and underweight rates were obtained from World Health Organization 2010. Wasting rates were obtained from UNICEF 2009. Rates are based on the 2006 WHO Child Growth Standards.

Note: Rates of underweight were not available for Bahrain, the Islamic Republic of Iran, Kuwait, Qatar, and the United Arab Emirates.

FIGURE 2.4

Incidence of Wasting and Stunting Relative to GDP per Capita (PPP) in the Middle East and North Africa, Selected Countries, c. 2009–12

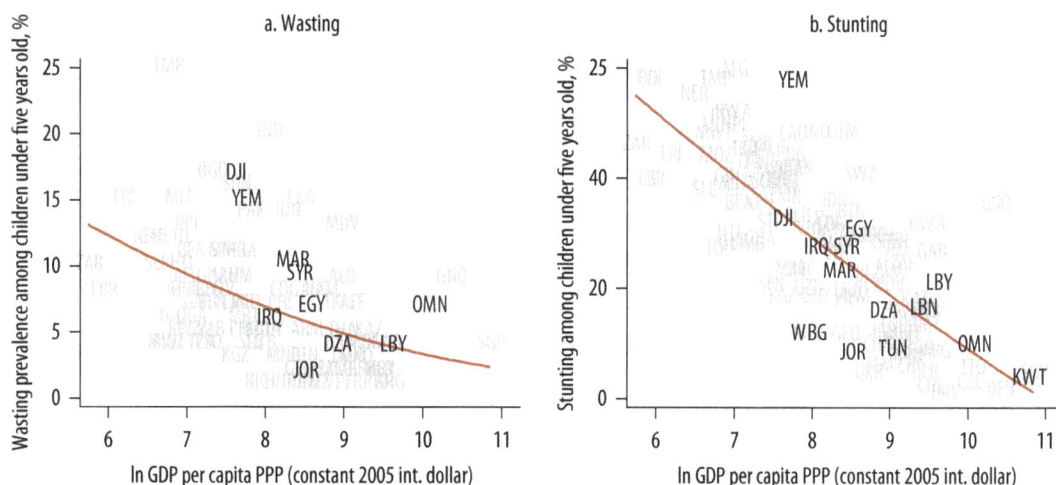

Sources: Authors' calculations using data on malnutrition from UNICEF 2009 and on GDP from World Bank 2012e.

Note: PPP = purchasing power parity.

FIGURE 2.5

Stunting, by Wealth Quintile, in the Middle East and North Africa, Selected Countries, 2006

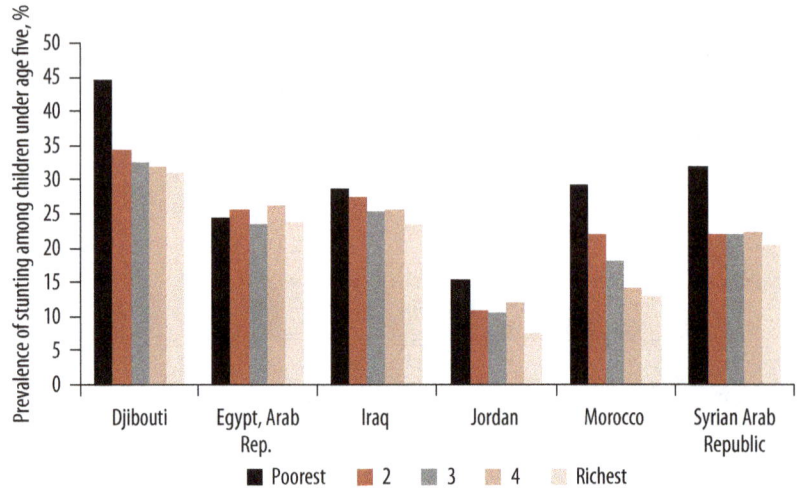

Sources: Authors' calculations based on data from UNICEF's latest available Multiple Indicator Cluster Surveys (MICS)[5] and Jordan Demographics and Health Survey (DHS) 2006.

In each Middle Eastern and North African country for which data are available, malnutrition is more prevalent among poor households, as reflected in the stunting findings shown in figure 2.5. In Morocco, stunting affects 29 percent of children in households in the lowest income quintile and is higher than the poverty rate (14 percent), which suggests inadequate food intake as well as poor nutrition practices (Horton et al. 2010). Similarly in Syria, stunting among children in the poorest quintile is approximately 33 percent, whereas stunting among children in the richest quintile is around 20 percent.

Looking at how malnutrition has evolved, the analysis shows that the levels of malnutrition have, for the most part, stagnated over time. In Algeria and Jordan, improvements were maintained, but in other countries the levels of stunting have not changed significantly. In Egypt in particular, stunting rates have been rising, even in the wealthy quintiles. Calculations based on household survey data show that in 2000, 26 percent of Egyptian children in the bottom quintile were stunted, with stunting rates dropping with each quintile, down to 11 percent of children in the richest quintile. Between 2000 and 2005, stunting rates in Egypt fell fairly equitably for all except the richest quintile, where they rose slightly. Surprisingly, despite a reduction in poverty between 2005 and 2008, stunting rates rose for all quintiles, and substantially so (by 6–12 percentage points) for all but the poorest quintile, where they rose by less than 1 percentage point. As shown in figure 2.5, this dynamic equalized stunting rates across quintiles in Egypt, but at a very high level.

Implications of Childhood Poverty for Human Capital Accumulation

Beyond malnutrition, the educational paths of poor and rich children diverge early in life, as early childhood education for young children is rare and often unaffordable for the poor. There is mounting evidence worldwide about the positive impact of early childhood development interventions on children's cognitive and socioemotional development, especially for children up to three years old. Long-term effects include higher schooling and earnings, lower dropout and repetition rates, more stable employment, and fewer arrests (Carneiro and Heckman 2003). Moreover, high-quality, affordable child care programs can also encourage higher labor force participation by women, which is currently very low in the Middle East and North Africa (World Bank 2012c).

All of these opportunities are currently lost because only 22 percent of young children in the Middle East and North Africa attend preschool, a rate exceeding only Sub-Saharan Africa (18 percent) and significantly lower than South Asia (47 percent) and Latin America and the Caribbean (69 percent), as figure 2.6 shows. In countries such as Djibouti, Iraq, and Syria, enrollment in preprimary education stands at less than 10 percent. Lack of access and high costs are the root of the problem, with children in the poorest wealth quintile in Egypt almost five times less likely to attend preprimary school than those in the richest quintile. With no better options for child care in Morocco, when parents go to work, 4 percent of children under 5 are left alone, and 10.6 percent are left in the care of children under 10. These proportions increase with poverty and distance to a capital city, and decrease with higher levels of mother's education (World Bank 2010e, 2012b). In Tunisia in 2009, 88 percent of kindergartens were run privately, and the coverage in Tunis and other urban areas was double that in rural areas (UNICEF 2009).

Once they enter school, poor children in the Middle East and North Africa have lower completion rates for primary education, higher dropout rates, and more limited access to higher education than nonpoor children. In Egypt, the primary noncompletion rate is 5.7 percent for children from poor households, while it is 0.5 percent for children from nonpoor households, as shown in table 2.3.

Lower primary completion rates in poor households are often attributed to circumstances that lead children (especially girls) to drop out of school, either to work or to care for younger siblings. In fact—and in spite

FIGURE 2.6

Preprimary School Gross Enrollment in the Middle East and North Africa, Compared with World and Developing-Country Averages, 2007–10

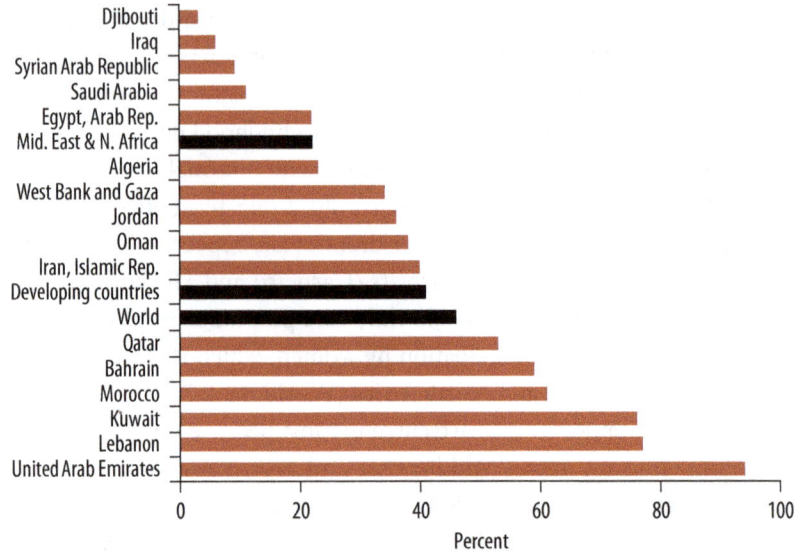

Source: UNICEF Child Info database, http://www.childinfo.org/education_preprimary.php.

of the significant progress in recent decades—dropout rates continue to be high and to depend strongly on economic background. Successful educational outcomes in the Middle East and North Africa are largely determined by access to some form of private education, whether tutoring or schooling. Average household spending on education varies widely across the region (1 percent in Egypt, 7 percent in Jordan, and 3.5 percent in Lebanon), and such variance is explained by differences in the availability of publicly funded education and in households' abilities to afford private educational services. In absolute terms, the richest 10 percent of Jordan's population spent 14 times more on education in 2008 than the poorest 30 percent (Galal and Taher 2010).

Access to higher education in the Middle East and North Africa is limited even for the poor youth who complete secondary schooling. Across the region, access to more prestigious higher-education degrees (such as in medicine, law, and engineering) is biased against the poor. Higher education in Egypt, Morocco, Syria, and Tunisia is publicly provided, but this does not ensure equity of access (Galal and Taher 2010). In Egypt, the poorest quintile of the population constitutes only 4 percent of higher-education students, while in Jordan there are three times as

TABLE 2.3

Education Outcomes of the Poorest and Richest Quintiles in the Middle East and North Africa, Selected Countries, 2006

		Primary noncompletion (%)	Dropout rates, ages 16–18 (%)	No formal education, ages 25–45 (%)	Average TIMSS score, 8th grade
Djibouti	Poorest	—	49.9	50.7	—
	Richest	—	41.5	39.2	—
Egypt, Arab Rep.	Poorest	5.7	58.8	54.8	380
	Richest	0.5	14.4	20.1	417
Iraq	Poorest	5.1	69.4	19.7	—
	Richest	0.5	47.1	8.4	—
Jordan	Poorest	0.7	30.3	42.9	412
	Richest	0.0	10.1	21.3	451
Morocco	Poorest	9.1	70.2	68.7	369
	Richest	1.6	16.6	16.2	426
Syrian Arab Republic	Poorest	1.1	74.1	27.0	—
	Richest	0.2	37.0	2.3	—
Yemen, Rep.	Poorest	4.5	79.4	65.1	—
	Richest	1.1	30.2	14.7	—

Source: Authors' calculations based on data from latest available MICS, DHS, and TIMSS data.

Note: DHS = Demographics and Health Survey; MICS = Multiple Indicator Cluster Surveys (UNICEF); TIMSS = Trends in International Mathematics and Science Study; — = not available.

many students from the richest quintile as those from the poorest quintile. Most higher-education institutions accept students based on general matriculation exams, but low-quality secondary education disadvantages students from poorer areas on these exams, and the prevalence of quotas and exceptions to admission further exacerbates the situation. For example, in Jordan, 10 percent of university placements are reserved for students from lower-income brackets, but these too are based on performance, often favoring students who attend private schools (Galal and Taher 2010). Quotas are used to allocate spaces for the children of Army and Ministry of Education retirees and graduates of schools from rural areas, but these are issued at the expense of the urban poor and students from refugee camps (Reiter 2002).

As in the case of education, access to basic health services is also skewed across income groups from early childhood, with lifelong consequences. Family wealth is a significant determinant of access to antenatal care, as seen in table 2.4. Vaccination rates also differ drastically by wealth, with children in the poorest wealth quintiles significantly less likely to have had all of their vaccinations. Lack of access to funds to cover health care costs is significant, and poorer households report this as a problem two to four times more often than those in the richest wealth quintile. In

TABLE 2.4

Access to Health Services in the Arab Republic of Egypt, Jordan, and Morocco, by Wealth Quintile, 2006

Country	Access to services indicator	Poorest Q1	Q2	Q3	Q4	Richest Q5
Egypt, Arab Rep.	Lack of antenatal coverage (% of pregnant women)	46	36	26	14	8
	Problems in accessing health care (distance to health facility) (% of women)	29	22	18	12	7
	Problems in accessing health care (getting money for treatment) (% of women)	70	56	47	36	16
	Problems in getting all vaccinations (% of children ages 12–23 months)	11	11	7	8	6
Jordan	Lack of antenatal coverage (% of pregnant women)	3	1	1	0	0
	Problems in accessing health care (distance to health facility) (% of women)	47	43	35	31	23
	Problems in accessing health care (getting money for treatment) (% of women)	49	39	33	24	17
	Problems in getting vaccinations (all vaccinations) (% of children ages 12– 23 months)	18	13	10	12	11
Morocco	Lack on antenatal coverage (% of pregnant women)	60	43	29	13	7
	Problems in accessing health care (distance to health facility) (% of women)	51	46	36	26	17
	Problems in accessing health care (getting money for treatment) (% of women)	55	53	48	38	24
	Problems in getting vaccinations (all vaccinations) (% of children ages 12–23 months)	19	15	9	5	3

Source: Authors' calculations based on data from latest available MICS surveys (UNICEF n.d.).

Note: Q = wealth quintile (1 = lowest, 5 = highest).

Morocco, 55 percent of the poor claim that cost constrains their access to health care, while almost 50 percent report that the distance to a health facility is also an impediment. Poor Jordanian households face similar constraints, whereas in Egypt, over 70 percent of poor households reported cost as a significant impediment to health care. In Iraq, reported distances to facilities such as public hospitals and health clinics were 15–25 percent longer for poor households than for rich ones. Given lack of access to health care providers, it is no wonder that a survey on child care in rural Morocco revealed a high prevalence of caretaker behaviors harmful to babies' health, such as declining exclusive breastfeeding, negative psycho-affective behavior, inadequate response in case of diarrhea, limited verbal communication with the baby, excessive swaddling, and incidents of violence (UNICEF 2007).

Under conditions of perfect equality of opportunity, circumstances such as a child's location or gender should have no impact on his or her basic human development outcomes, such that the distribution of outcomes would be the same for any circumstance group (Paes de Barros,

Vega, and Chanduvi 2008). However, in the Middle East and North Africa, the process by which children and young adults attain desirable health outcomes depends, to a large extent, on *circumstances* that are beyond their control, such as location at birth, family wealth, and parents' education. These circumstances play the preponderant role in determining outcomes such as receiving prenatal care and receiving adequate nutrition (see box 2.2).

BOX 2.2

Inequality of Opportunity Analysis for Early Childhood Health

Inequality of opportunities here is defined as inequality in access to basic services such as early childhood health care, which influence children's lives but are beyond their control. First, we will depict coverage rates of early childhood health outcomes; second, we will discuss the level and determinants of inequality in achieving these outcomes; last, we will present the human opportunity index (HOI), which is a combination of coverage rates and the degree of equity of the distribution of each outcome.

Coverage rates for early childhood health outcomes vary by country and outcome, as shown in table B2.2.1. "Not stunted" shows favorable coverage rates

(between 70 and 90 percent of children are not stunted in the countries of analysis), whereas other outcomes such as "vaccinations" (between 56 percent in Iraq and 83 percent in Egypt have all vaccinations) or "postnatal checkups" (48 percent in Egypt and 15 percent in Morocco) display lower coverage rates. Table 2.4 previously displayed coverage rates of basic health outcomes by wealth quintile in Egypt, Jordan, and Morocco. In all countries studied, coverage rates are highest for the richest quintile and lowest for the poorest.

Although coverage rates provide useful insights into how many health opportunities are available, they do not show how

TABLE B2.2.1

Average Coverage Rates for Selected Early Childhood Health Outcomes in the Middle East and North Africa, Selected Countries
percent

Health outcome	Egypt, Arab Rep.	Morocco	Iraq	Syrian Arab Republic	Yemen, Rep.
Postnatal checkup	48.44	15.51	—	—	—
Not stunted	74.04	91.31	71.85	71.67	—
All vaccinations	84.00	80.92	56.23	57.14	59.96

Source: Authors' calculations based on latest available DHS data.

Note: — = not available.

(box continued on next page)

BOX 2.2 *Continued*

equitably the available opportunities are distributed. The dissimilarity index indicates how equitably outcomes are distributed among different circumstance groups (see Paes de Barros et al. 2009). The index ranges between 0 and 1, with higher values suggesting higher inequality.

Among the outcomes studied, "postnatal checkups" display the highest dissimilarity index (0.35 in Morocco and 0.13 in Egypt), followed by "vaccinations" (ranging from 0.05 in Syria to 0.015 in Egypt) and "not stunted" (ranging from 0.03 in Syria to 0.013 in Egypt). In general, the dissimilarity index for the outcomes we looked at is lower in some countries (nota-

bly Egypt) than in others (such as Syria), hinting toward varying country-specific inequality of opportunities.

To understand how much an individual circumstance contributes to inequality in health outcomes, we conduct a Shapley decomposition of the index, as shown in figure B2.2.1. This analysis shows that especially parents' education and, to lesser extents, location and parents' wealth determine whether children will have positive health outcomes. In particular, the analysis looks at the likelihood that an individual who is 1–5 years old will have completed all vaccinations and will not be stunted. In Egypt and Morocco, we also look at the

FIGURE B2.2.1

Decomposition of Dissimilarity Index of Early Childhood Health Outcomes in the Middle East and North Africa, Selected Countries

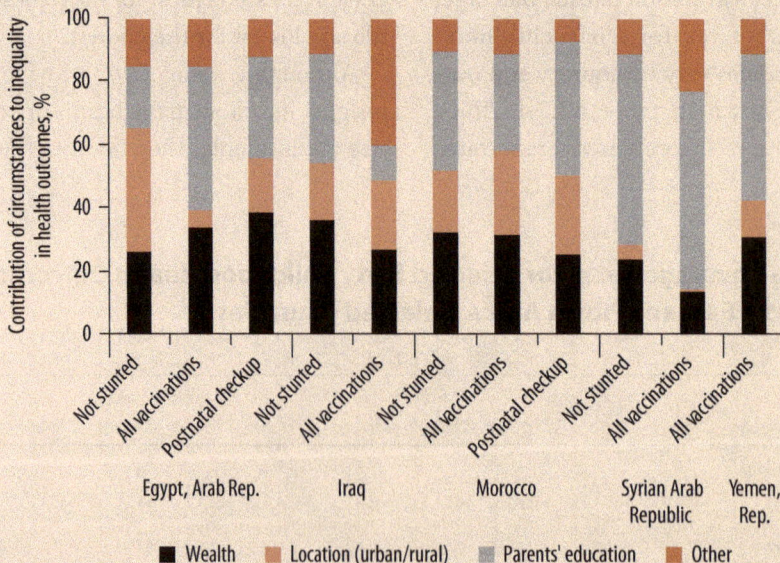

Source: Authors' calculations based on latest available DHS data.

Note: "Other" refers to the number of children in the household and gender.

BOX 2.2 *Continued*

completion of postnatal checkups. The variables measuring circumstances in the analysis were location (urban/rural), education of household head, and household wealth. "Other" factors in the analysis include considerations such as the number of children in a household and gender.

Combining coverage rates and the dissimilarity index, we calculate the human opportunity index (HOI) of early childhood health outcomes, as shown in figure B2.2.2. The HOI is a widely used measure of inequality of opportunities, which uses the coverage rate of a certain outcome and

then adjusts it according to how equitably the outcome is distributed among circumstance groups. The HOI ranges from 0 to 1, with higher values suggesting a more equitable outcome.

In the Middle Eastern and North African countries studied, the HOI is highest (hence, the distribution is most equitable) for "not stunted" and "all vaccinations" in Egypt and Morocco. The HOI is low and very similar for "all vaccinations" in Iraq, Syria, and the Republic of Yemen (0.54–0.57), hinting at low coverage rates in those countries.

FIGURE B2.2.2

Human Opportunity Index of Early Childhood Health Outcomes

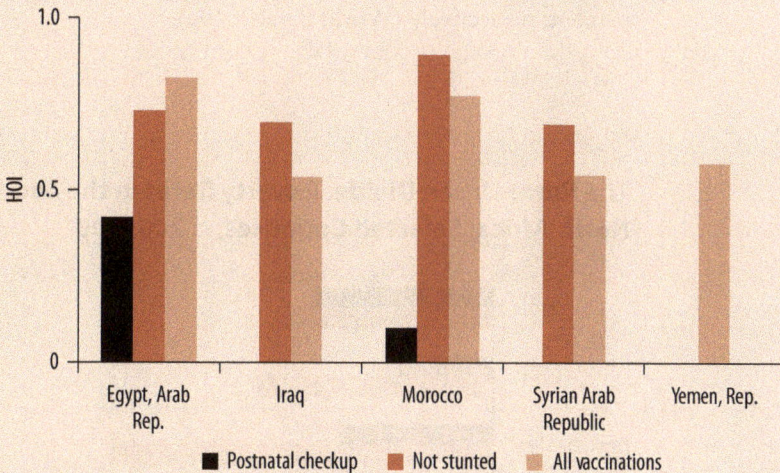

Source: Authors' calculations based on latest available DHS data.
Note: HOI = human opportunity index (0 = lowest, 1 = highest).

Poverty in Rural and Lagging Urban Areas

Middle-income countries have spatial pockets in rural areas and urban slums where extreme poverty is still prevalent. Although urbanization in the Middle East and North Africa increased in the past decade, a significant share of the population still resides in rural areas. In 2010, 38 percent of the region's total population were rural residents. There is substantial heterogeneity in urbanization between countries: although in Egypt and the Republic of Yemen, most of the population is rural, a third of Tunisia's population lives outside the cities, and in Djibouti and Lebanon rural population is slightly above 10 percent.

The Rural-Urban Divide

Most of the poor in the Middle East and North Africa live in urban areas because of high urbanization rates, but poverty incidence is significantly higher in the rural areas of Djibouti, Egypt, and Tunisia than it is in the urban areas of these countries. In Egypt, almost 31 percent of rural inhabitants are asset-poor, compared with 14 percent in urban settings (as shown in figure 2.7). In Iraq and the Republic of Yemen, around 40 percent of the rural population fall below the poverty line, compared with 16 and 21 percent, respectively, in urban areas.

In all Middle Eastern and North African countries with available data, the risk of being poor is twice or even three times as high for rural residents as it is for urban dwellers. For example, while Upper Egypt has 40 percent of the country's total population, it accounts for 60 percent of its poverty and 80 percent of severe poverty; its average rural per capita consumption lags behind urban levels in Jordan and Morocco by 24 and 46 percent, respectively (World Bank 2010d).

FIGURE 2.7

The Rural-Urban Divide: Poverty Rates in the Middle East and North Africa, Selected Countries, c. 2005–09

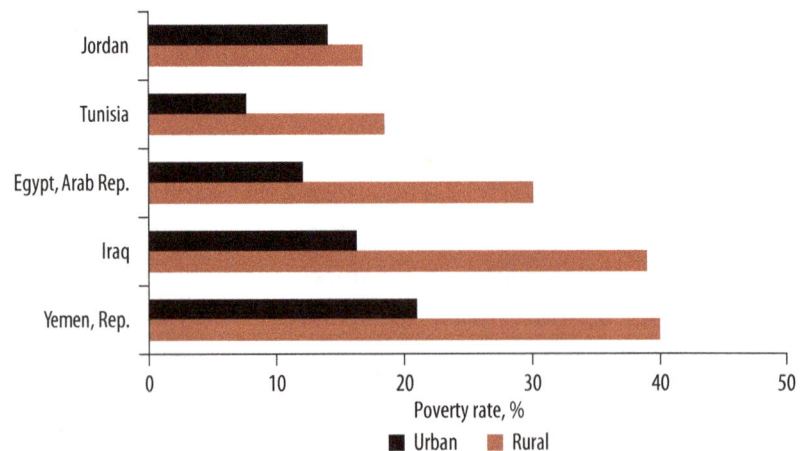

Sources: Authors' calculations based on HIES Egypt 2009; IHSES Iraq 2007; HBS Republic of Yemen 2006; World Bank (Poverty Reduction and Economic Management Network) staff estimates using HBS Tunisia 2005 and HBS Morocco 2006. For full descriptions of these surveys, see appendix A.

TABLE 2.5

Rural-Urban Divide: Access to Services in the Middle East and North Africa, Selected Countries, 2012

Country	Antenatal coverage (% of pregnant women)		Births attended by skilled personnel (%)		Improved drinking sources (%)		Primary school attendance (%)	
	Urban	Rural	Urban	Rural	Urban	Rural	Urban	Rural
Algeria	94	85	—	—	85	79	98	95
Djibouti	94	47	—	—	99	54	67	49
Egypt, Arab Rep.	85	67	87	59	100	99	91	87
Jordan	99	98	—	—	98	92	100	98
Morocco	85	48	85	40	98	61	96	83
Syrian Arab Republic	92	83	—	—	93	86	89	85
Yemen, Rep.	68	39	46	10	72	47	83	64

Source: Authors' calculations based on UNICEF Child Info database, http://www.childinfo.org.

Note: — = not available.

Demographic factors, such as higher dependency ratios as well as migration and education, explain a portion of the rural-urban divide (World Bank 2010d). However, disparities in access to services also play a role, exacerbating the disadvantages of rural inhabitants. Coverage by antenatal care and the share of births attended by a skilled health worker are all significantly lower in the rural areas of Egypt, Morocco, and the Republic of Yemen than in the urban areas, as shown in table 2.5. Rural residents in Djibouti, Morocco, and the Republic of Yemen are also much less likely to have access to improved drinking water sources and to send their children to preprimary or primary education. The accumulated lack of basic services is staggering: in rural Morocco, as many as 52 percent of women lack antenatal coverage; 39 percent of the population do not have access to improved drinking water sources; 17 percent of children of primary school age do not attend school; and the likelihood that a girl is married by the age of 18 is 79 percent. A child in Rural Upper Egypt is 3.4 times less likely than a child in Urban Lower Egypt to attend preprimary school.

In countries like Algeria, Jordan, Lebanon, and Syria, the urban-rural divide is less accentuated, but there are lagging areas that suffer from relative deprivation. For example, in the *wilaya* of Djelfa, Algeria, more than half of Djelfa's population older than six years of age are reported as not attending school compared with an almost universal primary education completion rate in the rest of Algeria. The average per capita household expenditure in Jordan's northeastern governorate Al-Mafraq is 51 percent of that of Amman. In Lebanon, poverty is significantly higher in pockets such as the rural Akkar and Dinniyeh regions and in concentrated slums around the cities (World Bank 2010d). In Syria, the mean per cap-

FIGURE 2.8

Out-of-School Rates by Location and Gender in the Middle East and North Africa, Selected Countries, c. 2006–10

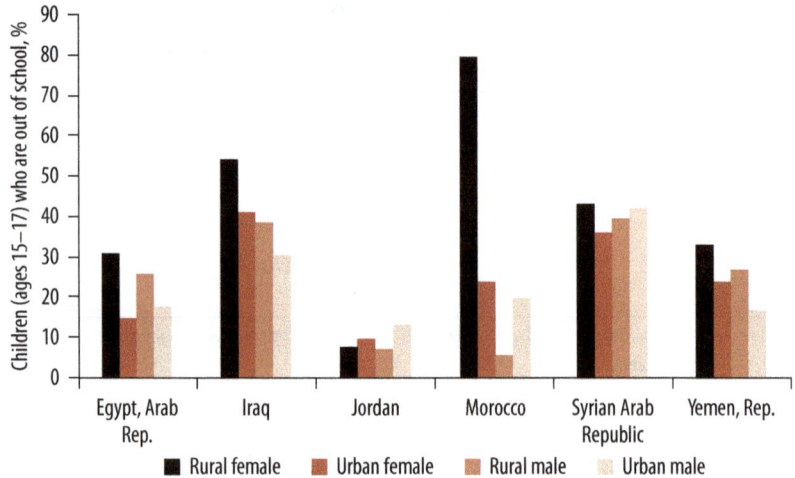

Sources: Authors' calculations based on data from latest MICS (UNICEF n.d.), DHS Egypt 2008, and MHYS Morocco 2010.

ita household expenditure in Aleppo is almost half of that of Damascus (the capital).

Rural Disadvantage Exacerbated for Females

Living in a rural area instantly puts one at a disadvantage when it comes to achieving favorable education outcomes, and this disadvantage is exacerbated for females. Figure 2.8 shows that in all Middle Eastern and North African countries except Jordan, rural females aged 15–17 have the highest probability of being out of school.

In Morocco, this difference is especially stark: 80 percent of rural girls are out of school compared with only 23 percent of urban girls. Moreover, based on data from the Morocco Youth Survey 2010, poverty starts contributing to the lower educational outcomes of rural females at an early age, with rural poor children and especially rural poor females having the highest out-of-school rate at ages 7–10. Indeed, 17 percent of rural females in the poorest quintiles are out of school in Morocco compared with 5 percent of urban poor females and virtually none of rural females in the top two quintiles.

The Poor in the Labor Market

The previous sections illustrated how the inequality of opportunities, combined with lack of access to basic services, severely limits the pros-

FIGURE 2.9

Work Status of Urban Wage-Employed Men (Aged 35–64) by Wealth Quintile in the Middle East and North Africa, Selected Countries, c. 2009–12

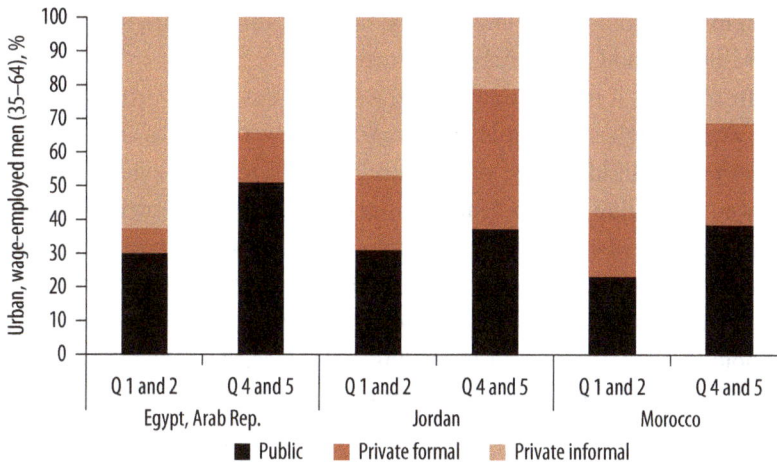

Sources: Authors' calculations based on data from MHYS Morocco 2010; Jordan ERF LMS 2012; and Egypt SYPE 2009.

Note: Q = wealth quintile (1 = lowest, 5 = highest).

pects of people growing up in poor households, particularly in rural areas, to accumulate essential human capital, including formal education, health, and skills. As an illustration, table 2.1 showed that, in most countries, most heads of poor households received no formal education.

Once in the labor market, individuals with low levels of human capital have limited chances to end up in jobs that will allow them and their families to escape poverty. Because the poor are mostly low-skilled, they are more likely to find themselves in precarious employment and to lack the means to move into better jobs. Figure 2.9 shows the work status of urban, wage-employed, prime-age males (35–64 years old) in Egypt, Jordan, and Morocco according to their household wealth. Adult males in poor families tend to be employed more in the informal sector, and in Egypt and Morocco they tend to have less access to public sector employment. Whereas the public sector offers social protection and the formal private sector offers high wages, the sectors where the poor tend to work are neither protected nor high-paying.

Doubly Disadvantaged in the Middle East and North Africa

Such labor market disadvantage is exacerbated in the context of Middle Eastern and North African countries, where job creation has been modest, and poor unskilled individuals compete with the better-skilled for scarce employment opportunities. In recent years, economic growth in the region has led to the creation of mostly low-quality, low-paid jobs (World Bank 2012c). Among those who do find a job, informality (defined as not having access to social security) is rampant, and especially so for young people, women, and the low-skilled. In fact, informality in the Middle East and North Africa (67 percent of the workforce) is higher than in other middle-income regions, such as Latin America (61 percent) and Europe and Central Asia (40 percent).

In addition, it is well known that the Middle East and North Africa has the world's highest unemployment rate, and how these jobs are allocated plays to the disadvantage of the poor. One-third of individuals interviewed by Gallup in non-Gulf Cooperation Council countries thought that the main obstacle to youth employment was the lack of acceptable jobs for new labor market entrants. Another fifth of respondents thought that the main challenge was that jobs are given only to the connected people (Gallup and World Bank 2009). Because the poor tend to have smaller networks in addition to lower human capital, they are at a double disadvantage in their chances to land a good job.

It is no surprise, then, that in some countries poor households are more likely to have no single member employed. As many as 23 percent of people in Morocco live in households with no employed member; in Jordan, 17 percent do so, and in Egypt, the figure is 10 percent. Households with no one employed are not necessarily poor, as they can receive other sources of income such as rent, pensions, or remittances. However, in Jordan and Morocco, households in the lower-income quintiles are indeed those most likely to have no member employed, with 25 and 36 percent of households, respectively, without a single member working. This is not so in Egypt, where only 7 percent of poor households are in this situation. Such patterns are likely to differ across countries according to migration opportunities and the propensity to cohabit in the absence of a male household head.

Starting Out Poor Often Leads to a Low-Productivity Path

Among young people, poverty strongly increases the chance to be out of school and out of work. Being neither in school nor at work captures the difficulty of labor market insertion as well as the lost potential of young people to become more productive adults later on. Available data from Egypt, Jordan, and Morocco demonstrate that the likelihood of poor young men to be in this state can be twice as high as that of young men in higher-income families. For instance, in rural Morocco, more than 40 percent of young men in the bottom two quintiles were out of school and out of work in 2010, compared with only 20 percent of those in the top two quintiles. As young, poor individuals in the Middle East and North Africa struggle to accumulate the two key assets to succeed in the labor

FIGURE 2.10

Likelihood of Refusing a Job, by Education Level, in the Middle East and North Africa, 2009

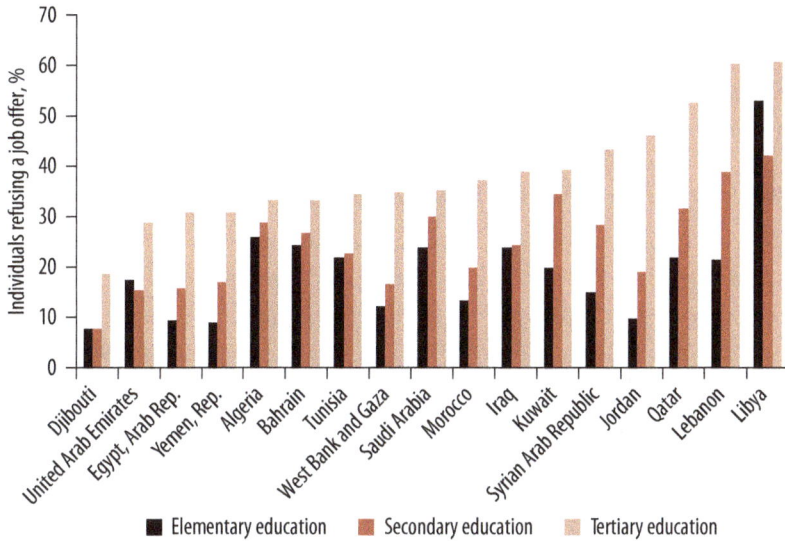

Source: Gallup Inc. 2009.

market—experience and postbasic education—joblessness at a young age is likely to affect earning potential later on.

Unemployment among the poor is less likely to be the result of choice, and more likely due to lack of work opportunities. Middle Eastern and North African countries experience the world's highest unemployment rates. However, the reasons for unemployment are heterogeneous. Among some groups, unemployment may be a strategic choice to maximize the chances of ending up in the desired job by increasing the search period. Among others, unemployment may simply be the result of the inability to find any job. The available evidence suggests that individuals who are poor and unemployed are more likely to be in this condition because they cannot find a job, not because they are waiting to find a better job (World Bank 2012c). For instance, the Gallup data in figure 2.10 show that the likelihood of refusing a job is far lower among the low-skilled (largely poor) than among the higher-skilled, signaling that unemployment for this group of individuals is less of a choice than for those who are better off.

Few Options and Incentives for Women in the Labor Force

Another factor explaining the high rate of joblessness in poor households relates to the labor force participation rate of unskilled women. Female labor force participation is historically low in the Middle East and North

Africa region except among highly educated women. Because women in poor households receive either no education or only a primary education, they are less likely to participate in the labor force, but the determinants of low female labor force participation are more complex than educational level. Women have few incentives to work in light of the low wages, low employability, and the low returns from education they can expect on the market.[6] They are also challenged by limited decision-making power and job opportunities (Lundberg and Wuermli 2012; World Bank 2012a).

Persistently Low Job Mobility for the Poor

Overall, poorer individuals show higher persistence in low-quality jobs, and a higher likelihood of falling out of good-quality jobs. The preceding figures have shown that poor individuals' jobs are more likely to be informal and low paying. Moreover, unlike in other regions, in the Middle East and North Africa, informality in the labor market is not a temporary phenomenon (Gatti et al. 2011).

Panel data from Egypt collected between 2008 and 2009 show us that the persistence of various labor market outcomes varies significantly according to individuals' household consumption level. Figure 2.11 shows the job transition rates of out-of-school males aged 15–34.[7] Among the youth with a low-paying informal job in the bottom two household quin-

FIGURE 2.11

Probability of Transition to a Good or Bad Job in 2009, by Consumption Quintile and Employment Condition of Young Egyptian Males in 2008

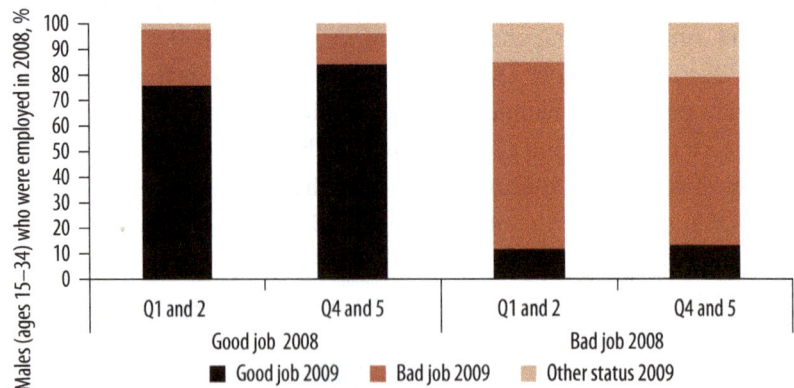

Source: Authors' calculations based on HIECS Egypt 2009.

Note: "Good job" is defined as offering social security or earnings above two-thirds of the median. "Bad job" is defined as informal and with earnings below two-thirds of the median. "Other status" is defined as being unemployed or out of the labor force. Q = consumption quintile (1 = lowest, 5 = highest).

tiles in 2008, 73 percent were in the same status a year later, compared with only 65 percent among the same cohort from the top two household wealth quintiles. Even in a relatively short time span, these rates indicate that wealthier workers are not only less likely to be in low-quality jobs but also better able to move out of them. Conversely, 76 percent of youth from low-income households who held a high-earning or protected job in 2008 remained in the same status a year later, compared with 84 percent among those from higher-income households.

Vulnerability to Poverty

Low Resilience to Shocks in the Middle East and North Africa

Poverty headcount ratios can inaccurately reflect the size of the population that SSN programs need to reach. Families and individuals who have insufficient resources to exit poverty are certainly a priority target group, but focusing exclusively on this group alone may be too restrictive. People who earn 1 percent more than the poverty threshold are not that different from those who earn 1 percent less; in other words, the population just above the poverty line is essentially equally at risk of falling under the poverty line in the event of a relatively minor individual shock or a slight worsening of economic conditions. Unfortunately, the vulnerability of these individuals near the poverty line often goes unrecognized.

In the Middle East and North Africa, vulnerable households make up a large share of the population. Although economic growth in the region has lifted many out of poverty, many of those people remain at risk of falling back into poverty if an economic contraction takes place, even if it is temporary. This vulnerability to poverty is illustrated in three different but complementary ways. First, defining the middle class as living between US$2 a day (poor by developing-country standards) and US$13 a day (poor by developed-country standards) (as in Ravallion 2010), the Middle East and North Africa stands out as having a large share of its population in the middle class by developing-country standards, many of whom remain fairly close to poverty. In fact, only 5 percent of the region's population live above US$13 a day. Second, a large share of the region's population is vulnerable to even smaller income loss. As many as 15–17 percent of Egyptians, Iraqis, Syrians, and Yemenis and 10 percent of Moroccans have consumption levels that are no more than US$0.50 per day above the US$2 poverty line, as shown in figure 2.12. Third, even using national poverty lines, household survey data in Egypt, Iraq, Syria, and the Republic of Yemen confirm that a high share of those countries' populations hovers just above the poverty line.

FIGURE 2.12

Share of Population Living on US$2–2.50 a Day in the Middle East and North Africa, Selected Countries

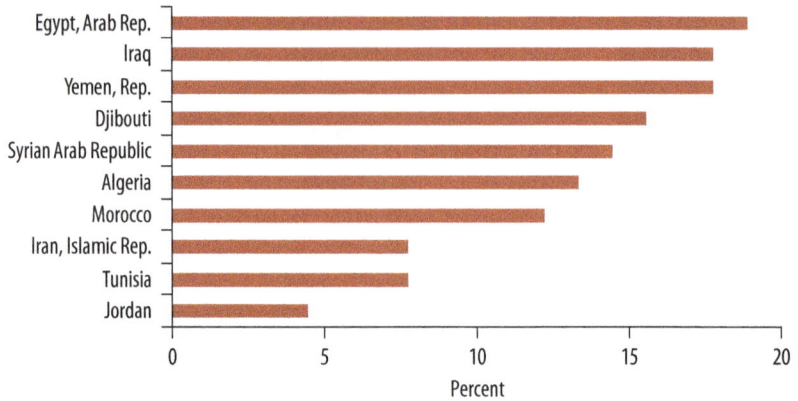

Source: Calculations from PovcalNet, http://iresearch.worldbank.org/povcalnet.

Overall, the data on vulnerability imply that many households frequently shift into and out of poverty. For example, between 2005 and 2008, the welfare of poor households in Egypt increased by 10 percent, but 55 percent of Egyptians experienced at least one poor (or near-poor) episode (Marotta et al. 2011). Almost one-fifth (17 percent) of the population experienced a deep fall in welfare, defined as moving more than two deciles down the welfare distribution; another fifth (21 percent) experienced a slight fall in welfare, moving down one decile; and 16 percent of the population preserved their rank as nonpoor.

The poor have low levels of disposable income and spend a high share of total expenditures on essentials that cannot be scaled down easily in the presence of shocks, as these examples show and figure 2.13 illustrates:

- In Jordan, the rising cost of food and basic goods caused an increase in the general poverty line (in Jordanian dinars) from JD 392 to JD 553 between 2002 and 2008. This was not met by a commensurate rise in wages, straining vulnerable households, who allocated 43.5 percent of household expenditures to food in 2008 (ESC 2010a). Asset ownership in 2008 represented only 0.9 percent of average household income, indicating limited scope for asset sales and resilience should Jordan experience another price shock. People in the three poorest quintiles in Jordan allocated 82 percent of the household budget to basic expenditures (45 percent of which was spent on food and 19 percent on rent).

- In Egypt, people in the three poorest quintiles allocated 88 percent of household consumption to basic goods (including 48 percent on

FIGURE 2.13

Expenditure Composition by Wealth Quintile in the Arab Republic of Egypt, Iraq, and Jordan, c. 2007–09

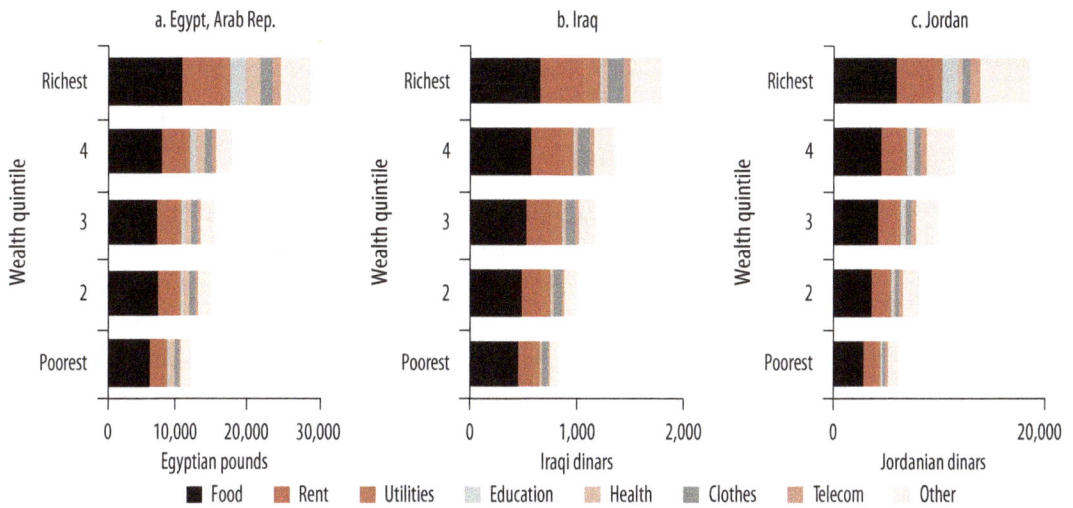

Sources: Authors' calculations based on data from HIES Egypt 2009; ESC 2010a (Jordan); IHSES Iraq 2007.

food and 19 percent on rent). In these quintiles, salaries accounted for 62 percent of household incomes while transfers provided another 33 percent. Meanwhile, consumption took up 86 percent of total income, leaving little room for spending on assets and other resilience capabilities.[8]

- Similarly, the three poorest quintiles in Iraq allocated 89 percent of consumption to basic expenditures (including 50 percent to food and 18 percent to rent).

As these examples suggest, households around the poverty line have very limited room for scaling down expenditures in times of economic hardship, seriously straining their capacity for resilience.

The absence of income support assistance for the unemployed, coupled with high informality, is an additional cause of high income vulnerability among most of the workforce in the Middle East and North Africa. Informality is mostly associated with low-quality jobs, with informal workers earning 10–50 percent lower salaries than formal workers with similar skills (Gatti et al. 2011). Informal employment is also associated with higher vulnerability to social risks because informal workers do not have access to the same social protection tools (including health insurance, pensions, and job stability) that protect the relatively small formal workforce. In Egypt and Tunisia, more than half of workers do not have a contract; in Egypt, the share without social security coverage increased by 10 percentage points between 1998 and 2006; and in Morocco, 80 percent of the population is not covered by a pension. No system of income support for the unemployed has been developed, and workfare programs in the region remain limited in scope and scale.

Crises at the Micro Level: Idiosyncratic Shocks from Health, Job, or Asset Loss

Households are exposed to multiple work- or business-, health-, and violence-related risks. When households are hit by these shocks, the result can be a significant loss of assets or income. Although household surveys usually do not capture household shocks and coping strategies, surveys conducted in Iraq, Morocco, and the Republic of Yemen are important exceptions and provide revealing information. Although some shocks are linked to the economy (for example, jobs and earnings losses are the most commonly reported major shock in Morocco), others relate to violence and conflict. (Loss of an asset or livestock due to violence and theft was the most commonly reported shock in Iraq during the war period, while death and serious illness of a household member were the most frequent shocks reported in the Republic of Yemen's capital, Sana'a, in 2009–10.) Table 2.6 shows the incidence of these shocks, by type, as reported by survey respondents.

As many as 15 percent of households in Iraq, Morocco, and Sana'a reported suffering at least one major shock during the previous 12 months. In the Republic of Yemen, the four worst shocks mentioned by households were death of a household member, serious injury or illness of a household member, loss of assets due to violence and theft, and job loss. The losses can be significant; for example, 58 percent of households in

TABLE 2.6

Incidence of Idiosyncratic Shocks in Iraq, Morocco, and the Republic of Yemen, 2009–10

Percentage of respondents reporting occurrence	Iraq	Morocco	Yemen, Rep. (Sana'a)
Lower wages or returns of family business	5	6	0
Unexpected job loss or bankruptcy of family business	7	5	2
Death of household member	2	4	5
Serious injury or illness of household member	3	0	4
Loss of asset or livestock due to violence and theft	13	1	2
Another major problem	2	1	3
At least one of the shocks mentioned above	15	15	15

Sources: Authors' calculations based on data from Republic of Yemen's Social Networks and Solidarity Mechanisms Survey 2010; IHSES Iraq 2009; and MHYS Morocco 2010.

Iraq who suffered a major shock reported that they reduced the quantity and quality of their food as a consequence.

Coping with Shocks to Individual Households

In the face of a major shock and in the absence of effective SSNs, households often rely on their own income, savings, and assets and on informal safety nets. In Morocco and Iraq, only about 1 percent of all households suffering major shocks reported receiving help from formal safety nets (that is, support from the government and nongovernmental organizations), as shown in figure 2.14. The most common coping strategies were using own income and savings and receiving help from informal safety nets (such as private support from family and neighbors). In this context, poorer families, with their limited incomes, savings, and assets, are again at greater risk.

Catastrophic and Impoverishing Effects of Health Care Costs

Although social health insurance schemes and free health services are extensive in most of the Middle East and North Africa, many households still face large—indeed, catastrophic—health care costs. *Catastrophic (health cost) effects* are commonly defined as occurring when a household's health care expenditures exceed 10 percent of its total expenditures or 40

FIGURE 2.14

Household Coping Mechanisms for Shocks in Iraq and Morocco, 2009–10

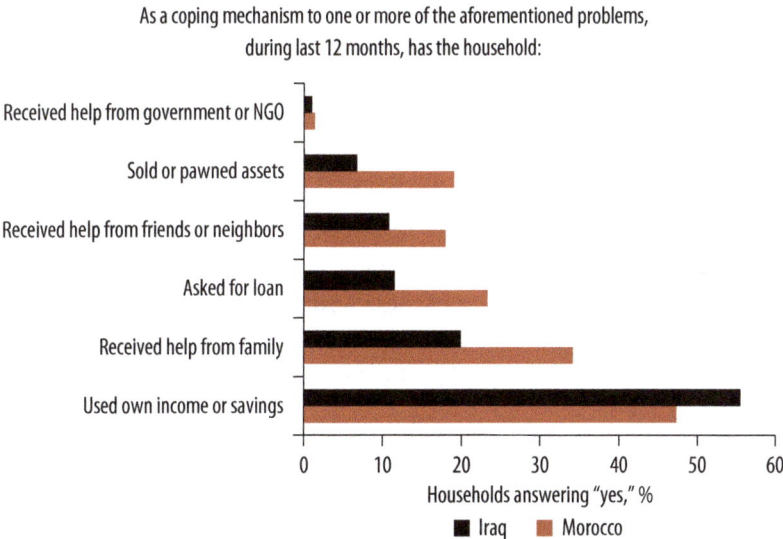

As a coping mechanism to one or more of the aforementioned problems, during last 12 months, has the household:

Sources: Authors' calculations using Iraq IHSES 2009 and Morocco MHYS 2010.

Note: NGO = nongovernmental organization.

FIGURE 2.15

Incidence of Catastrophic Health Expenditures in the Middle East and North Africa, Selected Economies, c. 2003–07

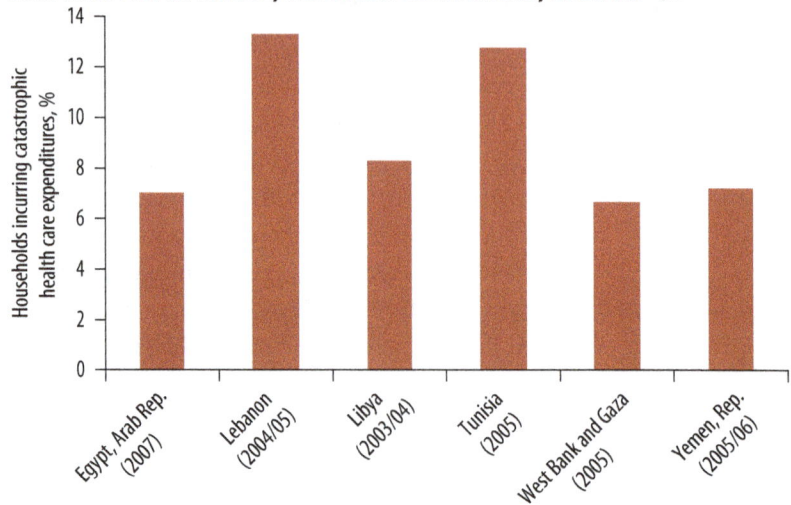

Sources: World Bank 2010c; data from national household surveys.

Note: "Catastrophic" health care expenditures are defined as expenditures exceeding 10 percent of a household's total expenditures or 40 percent of expenditures net of food spending.

percent of expenditures net of food spending. Related to but distinct from catastrophic effects, *impoverishment effects* occur when a household becomes poor following the need to pay for the health care services that it receives.

The Middle East and North Africa regional report on health (World Bank 2010c) found high levels of catastrophic health costs in several countries in the region. For example, in Lebanon in 2004/05, about 13 percent of households faced severe financial strain following the ill health of a household member (see figure 2.15). The study also found significant impoverishment effects related to health (see table 2.7), with an alarming increase in household poverty headcount ratios post-illness in a number of countries. The main driver of these health-related costs was the high out-of-pocket expenditures incurred by households, despite health fee waivers and services often paid for by the state.

The Toll on Households of Conflict and Violence

Wherever the likelihood of conflict and violence is high—as it is across the Middle East and North Africa—there are long-term human capital consequences for households. Injury and death of working members of households often precipitate the use of short-term coping strategies that

TABLE 2.7

Out-of-Pocket Health Care Spending and Impoverishment Effects in the Middle East and North Africa, Selected Economies

Economy	Prepayment poverty headcount (% households)	Postpayment poverty headcount (% households)	Absolute difference (% difference)	Relative difference (% difference)
Egypt, Arab Rep. (2007)	31.8	36.1	4.3	13.5
Iran, Islamic Rep. (2006)	13.6	15.4	1.8	13.2
Lebanon (2004/05)	27.5	31.6	4.1	14.9
Libya (2003/04)	1.7	1.8	0.1	5.6
Tunisia (2005)	3.7	4.4	0.7	17.8
West Bank and Gaza (2005)	13.7	25.1	11.4	82.9
Yemen, Rep. (2005/06)	20.3	21.9	1.6	7.9

Sources: World Bank 2010a; authors' calculations using data from national household surveys.

Note: An "impoverishment effect" is defined as when a household becomes poor following the need to pay for the health care services that it receives.

can damage long-term human capital accumulation. Such strategies include withdrawal of children from school, inadequate use of health care, and consumption of inadequate diets. In Iraq, conflict-related morbidity and mortality have been associated with increased asset sales by households, higher school dropout rates, and worse health outcomes for children (Silva and Thirumurthy 2010). In West Bank and Gaza, conflict threatens people's livelihoods and access to food, health, and education: approximately 40 percent of Gaza households live in extreme poverty, and 80 percent are dependent on food assistance (ILO 2008); in 2005, 32 percent of all fatalities were children, and as many as 1,709 were wounded (see UN-OCHA 2007); primary school enrollment decreased dramatically from around 95 percent in 2002 to 80 percent in 2005 (UNDP 2009). A recent United Nations Development Programme survey in West Bank and Gaza highlighted the significance of conflicts as a risk: when asked to specify the most important source of threat for themselves, respondents ranked "foreign occupation" as the most serious threat, followed by deteriorating economic conditions, deteriorating political conditions, and a lack of personal security (UNDP 2009).[9]

Crises at the Macro Level: Systemic Shocks

The macro-level shocks the Middle East and North Africa has suffered since 2008 have included rising commodity prices, reductions in remittances, and more recently, significant political upheaval. The region faced more of a price shock than a labor market shock following the global financial crisis, such that individuals' real income was reduced. A quantitative analysis shows that earnings fell for all workers between the ages of

25 and 58 in Egypt in 2008–09 (Cichello and Marotta 2011), but the effect was more pronounced for women, after controlling for initial levels of earning. Growth in remittances slowed to an 8.5 percent increase between 2007 and 2008 (in dollar terms) compared with 16 percent annual growth in the previous five years. The slowdown might not have affected poverty directly, as remittances typically go to better-off families, but it did affect the social balance in labor-sending countries in the region (World Bank 2010b). The political upheavals that began in 2011 have also had an economic impact, with disruption to daily commerce and the uncertainty surrounding the ultimate outcomes. In most cases, Middle Eastern and North African economies were able to rebound when the focus of the Arab Spring shifted from mass demonstrations to elections.

Such macro shocks (food price shocks, global financial crises, the Euro crisis, and so on) are expected to continue. The increasing volatility of commodity prices, as well as close links between the financial sector and the real economy, will likely increase the frequency of price shocks in the Middle East and North Africa relative to the 1980s and 1990s. The increased integration of the region's economies with international financial markets as a result of liberalization and structural reforms has brought many benefits (such as greater foreign direct investment). However, market irregularities elsewhere in the world now translate into greater economic growth shocks locally. Food price shocks in particular have a high impact in the region because as much as 50 percent of consumed food is imported.

Coping Strategies Show Resilience or Vulnerability

The impacts of high and volatile food prices on poverty, food security, and social cohesion are severe in many countries (World Bank 2012d).[10] The most common household responses to the 2007–08 crisis were to reduce the quality and quantity of meals consumed. In addition, households reduced nonfood consumption, sought more working hours, or diversified their income sources. Migration, and sometimes reverse migration, was another common response. Asset sales and loans from family and kin also provided important cushions for households. These trends can be organized into signs of vulnerability and resilience, as shown in table 2.8. Many of the coping strategies listed in the right column can lead to lasting welfare losses. In addition, box 2.3 describes coping strategies in the Republic of Yemen not necessarily captured in quantitative surveys but important nonetheless.

Mitigating Effects of Social Resilience—and Safety Nets

Crises can also frustrate expectations for upward mobility. Shocks can have social and psychological impacts during the critical formative years of a young person's life, with the severity depending on the person's age

TABLE 2.8

Household Coping Strategies in Response to Systemic Shocks

Evidence of resilience	Evidence of vulnerability
Living off savings	Cutting back basic consumption; fewer and less-nutritious meals
Migrating internally for opportunities	Cutting back essential nonfood consumption
Adapting business strategies	Forgoing health care
Cutting back nonessential spending	Selling assets needed for livelihood
Extending working hours	Accumulating unserviceable debt
Working more jobs	Dropping out of school; sending children to work; switching from private to public school
Striving to keep children in school	Engaging in high-risk income generating activities
Returning to education or training	Depleting community support networks
Engaging in communal meals	Engaging in theft, crime, drug selling
Joining mutual support groups; seeking support from family and friends	Resorting to divorce and abandonment, alcohol and drug use, high stress levels, domestic violence
Establishing savings or credit groups	Exhibiting lower resilience to other shocks

Source: World Bank 2012d.

BOX 2.3

Household Coping Strategies in the Republic of Yemen

Quantitative data do not often capture household coping strategies. Focus groups with rural communities in Omran governorate and in Noukem in Sana'a were conducted in 2010 to study the impact of the food price crisis on vulnerable households. The most common response in both rural and urban areas was that people reported eating differently, cutting out meat and chicken and relying more on vegetable stews. People ate smaller meals, making meals stretch, and skipped breakfast (especially affecting children who had to wait for lunch to be fed). Rural women said they gave children bread dipped in tea or mateed (a yogurt and tahini mix), whereas two years ago they could afford juice, meat, and fish. Some respondents reported chewing qat more often because it suppressed their appetite. Spending on other items and community events, such as weddings, also declined. There were reports of increased child labor, particularly begging or vending at street traffic lights.

Overall, the dominant message was that urban parents tried to keep their children in school and cut costs elsewhere. In rural areas, however, respondents thought that more children had been removed from school to work (for example, to sell qat). In the capital city of Sana'a, an increasing number of women sought home-based work or outside jobs. Depending on their level of education and skills, women found janitorial, hospital, or domestic service jobs, or they joined the police and armed forces. This was noted as a source of tension, as some men did not like competing with women for jobs, and some male household members disapproved of women working. The strain on households also resulted in noneconomic impacts, including reported higher levels of stress, more household disputes, and increased domestic violence.

Source: Hossain et al. 2010.

when the shock occurs and the extent to which mitigation measures are available to the child and parents and community (that is, social resilience) (Lundberg and Wuermli 2012). Social resilience is important for adolescents, especially because it affects their ability to develop their identities, autonomy, and future career orientation. Sources of social resilience during crises include services provided by community centers, churches, and mosques; family and community ties; and common narratives or ways of seeing the world that help promote resilience. Adolescents can also self-regulate their behavior to respond to a shock—for example, adapting to changing job markets by actively seeking out mentors and employment services (Lundberg and Wuermli 2012). When individuals, households, and communities respond to crises by self-regulating expectations and seeking psychosocial support, social resilience is the result.

However, vulnerable groups in the Middle East and North Africa rarely benefited from social protection programs during the food, fuel, and financial crises that started in 2008, according to a global qualitative study of the impact of food, fuel, and financial crises on households (World Bank 2012d). Reported problems with formal safety nets include poor targeting, low generosity, and downscaling during the crisis as constraints on public spending increased. Free and subsidized education, on the other hand, was important in keeping children in school, and subsidized health services were appreciated by recipients. A World Food Programme survey in 2008 found that one-third of respondents in the Republic of Yemen received some form of cash or food assistance (WFP 2008). Focus groups there had considerable awareness of the Social Welfare Fund (the government's main cash transfer program) and its designated target groups. According to the findings, people who did not receive official assistance felt that those that did were particularly needy. Other official sources of assistance appear to have declined or have been withdrawn, including noncash benefits for soldiers. Households in Sana'a resorted to multiple sources of assistance, most commonly borrowing from family and neighbors. Food distributed during Ramadan and Eid by mosques and local councils was another source of assistance cited (Hossain et al. 2010).

Climate-Related Shocks

According to preliminary analysis, climate change impacts are likely to be particularly significant in most parts of the Middle East and North Africa (World Bank 2009, 2010e)—generating more frequent challenges and demands for governments' rapid response. Higher temperatures and reduced precipitation, which lead to increased occurrences of droughts, are already materializing in the Maghreb. Among the predicted effects are the following:

- An estimated 80–100 million more people will be exposed to water stress by 2025, which is likely to result in increased pressure on groundwater resources and an attendant rise in potential conflict, diarrheal diseases, and malnutrition.

- Agriculture yields, especially in rainfed areas, are expected to fluctuate more widely, ultimately falling to a significantly lower long-term average.

- In urban areas in North Africa, a temperature increase of 1–3 degrees Celsius could expose 6–25 million people to coastal flooding. Communities in low-lying coastal areas of Egypt, Kuwait, Libya, Qatar, Tunisia, and the United Arab Emirates are at particular risk. Flooding will affect communities in both urban (port cities) and rural areas. All households across a subregion may be at risk, but particular pockets that are already poor (for example, fishing communities) may have fewer resources to cope and rebuild livelihoods.

Widespread Effects, with Agricultural Households Most Vulnerable

For rural agricultural households, the principal vulnerability is from weather-related shocks—shocks that are increasing as a result of climate change. In Morocco, a climate shock and agriculture module was fielded as part of the 2010 Household and Youth Survey (MHYS). Results indicate that 22 percent of all households in Morocco reported having experienced a major weather shock, such as drought, flood, pest infestation, or crop and livestock diseases, in the previous five years. The only type of shock reported more frequently than weather was an unexpected increase in prices of food or other essential commodities consumed (72 percent of all households experienced this shock). Weather shocks were more common than job-, business-, health-, and violence-related shocks. Moreover, 77 percent of households who suffered this type of shock reported that they had not yet recovered from its negative consequences.

Moreover, the consequences of these types of shocks are severe among agricultural households. In Morocco, 28 percent of households had at least one member engaged in agriculture or agriculture-related activities, of which 30 percent reported having had a serious or very serious financial loss due to climate-related factors. The five most commonly reported climate-related shocks were

- Reduction of agricultural yield due to inadequate rainfall (periodic and recurrent water scarcity due to droughts) (reported by 62 percent of households);

- Reduction of job opportunities in the agricultural sector (44 percent of households);

- Reduction of agricultural yields because of too much water (too much rain or flooding) (38 percent of households);

- Reduction of agricultural yields because of changing and unpredictable climate and temperatures (too hot, too cold, too rainy, too dry) (35 percent of households); and

- Reduction in livestock due to less grazing land because of droughts and floods (32 percent of households).

For these households, climate change brings frequent and significant shocks that can have large impacts. These impacts create new needs to which SSNs have to adapt (Heltberg, Siegel, and Jorgensen 2009, 2010).

SSNs Crucial to Climate Change Adaptation

The Middle East and North Africa is one of the most vulnerable regions in the world to climate change, and traditional SSNs can be adapted to provide a broader response. Those countries with increasing urbanization in low-lying coastal areas and river deltas are at higher risk of weather-related events (Verner and Biroscak 2010). The recent Intergovernmental Panel on Climate Change report (IPCC 2012) forecasts increasing climate and weather variability as well as more frequent and severe natural hazards. These phenomena will have an intricate and negative effect on health as well as on food and water security. Thus, poverty and vulnerability might increase.

These forecasts imply an increasing challenge for SSNs. Countries in Sub-Saharan Africa are pioneers in this respect, having adopted an approach that integrates SSNs with climate change adaptation and disaster risk management schemes (Davies, Oswald, and Mitchell 2009). These programs aim to increase *resilience* of vulnerable households and communities by strengthening and protecting livelihoods and by building assets that are useful for communities: for example, public works projects geared at improving water resource management and cash transfers conditional on participation in resilience-building activities. Such projects help build human capital while promoting sustainable development and helping to mitigate climate-related risk. It is important for these programs to be flexible, responsive, and easily scalable to efficiently respond to changing conditions (Heltberg, Siegel, and Jorgensen 2010). There are new easily accessible technologies such as geographic information systems, spatial data infrastructures, and information and communications technologies that could be used innovatively to achieve better results (Siegel, Gatsinzi, and Kettlewell 2011). Countries such as Ethiopia, Kenya, and Rwanda have recently started such initiatives and have been fairly successful at adopting climate-related approaches to SSNs (GEF 2007; Siegel, Gatsinzi, and Kettlewell 2011; World Bank 2010e).

Social Exclusion

Even apart from the effects of poverty and economic or weather-related shocks, social exclusion explains why some groups of people remain poorer than others, are less economically or politically involved, or benefit less from services. Social exclusion in the Middle East and North Africa is multifaceted and takes on many forms. Some of the excluded groups in the region are women, people with disabilities, and displaced people. Often the conditions of social exclusion are interconnected, and they most clearly play out in the labor market and the ability of socially excluded groups to access employment or health insurance benefits.

Gender-Based Exclusion

Although ability is evenly distributed between the genders, opportunities to exit poverty in the Middle East and North Africa are not. In particular, in the region during the past decade, while the average level of education has increased significantly among women, the opportunities available to them in terms of labor market participation, the percentage of seats held in parliament by women, and the ratio of women to men in nonagricultural wage employment have remained low (World Bank 2012c).[11]

Cultural barriers, weak support systems (such as public transportation and child care services), and wage discrimination are some of the main factors hindering female labor force participation in the region (UNDP 2005; World Bank 2004). A comparative household survey conducted by the World Bank in Amman, Cairo, and Sana'a shows that social norms and conservative attitudes play a significant role in preventing women from entering the labor force: less than 10 percent of women living in households with a member who opposes their work actually do participate in the labor market. This is particularly of concern because more than 30 percent of young men (aged 15–44) oppose female participation in labor markets (Chamlou, Muzi, and Ahmed 2008a, 2008b).

Furthermore, tax- and employment-related benefits to families are channeled through men. A woman can receive such benefits only if she is officially the head of the household (that is, if she is widowed or proves that her husband is old or incapacitated). In Jordan, women's social security and pensions cannot be passed on to their husbands and children after their deaths. A woman cannot apply for a family allowance unless she can prove that her husband is deceased or disabled or that she is the primary family breadwinner. A lower mandatory retirement age for women, while designed to protect them, also leads women to accumulate less in social benefits than their male counterparts (ESC 2010b). Gender-based regulations—including, in some countries, restrictions on the type and hours of work as well as requirements for the husband's permission to work and travel—pose additional challenges.

Disability-Based Exclusion

As in other regions, countries in the Middle East and North Africa have not effectively addressed the difficulties that persons with disabilities consistently face. Although a precise estimate is elusive, the incidence of disability in the Middle East and North Africa is between 1 and 12 percent of the population (Peters 2009).

The disadvantages that disabled people encounter are clearer: high unemployment rates, inaccessible and unaffordable health care, low educational attainment, inaccessible transportation and infrastructure, and stigmatization resulting in social exclusion and marginalization (WHO and World Bank 2011). For example, in Syria, only 20 percent of women with disabilities are literate, compared with 66 percent of the total female population and 40 percent of men with disabilities (UNICEF 2002). In addition, the physical infrastructure to aid mobility is lacking for people with disabilities. Very few public schools accommodate disabled students, and very few countries have publicly funded programs to help the disabled integrate into society or build their skills (UN-ESCWA 2007). Moreover, people with disabilities in the Middle East and North Africa have poor access to health and social provisioning as well as inadequate rehabilitation services (UN-ESCWA 2007).

To confront these challenges, people with disabilities require a range of services, from relatively minor and inexpensive interventions to complex and costly ones. In 2006, a national study in Morocco estimated the expressed need for improved access to a range of services. People with disabilities in the study expressed a strong need for better health care and rehabilitation services (55.3 percent), medications (21.3 percent), technical devices (17.5 percent), and financial help for basic needs (52.5 percent) (Kingdom of Morocco 2006). In combination with better provision of services, unconditional cash transfers for people with disabilities can help to address the additional barriers faced by this group in accessing health care and rehabilitation, transport, education, and working, among other things. Many countries provide income support through such transfers to these households, including poor households with a disabled member and directly to individuals with disabilities (for example, Bangladesh, Brazil, India, and South Africa [WHO and World Bank 2011]).

Exclusion of Displaced People

The Middle East and North Africa hosts almost half of all the registered externally displaced people in the world, according to the United Nations High Commissioner for Refugees (UNHCR) and the United Nations Relief and Works Agency for Palestine Refugees in the Near East. Among them are 7.5 million Palestinians and Iraqis displaced in Jordan and Syria (UNDP 2009). The UNHCR also estimates that the total number of internally displaced persons in the region is around 10 million.

However, Middle Eastern and North African countries grant few citizenship rights to externally displaced people, thus excluding the long-term displaced from labor markets, political participation, public education, health care, and other social benefits in their host countries. The integration of the displaced varies substantially from country to country, and often by particular group. In Jordan, for example, Palestinians who have not been granted Jordanian citizenship (or who hold temporary two-year passports) are denied access to free basic public education, have to pay higher non-national university fees, and face more expensive health care services. Furthermore, access to formal sector professions is denied because working in organized occupations such as medicine, law, and engineering requires Jordanian citizenship to belong to the relevant professional association. Mobility is also constrained because foreigners' driver's licenses are more expensive and shorter in duration (Human Rights Watch 2010).

In countries with ongoing conflicts or returning displaced people, the UNHCR and NGOs often take on the role of providing basic services to these groups. For example, international NGO programs within Syria and Jordan have provided cash and in-kind support to displaced Iraqi families, with a focus on vulnerable children and women, including vocational training for girls, community centers, and remedial education.

Conclusions

This chapter has used the most recent data in the Middle East and North Africa to identify structural factors and emerging risks faced by the poor and vulnerable—the targeted population for SSN programs. The data show that the opportunities associated with continued economic growth, poverty reduction, and a growing middle class in the region are dampened by the effects of poverty, exclusion, high vulnerability to shocks, and rising economic volatility, as summarized here.

Poverty

Children are at particular risk for poverty, which is correlated with poor human development outcomes, such as malnutrition. Being born into poverty puts a child at a significant disadvantage relative to his or her peers. Poor children are at a higher risk for malnutrition, a risk aggravated by lack of health-related services. Due to this inequality of opportunities, the paths of poor and rich children diverge early in life, which manifests itself among poor children in lower preprimary enrollment, higher dropout rates, and lower completion rates.

Precarious employment and joblessness go hand in hand with poverty because the poor and low-skilled tend to have fewer labor market opportunities and more unstable employment conditions, which perpetuates their poverty status. The scarcity of jobs and how they are allocated particularly affects poor individuals. The available evidence suggests that individuals who are poor and unemployed are more likely to be in this condition because they cannot find a job, not because they are waiting to find a better job. Indeed, poor individuals are more likely to work in informal and low-paying jobs. They are also more likely to stay in low-quality jobs and less likely to keep good-quality jobs.

The region also has important geographic disparities, with those born in lagging areas of even relatively rich countries lacking opportunities. There are spatial pockets of poverty in middle-income countries where extreme poverty is prevalent, access to basic services is lacking, and human development indicators are considerably below the country's average. The disadvantageous circumstances of these areas are likely to undermine the potential of those born there, independent of their level of effort.

Vulnerability to Shocks

The extent of vulnerability to shocks is high, with a large share of the population in the Middle East and North Africa living just above the poverty line. In the absence of reliable and effective SSNs, regular idiosyncratic shocks (such as employment and health shocks) as well as increasingly frequent systemic, macro-level crises can plunge many into persistent poverty that can have irreversible effects on human capital because of ineffective coping strategies. New risks associated with climate change also pose new challenges.

Social Exclusion

The social exclusion of some groups in the region—particularly women, people with disabilities, and displaced people—explains why these groups remain poorer than others, are less economically or politically involved, or benefit less from services. Cultural barriers, weak support systems, and wage discrimination are some of the main factors hindering female labor force participation in the Middle East and North Africa. Exclusion of migrants occurs through a lack of legal and political rights; a lack of security; and limited access to services, housing, and employment in the receiving country. Countries in the region face challenges in effectively addressing the difficulties that persons with disabilities consistently face, including high unemployment rates, inaccessible and unaffordable health care, low educational attainment, inaccessible transportation and infrastructure, and stigmatization resulting in social exclusion and marginalization. To promote more equitable access to services, SSN design should address these groups' particular needs and ensure their active participation in interventions.

Finally, Why?

The high prevalence of lost opportunities for poor and vulnerable households indicates that SSNs in the Middle East and North Africa are falling short of protecting the poor from deprivation, promoting human capital formation among the poor, and ensuring them against long-term losses brought about by short-duration shocks. But why is this so? The next chapter examines in detail the performance of SSN programs in the region, benchmarking them against SSN performance in other regions and countries.

ANNEX 2A

Demographic Statistics and Poverty Incidence in the Middle East and North Africa, Selected Countries, c. 2006–10

	Egypt, Arab Rep. 2009		Iraq 2007		Yemen, Rep. 2006		Jordan 2010		Morocco 2010		Syrian Arab Rep. 2006	
	% population	Poverty incidence (%)	% population	Poverty incidence (%)	% population	Poverty incidence (%)	% population	Poverty incidence (%)	% population	Q1 incidence (%)	% population	Q1 incidence (%)
Urban	48	12	68	16	26	21	83	14	53	6	56	37
Rural	53	30	33	39	74	40	17	17	47	33	44	4
Elderly (>65)	5	14	3	17	3	30	5	7	5	13	7	24
Infants (0–1)	2	30	3	37	3	27	2	16	2	31	2	19
Children under 5	11	29	15	28	15	30	11	17	9	26	10	20
Children (0–14)	33	29	40	27	46	36	34	20	28	25	33	20
Youth (15–29)	28	20	30	28	30	36	30	11	31	16	30	8
Members of female-headed households	12	20	9	20	5	29	9	11	—	—	8	20
Members of male-headed households	88	22	91	23	95	35	91	15	—	—	92	18
People with disabilities	1	38	3	24	11	35	2.4	28	—	—	—	—
Members of households whose head is illiterate	31	31	20	32	39	43	8	26	—	—	—	—
Total	100	22	100	23	100	36	100	14	100	20	100	20

	DHS 2008	MICS 2006	MICS 2006	DHS 2007	DHS 2004	MICS 2006
ANC by trained medical staff	74	84	97	99	68	84
Birth delivery by trained medical staff	79	93	98	99	63	93
Birth delivery in a health facility	72	—	99	99	61	—

Sources: Authors' calculations based on Egypt HIES 2009, Egypt DHS 2008; Iraq HSES 2007, Iraq MICS 2006; Jordan LMPS 2010, Jordan DHS 2007; Morocco MHYS 2010, Morocco DHS 2004; Republic of Yemen HBS 2006, Republic of Yemen MICS 2006; Syria HIES 2006, Syria MICS 2006.

Note: ANC = antenatal care; DHS = Demographic and Health Survey; MICS = Multiple Indicator Cluster Survey (UNICEF); Q = wealth quintile (1 = lowest, 5 = highest); — = not available.

Notes

1. Weakly relative poverty lines assume that a rise in the overall living standards in a country increases the minimum consumption level needed to not be deemed "poor." This concept differs from the strongly relative poverty lines in that, with the former, poverty rates fall in the presence of distribution-neutral growth. The estimates of weakly relative poverty presented in the report are anchored to private consumption from the national accounts (Chen and Ravallion 2012).

2. The PovcalNet website also included aggregate poverty numbers for the Middle East and North Africa region for 2008 (15 percent at US$2/day at 2005 PPP). However, those numbers are based on data that cover less than 50 percent of the population, creating uncertainty about the estimated poverty rate at the regional level for 2008.

3. Other groups that are at high risk of poverty, such as the disabled, are discussed later in the chapter. A third group with high risk of poverty relates to households headed by illiterate individuals, whose profile, however, tends to overlap with the rural households and households with child poverty.

4. In countries where malnutrition extends into the middle and higher quintiles, international experience suggests that the problem is not just lack of income but also lack of knowledge or practice. In these situations, SSNs can be a helpful delivery mechanism, but a transfer per se might not be the main tool; that is, in cases where a targeted (conditional or unconditional) cash transfer or a workfare program is going to be implemented, an associated component can create incentives to change behaviors. This is now being done in Djibouti and has attracted a high degree of buy-in from the government and donors.

5. The Multiple Indicator Cluster Surveys (MICS) is an initiative conducted by the United Nations Children's Fund (UNICEF) to assist countries in collecting and analyzing data to fill data gaps for monitoring the situation of children and women. For information, see http://www.childinfo.org/mics.html.

6. Although unemployment is a serious problem in the region for both sexes, especially among first-time job seekers, it is more acute among women. The average female worker in Jordan is likely to have 12.3 years of education, compared with 9.3 years for a male counterpart holding the same job (ILO 2010).

7. Using youth as an illustration also ensures that the household income quintile is less likely to be driven by their labor market status than if the whole adult population had been taken into account. Because the time span is only one year, even relatively small differences are significant—although the crisis year of 2008–09 may have increased the dynamism of the labor market and may not be a representative year.

8. Data from Egypt Household Income, Expenditure, and Consumption Survey (2009).

9. For more details on the effects of conflicts on poverty, see UNDP (2009).

10. Countries included in the research were Bangladesh, Cambodia, the Central African Republic, Kazakhstan, Kenya, Mongolia, Senegal, and Thailand.

11. Evidence from Lebanon and Syria shows that the gap in earnings between men and women is higher in the informal sector than in the formal sector.

Moreover, women in Lebanon and Syria stay in informal jobs longer than men, although women tend to drop out of the labor force with age. The share of women with formal jobs increases with age more than the share of men, which suggests that women who have formal jobs tend to remain in the labor force. When it comes to job benefits, the gap between men and women is larger in informal jobs. Furthermore, informal jobs are 30 percent less likely to offer maternity leave than formal jobs in Lebanon (Silva, Alloush, et al. 2011; Silva, Chartouni, et al. 2011).

References

Ackland, R., S. Dowrick, and B. Freyens. 2006. "Measuring Global Poverty: Why PPP Methods Matter." Working Paper, Research School of Social Sciences, Australia National University, Canberra.

Bhalla, A. S., and F. Lapeyre. 1999. *Poverty and Exclusion in a Global World*. New York, NY: Palgrave Macmillan.

Burchardt, T., J. Le Grand, and D. Piachaud. 2002. "Introduction." In *Understanding Social Exclusion*, edited by J. Hills, J. Le Grand, and D. Piachaud, 1–12. Oxford, U.K.: Oxford University Press.

Carneiro, P., and J. Heckman. 2003. "Human Capital Policy." In *Inequality in America: What Role for Human Capital Policies?* edited by J. J. Heckman, A. B. Krueger, and B. M. Friedman, 77–238. Cambridge, MA: MIT Press.

Chamlou, N., S. Muzi, and H. Ahmed. 2008a. "Female Home-Based Work and Entrepreneurship in MENA: Evidence from Amman, Cairo, and Sana'a." PowerPoint presentation, World Bank, Washington, DC.

———. 2008b. "Women's Labor Force Participation, Education and Non-Economic Factors: The Case of Middle East and North Africa Countries." Unpublished manuscript, World Bank, Washington, DC.

Chen, S., and M. Ravallion. 2012. "More Relatively-Poor People in a Less Absolutely-Poor World." Policy Research Working Paper 6114, World Bank, Washington, DC.

Cichello, P., and D. Marotta. 2011. "Falling Real Earnings in Egypt 2008–2009 and How the Declines Differ by Gender and Initial Earnings." Paper presented at 18th Economic Research Forum, World Bank, Washington, DC.

Coudouel, A., and J. Hentschel. 2000. "Poverty Data and Measurement." Unpublished draft for *A Sourcebook for Poverty Reduction Strategies*, edited by J. Klugman. Washington, DC: World Bank.

Coudouel, A., J. Hentschel, and Q. Wodon. 2002. "Poverty Measurement and Analysis." In *A Sourcebook for Poverty Reduction Strategies*, edited by J. Klugman, 29–70. Washington, DC: World Bank.

Davies, M., K. Oswald, and T. Mitchell. 2009. "Climate Change Adaptation, Disaster Risk Reduction and Social Protection." In *Promoting Pro-Poor Growth: Social Protection*. Prepared by the DAC Network on Poverty Reduction (POVNET), Organisation for Economic Co-operation and Development (OECD), Paris.

ESC (Economic and Social Council). 2010a. "Assessing the Middle Class in Jordan." Policy paper, ESC, Amman.

——. 2010b. "Female Labour Force Participation in Jordan." Economic and Social Council Policy Papers, ESC, Amman.

Galal, A., and K. Taher. 2010. *Financing Higher Education in Arab Countries*. Policy Research Report 34, Economic Research Forum, Cairo.

Gallup Inc. 2009. World Poll Survey (database). The Gallup Organization, Washington, DC. http://www.gallup.com/se/126845/Action.aspx.

Gatti, R., D. Angel-Urdinola, J. Silva, and A. Bodor. 2011. *Striving for Better Jobs: the Challenge of Informality in the Middle East and North Africa*. Directions in Development Series. Washington, DC: World Bank.

GEF (Global Environment Fund). 2007. *Kenya Adaptation to Climate Change in Arid Lands (KACCAL)*. Executive Summary, Project P091979, World Bank, Washington, DC.

Gore, C., and J. B. Figueiredo, eds. 1997. *Social Exclusion and Anti-Poverty Policy: A Debate*. Geneva: International Institute for Labour Studies.

Heltberg, R., P. B. Siegel, and S. L. Jorgensen. 2009. "Addressing Human Vulnerability to Climate Change: Toward a 'No Regrets' Approach." *Global Environmental Change* 19 (1): 89–99.

——. 2010. "Social Policies for Adaptation to Climate Change." In *Social Dimensions of Climate Change: Equity and Vulnerability in a Warming World*, edited by R. Mearns and A. Norton, 259–75. Washington, DC: World Bank.

Horton, S., M. Shekar, C. McDonald, A. Mahal, and J. Brooks. 2010. *Scaling Up Nutrition: What Will It Cost?* Directions in Development Series. Washington, DC: World Bank.

Hossain, N., R. Fillaili, G. Lubaale, M. Mulumbi, M. Rashid, and M. Tadros. 2010. *The Social Impacts of Crisis: Findings from Community-Level Research in Five Developing Countries*. Research report, Institute of Development Studies, Brighton, U.K.

Human Rights Watch. 2010. *Stateless Again: Palestinian-Origin Jordanians Deprived of their Nationality*. Report 1-56432-575-X, New York, NY.

ILO (International Labour Organization). 2008. *The Situation of Workers of the Occupied Arab Territories*. Report of the director general, International Labour Conference, 97th Session, June 2008, Geneva.

——. 2010. *Pay Equity in Jordan*. Policy brief, ILO Regional Office for Arab States, Beirut.

IPCC (Intergovernmental Panel on Climate Change). 2012. *Managing the Risks of Extreme Events and Disasters to Advance Climate Change Adaptation*. Special report of IPCC. Cambridge, U.K.: Cambridge University Press.

Kingdom of Morocco. 2006. *Childhood and Disabled Persons: The National Survey on Disability*. Secretariat of Family, Kingdom of Morocco, Rabat.

Lundberg, M., and A. Wuermli. 2012. *Children and Youth in Crisis Protecting and Promoting Human Development in Times of Economic Shocks*. Directions in Development Series. Washington, DC: World Bank.

Marotta, D. M., Y. Ruslan, H. El-Laithy, H. Abou-Ali, and S. Al-Shawarby. 2011. "Was Growth in Egypt between 2005 and 2008 Pro-Poor? From Static to Dynamic Poverty Profile." Policy Research Working Paper 5589, World Bank, Washington, DC.

Paes de Barros, R., H. Francisco, J. R. M. Vega, and J. S. Chanduvi. 2009. *Measuring Inequality of Opportunities in Latin America and the Caribbean*. Washington, DC: World Bank.

Paes de Barros, R., J. R. M. Vega, and J. S. Chanduvi. 2008. "Measuring Inequality of Opportunities for Children." Working Paper 4659, World Bank, Washington, DC.

Peters, S. 2009. "Review of Marginalisation of People with Disabilities in Lebanon, Syria and Jordan." Background paper for the Education for All Global Monitoring Report 2010, United Nations Educational, Scientific, and Cultural Organization, Paris.

Ravallion, M. 1996. "Issues in Measuring and Modeling Poverty." Policy Research Working Paper 1615, World Bank, Washington, DC.

———. 2010. "The Developing World's Bulging (but Vulnerable) Middle Class." *World Development* 38 (4): 445–54.

Reiter, Y. 2002. "Higher Education and Sociopolitical Transformation in Jordan." *British Journal of Middle Eastern Studies* 29 (2): 137–64.

Sen, A. 2000. "Social Exclusion: Concept, Application and Scrutiny." Social Protection Paper 1, Office of Environment and Social Protection, Asian Development Bank, Manila.

Siegel, P., J. Alwang, and S. L. Jorgensen. 2003. "Rediscovering Vulnerability through a Risk Chain: Views from Different Disciplines." *Quarterly Journal of Agriculture* 42 (3): 351–70.

Siegel, P. B., J. Gatsinzi, and A. Kettlewell. 2011. "Adaptive Social Protection in Rwanda: 'Climate-Proofing' the Vision 2020 Umurenge Programme." *IDS Bulletin* 42 (6): 71–78.

Silva, J., and H. Thirumurthy. 2010. "The Impact of the Iraq War on Labor Market and Human Development Outcomes." Unpublished manuscript, World Bank, Washington, DC.

Silva, J., M. Alloush, H. Sayed, and M. Wazzan. 2011. "The Challenges of Informality and Job Quality for Women in Lebanon Using Matched Employer-Employee Data." Unpublished manuscript, World Bank, Washington, DC.

Silva, J., C. Chartouni, H. Sayed, and M. Wazzan. 2011. "The Challenges of Informality and Job Quality for Women in Syria Using Matched Employer-Employee Data." Unpublished manuscript, World Bank, Washington, DC.

UNDP (United Nations Development Programme). 2005. *Arab Human Development Report 2005: Towards the Rise of Women in the Arab World*. New York, NY: UNDP.

———. 2009. *Arab Human Development Report 2009: Challenges to Human Security in the Arab Countries*. New York, NY: UNDP.

UN-ESCWA (United Nations Economic and Social Commission for Western Asia). 2007. "Social Exclusion in the ESCWA Region." *Social Development Bulletin* 1 (3).

UNICEF (United Nations Children's Fund). 2002. *The State of the World's Children 2002.* New York, NY: UNICEF.

———. 2007. *La situation des enfants au Maroc. Analyse selon l'approche basée sur les droits humains.* Summary report, Rabat. http://www.unicef.org/morocco/french/SITAN2007resume-fr.pdf.

———. 2009. *The State of the World's Children 2009.* New York: UNICEF.

———. n.d. Child Info (database). http://www.childinfo.org.

———. n.d. Multiple Indicator Cluster Surveys (database). http://www.childinfo.org/mics.html.

UN-OCHA (United Nations Office for the Coordination of Humanitarian Affairs). 2007. *The Humanitarian Impact on Palestinians of Israeli Settlements and Other Infrastructure in the West Bank.* New York, NY.

Verner, D., and J. Biroscak. 2010. "Climate Change and the Middle East." *Development Horizons* First/Second Quarter 2010: 4–9.

WFP (World Food Programme). 2008. *Impact of Rising Food Prices on Household Food Security in Yemen.* Report, Rome.

WHO (World Health Organization). 2010. *World Health Statistics.* Geneva: WHO.

———. n.d. The WHO Child Growth Standards. http://www.who.int/childgrowth/en/.

WHO (World Health Organization) and World Bank. 2011. *World Report on Disability.* Geneva: WHO.

World Bank. 2004. *Gender and Development in the Middle East and North Africa: Women in the Public Sphere.* MENA Development Report Series, Washington, DC: World Bank.

———. 2009. *Building Resilient Communities: Risk Management and Response to Natural Disasters through Social Funds and Community-Driven Development Operations.* Resource toolkit, Washington, DC: World Bank.

———. 2010a. *Implementation Completion and Results Report: Ethiopia Productive Safety Nets.* APL II Project, Report ICR00001676, Washington, DC: World Bank.

———. 2010b. *Labor Migration from North Africa: Development Impact, Challenges, and Policy Options.* Vol. I: Main report. Washington, DC. http://siteresources.worldbank.org/INTMENA/Resources/MIGRATIONREPORT.pdf.

———. 2010c. *Meeting the Challenges of Health Transition in the Middle East and North Africa Region: Building Partnerships for Results Time for Strategic Action.* Health study, Washington, DC: World Bank.

———. 2010d. *Poor Places, Thriving People: How the Middle East and North Africa Can Rise above Spatial Disparities.* Washington, DC: World Bank.

———. 2010e. *World Development Report 2010: Development and Climate Change.* Washington, DC: World Bank.

———. 2013a. *Jobs for Shared Prosperity: Time for Action in the Middle East and North Africa.* Washington, DC: World Bank.

———. 2012b. *Ciblage et Protection Sociale au Maroc. Note d'Orientation Strategique.* Washington, DC: World Bank.

————. 2012c. *Gender Opening Doors: Gender Equality in the Middle East and North Africa*. Washington, DC: World Bank.

————. 2012d. *Living through Crises: How the Food, Fuel and Financial Shocks Affect the Poor*. Washington, DC: World Bank.

————. 2012e. *World Development Indicators 2012*. Washington, DC: World Bank.

CHAPTER 3

The Current State of Social Safety Nets in the Middle East and North Africa

Introduction

To perform an assessment of the multiple challenges concerning social safety nets (SSNs) in the Middle East and North Africa today, this chapter will use household survey data and administrative data from a variety of sources to answer two main questions:

1. How much does the region spend on SSNs, both overall and disaggregated by program type?

2. How well do the region's SSNs perform in terms of coverage, targeting, generosity, and impact on poverty and inequality?

The average Middle Eastern and North African country spends about 6 percent of gross domestic product (GDP) (or more than 85 percent of total SSN resources) on nontargeted food and energy subsidies. Most of the region's countries provide food subsidies, fuel price subsidies, or both. In addition, some countries, such as Iraq and the Arab Republic of Egypt, also provide food for the poor through ration cards.

Although subsidy programs are usually popular and are based on good intentions to guarantee access to basic goods for everyone, such programs are expensive for governments to maintain. Thus, they capture substantial financial resources that could be spent on more efficient and effective SSN programs. In addition, subsidy budgets fluctuate with the world market price of the subsidized goods, which undermines a government's ability to predict expenditures. Besides imposing a sizable and unpredictable fiscal burden, subsidies suffer from high levels of leakage to the nonpoor and may even be regressive if the rich consume more of the subsidized goods than the poor do, as is the case with most types of fuel. Subsidies can also distort consumption patterns when people overuse subsidized products, and they can have adverse effects on producers' incentives. Finally, subsidies are vulnerable to fraud because intermediaries have an incentive to sell subsidized goods at market prices.

Price subsidies aside, SSNs in the Middle East and North Africa are very small (with all but one country covering less than 30 percent of the bottom wealth quintile) and highly fragmented. Countries in the region adopt one of two approaches to SSNs: (a) relying primarily on subsidies or ration programs, as Iraq and the Republic of Yemen do; or (b) offering a multitude of small and fragmented programs that serve similar objectives but are implemented by different agencies, as in Jordan and Morocco (where 12 programs all aim at increasing school enrollment). Aside from the Public Distribution System food ration card, Iraq's only other program is the Social Safety Net (also known as the Social Protection Network), which covers 0.3 percent of the population and only 0.09 percent of the bottom quintile. In Jordan, both the National Aid Fund (NAF) and the Ministry of Social Development provide emergency assistance, but there is a lack of coordination between the two agencies. Low coverage and high fragmentation make SSNs unreliable, limiting their ability to protect people from destitution or to prevent short-term shocks from having adverse long-term consequences.

Moreover, the Middle East and North Africa region lags behind other regions in the efficient use of SSN resources, with the average program in the region distributing only 23 percent of its benefits to the bottom quintile, versus an average of 59 percent in the comparator sample of programs in Latin America and the Caribbean and in Eastern Europe and Central Asia. The disparity stems from (a) overreliance on subsidies and (b) low coverage, fragmentation, and ineffective targeting of nonsubsidy SSNs.

As mentioned above, subsidies and ration cards tend to be universal, so their use is not explicitly restricted to the poor. However, other SSN programs in the region, specifically cash transfer programs, suffer from poor targeting. Many countries target cash transfers categorically—to single mothers, widows, orphans, the unemployed, the elderly, and the disabled—irrespective of poverty level. Even though geographic targeting can be highly effective in principle, in the Middle East and North Africa it has been applied without the required updated poverty maps. In Egypt, Tunisia, and the Republic of Yemen, all cash transfer programs target specific categories of the population in certain geographic regions. For example, Tunisia's National Program of Assistance to Needy Families (*Programme National d'Aide aux Familles Nécessiteuses*; PNAFN) cash transfer program targets the country's Center-West and North-West regions based on outdated poverty estimates. Eligibility for other programs in the region is based on the discretion of the relevant agencies. Such targeting approaches lead to considerable leakage of program resources to the nonpoor and to undercoverage of the poor who do not fit the predefined categories or do not live in targeted regions.

Although categorical or geographic targeting can be effective in the presence of concentrated poverty, such targeting makes it difficult for governments to scale up SSNs in times of crisis. Only a handful of programs in the region have begun implementing individual assessment targeting, such as the income (or means) test used in Jordan's NAF. West Bank and Gaza was the first country in the region to target its Cash Transfer Program using proxy means testing (PMT), which relies on observable household characteristics rather than hard-to-verify income to assess welfare. Lebanon's new National Poverty Targeting Program and the Republic of Yemen's Social Welfare Fund (SWF) now also use PMT to assess eligibility.

To formulate policies that can address the challenges outlined above, it is vital to assess the current performance of key SSN programs in the Middle East and North Africa. This chapter analyzes the expenditure levels, coverage rates, targeting performance, and poverty and inequality impact of existing SSN programs in selected countries. The selection of countries was driven by the availability of the necessary data, as described in the next section. The remaining sections present the results of this assessment.

Data and Methodology

The most important prerequisite (and the most frequently cited constraint) for the analysis of SSN performance is high-quality data. This study uses two sources of data to assess the effectiveness of current SSNs: household survey data and a new compilation of administrative data on existing SSN programs in the Middle East and North Africa.

Household Survey Data

The first type of data, existing household surveys, are used mainly to assess coverage, targeting, generosity, and overall impact on poverty and inequality. Availability of and access to microdata are essential to assess the performance and incidence of the different fiscal efforts invested in subsidies and SSNs. Microdata allow for precise identification of the beneficiaries of different SSN programs, as well as for estimation of the impact that SSN programs have on poverty and inequality.

For an SSN performance assessment, household surveys had to include questions about respondents' participation in SSN programs and

TABLE 3.1

Household Surveys Used in the Middle East and North Africa SSN Study

Economy	Survey	Year
Djibouti	Djibouti Household Survey (*Enquete Djiboutienne Auprès des Ménages*; EDAM-IS2)	2002
Egypt, Arab Rep.	Household Income, Expenditure, and Consumption Survey (HIECS)	2009
Iraq	Iraq Household Socio-Economic Survey (IHSES)	2007
Jordan	Household Income and Expenditure Survey (HIES)	2010
Morocco	Morocco Household and Youth Survey (MHYS)	2010
West Bank and Gaza	Expenditure and Consumption Survey (ECS)	2009
Yemen, Rep.	Household Budget Survey (HBS)	2005/06

the SSN transfer income received by their households. Such surveys were available for seven of the region's economies: Djibouti, Egypt, Iraq, Jordan, Morocco, West Bank and Gaza, and the Republic of Yemen. Table 3.1 lists the household surveys that served as the core data sources for this report.[1]

Administrative Data: MENA SSN Inventory

Using household survey data to analyze the performance of SSN programs has limitations because household surveys cannot capture the full range of transfers provided through public spending. In addition, depending on the year of the latest available household survey, an analysis based entirely on this source might give a dated perspective on SSNs. Therefore, a new inventory of SSNs in the Middle East and North Africa was compiled to complement the household survey analysis with administrative data on SSN spending and scope.

This study spearheaded the creation of the Middle East and North Africa (MENA) SSN Inventory through a major data collection effort involving a variety of counterparts and instruments. A standard questionnaire template was formulated to obtain detailed information on SSN programs, such as their objectives, targeted population, implementing agencies, eligibility criteria, and type of instrument used. Moreover, the questionnaire collected the number of beneficiaries and budgetary costs for the latest available years. The template was completed by triangulating a variety of sources, starting with desk reviews of relevant documents (such as Poverty Assessments, Public Expenditure Reviews, and Social Safety Net Assessments) and adding information from the websites of ministries of social affairs and national statistical offices. Following data collection, representatives of relevant entities were interviewed, using entry points in existing policy dialogue in Egypt, Jordan, and Tunisia, as well as by canvassing participants of the 2012 SSN consultation workshops held in Lebanon, Oman, and Tunisia. Data collection for the inventory required extensive consultations with key informants who had intimate knowledge of the SSN programs. The collected MENA SSN Inventory contains a wealth of administrative data on existing SSNs in the Middle East and North Africa, and it is used extensively throughout this chapter (for a list of programs in the inventory, see appendix C.

Methodology

Because the performance of SSNs depends in part on the resources at their disposal, the study first turns to the assessment of SSN expenditure levels in the Middle East and North Africa. Overall SSN expenditure, measured as a percentage of GDP, is benchmarked against other country comparators and then disaggregated by program type, such as universal price subsidies and targeted cash transfer programs, to reveal the relative extent of resource use efficiency. This comparative analysis relies mostly on administrative data.

This study analyzes SSN programs through four performance indicators:

- *Coverage rate*, defined as the portion of the population in a given quintile that receives the transfer

- *Targeting accuracy*, measured by the *incidence of beneficiaries* (proportion of program beneficiaries belonging to each quintile) and *incidence of benefits* (proportion of total transfers received by beneficiaries in each quintile)

- *Generosity*, measured as the average magnitude of the transfer as a share of the welfare of a given quintile of beneficiaries

- *Poverty and inequality impact*, measured as the difference between the actual poverty (inequality) indicator and a simulated poverty (inequality) indicator in the absence of the SSN program.

As much as possible, the methodology for the SSN performance assessment was standardized across countries to improve comparability.[2] For instance, the study uses the bottom quintile of welfare (as measured by consumption, expenditure, or asset-based wealth index) in the assessment of coverage, targeting, and generosity instead of relying on national poverty lines. For more information about methodology in this study, see annex 3B.

Spending on SSNs

The comparison of SSN expenditures between those of the Middle East and North Africa and those of the countries of other regions depends, in large part, on the definition of SSNs—in particular, whether SSNs include food and fuel subsidies. To benchmark the spending in 11 of the region's economies, a sample of other developing countries was constructed from an International Monetary Fund data set of spending on subsidies and transfer programs. The resulting average expenditure on SSNs (including food and fuel subsidies) for 35 comparator developing countries is 2.1 percent of GDP, or less than a third of the average 6.4 percent of GDP spent by Middle East and North African countries (including subsidies and ration cards).[3]

Subsidy spending in the region is much higher in both absolute and relative terms than it is elsewhere. The average Middle Eastern and North African country spends 5.7 percent of GDP on food and fuel subsidies, as opposed to 1.3 percent of GDP in the average benchmark country. Moreover, subsidy spending as a share of total SSN spending is much higher in the Middle East and North Africa (at 84 percent) than in the comparator country sample (55 percent). Excluding the subsidy category from SSNs reduces the region's spending drastically, making it almost 10 percent lower than the average spending of benchmark developing countries. Indeed, without subsidies, the region's countries spend, on average, 0.74 percent of GDP on SSNs, while benchmark countries spend, on average, 0.8 percent of GDP, as shown in figure 3.1.

Within the Middle East and North Africa, there is substantial heterogeneity in overall SSN spending, with expenditures ranging from 0.6 percent of GDP in Lebanon to more than 14 percent of GDP in the Republic of Yemen. The wide disparity in spending is driven almost entirely by differences in expenditures on subsidies, as nonsubsidy spending has a very narrow range: from 0.04 percent of GDP in Kuwait to 1.9 percent of GDP in Iraq. On the other hand, subsidy spending ranges widely, from 0.4 percent of GDP in Lebanon to 13.7 percent of GDP in the Republic of Yemen.

One would expect that, as a country develops, it would spend more on protecting its poor and vulnerable populations. Figure 3.2 looks at SSN spending with and without subsidies in the Middle East and North Africa relative to the constructed sample of comparator countries, controlling for the countries' level of GDP per capita. The conclusions are striking: if one includes subsidies in SSN expenditures, most Middle Eastern and North African countries (Egypt, Iraq, Jordan, Morocco, Tunisia, and the Republic of Yemen) spend much more on SSNs than predicted by their

FIGURE 3.1

SSN Spending, with and without Subsidies, in the Middle East and North Africa Compared with Other Developing Countries, c. 2008–11

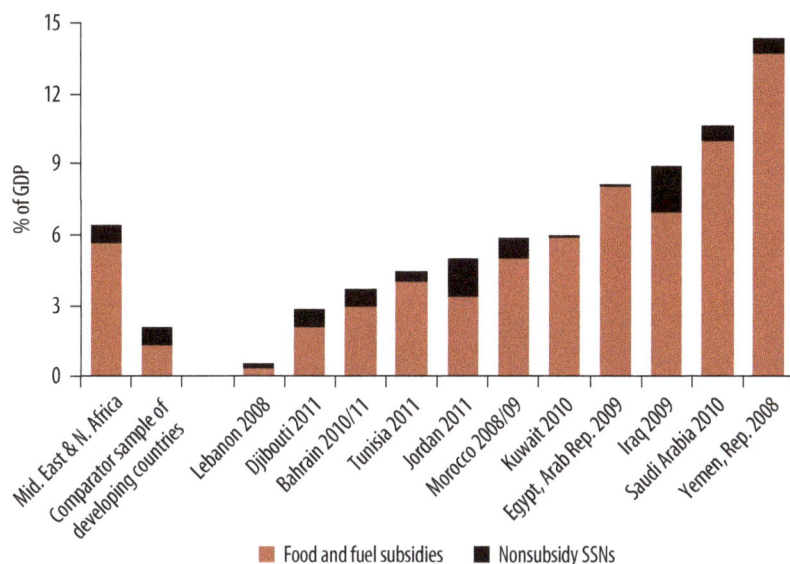

Sources: Authors' calculations based on data from World Bank 2010c, 2011a, 2011b, 2012b; Government of Jordan 2011b; World Bank, FAO, and IFAD 2009; IMF Fiscal Affairs Department database; IMF staff reports; various publications.

Note: SSN = social safety net.

level of development. However, if subsidies are taken out, most underspend on SSNs compared with their development peers. The spending of all but two of the region's countries (Iraq and Jordan) is at or below the trend line. In Egypt, Lebanon, and Tunisia, the level of SSN spending net of subsidies is far below that of their respective development peers.

Subsidies: Fuel over Food

On average, Middle Eastern and North African countries spend much more on fuel subsidies (4.5 percent of GDP) than on food subsidies (1.1 percent of GDP). The predominance of fuel subsidies is evident in figure 3.3: fuel subsidies make up, on average, almost three-fourths (73 percent) of total subsidy spending in the region. Still, there is much heterogeneity in terms of reliance on fuel versus food subsidy spending. The Republic of Yemen represents one end of the spectrum, with 13.6 percent of GDP spent on fuel subsidies and only 0.1 percent of GDP spent on food subsidies. Two countries (Iraq and Lebanon) spend more on food subsidies than on fuel subsidies, with Iraq, whose Public

FIGURE 3.2

Spending on SSNs, with and without Subsidies, in the Middle East and North Africa, Selected Countries, Compared with Other Developing Countries

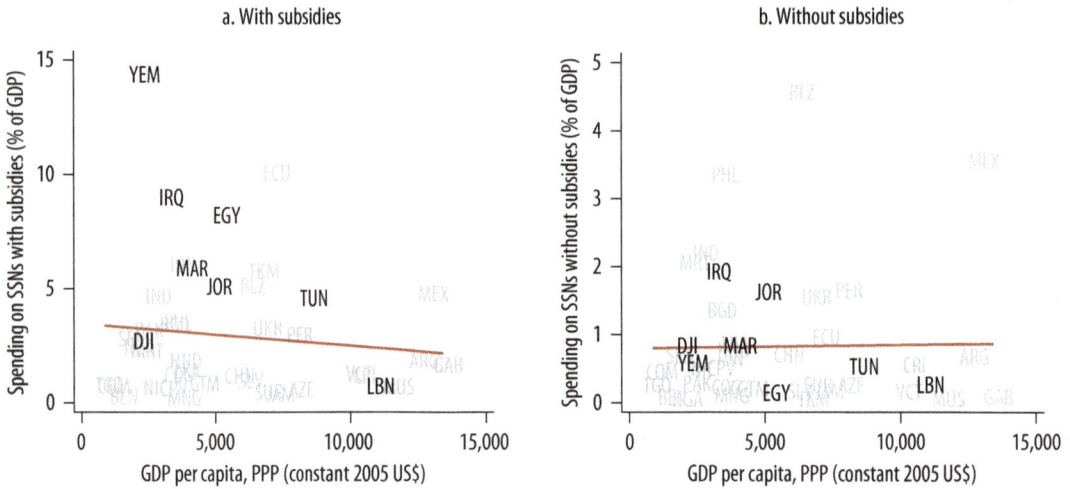

a. With subsidies

b. Without subsidies

Sources: Authors' calculations based on data for Middle East and North Africa from the IMF Fiscal Affairs Department database and World Bank publications. Data for comparator countries from the IMF Fiscal Affairs Department database. GDP data from *World Development Indicators* (World Bank various years).

Note: Bahrain, Kuwait, and Saudi Arabia were excluded from this graph, given their high level of GDP per capita and the absence of their development peers in the data set. PPP = purchasing power parity; SSN = social safety net.

FIGURE 3.3

Expenditures on Food and Fuel Subsidies in the Middle East and North Africa, Selected Countries, c. 2008–11

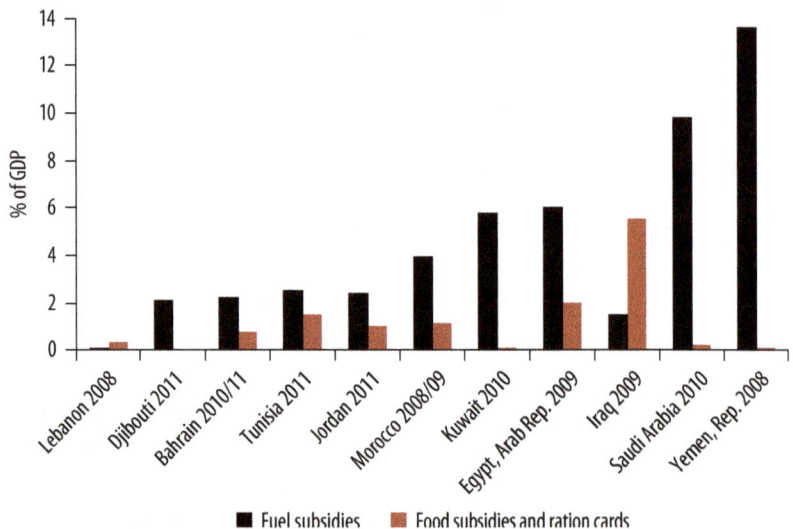

■ Fuel subsidies   ■ Food subsidies and ration cards

Sources: Authors' calculations based on data from World Bank 2010c, 2011a, 2011b, 2012b; Government of Jordan 2011b; World Bank, FAO, and IFAD 2009; IMF Fiscal Affairs Department database; IMF staff reports; various publications.

FIGURE 3.4

Comparison of Subsidy and Nonsubsidy SSN Expenditures for the Poor in the Middle East and North Africa, Selected Countries, c. 2008–11

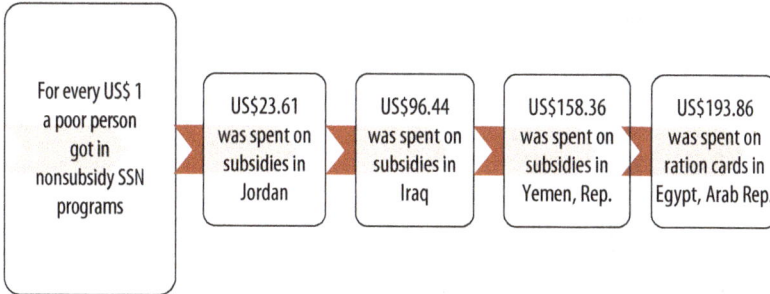

| For every US$ 1 a poor person got in nonsubsidy SSN programs | US$23.61 was spent on subsidies in Jordan | US$96.44 was spent on subsidies in Iraq | US$158.36 was spent on subsidies in Yemen, Rep. | US$193.86 was spent on ration cards in Egypt, Arab Rep. |

Sources: Authors' calculations based on latest household surveys, subsidy expenditure data, and World Bank 2009, 2010a, 2011b; Government of Jordan 2011b; IMF Fiscal Affairs Department database.

Note: SSN = social safety net.

Distribution System ration cards reach virtually all Iraqis, spending the most on food subsidies (5.5 percent of GDP).

Although the intention to provide affordable fuel to citizens is laudable, this objective is achieved at a high social cost. The substantial financial resources expended on fuel subsidies could be spent on more efficient and effective SSN programs or on other priority sectors, such as health and education. Currently, for every US$1 a poor person receives in nonsubsidy SSN programs in Jordan, Iraq, the Republic of Yemen, and Egypt, around US$24, US$96, US$158, and US$194, respectively, are spent on subsidies or ration cards (see figure 3.4).[4] For example, our analysis of household survey data reveals that poor Egyptians received about LE 430 million (Egyptian pounds) in 2009; at the same time, the combined expenditures on untargeted fuel and food subsidies and ration cards were close to LE 83.4 billion. Indeed, as demonstrated by Fattouh and El-Katiri (2012), the 2008 spending on fuel subsidies in Egypt was equal to all health and education expenditures combined, while in the Syrian Arab Republic and the Republic of Yemen, fuel subsidies absorbed more than 1.5 times the combined health and education expenditures.

Nonsubsidy SSNs: Small, Fragmented Programs

Subsidies aside, SSNs in the Middle East and North Africa are fragmented among many small programs. Figure 3.5 presents the data on SSNs from the MENA SSN Inventory of administrative data (by program type).

FIGURE 3.5

Nonsubsidy SSN Program Mix by Type, Middle East and North Africa, c. 2008–11

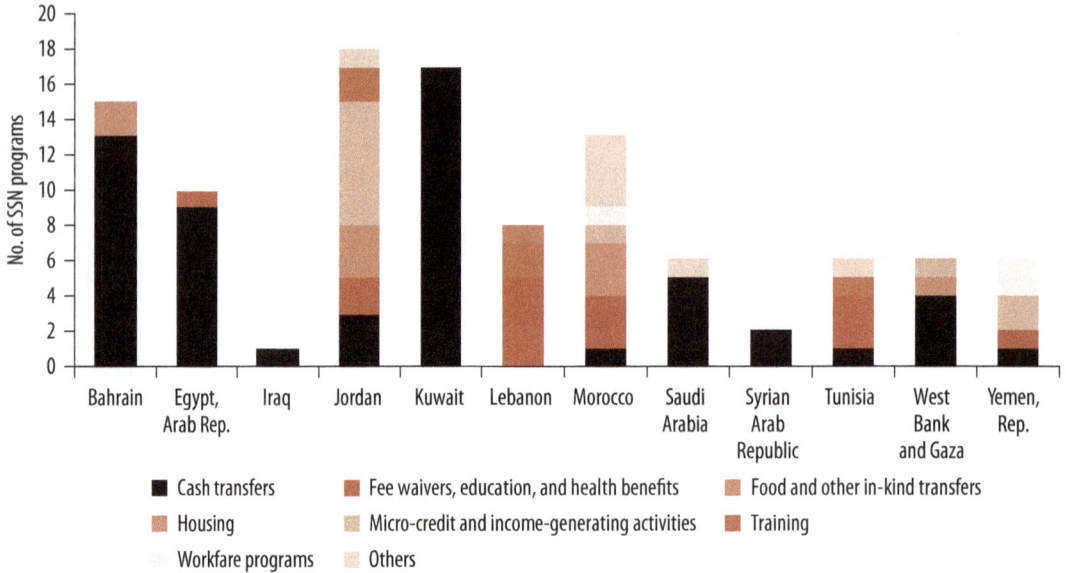

Source: Authors' calculations based on MENA SSN Inventory. For specific programs covered, see appendix C.

The programs available in each country vary greatly in number. Some countries, such as Iraq and Syria, have only a few SSN programs. Others, such as Bahrain, Jordan, Kuwait, and Morocco, have more than 10 SSN programs. Program fragmentation is especially evident in Jordan and Morocco, where many programs attempt to achieve the same objective (as previously noted concerning Morocco's multitude of education programs). This snapshot reveals that Bahrain, Egypt, Kuwait, Jordan, Lebanon, and Morocco have more than five programs in one category, which implies intense competition for limited fiscal resources and a high probability of overlap.

In terms of spending, most Middle Eastern and North African countries concentrate on cash transfer programs (see table 3A.1). However, in Lebanon, the bulk of spending goes toward fee waivers for education and hospitals. In the Republic of Yemen, half of the nonsubsidy SSN expenditure is on workfare, while in Morocco, noncash programs such as community infrastructure projects take precedence. Finally, in Jordan, training and micro-credit programs consume a substantial share of the SSN budget. The next section assesses the performance of some of these programs, focusing especially on principal cash transfer programs, described in box 3.1. Because subsidies constitute such a significant share of spending on SSNs in the Middle East and North Africa, a later section evaluates the performance of subsidies as SSNs.

BOX 3.1

Principal Cash Transfer Programs in the Middle East and North Africa, Selected Countries

Most of the principal cash transfer programs in the region target specific populations assumed more likely to be poor, such as orphans, widows, individuals with disabilities, and families of prisoners. This box describes the main features of these programs.

Egypt: Monthly Social Pension (formerly Sadat Pension)

The program was legislated in 1980 and is implemented by the Ministry of Insurance and Social Affairs. Its objective is to help families without able-bodied males. Beneficiary households are paid about LE 145–205 per month depending on household size.

Iraq: Social Safety Net (SSN)

Founded in 2006, the SSN (also known as the Social Protection Network, or SPN) is implemented by the Social Welfare Department. The program targets orphans, children of divorced women, the handicapped, the unemployed, and families of prisoners. Households receive US$110–170 per month depending on household size.

Jordan: The National Aid Fund (NAF)

The NAF was established in 1986 as an administratively and financially independent organization to protect and support needy individuals and families by extending recurring or emergency financial aid as well as vocational training and free health insurance. The cash transfer is implemented by the NAF Directorate within the Ministry of Social Development. Households receive around US$56–254 per month depending on household size and the number of handicapped people in the household. Besides regular cash assistance, the NAF also provides free health insurance coverage and emergency assistance.

Morocco: Tayssir Program

Initially a pilot study implemented by the Ministry of Higher Education and Scientific Research in 2008, this program was a conditional cash transfer targeting 6- to 12-year-old students living in poor communities. Its objective was to promote primary school enrollment and to reduce dropouts of poor primary school students. Each student received US$8–13 per month, with higher amounts conditional on attendance and higher grades. An impact evaluation revealed that dropout rates were reduced, especially in higher grades (with stronger impacts on dropouts for girls), and provided some evidence of improvement in math achievement for boys.

Tunisia: National Program of Assistance to Needy Families (Programme National d'Aide aux Familles Nécessiteuses; PNAFN)

Founded in 1986, the PNAFN is implemented by the Ministry of Social Affairs. The program covers about 7.2 percent of the population and mainly targets the elderly poor, poor widows, and handicapped individuals of the poor regions in the

(box continued on next page)

BOX 3.1 *Continued*

Center-West and North-West. The average monthly transfer is about US$45 per month. A child allowance supplement of US$6 per school-age child is also provided, up to a limit of three children.

Republic of Yemen: Social Welfare Fund (SWF)

The SWF was established in 1996 as an independent government institution whose board is chaired by the Minister of Social Affairs and Labor. The fund provides both temporary and permanent SSNs. Since 2007, the SWF has used PMT to assess eligibility for its permanent cash transfer program. The SWF covers more than 1 million households, with transfers of up to US$4.66 per month for individuals and up to US$9.32 per month for families.

Performance of SSNs Excluding Subsidies

This section assesses the performance of the Middle East and North Africa's principal SSN programs other than subsidies and ration cards. In particular, these programs are evaluated on

- *Coverage rates:* the extent to which they reach the neediest beneficiaries;

- *Targeting accuracy:* the extent to which program resources are distributed efficiently; and

- *Benefit generosity:* the extent to which these transfers provide adequate income support.

All of these features combine into the most important indicators of poverty and inequality impact—observable effects on reducing poverty and decreasing inequality.

Coverage Rates

The MENA SSN Inventory collected information on the number of beneficiaries in SSN programs. Figure 3.6 aggregates these data and presents them as shares of the selected countries' total populations. It is important to note that the Inventory does not capture the overlap between different programs (the same person in the Republic of Yemen could receive assistance from the Social Welfare Fund and the Social Fund for Development, for example, and be counted twice in the figure). The estimates presented in the figure should thus be treated as the upper bounds on nationwide coverage of SSNs. The inventory shows that the

FIGURE 3.6

Nationwide Coverage of Nonsubsidy SSNs, by Program Type, in the Middle East and North Africa, c. 2008–11

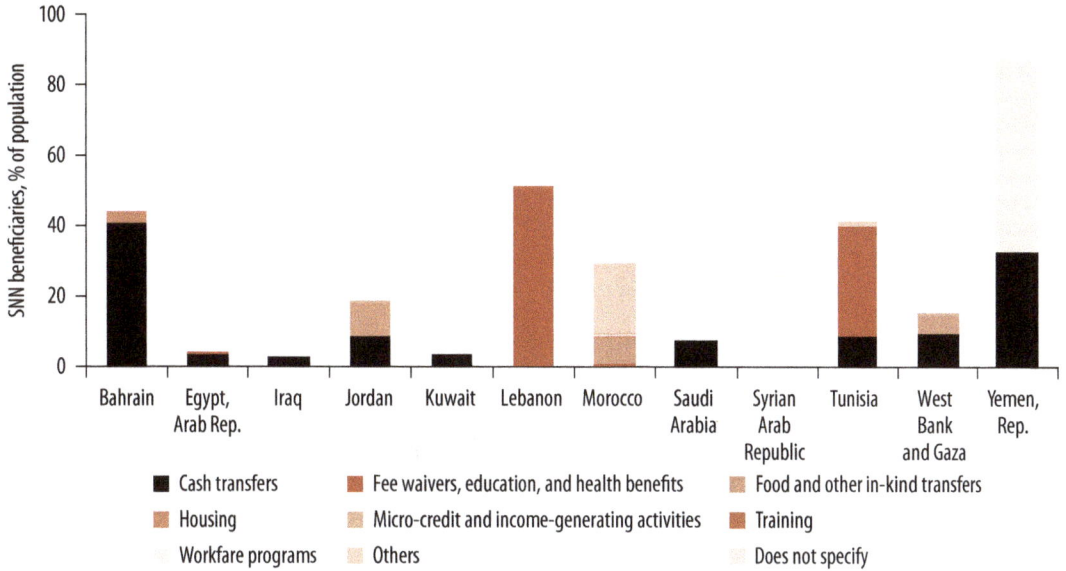

Source: MENA SSN Inventory. For a complete list of programs, see appendix C.

Note: SSN = social safety net. Each program's coverage is added independently of others; this calculation assumes no overlap between SSN programs and thus represents the upper-bound estimate of SSN coverage.

region's countries vary widely in their SSN coverage—demonstrating that in some countries (such as Egypt, Iraq, Kuwait, and Syria), nationwide coverage is quite low, while coverage is the Republic of Yemen is extensive. Coverage by cash transfers is highest in Bahrain and the Republic of Yemen, and in Lebanon, hospital fee waivers reach a large share of the population.

There are large gaps in SSNs' coverage of the poor and vulnerable throughout the Middle East and North Africa. Figure 3.7 depicts the coverage rates of SSN programs for the poorest quintile in selected countries. Overall, two out of three people (more than 70 percent) in the poorest quintile receive no income support transfers. The only exception is West Bank and Gaza, where government, donor, and NGO programs cover more than half of the poorest quintile.

How do the observed coverage rates of the region's SSNs compare with those of other regions? To answer this question, the *2011 Atlas of Social Protection: Indicators of Resilience and Equity* (ASPIRE) (World Bank 2012a) is used to compare the population-weighted regional and world averages of SSN coverage for the bottom quintile. The right side of figure 3.7 reveals that the Middle East and North Africa leaves a much larger

FIGURE 3.7

Coverage by Nonsubsidy SSN Programs in the Middle East and North Africa Compared with World and Other Regional Averages, c. 2002–10

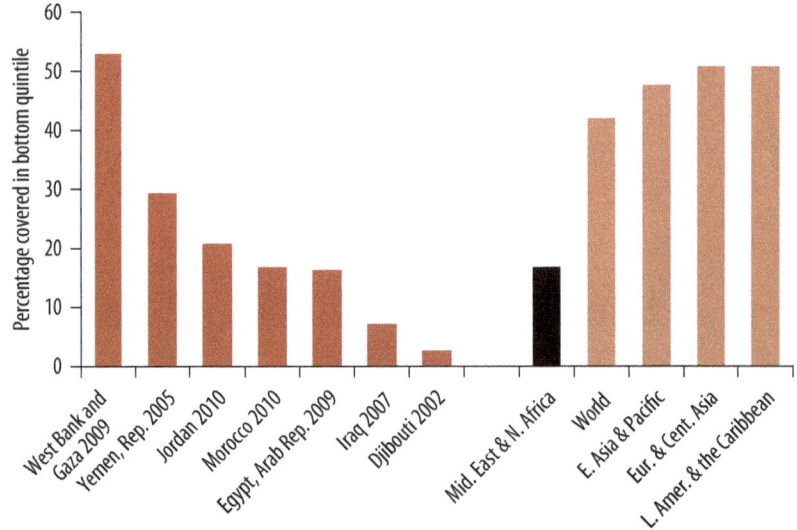

Sources: Middle East and North Africa: Authors' calculations based on data from national household surveys; data for other regions from World Bank 2012a.

Note: SSN = social safety net. Regional averages are population-weighted.

share of its bottom quintile uncovered by SSN programs than all other regions. Whereas only 16 percent of people in the bottom quintile in the Middle East and North Africa receive any SSN transfers, the corresponding share is higher than 50 percent in Europe and Central Asia as well as Latin America and the Caribbean. In the Middle East and North Africa, coverage of the bottom quintile by SSNs is less than half the world average and less than a third of the average in Europe and Central Asia and Latin America and the Caribbean.

Six out of seven Middle Eastern and North African countries also underperform their development peers in terms of undercoverage of the bottom quintile. We use country-specific data from ASPIRE to analyze the relationship between undercoverage rates and economic development, as measured by GDP per capita. The results of this analysis can be found in figure 3A.1, panel a. The downward-sloping trend line shows a negative correlation between economic development and coverage of the bottom quintile by SSNs: as countries attain greater fiscal space, they can cover more of the poor and vulnerable, thus reducing undercoverage rates. However, throughout the Middle East and North Africa except in West Bank and Gaza, undercoverage rates are above the level predicted by the trend line, implying that, at least in principle, there can be sufficient fiscal space to reduce undercoverage. Of course, in the Middle East and North Africa, the reality is that food and fuel subsidies are taking up most of this fiscal space (their performance is discussed in the next section).

Virtually all SSN programs in the Middle East and North Africa fail to cover even 20 percent of the bottom quintile, while some programs cover a substantial proportion (up to 11–12 percent) of the top quintile. In Egypt, for example, the Monthly Social Pension (or Sadat Pension) program covers only 8 percent of the poorest quintile. In Jordan, the NAF reaches only 16.5 percent of the poorest quintile. And Djibouti's programs and Iraq's SSN are almost nonexistent in terms of coverage, reaching less than 2 percent of the poorest quintile. Indeed, the highest coverage of the poorest quintile (exceeding 50 percent) is again in West Bank and Gaza, where assistance is provided primarily by the United Nations (UN).

Although low coverage of the poor is a key signal that SSN programs need expansion, substantial coverage of the rich indicates a high degree of inefficiency. In practice, high coverage rates for the poor are difficult to attain without some leakage. Nevertheless, at the very least, coverage rates should decrease progressively from the poorest to the richest quintiles. Specifically, coverage rates should have a negative slope across wealth quintiles. We test this hypothesis as shown in figure 3A.2: the Monthly Social Pension (or Sadat Pension) and Zakat in Egypt; the NAF and Zakat in Jordan; the SWF and the Social Security Fund in the Republic of Yemen; Reintegration for the Demobilized in Djibouti; and assistance from all entities in West Bank and Gaza do portray a somewhat negative gradient. Conversely, Iraq's SSN program actually has a positive slope, as does the disability assistance in Djibouti for all but the richest quintile. Meanwhile, in Morocco, coverage rates for programs that promote school enrollment and literacy fluctuate across wealth quintiles.

To benchmark the region's program coverage rates, a household survey analysis similar to that performed for Europe and Central Asia and Latin America and the Caribbean is used. Benchmarking the Middle East and North Africa's program coverage rates of the bottom quintile reveals that they are 50 percent lower, on average, than in Europe and Central Asia or in Latin America and the Caribbean. It is important to note that coverage depends on program type because family allowances—such as that of Uruguay's *Asignación Familiar* or Russia's child allowance—achieve very high coverage because of their universal nature. Still, it is illustrative to observe that, in the Middle East and North Africa, only the UN assistance in West Bank and Gaza covers as much of the bottom quintile as other signature programs in Europe and Central Asia or Latin America and the Caribbean, with the region's other programs trailing far behind, as shown in figure 3.8.

FIGURE 3.8

Coverage Rates of the Bottom Quintile by Specific Nonsubsidy SSN Programs

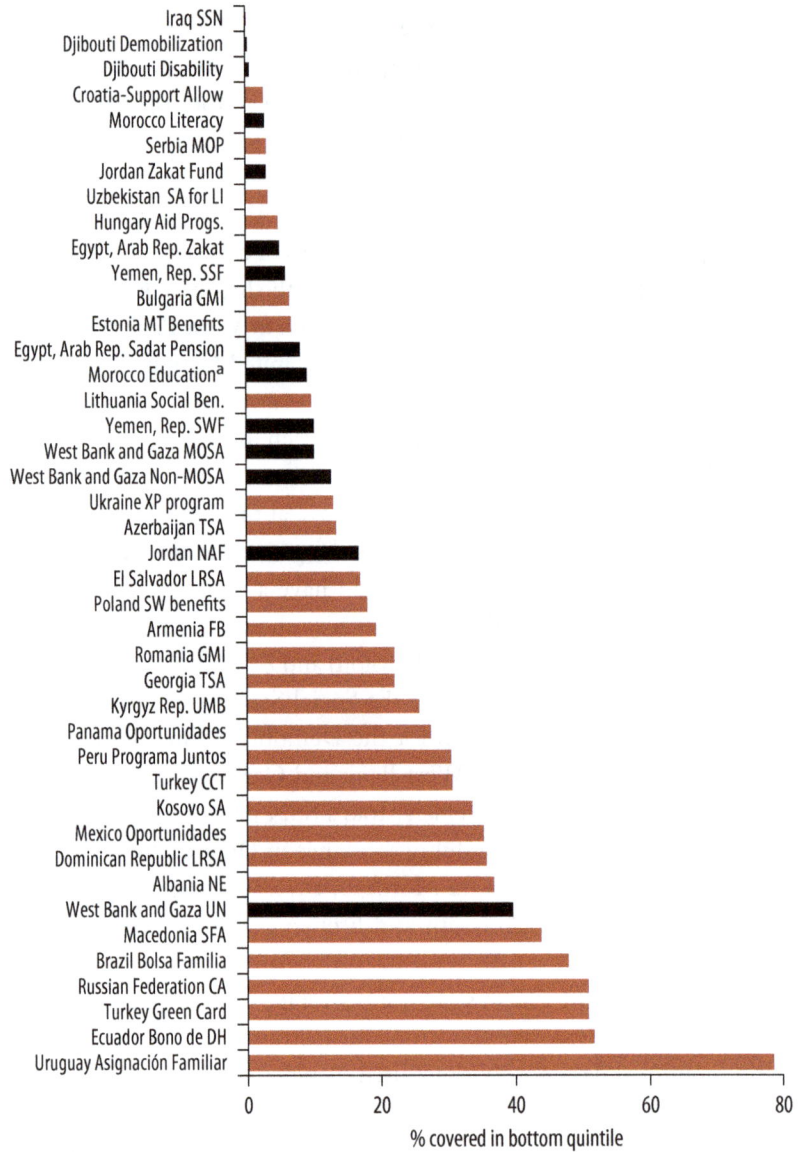

Horizontal bar chart. Y-axis lists programs (top to bottom): Iraq SSN; Djibouti Demobilization; Djibouti Disability; Croatia-Support Allow; Morocco Literacy; Serbia MOP; Jordan Zakat Fund; Uzbekistan SA for LI; Hungary Aid Progs.; Egypt, Arab Rep. Zakat; Yemen, Rep. SSF; Bulgaria GMI; Estonia MT Benefits; Egypt, Arab Rep. Sadat Pension; Morocco Education[a]; Lithuania Social Ben.; Yemen, Rep. SWF; West Bank and Gaza MOSA; West Bank and Gaza Non-MOSA; Ukraine XP program; Azerbaijan TSA; Jordan NAF; El Salvador LRSA; Poland SW benefits; Armenia FB; Romania GMI; Georgia TSA; Kyrgyz Rep. UMB; Panama Oportunidades; Peru Programa Juntos; Turkey CCT; Kosovo SA; Mexico Oportunidades; Dominican Republic LRSA; Albania NE; West Bank and Gaza UN; Macedonia SFA; Brazil Bolsa Familia; Russian Federation CA; Turkey Green Card; Ecuador Bono de DH; Uruguay Asignación Familiar. X-axis: % covered in bottom quintile, from 0 to 80.

Sources: Middle East and North Africa: Authors' calculations based on data from national household surveys; data for other regions from the World Bank's Europe and Central Asia Household Survey Database; the Organisation for Economic Co-operation and Development Social Expenditure Database (www.oecd.org/els/social/expenditure); and the World Bank's Latin America and the Caribbean SSN inventory (forthcoming).

Note: CA = Child Allowance; CCT = conditional cash transfers; DH = human development (*desarollo humano*); GMI = Guaranteed Minimum Income; LRSA = Last Resort Social Assistance; MOP = Maternal Support to Families (*Materijalno obezbeđenje porodice*); MOSA = Ministry of Social Affairs; MT = Means Tested; NAF = National Aid Fund; NE = Economic Assistance (*Ndihma Ekonomike*); SA = Social Assistance; SA for LI = Social Assistance for Low Income; SFA = Social Financial Assistance; SSF = Social Security Fund; SSN = social safety net; SWF = Social Welfare Fund; TSA = Targeted Social Assistance; UMB = United Monthly Benefit; UN = United Nations; XP = Extremely Poor.

a. Excludes the "One Million Satchels" (*Un Million de Cartables*) school supplies program.

The evidence presented above is unambiguous: the coverage of nonsubsidy SSNs in the Middle East and North Africa is very low, with the vast majority of the poor being left to fend for themselves in times of need. A dependable SSN is vital not only for protecting those who cannot work (such as the elderly and the disabled) from destitution, but also for preventing temporary income shocks from becoming permanent poverty traps because of inefficient coping strategies (for example, taking children out of school or selling productive assets). The coverage rate is one indicator that signals the effectiveness of SSNs in reaching those in need; clearly, the region's countries have significant scope to improve the *reach* of their safety nets to the poor and vulnerable population.

Targeting Accuracy

Different targeting methods are applicable in different contexts. In the Middle East and North Africa, SSN programs overwhelmingly use categorical and geographical targeting methods, which work well in environments where poverty is concentrated but not where poverty is multifaceted and spatially dispersed. In the latter case, methods that identify households or individuals based on their means or correlates of poverty (through PMT) are preferable.

The MENA SSN Inventory has collected valuable information on targeting methods used by different SSN programs. Using these data, figure 3.9 vividly illustrates the predominance of categorical targeting in the region. Indeed, many countries (Bahrain, Egypt, Iraq, Kuwait, Saudi Arabia, and Syria) rely exclusively on categorical targeting. The second favorite targeting method is geographic, with Morocco and the Republic of Yemen relying heavily on SSN programs that target different regions. The use of individual assessment criteria (such as means tests or PMT) is much less common. A couple of programs in Jordan and Tunisia use income thresholds as eligibility cutoffs. PMT for targeting SSNs is an emerging trend, with programs in Lebanon, Morocco, West Bank and Gaza, and the Republic of Yemen starting to use it fairly recently. A few programs in Jordan and Morocco are self-targeted.

Although in theory SSN programs are intended for the poor and vulnerable, in the Middle East and North Africa, the wealthy tend to constitute a significant share of SSN beneficiaries. On average, only a quarter of nonsubsidy SSN beneficiaries in the region come from the poorest quintile, while about 15 percent come from the richest quintile, as shown on the left side of figure 3.10. In Egypt, Jordan, and West Bank and Gaza, only 1 in 10 SSN beneficiaries may come from the top quintile; this indicates some degree of targeting accuracy, but still fewer than half of all SSN beneficiaries in these countries are from the poorest quintile.

FIGURE 3.9

Nonsubsidy SSN Program Mix by Targeting Type, Middle East and North Africa, c. 2008–11

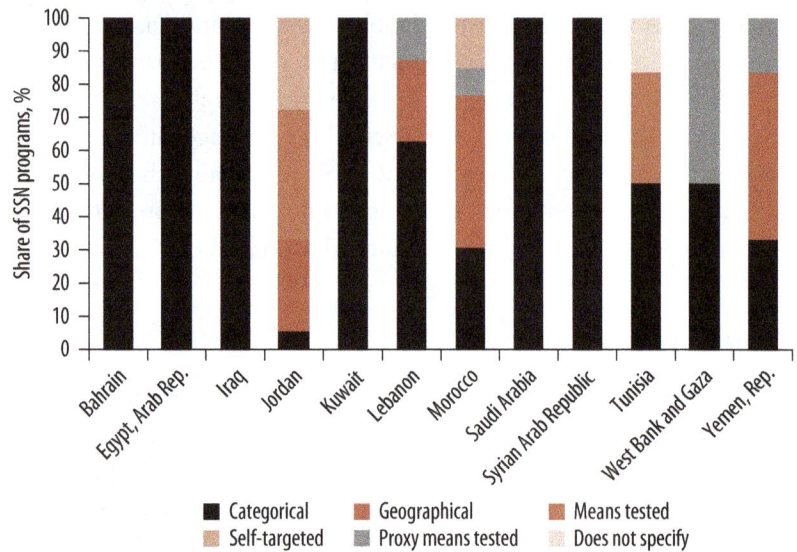

Source: Authors' calculations based on MENA SSN Inventory. For a list of programs in the inventory, see appendix C.

Note: SSN = social safety net.

Since 2009, targeting performance in West Bank and Gaza has improved further, given the creation of the unified Cash Transfer Program (CTP) in 2010, which uses a PMT targeting mechanism and a unified payment scheme. Indeed, a recent targeting assessment of the CTP confirmed that more than 80 percent of beneficiaries of this program are in the bottom 20 percent of the population. Thus, CTP is poised to become one of the most advanced cash assistance programs in the Middle East and North Africa and may serve as a model of best practices elsewhere in the region.

In contrast, in Djibouti and Morocco, the richest quintile represents the same share of SSN beneficiaries as the poorest quintile, implying little targeting, if any. In the most extreme case of Iraq, the distribution of beneficiaries is skewed toward the rich, with the top quintile making up almost 30 percent of all SSN beneficiaries. A comparison with other regions, using ASPIRE, confirms the underperformance of the Middle East and North Africa's SSNs in terms of beneficiary incidence: in all the other three regions in the comparison, the bottom quintile constitutes 30 percent or more of SSN beneficiaries, with Latin America and the Caribbean leading the world at 36 percent.

There is a strong positive correlation between targeting accuracy and economic development (as shown in figure 3A.1, panel b), but there is

FIGURE 3.10

FIGURE 3.10

Beneficiary Incidence of Nonsubsidy SSNs in the Middle East and North Africa Compared with World and Other Regions, c. 2002–10

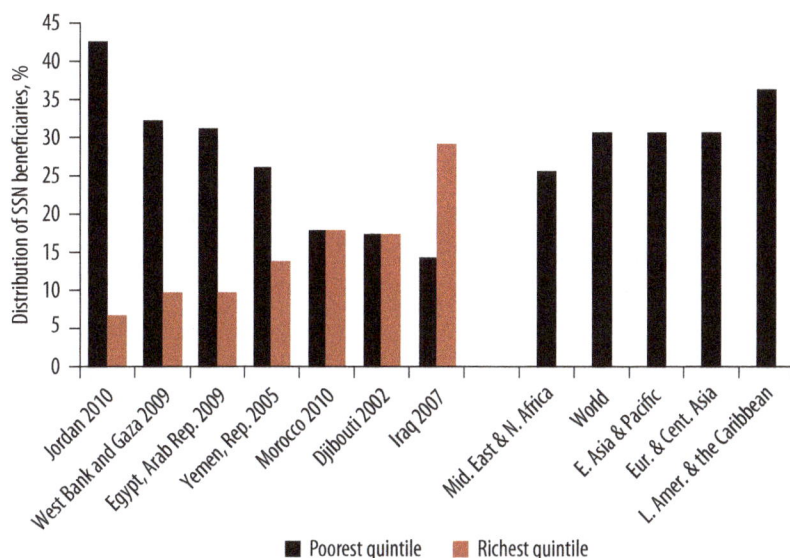

Sources: Middle East and North Africa: Authors' calculations based on data from national household surveys; data for other regions and world from World Bank 2012a.

Note: SSN = social safety net. All regional averages are population-weighted.

great dispersion in the performance of Middle Eastern and North African economies relative to development peers. Egypt, Jordan, West Bank and Gaza, and the Republic of Yemen are above the trend line, which means that the targeting accuracy of their SSNs is higher than would be predicted by their levels of GDP per capita. On the other end of the spectrum, Djibouti, Iraq, and Morocco all find themselves below the trend line, so their SSNs' targeting is worse than that of their development peers.

In a well-targeted, progressive SSN program, the bottom quintile receives the most transfers, with the share of transfers declining as wealth increases. As shown in figure 3A.2, the only program in the Middle East and North Africa that appears to fit this description is Jordan's NAF, which has a steep negative gradient, with the richest two quintiles cumulatively receiving less than 20 percent of all NAF transfers (see box 3.2 for a description of NAF's targeting methods). In contrast, in Iraq, a mere 2 percent of all SSN benefits go to the poorest quintile, while the richest quintile captures 43 percent of program resources, making this program highly regressive. In terms of benefit incidence, therefore, Jordan's NAF

BOX 3.2

The National Aid Fund in Jordan

The National Aid Fund (NAF) administers the largest cash safety net program in Jordan. It was established in 1986 as a response to increasing poverty and inequality in the country. A semiautonomous institution, the NAF is governed by a board of directors chaired by the Minister of Social Development. NAF assistance is administered through district offices throughout Jordan. In terms of program resources, public spending on the NAF in 2009 represented only 0.5 percent of GDP and 2 percent of government spending.

NAF assistance is targeted at poor and disadvantaged people belonging to various categories perceived as incapable of engaging in income-generating activities. Such categories include women with young children, orphans, the elderly, persons with disabilities, families headed by divorced or abandoned women, and households where the main breadwinner is in prison. Although the first eligibility criterion for NAF assistance is belonging to one or more of the above categories, the second criterion is a means test: families' income must fall short of a preset per capita threshold. This income test falls between a semiverified test for formal incomes and an unverified test for other sources of income.

In terms of benefits, the NAF provides regular and emergency cash transfers, with minimum benefits in 2009 of JD 40 (Jordanian dinars) per month (71 percent of the adult equivalent poverty line) and a maximum of JD 180 per family per month for a family of five or more persons. In addition to cash support, beneficiary families are automatically eligible for free government health insurance and vocational training programs.

Sources: Adapted from Government of Jordan 2011b and World Bank 2007.

---

is the regional leader in targeting accuracy, and Iraq's SSN program is the most regressive program in the region.

The Monthly Social Pension (or Sadat Pension) in Egypt and the SWF in the Republic of Yemen each have a progressive benefit incidence, but not significantly so. However, these two countries differ in their targeting of the poor, given the difference in their respective poverty lines. Given the Republic of Yemen's high poverty rate (about 35 percent), the share of the SWF going to the poor is 48 percent, whereas Egypt's poverty rate of 22 percent implies that only 26 percent of Monthly Social Pension (or Sadat Pension) benefits reach the poor. Finally, in West Bank and Gaza, assistance received from the UN in 2009 was relatively better targeted than the rest of the programs there. Both Ministry of Social Affairs (MOSA) and non-MOSA programs reach the poor but cannot avoid leakage to the better-off. As mentioned above, however, West Bank and Gaza has made tremendous progress in targeting performance since 2009.

Benchmarking the incidence of benefits in specific SSN programs demonstrates highly inefficient resource use in the Middle East and North Africa. Figure 3.11 shows the benefit incidence for the bottom quintile of SSN programs in the region against comparator programs in Europe and Central Asia and Latin America and the Caribbean. The average program in the Middle East and North Africa distributes 23 percent of its benefits to the bottom quintile, whereas the average comparator program distributes more than twice that percentage—59 percent—to the bottom quintile.

It is important to note that benefit incidence is necessarily lower for large programs, such as *Oportunidades* in Mexico (which covers around 30 percent of the total population), than it is for small programs, which can target resources more precisely. All of the Middle Eastern and North African economies lag behind their comparators in terms of targeting performance. Indeed, four programs in the region—the SSN in Iraq, the Zakat Fund in Jordan, the MOSA assistance in West Bank and Gaza, and the cash assistance from the Social Security Fund in the Republic of Yemen—transfer less than 20 percent of their program resources to the bottom quintile, which makes all of these programs regressive (figure 3A.3).

SSNs in the Middle East and North Africa suffer from significant leakages of resources to the nonpoor and even the wealthy, which means the region has significant scope to improve the allocative efficiency of its SSN programs. Because of its reliance on outdated categorical and geographic targeting methods, the region lags behind others that have switched to individual assessments of either incomes (through means tests) or expenditures (through PMT), in some cases complemented by community-based targeting. Within the Middle East and North Africa, Jordan, West Bank and Gaza, and the Republic of Yemen have begun to improve their targeting methods. For example, Jordan's NAF relies on a semiverified means test together with categorical targeting, while West Bank and Gaza, the Republic of Yemen, and, most recently, Lebanon, have introduced PMT-based targeting for their signature SSN programs.

Benefit Generosity

The basic question in designing an SSN program is the transfer size, which should be commensurate with the desired impact on intended outcomes, such as poverty reduction (Grosh et al. 2008). As shown in figure

FIGURE 3.11

Benefit Incidence for Bottom Quintile of Selected Nonsubsidy SSN Programs

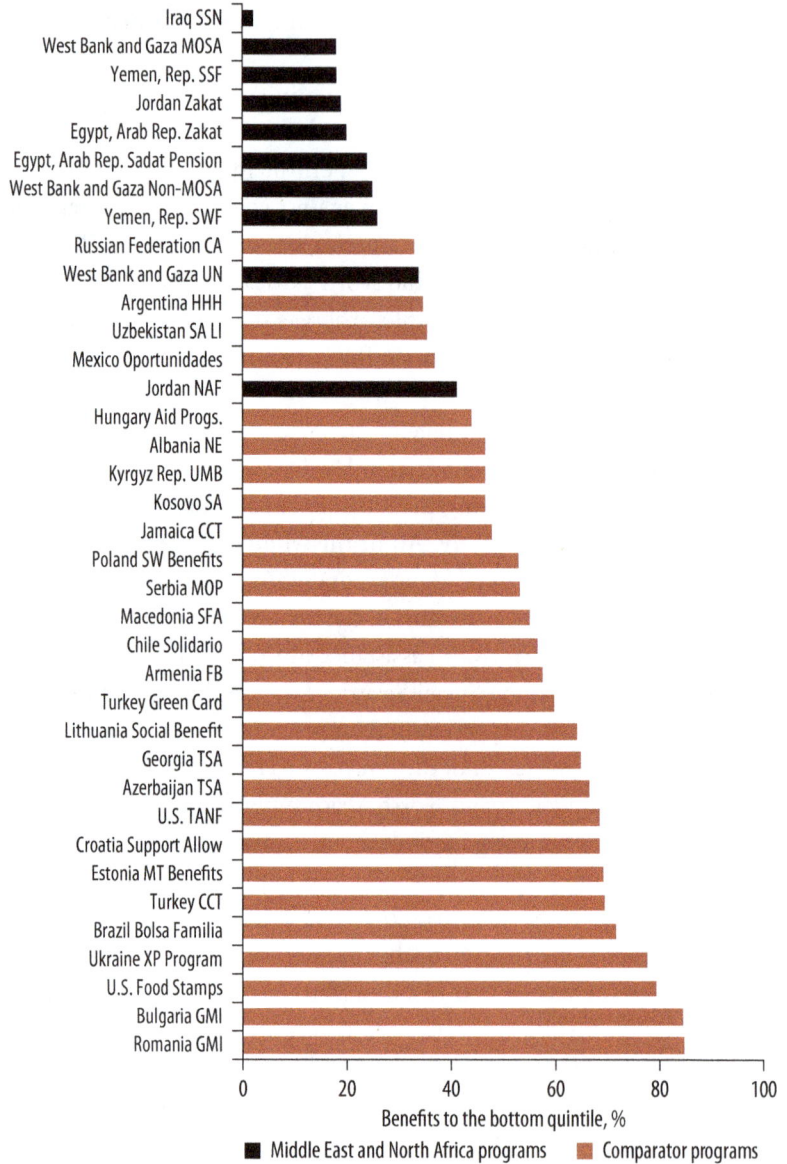

Benefits to the bottom quintile, %

■ Middle East and North Africa programs   ■ Comparator programs

Sources: Middle East and North Africa: Authors' calculations based on data from household surveys. Europe and Central Asia data from the World Bank Social Protection database and the Organisation for Economic Co-operation and Development Social Expenditure Database (www.oecd.org/els/social/expenditure). Latin America and the Caribbean data from LAC SSN inventory (forthcoming).

Note: CA = Child Allowance; CCT = conditional cash transfers; FB = Family Benefit; GMI = Guaranteed Minimum Income; HHH = Heads of Households; MOP = Material Support to Families (*Materijalno obezbeđenje porodice*); MOSA = Ministry of Social Affairs; MT = Means Tested; NAF = National Aid Fund; NE = Economic Assistance (*Ndihma Ekonomike*); SA = Social Assistance; SA LI = Social Assistance for Low Income; SFA = Social Financial Assistance; SSF = Social Security Fund; SSN = social safety net; SW = Social Welfare; SWF = Social Welfare Fund; TANF: Temporary Assistance for Needy Families; TSA = Targeted Social Assistance; UMB = Unified Monthly Benefit; UN = United Nations; XP = Extremely Poor.

FIGURE 3.12

Benefit Generosity of Nonsubsidy SSNs, Middle East and North Africa, Compared with World and Other Regions, c. 2005–10

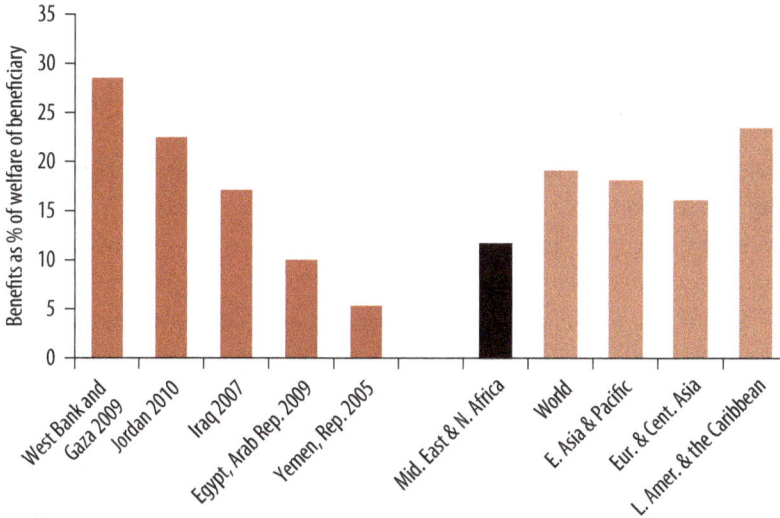

Sources: Middle East and North Africa: Authors' calculations based on data from national household surveys; data for world and other regions from World Bank 2012a.

Note: All regional averages are population-weighted.

3.12, the generosity of SSN programs that reach the bottom quintile in the Middle East and North Africa is low, constituting less than 15 percent of the bottom quintile's welfare. The greatest impact of SSN transfers on the welfare of the poorest quintile is in West Bank and Gaza, followed by Jordan. Elsewhere, such as in the Republic of Yemen, the consumption levels of beneficiaries in the bottom quintile are barely affected.

At the same time, one would expect SSNs to represent a negligible share of consumption for the richest quintile. In the Middle East and North Africa, this is not the case. Indeed, in Egypt, SSNs are more generous for the richest quintile than for the poorest one. Iraq and West Bank and Gaza also provide substantial income support to the richest quintile, comprising 10 and 18 percent, respectively, of that quintile's welfare.

Using ASPIRE to benchmark the region's SSN generosity for the bottom quintile against that of other regions reveals that SSN transfers in the Middle East and North Africa are much more modest than elsewhere. Whereas the average SSN system in the world provides transfers of almost 20 percent of the bottom quintile's welfare, in the Middle East and North Africa, this figure stands at only 12 percent, far below the other regions.

Plotting benefit generosity for the bottom quintile against GDP per capita demonstrates that richer economies provide more generous benefits to their poor and vulnerable populations (see figure 3A.1, panel c). West Bank and Gaza appears above the trend line, most likely because cash assistance is provided by international donors, such as the UN and international NGOs. On the other hand, Egypt and the Republic of Yemen (and, to a lesser extent, Iraq) are below the trend line, implying that compared with their development peers, SSN transfers in these countries are much more modest.

Figure 3.13 compares the generosity of some SSN programs in the Middle East and North Africa with similar programs in Europe and Central Asia. Most Middle Eastern and North African programs lag behind the comparator programs in providing sufficient income support for the poorest quintile. West Bank and Gaza and Jordan's NAF are regional leaders in terms of benefit generosity.

Setting the benefit size for an SSN program is an important but difficult policy decision. On the one hand, a robust safety net should deliver adequate consumption protection for the most vulnerable members of a society: those who cannot provide for themselves due to age or disability and those who need temporary assistance to rebound from an economic or health shock. On the other hand, overly generous benefits may discourage working-age, able-bodied adults from participating in the labor force and instead encourage them to depend on the SSNs provided by the government. Based on the international comparisons presented above, the benefit generosity of SSNs in the Middle East and North Africa can be increased without triggering work disincentives.

The Role of Zakat as Informal Safety Net

In the Middle East and North Africa, a significant complement in all countries to the formal or public SSN system is the privately provided Zakat, which is often perceived as the largest transfer system to the poor and vulnerable. Zakat consists of informal social transfer from better-off to poorer households. One of the Five Pillars of Islam, it is a system ingrained in Islamic society whereby it is a duty to give part of one's income and assets to help the poor and needy. The amount is computed using a formula that differs by type of asset, which may include gold, land, livestock, minerals, and cash savings. Interpretation of this formula varies from country to country.

Typically, Zakat targets categories of beneficiaries that the Qur'an defines as being especially in need. In some countries, the collection and distribution is institutionalized by the government in the form of an obligatory tax, but in others, such as the Republic of Yemen, it remains largely a private affair—being not an obligatory tax but a transfer whose amount is calculated by the giving household and that is mostly either distributed

FIGURE 3.13

Benefit Generosity for the Bottom Quintile of Selected Nonsubsidy SSN Programs, Middle East and North Africa Compared with Europe and Central Asia

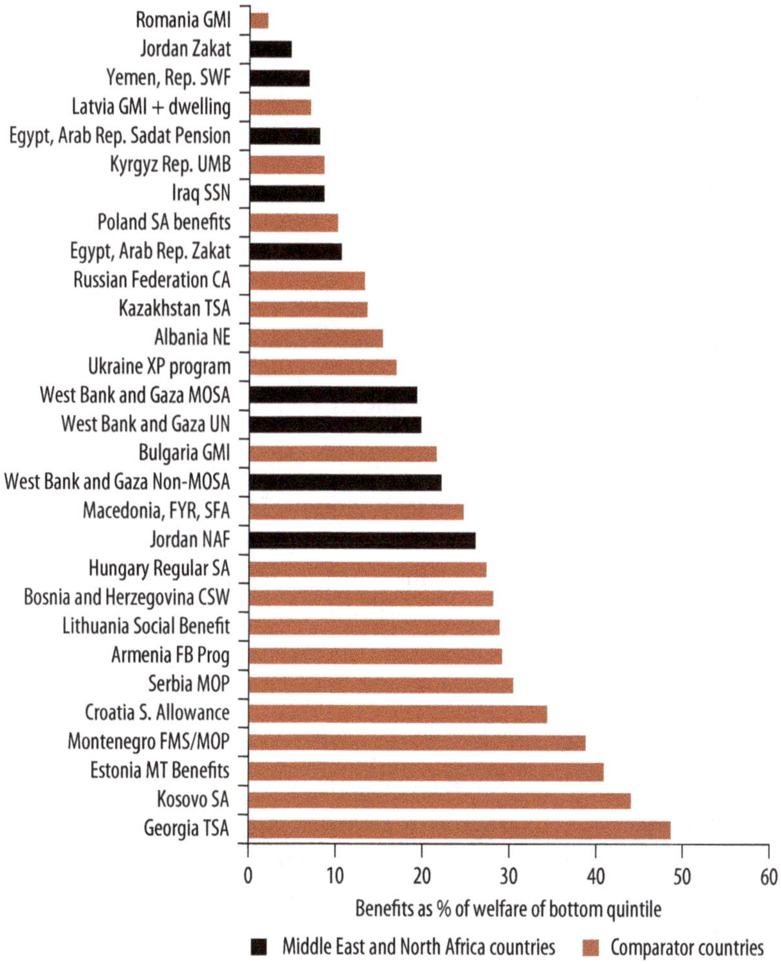
Romania GMI
Jordan Zakat
Yemen, Rep. SWF
Latvia GMI + dwelling
Egypt, Arab Rep. Sadat Pension
Kyrgyz Rep. UMB
Iraq SSN
Poland SA benefits
Egypt, Arab Rep. Zakat
Russian Federation CA
Kazakhstan TSA
Albania NE
Ukraine XP program
West Bank and Gaza MOSA
West Bank and Gaza UN
Bulgaria GMI
West Bank and Gaza Non-MOSA
Macedonia, FYR, SFA
Jordan NAF
Hungary Regular SA
Bosnia and Herzegovina CSW
Lithuania Social Benefit
Armenia FB Prog
Serbia MOP
Croatia S. Allowance
Montenegro FMS/MOP
Estonia MT Benefits
Kosovo SA
Georgia TSA
0
10
20
30
40
50
60
Benefits as % of welfare of bottom quintile
Middle East and North Africa countries
Comparator countries

Sources: Middle East and North Africa data from authors' calculations based on household surveys; other data from World Bank's ECA (Europe and Central Asia) Household Survey Database.

Note: CA = Child Allowance; CSW = Centres for Social Work; FB = Family Benefit; FMS = Family Material Support; GMI = Guaranteed Minimum Income; MOP = Material Support to Families (*Materijalno obezbeđenje porodice*); MOSA = Ministry of Social Affairs; NAF = National Aid Fund; NE = Economic Assistance (*Ndihma Ekonomike*); SA = Social Assistance; SFA = Social Financial Assistance; SSN = social safety net; SWF = Social Welfare Fund; TSA = Targeted Social Assistance; UMB = United Monthly Benefit; UN = United Nations; XP = Extremely Poor.

directly to the chosen beneficiary or delivered for distribution to the mosque or sherif (neighborhood leader). (Delivery to the government or an NGO is less frequent.) Zakat is normally given in the form of cash, once or twice a year (during Ramadan and Eid). According to the United Nations Development Programme's Arab Human Development Report

(UNDP 2002), the system of Zakat may be enabling large segments of the Arab and Muslim populations to escape visible poverty and need.

Quantitative data on this issue are scarce, but new data on the Republic of Yemen reveals that Zakat

- Is an important SSN;

- Does not serve all the functions of an SSN (such as promotion of resilience and of human capital formation) and overlaps with (thus does not fully crowd out) other private and public SSNs; and

- Poses interesting political economy issues (see box 3.3 and Silva, Alloush, and Wodon 2012).

BOX 3.3

A Private, Informal Safety Net: Zakat in the Republic of Yemen

Data

As part of the SSN review, the World Bank piloted the Yemen Survey on Social Networks and Solidarity Mechanisms. The survey included traditional modules on socioeconomic characteristics in addition to new modules that specifically targeted the giving and receiving of Zakat as well as attitudes toward Zakat. It also included modules on social networks, the incidence of shocks, risk coping mechanisms, and household decision making. A sample of 795 households (5,500 individuals) was surveyed. The sample was representative of the capital city of Sana'a. The data have been used to study the determinants of giving and receiving Zakat and its effects on poverty (Silva, Alloush, and Wodon 2012).

Facts on Zakat

Giving Zakat: Do most households give? How much do households give? Thirty percent of all households in Sana'a indicated they have given Zakat, and the financial ability to give was the most important determinant of both the likelihood of giving and the amount given. Other important determinants of giving were social networks, trust in personal connections, and religiosity. On average, the reported amounts were below 2.5 percent of annual income.

Receiving Zakat: Is Zakat an important source of financial support for the poor? Among receivers in the poorest income decile, it represents about 25 percent of their pre-Zakat income. Does it provide good coverage of the poor? It reaches over 35 percent in the poorest quintile—higher coverage than that of formal SSN programs in Sana'a. Is it well targeted? Yes, the data show that more than 70 percent of Zakat recipients were in the lowest wealth quintiles.

What do receivers use Zakat assistance for? Zakat is used mostly for necessities, and the most common reason for receiving Zakat is financial difficulty. However, having

---

BOX 3.3 *Continued*

suffered a shock is not significantly associated with a higher likelihood of receiving Zakat. Nor do income losses significantly increase the probability of receiving Zakat, but decreases in wealth do, suggesting that Zakat is more likely to focus on the chronically poor than the transitory poor.

Who falls through the cracks? Zakat reaches more poor households in Sana'a than other safety nets, and those who receive it are poor. However, the receivers are usually related to or live near the givers: 82 percent of givers said that the person to whom they gave Zakat was related to them or their households, and 60 percent of givers say the person to whom they gave Zakat last year had already received Zakat from them for more than three years. Silva, Al-

loush, and Wodon (2012) show that social networks of the household head are significant determinants of the likelihood of receiving Zakat.

Is Zakat perceived positively as an SSN? Zakat is a well-respected institution that is perceived positively. People trust Zakat and think it is an important part of society. It sets a high standard for formal SSN targeting and distribution. However, its role is to ameliorate poverty, not to promote the formation of human capital, which calls for the use of other forms of SSN to complement it. In Sana'a, people's attitudes about making SSNs conditional on behaviors conducive to human capital formation were positive.

In the context of this report, an interesting survey was conducted: the Yemen Survey on Social Networks and Solidarity Mechanisms. This household-level survey added modules on giving and receiving Zakat, attitudes toward Zakat as a form of SSN, and complementarities between receiving Zakat and other forms of SSN, to other modules on socioeconomic characteristics and income. Its main findings were threefold:

- First, Zakat is an important SSN because it is an important source of financial support for the poor, and most households that receive it are poor and vulnerable.

- Second, for full coverage of the poor and of all the functions of an SSN, Zakat needs to be complemented by other forms of SSN because (a) part of the chronically poor are not benefiting from Zakat, which reaches about one-third of the poor (based on the survey in Sana'a)—a coverage nevertheless better than other existing SSNs in Sana'a—and although those who get it are poor, because it entails an existing link between receiver and giver, poor households that are not well connected to social networks are systematically excluded; and (b) Zakat does not serve all the functions of an SSN because it does not *promote* spending on human capital formation or health. Public programs focused on that function could leverage the effect of Zakat *protection*. As a lump-sum donation given once or twice a year, Zakat is also not a very effective instrument for risk *prevention* because it neither facilitates consumption smoothing nor appears to help households.

- Third, Zakat overlaps with (thus does not fully crowd out) other private and public SSNs.

Impact on Poverty and Inequality

The most important indicator of SSN effectiveness is the impact on poverty and inequality. This indicator combines the separate forces of coverage, targeting, and generosity of SSN programs and assesses the overall effect of the presence of SSNs on the welfare distribution of the country. This analysis is performed through a static simulation of welfare net of SSN transfers, without attempting to simulate any behavioral adjustments to the absence of SSNs. Still, for the purposes of this regional study, this analysis allows for comparison of the effectiveness of existing SSNs in reducing poverty and inequality in different areas of the Middle East and North Africa.

With the exception of West Bank and Gaza and Jordan, SSNs in the region have little effect on poverty rates, as shown in figure 3.14. SSN presence in Egypt, Iraq, and the Republic of Yemen reduces poverty rates in these countries by at most 4 percent. Benchmarking the region's performance to other regions and the world average is revealing: SSNs in the Middle East and North Africa perform better in terms of poverty impact than SSNs in East Asia but much worse than the world average or in Europe and Central Asia or Latin America and the Caribbean. Notably, however, SSNs in West Bank and Gaza have a higher impact on poverty than those in the best-performing region (Europe and Central Asia).

A similar picture emerges for the nonsubsidy SSN impact on the poverty gap. The poverty gap measures the average shortfall from the poverty line (with the nonpoor having zero shortfall) as a percentage of the poverty line. Thus, the poverty gap reflects both the depth and the incidence of poverty. As with the poverty rate, SSNs in Jordan and West Bank and Gaza appear to have a noticeable effect on the poverty gap (reducing it by 23 and 42 percent, respectively). The rest of the region performs significantly worse compared with the 22 percent average world reduction in the poverty gap due to SSNs. Egypt's and Iraq's SSNs reduce the gap by about 7 percent, and those of the Republic of Yemen, by 4 percent. Overall on this measure, the Middle East and North Africa is on par with East Asia but performs worse than Europe and Central Asia or Latin America and the Caribbean.

FIGURE 3.14

Poverty Rate Impact of Nonsubsidy SSNs, Selected Economies in the Middle East and North Africa Compared with World and Regional Averages, c. 2005–10

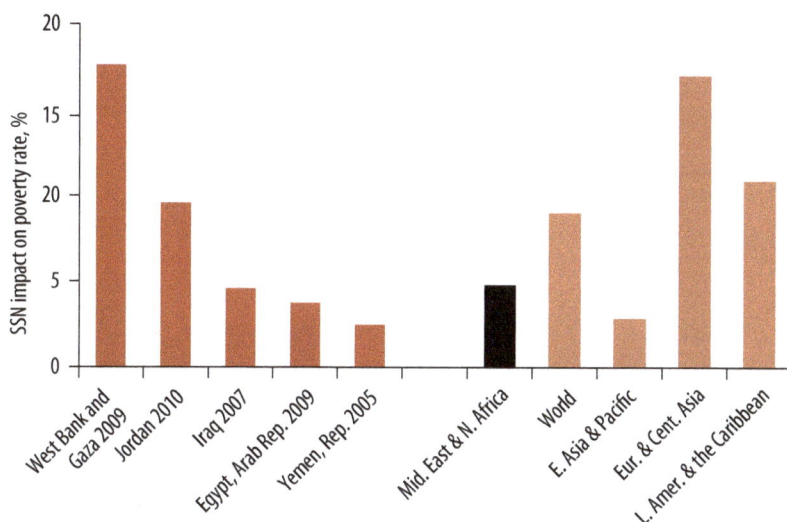

Source: Middle East and North Africa: Authors' calculations based on data from national household surveys; data for world and other regions from World Bank 2012a.

Note: SSN = social safety net.

Regarding the impact on inequality, the regional leader is again West Bank and Gaza, with its SSNs reducing the Gini coefficient by more than 7 percent, as shown in figure 3.15. Most other SSNs in the region have little impact in this regard. In Egypt, Iraq, and the Republic of Yemen, SSNs have an imperceptible effect on welfare distribution, with the Gini coefficient declining by less than 1 percent. Comparisons with other regions demonstrate that in terms of reducing inequality, the region's performance is in the middle of the rankings, below Europe and Central Asia and Latin America and the Caribbean but above East Asia.

In figure 3A.1, panels d and e benchmark Middle Eastern and North African economies against those of other regions that are at the same level of economic development. As economies develop, the impact of their SSN systems on poverty and inequality tends to improve, as demonstrated by the positive trend lines. SSNs in Egypt, Iraq, Jordan, and the Republic of Yemen reduce poverty and inequality by less than would be predicted given their level of GDP per capita. Within the region, only West Bank and Gaza outperforms its development peers in terms of both poverty and inequality reduction due to SSNs. In fact, it is one of the top 10 performers in the world in terms of reducing inequality.

FIGURE 3.15

Inequality Impact of Nonsubsidy SSNs, Selected Economies in the Middle East and North Africa Compared with World and Regional Averages, c. 2005–10

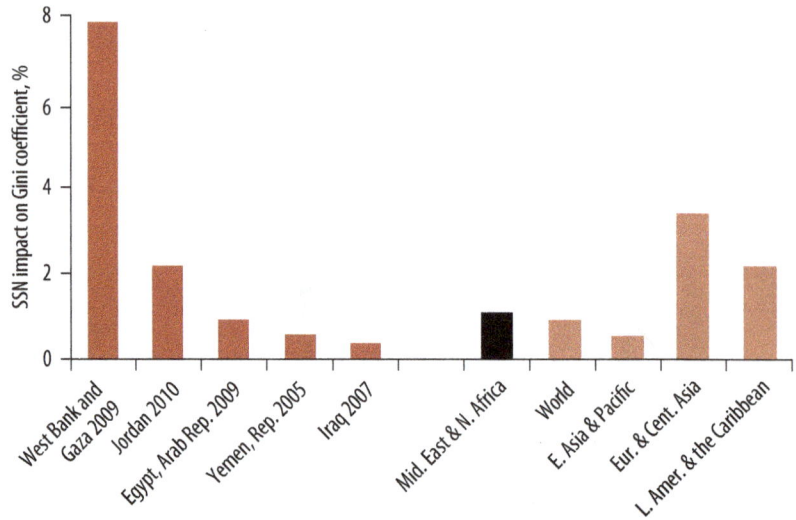

Source: Middle East and North Africa: Authors' calculations based on data from national household surveys; data for world and other regions from World Bank 2012a.

Note: SSN = social safety net.

As seen above, the coverage and generosity of nonsubsidy SSNs in the Middle East and North Africa leave much scope for improvement, and the expenditures absorbed by these programs are very small, especially in comparison with spending on subsidies. So, the negligible effects of the region's SSNs on poverty rates and poverty gaps do not come as a big surprise. The impact on inequality measures the effect of SSNs on welfare distribution; as such, it is directly tied to targeting accuracy. Even excluding subsidies and ration cards, the region's SSNs are not adequately targeted to the poor and vulnerable, which explains the negligible effect on the Gini coefficient. Notably, if subsidies were included, this barely positive effect on inequality might even turn negative in some countries, given the regressive nature of most subsidies. The next section assesses the extent to which subsidies achieve their intended safety net objectives.

Performance of Subsidies as SSNs

Subsidies and ration cards are introduced by governments to achieve a variety of objectives, among them,

- To expand access to the subsidized goods (for example, to reduce energy poverty);

- To spur the development of certain sectors (industry for fuel subsidies and agriculture for food subsidies);

- To offset temporary commodity price fluctuations;

- To avoid inflationary pressures; and, of course,

- To maintain popular support (Fattouh and El-Katiri 2012).

Yet the most frequently cited objective for reliance on subsidies is to protect the poor by guaranteeing access to food and other essential items at affordable prices (Grosh et al. 2008). Previously the chapter showed that Middle Eastern and North African countries rely extensively on subsidies to provide safety nets for their poor and vulnerable populations. How effective are these subsidy-based SSNs? This section takes a brief look at the coverage, targeting, and poverty impact of subsidies and ration cards in the region.

Although subsidy programs are intended to benefit all poor and vulnerable people, such coverage depends on whether these groups consume the subsidized goods. Household survey evidence suggests that fuel subsidies in Egypt, Morocco, and the Republic of Yemen, as well as food subsidies and ration cards in Iraq and Morocco, cover almost everyone in the country. However, Egypt's food ration cards, which require registration, miss about 20 percent of the bottom quintile.

In terms of their benefit incidence, subsidies are at best neutral; up to 60 percent of fuel subsidies in the Middle East and North Africa are captured by the richest quintile. A review of fuel subsidies in 20 developing countries revealed that the top consumption quintile captures six times more in subsidy benefits than the bottom quintile, as shown in table 3.2 (Del Granado, Coady, and Gillingham 2010). Even subsidies for kerosene, a fuel used predominantly by the poor, while less regressive, cannot compare in targeting efficiency with a targeted cash transfer program. It comes as no surprise, then, that price subsidies and ration cards have the highest leakage rates of all types of SSN programs in the Middle East and North Africa.

Figure 3.16 depicts the percentage of expenditures incurred by each quintile on food or fuel subsidies in selected countries. The benefits of food subsidies in Jordan and ration cards in Iraq are equally distributed across quintiles because the poor spend a large portion of their income on food. In contrast, the richest 20 percent of the population capture 40–60 percent of all fuel subsidy benefits because the rich consume more energy products. Thus, the benefit incidence curves of fuel subsidies in Egypt,

TABLE 3.2

Average Distribution of Food Subsidy Benefits by Consumption Quintile in 20 Developing Countries
percentage

| | Consumption quintile | | | | | |
	Poorest	2	3	4	Richest	All housholds
Total impact	7.1	11.4	16.2	22.5	42.8	100.0
Total direct impact	7.1	10.7	14.0	19.9	47.6	100.0
Gasoline	3.0	5.7	9.7	19.4	61.3	100.0
Kerosene	19.0	19.7	20.6	20.1	20.6	100.0
LPG	3.8	7.6	12.6	20.8	53.8	100.0
Indirect impact	7.3	11.7	16.3	22.6	42.0	100.0

Source: Del Granado, Coady, and Gillingham 2010.
Note: LPG = liquefied petroleum gas.

FIGURE 3.16

Benefit Incidence of Subsidies and Ration Cards in the Middle East and North Africa, Selected Countries, c. 2005–10

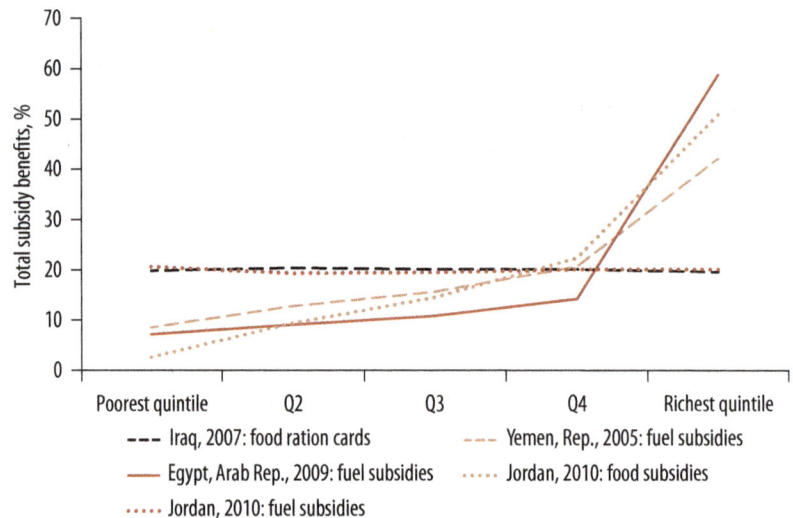

Source: Authors' calculations based on data from national household surveys.
Note: Subsidy incidence calculated using consumption incidence and aggregating across subsidized fuel or food products; thus, it assumes the same subsidization rates across these products. Q = quintile (1 = lowest, 5 = highest).

Jordan, and the Republic of Yemen have a very steep positive gradient across wealth quintiles.

When used as SSNs, subsidies and ration cards suffer from significant deficiencies in targeting accuracy because there is a high propensity for fraud and corruption. The inefficiencies due to leakages of subsidies are

BOX 3.4

The Food Subsidy Program in Tunisia

The Food Subsidy Program has been an important part of Tunisia's safety net since the 1970s, providing universal access to food subsidies on selected consumer products (cooking oil, sugar, milk, meat, and cereals). By the mid-1980s, subsidies accounted for 10 percent of government expenditures and 4 percent of GDP, representing a substantial budgetary burden. At the same time, studies showed that the wealthiest income group captured twice as much of the subsidy per capita as the poorest income group. In the early 1990s, Tunisia launched a series of reforms, including reducing or eliminating subsidies for some commodities and cutting production and distribution costs of subsidized goods.

One major achievement of the reforms was improvement in the targeting of subsidies, achieved by reliance on self-targeting through innovative use of packaging and marketing. For instance, the government introduced different subsidy levels for nutritionally equivalent forms of milk in different packages. The highest subsidy was on reconstituted powdered milk packaged in small plastic bags that would not stand up in the refrigerator. The packages that did stand up in the refrigerator had a lower subsidy, while the lowest subsidy was on fresh bottled milk. For cooking oil, the government maintained the subsidy on oil labeled only as "cooking oil" and dispensed from bulk drums but sold oil labeled as "olive oil" and dispensed in appealing bottles at market prices. As a result, many wealthier consumers switched to the unsubsidized products, which they found more attractive and convenient. Similar reforms were implemented for bread, thus eliminating the subsidy on refined baguette-type bread while preserving it for lower-quality bread.

Although such tinkering with packaging and marketing can appear minor, the reforms led to a significant decrease in government expenditure on food subsidies (from 4 percent of GDP in 1984 to 1.5 percent in 1998). Perhaps even more important, the share of subsidy transfers captured by the poorest quintile increased from 8 to 21 percent. Nevertheless, the subsidy reforms might have had an adverse effect on nutrition: an early analysis of consumption revealed a drop in calorie and protein intake in the poorest quintile.

Sources: Alderman 2002; Grosh et al. 2008; Tuck and Lindert 1996.

staggering: for instance, the government of Egypt could save 73 percent of the cost of food subsidies if it eliminated leakages and decreased coverage (World Bank 2010a). This is especially true for the subsidized *baladi* bread, where the cost of transferring LE 1 to a needy household is almost LE 3 because almost two-thirds of the benefits go to the non-needy (Ahmed et al. 2001; Grosh et al. 2008; World Bank 2005). Similarly, in Iraq, for every US$1 received by the poor in the form of food rations, the government spent US$6 because of inefficiencies and vulnerability to waste, theft, and corruption (World Bank 2010b).

One way to increase the efficiency of subsidies as an SSN instrument is through self-targeting, achieved by focusing on inferior goods (goods consumed primarily by the poor, such as kerosene) or by packaging and marketing subsidized goods in a way that promotes self-targeting. Tunisia's reform of its Food Subsidy Program in the 1990s is one of the most successful examples of the latter (see box 3.4).

As shown above, although subsidies suffer from extremely high leakages and do not provide a reliable safety net, simple removal of subsidies would have significant impoverishing effects in many Middle Eastern and North African countries. Figure 3.17 shows the poverty impacts of the region's subsidies based on existing studies. It is evident that given their wider coverage and generosity (in terms of subsidization rates of essential consumer goods), subsidies have major impacts on keeping people out of poverty. In Egypt and Iraq, the presence of food subsidies and ration cards reduced poverty rates by about 30 percent. Notably, fuel subsidies have less impact on poverty than food subsidies; still, fuel subsidies in Egypt decreased poverty incidence in 2004 by more than 18 percent. In Jordan, removal of the water subsidy would have a higher effect on poverty than removal of food or gas subsidies. Finally, in the Republic of Yemen, the direct impact of petroleum subsidies on poverty was only 5.7

FIGURE 3.17

Poverty Impact of Subsidies in the Middle East and North Africa, Selected Countries, c. 2004–10

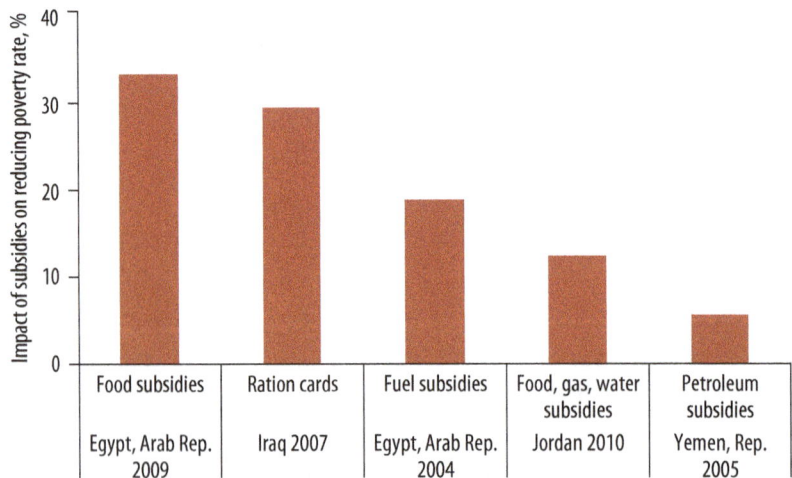

Sources: Government of Jordan 2011a; Government of Yemen, World Bank, and UNDP 2007; World Bank 2005, 2010a, 2010b.

percent—still very high relative to the 2 percent impact from the presence of nonsubsidy SSNs. These results imply that subsidy reform should be accompanied by expansion of nonsubsidy SSNs that promote livelihood and resilience.

Conclusions

This chapter has demonstrated that SSNs in the Middle East and North Africa are ripe for reform. The region relies too heavily on untargeted price subsidies and ration cards, which waste the scarce resources of governments because of high leakage rates and a high propensity for waste, fraud, and corruption. Subsidies aside, SSNs in the region are underresourced and fragmented. Most of the poor and vulnerable fall through the cracks of the small and categorically or geographically targeted programs. Moreover, poor targeting methods result in significant leakages of SSN benefits to the nonpoor, siphoning off resources that could be used elsewhere to decrease poverty and improve the distribution of welfare in the Middle East and North Africa.

Although subsidies are inefficient and frequently ineffective relative to other SSN interventions, large numbers of the poor and vulnerable populations depend on them to stay out of poverty. So if the region's countries are to move from the status quo toward more effective, reliable, and equitable social safety nets, how should they proceed? The most difficult questions always revolve around the political economy of reform, and chapter 4 will move from the "what" to the "how."

Annex 3A

Additional Figures and Tables

Share of Nonsubsidy SSN Spending by Economy and Program Type, Middle East and North Africa, c. 2008–11

percent

	Cash transfers	Fee waivers, education, and health benefits	Food and other in-kind transfers	Housing	Micro-credit and income-generating activities	Training	Workfare programs	Others
Bahrain	100.0	n.a.	n.a.	n.a.	n.a.	n.a.	n.a.	n.a.
Egypt, Arab Rep.	91.9	8.1	n.a.	n.a.	n.a.	n.a.	n.a.	n.a.
Iraq	100.0	n.a.	n.a.	n.a.	n.a.	n.a.	n.a.	n.a.
Jordan	44.5	0.5	8.7	1.1	29.6	15.6	n.a.	n.a.
Kuwait	100.0	n.a.	n.a.	n.a.	n.a.	n.a.	n.a.	n.a.
Lebanon	n.a.	82.9	n.a.	n.a.	n.a.	0.1	n.a.	17.1
Morocco	2.5	4.9	20.8	3.7	n.a.	n.a.	16.6	51.6
Saudi Arabia	100.0	n.a.	n.a.	n.a.	n.a.	n.a.	n.a.	n.a.
Syrian Arab Republic	100.0	n.a.	n.a.	n.a.	n.a.	n.a.	n.a.	n.a.
Tunisia	69.0	27.9	n.a.	n.a.	n.a.	0.2	n.a.	2.8
West Bank and Gaza	64.0	n.a.	34.3	n.a.	1.7	n.a.	n.a.	n.a.
Yemen, Rep.	55.5	3.7	n.a.	n.a.	n.a.	n.a.	40.8	n.a.

Source: Authors' calculations based on MENA SSN Inventory. For a list of programs in the inventory, see appendix C.

Note: n.a. = not applicable.

FIGURE 3A.1

Performance of Nonsubsidy SSNs in the Middle East and North Africa, Selected Economies, Relative to Development Peers

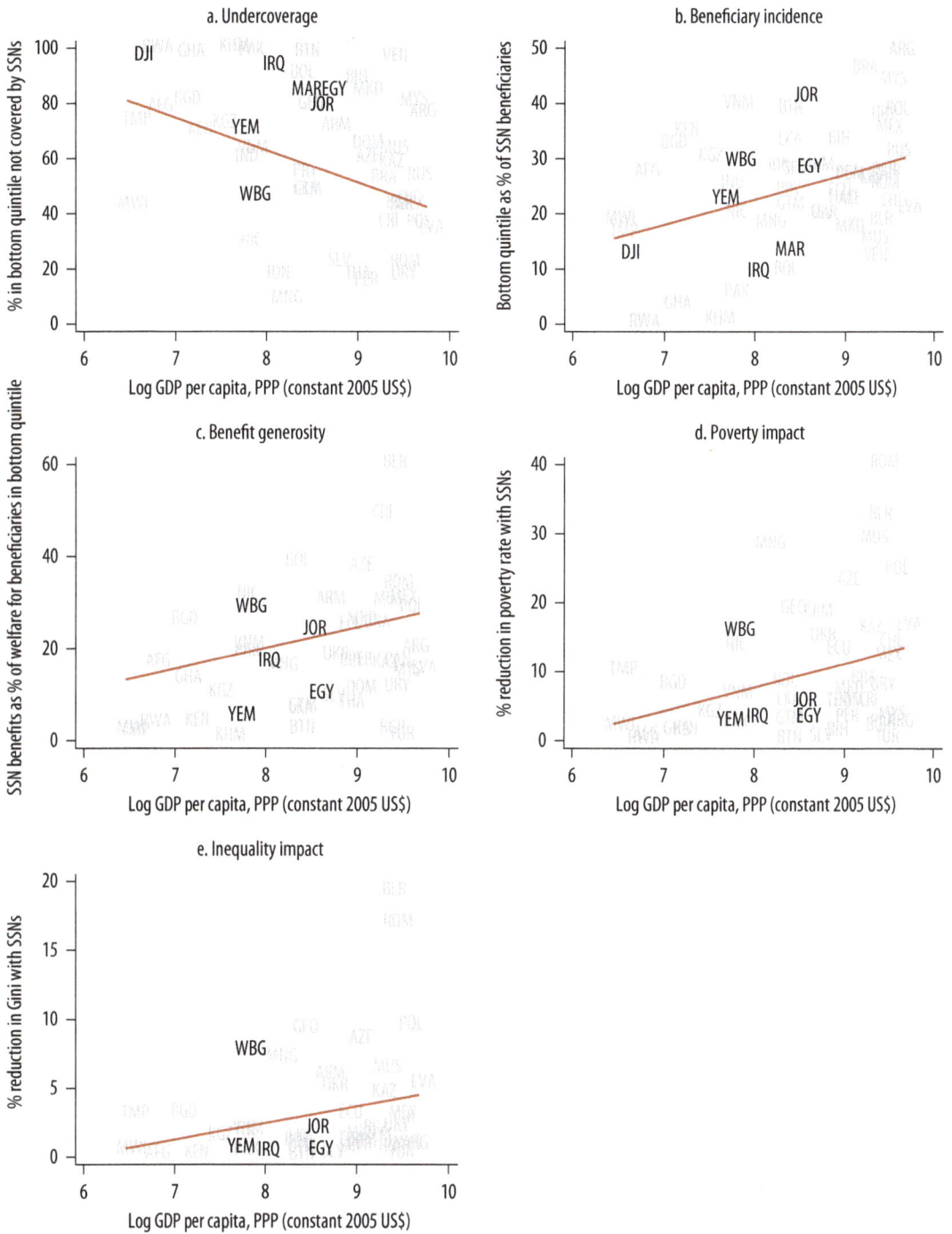

Sources: Middle East and North Africa data from national household surveys; other data from World Bank 2012a.

Note: PPP = purchasing power parity; SSN = social safety net. Trend lines are not weighted by population.

FIGURE 3A.2

Coverage Rates of Main Nonsubsidy SSN Programs by Wealth Quintile in the Middle East and North Africa

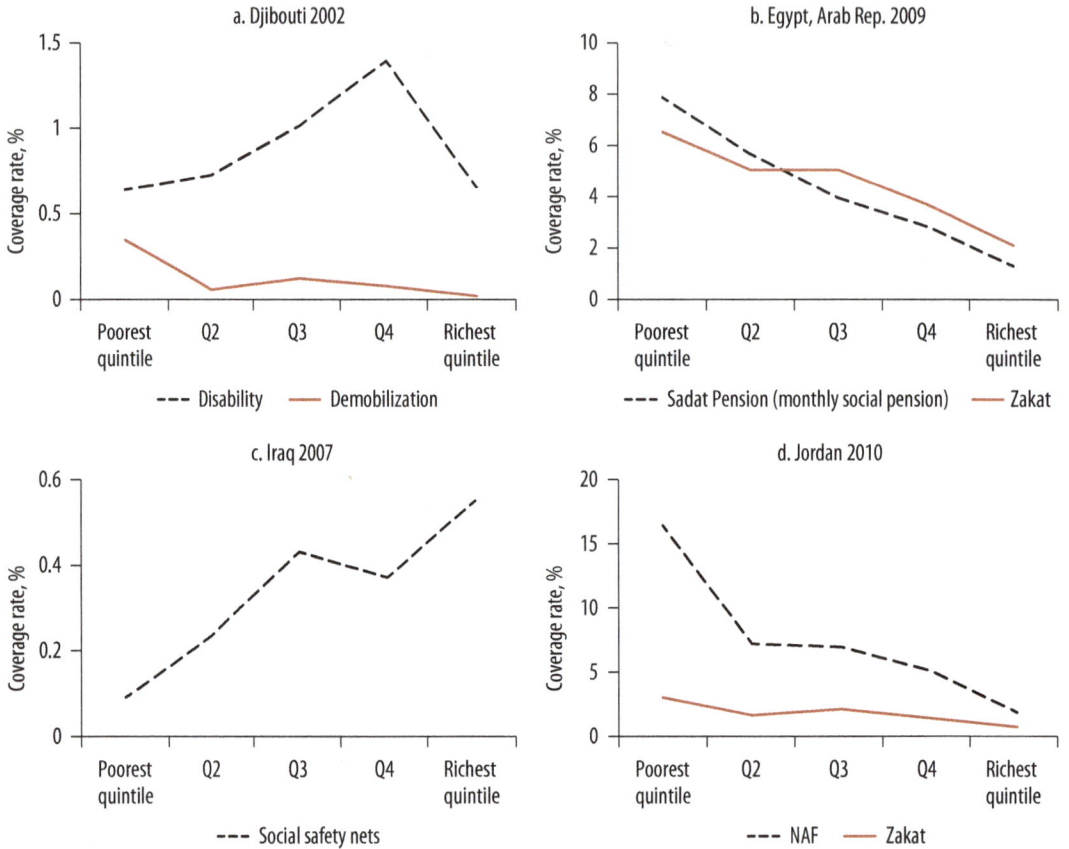

a. Djibouti 2002

b. Egypt, Arab Rep. 2009

c. Iraq 2007

d. Jordan 2010

FIGURE 3A.2 *Continued*

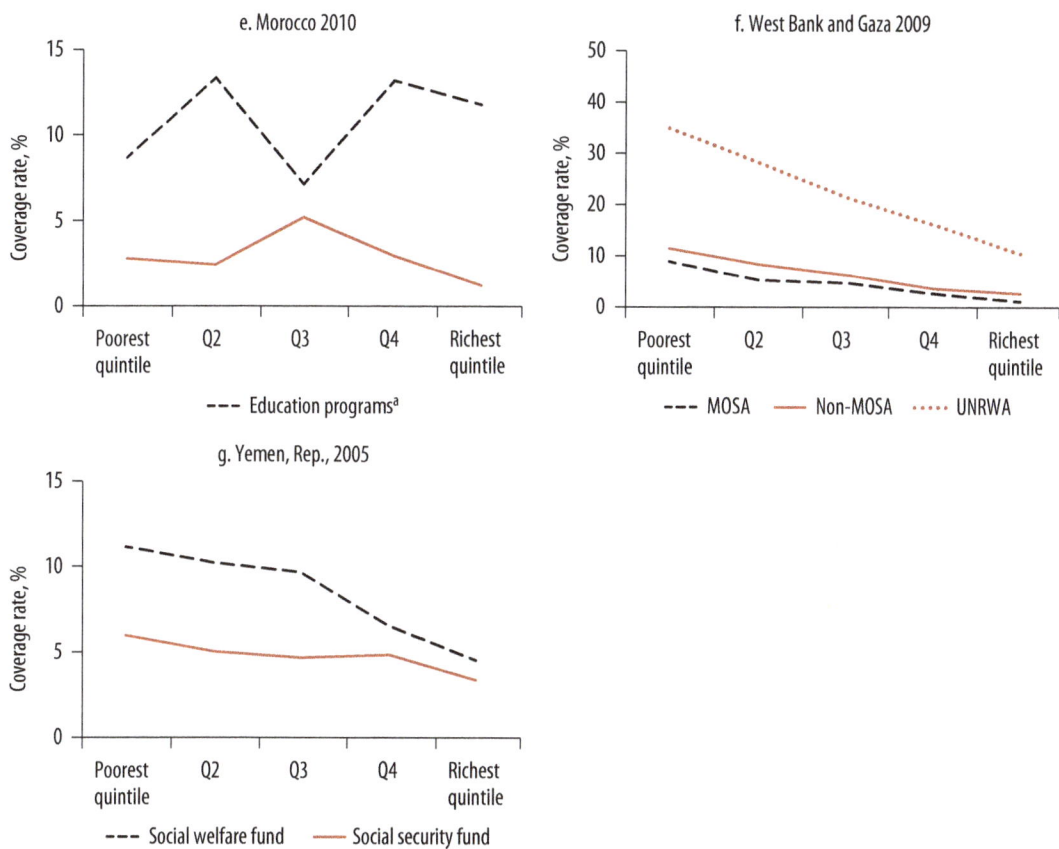

e. Morocco 2010

f. West Bank and Gaza 2009

--- Education programs[a]

--- MOSA ——— Non-MOSA ····· UNRWA

g. Yemen, Rep., 2005

--- Social welfare fund ——— Social security fund

Source: Authors' calculations based on data from national household surveys.

Note: MOSA = Ministry of Social Affairs; NAF = National Aid Fund; SSN = social safety net; UNRWA = United Nations Relief and Works Agency for Palestine Refugees in the Near East.

a. Excludes the "One Million Satchels" (*Un Million de Cartables*) school supplies program.

FIGURE 3A.3

Distribution of Benefits from Main Nonsubsidy SSNs by Wealth Quintile, Middle East and North Africa, Selected Economies

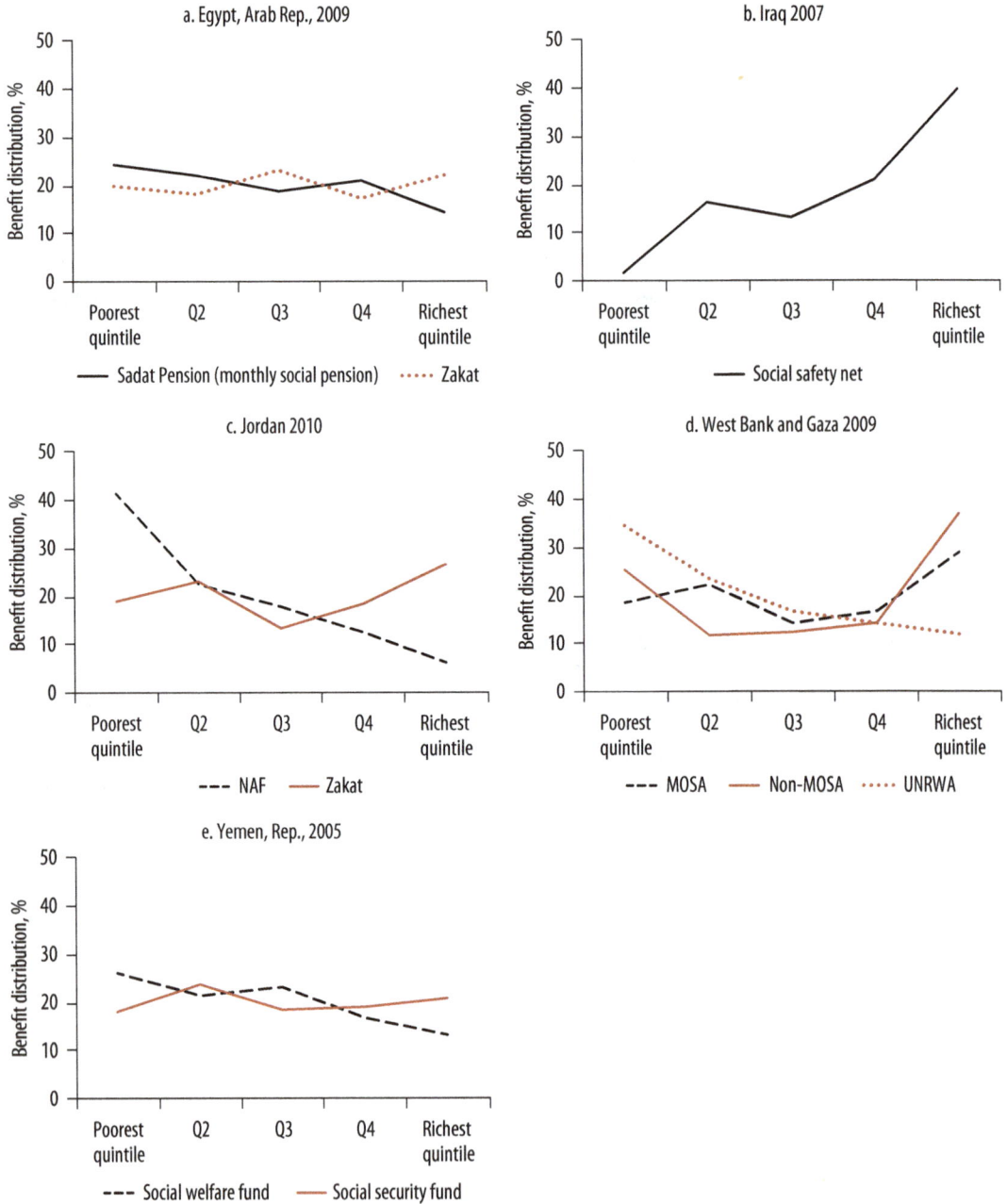

a. Egypt, Arab Rep., 2009

— Sadat Pension (monthly social pension) ····· Zakat

b. Iraq 2007

— Social safety net

c. Jordan 2010

--- NAF — Zakat

d. West Bank and Gaza 2009

--- MOSA — Non-MOSA ····· UNRWA

e. Yemen, Rep., 2005

--- Social welfare fund — Social security fund

Source: Authors' calculations based on data from national household surveys.

Note: MOSA = Ministry of Social Affairs; NAF = National Aid Fund; SSN = social safety net; UNRWA = United Nations Relief and Works Agency for Palestine Refugees in the Near East.

Annex 3B

Methodological Annex

Program coverage—the portion of the population in a specific group that receives the transfer. Specifically, the program coverage rate of a quintile is calculated in this study as the number of individuals in the quintile who live in a household where at least one member receives the transfer, divided by the total number of individuals in the quintile. For countries where questionnaires include explicit questions on program participation,[5] a binary variable is set equal to one if the person lives in a household where at least one member receives the program, and equal to zero otherwise. When program participation questions are not included in the questionnaires,[6] coverage is calculated by creating a binary variable equal to one if the person lives in a household receiving positive transfers from the program, and equal to zero otherwise. In the latter case, results should be interpreted with caution because respondents might report no or null transfers while still participating in an SSN program. The report also presents indicators of *undercoverage*, which is the percentage of poor individuals who do not receive the SSN program transfer.

Targeting accuracy—the incidence of beneficiaries and benefits as well as indicators of leakage, defined as follows:

- *Beneficiary incidence* is the proportion of beneficiaries in each group. Specifically, beneficiary incidence is calculated here as the number of individuals in the quintile who live in a household where at least one member receives the transfer divided by the total number of direct and indirect beneficiaries.

- *Benefit incidence* is the transfer amount received by a specific group as a percentage of total transfers received by the population. For the purposes of this study, a program's benefit incidence for a quintile is equal to the sum of all transfers received by all individuals in that quintile divided by the sum of all transfers received by all individuals in the population.

- *Leakage of beneficiaries* is the percentage of individuals who receive transfers and are not poor.

- *Leakage of benefits* is the percentage of benefits that is received by individuals who are not poor.

Generosity—the mean value of the share transfer amount received by all beneficiaries in a group as a share of the total welfare aggregate of the beneficiaries in that group.[7]

TABLE 3B.1

Welfare Aggregates in Middle Eastern and North African Economies under Study

Country	Welfare indicator
Djibouti	Adult equivalent expenditure
Egypt, Arab Rep.	Actual consumption per capita
Iraq	Expenditure per capita
Jordan	Expenditure per capita
Morocco	Asset-based wealth index
West Bank and Gaza	Adult equivalent expenditure
Yemen, Rep.	Actual consumption per capita

Sources: Data from the following household surveys (as detailed in appendix B): Djibouti EDAM-IS2 2002; Egypt HIECS 2009; Iraq IHSES 2007; Jordan HIES 2010; Morocco MHYS 2010; Syria HIES 2004; West Bank and Gaza ECS 2009; Republic of Yemen HBS 2006.

For this study, generosity is calculated as the average of the ratio of transfer amounts received by all beneficiaries in a quintile over the total welfare aggregate of the beneficiaries in that quintile.

Poverty (or inequality) impact—*the difference between the actual poverty (or inequality) indicator and a simulated poverty (or inequality) indicator in the absence of the SSN program.*

For this study, the poverty rate is used (defined as the share of the population below the poverty line) as the poverty indicator, and the Gini coefficient is used as the indicator of inequality. One important assumption made in the simulation of poverty and inequality impact is that, in the absence of the program, household welfare diminishes by the full value of the program transfer. This assumes no behavioral adjustments in response to the absence of the program.

The analysis of coverage, targeting, generosity, and poverty or inequality impact of SSN programs uses an expenditure or consumption-based welfare aggregate to divide the population into wealth quintiles and identify poverty status. When consumption or expenditure data are not available, an asset index is calculated to construct wealth quintiles (for example, in Morocco). In this latter case, almost all assets and utility services are used, including country-specific items. The reason for using many indicator variables rather than a few selected items is the improvement in the distribution, with fewer households concentrated on certain index scores. Generally, any item that can potentially be correlated with economic status is included. Finally, following the recommendations of Filmer and Pritchett (2001), Principal Components Analysis (PCA) aggregates several binary asset ownership variables into a single dimension. A PCA index is calculated so that households can be ranked from the lowest to the highest socioeconomic level. Table 3B.1 presents the welfare aggregates used for the different countries under study.

As much as possible, the methodology for the SSN performance assessment was standardized across countries to improve comparability.[8]

Notes

1. The transfer income and SSN participation modules for Lebanon and Tunisia were not available for this study.
2. For the sake of such comparability, posttransfer welfare is used to divide each country's population into quintiles. Although pretransfer welfare is generally preferable, some household surveys only have indicator variables for transfer receipt and not the transfer amounts (for example, in Djibouti and Morocco).
3. These are simple (not population-weighted) averages.
4. The results were computed as follows: $\frac{\text{Total expenditure on subsidies}}{\text{Amount of nonsubsidy SSN benefits going to the poor}}$. The numerator uses administrative data on subsidies, while the denominator uses data from household surveys.
5. Countries include Djibouti, Iraq, and Morocco.
6. Economies include Egypt, Jordan, Syria, West Bank and Gaza, and the Republic of Yemen.
7. See table 3B.1 for more information on welfare aggregates.
8. For the sake of such comparability, posttransfer welfare is used to divide each country's population into quintiles. Although pretransfer welfare is generally preferable, some household surveys only have indicator variables for transfer receipt and not the transfer amounts (for example, in Djibouti and Morocco).

References

Ahmed, A. U., H. Bouis, T. Gutner, and H. Lofgren. 2001. *The Egyptian Food Subsidy System: Structure, Performance, and Options for Reform*. Research report 119, International Food Policy Research Institute, Washington, DC.

Alderman, H. 2002. "Subsidies as a Social Safety Net: Effectiveness and Challenges." Social Safety Net Primer Series, Discussion Paper 0224, World Bank, Washington, DC.

Del Granado, J. A., D. Coady, and R. Gillingham. 2010. "The Unequal Benefits of Fuel Subsidies: A Review of Evidence for Developing Countries." Working Paper 10/202, International Monetary Fund, Washington, DC.

Fattouh, B., and L. El-Katiri. 2012. *Energy Subsidies in the Arab World*. Arab Human Development Report Research Paper Series, United Nations Development Programme, New York.

Filmer, D., and L. Pritchett. 2001. "Estimating Wealth Effects without Expenditure Data—or Tears: An Application to Educational Enrollments in States of India." *Demography* 38 (1): 115–33.

Government of Yemen, World Bank, and UNDP (United Nations Development Programme). 2007. *Yemen Poverty Assessment*. Washington, DC: World Bank.

Government of Jordan. 2011a. *An Analysis of Consumption Subsidies*. Unpublished report, Amman.

———. 2011b. *Social Protection Review*. Unpublished report, Amman.

Grosh, M., C. Del Ninno, E. Tesliuc, and A. Ouerghi. 2008. *For Protection & Promotion: The Design and Implementation of Effective Safety Nets*. Washington, DC: World Bank.

OECD (Organisation for Economic Co-operation and Development). n.d. Social Expenditure Database (SOCX). http://www.oecd.org/els/social/expenditure.

Silva, J., M. Alloush, and Q. Wodon. 2012. "Middle East and North Africa: Zakat as a Social Safety Net in Yemen." Unpublished manuscript, World Bank, Washington, DC.

Tuck, L., and K. Lindert. 1996. "From Universal Food Subsidies to a Self-Targeted Program: A Case Study in Tunisian Reform." Discussion Paper 351, World Bank, Washington, DC.

UNDP (United Nations Development Programme). 2002. *Arab Human Development Report 2002: Creating Opportunities for Future Generations*. New York: UNDP.

World Bank. 2005. *Egypt: Toward a More Effective Social Policy: Subsidies and Social Safety Net*. Report 33550-EG, World Bank, Washington, DC.

———. 2007. *Hashemite Kingdom of Jordan: A Note on Strategy for Modernization of the Social Safety Nets*. World Bank, Washington, DC.

———. 2009. *Iraq: Poverty Assessment 2009 Report*. World Bank, Washington, DC.

———. 2010a. *Egypt's Food Subsidies: Benefit Incidence and Leakages*. Report 57446, World Bank, Washington, DC.

———. 2010b. *Iraq: First Programmatic Fiscal Sustainability DPL Program Document*. Report 51528–IQ, World Bank, Washington, DC.

———. 2010c. *Yemen: Private Sector Growth and Social Protection Development Policy*. Grant Program Document, Report 55649–YE, World Bank, Washington, DC.

———. 2011a. *Poverty in Egypt 2008–09: Withstanding the Global Economic Crisis*. Report 60249–EG, World Bank, Washington, DC.

———. 2011b. *Royaume du Maroc: Note Strategique sur le Ciblage et la Protection Sociale*. Ciblage et protection sociale: Note d'orientation stratégique. Report AAA65-MA, World Bank, Washington, DC.

———. 2012a. *Atlas of Social Protection: Indicators of Resilience and Equity (ASPIRE)*. Washington, DC: World Bank. http://www.worldbank.org/spatlas.

———. 2012b. *Republic of Iraq: Public Expenditure Review (towards More Efficient Spending for Better Service Delivery in Iraq)*. Report 68682-IQ, World Bank, Washington, DC.

———. Various years. *World Development Indicators*. Washington, DC: World Bank.

———. Forthcoming. *LAC SSN inventory*. Unpublished report, World Bank, Washington, DC.

World Bank, FAO (Food and Agriculture Organization of the United Nations), and IFAD (International Fund for Agricultural Development). 2009. *Improving Food Security in Arab Countries*. Joint report, Washington, DC.

CHAPTER 4

The Political Economy of SSN Reforms in the Middle East and North Africa: What Do Citizens Want?

Introduction

Like other policy areas that involve redistributing resources, social safety nets (SSNs) are a politically sensitive topic. Although a number of the technical shortcomings of the existing safety nets in the Middle East and North Africa have been documented in the past, political economy considerations have probably been a major reason why the SSN reforms have largely stalled across the region.

Disentangling the political economy of safety nets is complex. The approach of this chapter is to collect cross-country evidence regarding citizens' perceptions and aspirations about SSNs, with the objective of informing decision makers on possible entry points for SSNs' renewal and reform that the poor and middle classes are likely to support and that can draw from positive international experience. For example, in cash transfer programs in Latin America, the main reason for making the providers of the program and its beneficiaries jointly responsible for building human capital was to maximize the program's impact on intergenerational poverty. However, this feature also proved critical in changing the political acceptability of SSN programs in Latin America (Grosh et al. 2008). In this sense, the report does not undertake a full political economy analysis of reform but rather highlights its feasibility from the perspective of the general public and helps decision makers by reducing the risks associated with reforming under complete uncertainty.

This chapter focuses on the following six questions, in light of what the existing literature has found to be relevant on the political economy of SSNs—specifically SSNs in the Middle East and North Africa:

- What are the perceived causes of poverty and economic success?

- What are the main correlates of the appetite for redistribution?

- What do people think the role of the state is, and how satisfied are they about the state's role with regard to the provision of SSNs to the poor?

- What design features do people think SSNs should include?

- What is the acceptability of price subsidy reform and the politically viable options for their reform?

- What are the characteristics of effective SSNs that have gained broad acceptance among populations around the world?

The evidence presented in this chapter is based on newly collected data from the MENA SPEAKS surveys in the Arab Republic of Egypt, Jordan, Lebanon, and Tunisia and from the Jordan Gives behavioral experiment. These data address important knowledge gaps on the subject.

The MENA SPEAKS surveys are four nationally representative opinion surveys on knowledge and attitudes about safety nets and social preferences, fielded by Gallup in Egypt, Jordan, Lebanon, and Tunisia. These cross-country comparable surveys interviewed citizens on the Social Protection Evaluation of Attitudes, Knowledge, and Support (SPEAKS).

The second set of data derives from a behavioral experiment conducted among a nationally representative sample of the lower, middle, and upper-middle classes in Jordan. The Jordan Gives experiment collected fact-based information on individuals' preferences for various forms of SSNs by observing their decisions on whether and how to allocate various forms of SSNs to poor individuals. Little to no data had existed for MENA countries regarding these issues.[1] No cross-country data previously existed regarding public awareness and preferences toward SSNs and subsidy reform, and little knowledge existed regarding the appetite for redistribution and perceptions about inequality, as part of the World Values Survey (WVS n.d.). Box 4.1 summarizes the methodology adopted to collect these data, and annex 4B presents the methodology in greater detail.

The data on awareness of existing SSN programs and subsidies reflect the overall state of fragmentation, low coverage, and regressiveness of the current system. Among the key findings, are the following:

- Awareness of SSN programs is generally low among their intended beneficiaries, particularly in Egypt, while it is somewhat higher among the rich.

- The rich also tend to be more likely than the poor to know a program beneficiary.

- Regarding subsidies, the poor are mostly aware of food subsidies but know far less about energy subsidies, though awareness of the latter

BOX 4.1

Listening to Citizens: The MENA SPEAKS Surveys and the Jordan Gives Experiment

Two data collection projects were conducted as part of this regional study. The findings presented in this report represent an unprecedented attempt to shed light on the specificities of the political economy of SSNs in the region through nationally representative data. These data are also unique in their application of behavioral economics to study the preferences for SSNs in the Middle East and North Africa.

MENA SPEAKS: MENA Social Protection Evaluation of Attitudes, Knowledge, and Support (SPEAKS)

MENA SPEAKS surveys are four nationally representative surveys conducted as part of the Spring 2012 wave of Gallup's World Poll in Egypt, Jordan, Lebanon, and Tunisia. The surveys collected data from 1,000 randomly selected households in each country about their subjective income; perceptions on existing inequality; the role of the state as the main provider of SSNs; knowledge of existing SSN programs; preferences on SSN design features; knowledge of existing subsidies; and preferences regarding subsidy removal and different compensation packages. For an example of a MENA SPEAKS questionnaire (Egypt), see annex 4A.

Jordan Gives: Jordan Behavioral Experiment on Redistribution Preferences

Jordan Gives is a behavioral game that collected information on people's preferences and support for several redistribution alternatives. The value added of the game through a simple survey is that participants tend to think more deeply about trade-offs when the consequences of their choices translate into concrete monetary costs and benefits. Thus, the information elicited through their decisions should be a more reliable measure of their true preferences for redistribution.

The game was carried out in Jordan with 42 groups of 10 citizens each by the Center for Strategic Studies at the University of Jordan. The sampling units were drawn from a sample of the Jordanian middle class (explained further below). In each randomly selected primary sampling unit (PSU), two groups (treatment and control) played simultaneously in separate rooms, with participants randomly assigned to one of the groups. At the beginning of the game, each participant received fuel vouchers issued by Jordan Petroleum Refinery: a JD 5 (Jordanian dinars) voucher as a show-up fee and a JD 10 voucher to play the game. The magnitude of the voucher for the game (JD 10) is essentially equivalent to the minimum daily wage. Participants were offered four independent proposals, and for each proposal they had to decide whether to accept it (implying willingness to give up the JD 10 voucher to have the proposal implemented) or to reject it (implying a preference to keep the JD 10 voucher instead of implementing the proposal.

(box continued on next page)

BOX 4.1 *Continued*

The proposals, which portrayed as closely as possible different SSN designs, were the following:

- [Cash transfer] You give up your JD 10 voucher. Our team gives JD 20 cash per family to five poor families in this community. Do you accept or reject the proposal?

- [In-kind transfer] You give up your JD 10 voucher. Our team gives a food basket worth JD 20 per family to five poor families in this community.

- [Conditional cash transfer] You give up your JD 10 voucher. Our team gives JD 20 cash per family to five poor families in this community conditional on their completion of a free training program on work-related skills.

- [Cash transfer and money to the local school] You give up your JD 10 voucher. Our team gives JD 20 cash per family to two poor families in this community, and JD 60 cash will go to the local school.

The difference in acceptance rates between the presented alternatives can be attributed to the differences in preferences for par-

ticular proposal features (cash versus in-kind, conditional versus unconditional, private goods only versus private and public). The difference in the game played in the treatment groups as opposed to the control groups consisted of additional information provided only to the treatment groups. This information appealed to the Arab values of solidarity and listed the potential "shopping cart" a poor family could buy with JD 20. Moreover, treatment groups were offered the option to accompany the facilitator after the game to witness the implementation of the proposal if the selected decision was "accept." This activity was complemented by evidence collected through a questionnaire. The sample was nationally representative of the middle class to represent the median voter, who was expected to have lower self-interest in increasing redistribution and to be more likely to actively oppose SSN reform.

Because of the national scale of the experiment and to ensure homogeneity of implementation across groups, a video in the local language was used in all groups. This video provided detailed instructions to the participants and projected each of the proposals on the screen.

tends to increase among wealthier people (who absorb most of the subsidy benefits, as shown in chapter 3).

- Contrary to the oft-cited perception that SSNs in the Middle East and North Africa are seen as the responsibility of religious or charitable organizations, the region's citizens unambiguously see their governments as most responsible for assisting the poor. Yet in two out of the four countries studied through the MENA SPEAKS surveys, the vast majority reported being dissatisfied with the effectiveness of the existing SSNs.

- The subjective poor (those who are not in the bottom quintile of income but who perceive themselves to be in the bottom of the four income groups) are a constituency that feels particularly unsatisfied with existing SSNs while showing great demand for more redistribution.

- People who perceive inequality to be high, those who expect a drop in living standards, and those who believe that poverty is socially (as opposed to individually) caused are more likely to demand redistributive policies.

- Looking toward the future, citizens (particularly the poor) would rather see SSNs with cash-based benefits, are in favor of poverty-based targeting, and are generally averse to imposing conditionalities—though preferences on the latter are heterogeneous across classes and countries.

- Opposition to subsidy reform varies strongly by country—and it is higher in Egypt and Jordan. Generally there is lower resistance to reforming energy subsidies than food subsidies.

- In case of reform, most citizens would rather see the country's savings converted into cash-based transfers targeted to the poor, coupled in some cases, with higher spending on the social sector.

The next section discusses the evidence on the determinants of the demand for redistribution in the Middle East and North Africa, including beliefs on poverty and individual success. Subsequent sections discuss how citizens regard the existing SSNs and lay out the most-accepted options for subsidy reform. The final section presents international experiences of program design features that are likely to enhance acceptability of reform among citizens.

Demand for Redistribution among Citizens of the Middle East and North Africa

Attitudes toward redistribution vary largely across countries, and in the Middle East and North Africa, comparable data on citizens' preferences for redistribution, such as those collected by the World Values Survey (WVS), are limited to a few countries (Egypt, the Islamic Republic of Iran, Jordan, and Morocco). As a result, this issue—a crucial determinant of the demand for SSNs—is poorly studied in the region. The MENA

SPEAKS survey and the Jordan Gives game provide new insights on these issues.

Attitudes toward redistribution are shaped by multiple factors, and this section will focus on three major individual determinants: (a) beliefs on causes of poverty and success, (b) self-perceptions of one's status in the welfare distribution, and (c) perceptions of prospects for upward mobility.

- *Beliefs on causes of poverty and success.* On an individual level, people who think that poverty is caused by lack of willpower or laziness and that success is a result of effort and hard work believe in a "just world," where everyone gets what they deserve. Such a belief implies a lower preference for redistributive policies (Alesina and Angeletos 2005; Alesina and Giuliano 2009; Bénabou and Tirole 2006).

- *Self-perceived status in the welfare distribution.* Preferences for redistribution, and consequently for SSN reform, depend, in part, on whether people perceive themselves to be potential net beneficiaries or benefactors of SSN programs. This, in turn, is determined by self-perceived rank in the welfare distribution, which is only partly reflected in objective measurements such as income or consumption (Cruces, Truglia, and Tetaz 2011; Ravallion and Lokshin 2000).

- *Perceptions on prospects for upward mobility.* When thinking about long-lasting redistributive policies, people take into account not just their current status and position in the welfare distribution but also their expected future position (Bénabou and Ok 2001; Ravallion and Lokshin 2000). Thus, people who are hopeful about future upward mobility are less likely to support redistributive SSN programs than people who do not hold such optimistic views about their future prospects.

Beliefs on the Causes of Poverty and Success

Among the Jordanian middle class, injustice in society is more frequently deemed to be the main cause of poverty, as opposed to laziness. This perception is halfway between those held in regions like Latin America and the Caribbean and continental Europe, where SSNs are more developed, and the United States and China, where most citizens believe that poverty is a result of laziness and lack of willpower, as shown in table 4.1.

Although this belief prevails at the mean, the perceptions differ between lower-middle- and upper-middle-class individuals. Data from Jordan reveal that middle-class individuals who report being closer to being poor are more likely than upper-middle-class individuals to believe that poverty is a result of injustice in society or of bad luck, as figure 4.1 il-

TABLE 4.1

Perceptions of Poverty in Jordan, Latin America and the Caribbean, Europe, and the United States, c. 2006–12

	% who believe "the poor are poor because…"	
	"… society is unjust" or "… they are unlucky"	"… they are lazy"
China	41.6	58.4
Europe[a]	78.3	21.7
India	57.9	42.1
Jordan (middle class only)	61.7	38.3
Latin America and the Caribbean	73.5	26.5
United States	38.4	61.6

Sources: Authors' calculations based on World Values Survey (WVS) 2006; Jordan Gives 2012.

a. Continental Europe.

FIGURE 4.1

Perceived Causes of Poverty among Jordanian Middle Class, by Subjective Income Group, 2012

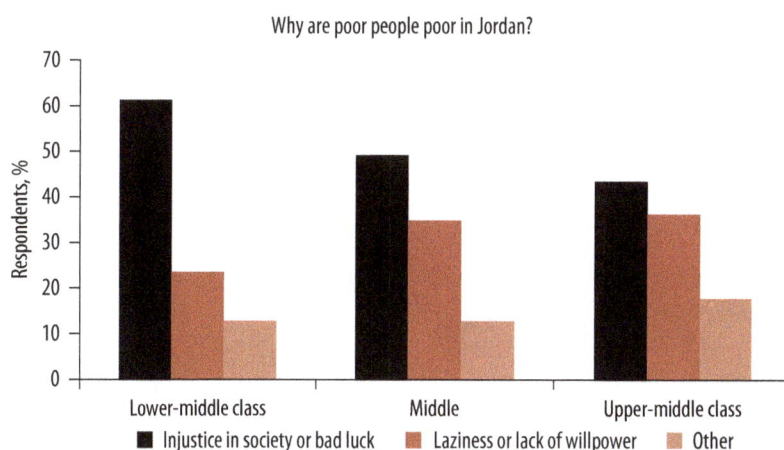

Source: Authors' calculations based on Jordan Gives 2012.

lustrates. In fact, the share of individuals who believe that laziness is at the core of poverty increases with income and is as high as 37 percent among the upper-middle class in Jordan.

The Jordan Gives experiment indicates that perceptions about the poor are associated with the level of support for redistribution. Regression analysis on data from the Jordanian middle class (shown in annex 4D) indicates that those who believe that the poor are in this economic condition out of laziness (as opposed to injustice or bad luck) support significantly less redistributive intervention by the government. These findings are consistent with the evidence from high-income countries. Alesina and Giuliano (2009) have shown that people tend to prefer more redistribution to the poor if they believe that poverty is caused by factors beyond an individual's control. In an empirical study based on a U.S. survey, Fong (2001) concluded that people who believe that earnings depend on individual effort such as hard work and willpower do not support redistribution programs for the poor; usually these are people with high-mean and low-variance income. The same study also concluded that people who believe that poverty is caused by exogenous factors, such as bad luck or lack of opportunity, have higher support for redistribution.

The regression analysis on the Jordanian data also shows that there does not seem to be a significant correlation between private social safety nets and lower demand for redistribution: those who reported being able to rely on family and friends in times of need actually supported significantly more redistributive policies by the government than those who felt unable to rely on informal safety nets.

Subjective Poverty and the Demand for Redistribution

In Egypt and Tunisia, a third of people define themselves as poor—a much higher rate than the actual poverty rate. In the MENA SPEAKS survey, individuals were asked to place their household's income in one of four categories and were shown four coin stacks of different heights to help visualize the income categories—from poorest (one coin) to richest (many coins). More than 30 percent of all Egyptians and Tunisians characterized themselves as being within the poorest income category in their country (the "self-reported poor"). In Jordan and Lebanon, this share hovered at 20 percent. Lebanon stands out as the only Middle Eastern and North African country out of the four where the self-reported poor were actually fewer than what the actual poverty rate indicated.

In addition, a sizable share of those in the middle class—and up to 20 percent of the upper middle class in both Egypt and Tunisia—reported themselves as being poor (the "subjective poor") in spite of not belonging to the bottom income quintile, as table 4.2 shows. In particular, in Egypt, a third of people in the second and third quintiles felt poor; in Lebanon and Jordan, a quarter of the second quintile felt poor; and in Tunisia, almost half of the people in the second quintile felt poor, as figure 4.2 shows.

The previously mentioned regression analysis also indicated that among the Jordanian middle class, those who defined themselves as nonpoor were significantly less likely to support redistribution policies than

TABLE 4.2

Do People Feel Poorer than They Are? Self-Reported Poverty and Subjective Poverty in the Middle East and North Africa, Selected Countries, 2012

percent

Country	Poverty rate	"Self-reported poor"	"Subjective poor"
Egypt, Arab Rep.	23.00	34.79	22.44
Jordan	14.40	21.23	8.88
Lebanon	28.50	20.98	10.54
Tunisia	11.00	33.62	19.66

Sources: Authors' calculations based on latest available household surveys, national estimates, and MENA SPEAKS survey 2012.

Note: "Self-reported poor" = individuals who say they feel poor from all wealth quintiles; "subjective poor" = individuals who say they feel poor excluding the bottom wealth quintile.

FIGURE 4.2

Who Feels Poor, by Income Quintile, in the Middle East and North Africa, Selected Countries, 2012

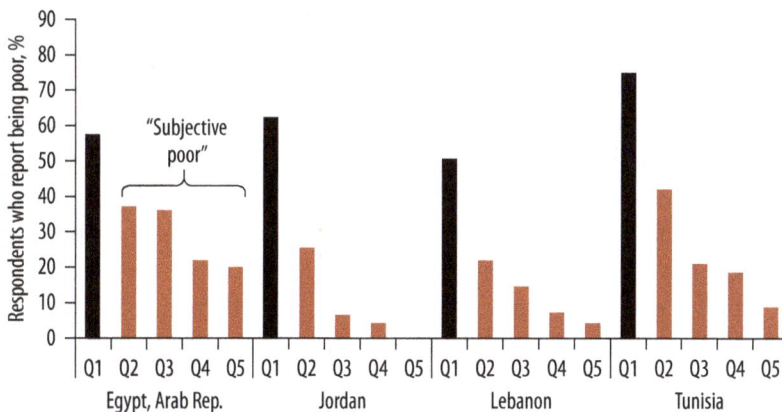

Source: Authors' calculations based on MENA SPEAKS Survey 2012.

Note: Income quintiles calculated based on Gallup income variable. Q = income quintile (1 = lowest, 5 = highest).

those who defined themselves as poor. In fact, part of the literature suggests that the subjective perception of poverty, and not just income poverty, may strongly affect the demand for redistribution. Although some authors believe that the inclination for redistribution programs reduces monotonically with income levels (Gelbach and Pritchett 2002; Meltzer and Richard 1981; Pritchett 2005; T. Romer 1975), other studies indicated that an individual's perception about own income relative to others is a better determinant of support for redistribution programs (Alesina and La Ferrara 2005). Based on a randomized experiment in Argentina,

Cruces, Truglia, and Tetaz (2011) found that individuals who overestimated their relative position in the income table (thinking themselves richer than they were), once they found out their actual standing, demanded more redistribution. Another study based on a U.S. survey suggested that awareness about greater poverty may increase demand for redistribution programs through altruism (Fong 2001).

Perceptions of Inequality and Social Mobility

The MENA SPEAKS surveys also reveal that between one-third and one-half of the citizens in the four countries, particularly those of lower income, perceive inequality to be extremely high. People were asked what portion of their country's total wealth they believed was held by the rich. The options were (a) almost all, (b) more than half, (c) half, or (d) less than half of the total wealth held by individuals. The share of individuals that selected "almost all" was 56 percent in Egypt, 38 percent in Lebanon, 36 percent in Tunisia, and 29 percent in Jordan. Although these answers show that inequality is perceived as extreme by only a subset of the population, it is noteworthy that the poor are more likely to believe that the rich own almost all of the wealth in each country.

The data also show that the "subjective poor" systematically perceive higher inequality than the average population does. In particular, the poorer one is, the more likely one is to feel that the rich own almost all the wealth. But the "subjective poor" stand out as having a stronger perception of inequality than any other income group (including the poorest quintile), as shown in figure 4.3.

Higher inequality does not systematically breed greater demand for redistribution. The demand depends on whether individuals believe that their society is upwardly mobile. Regression analysis from the MENA SPEAKS survey suggests that in Egypt, Jordan, and Tunisia, the perception of high inequality is lower among those whose living standard has been improving (see annex 4E). In fact, the literature suggests that individuals will be less inclined to support SSN programs if they are hopeful about upward mobility in the future. A study by Alesina and Giuliano (2009) suggested that if people are less optimistic about their future income, they will be more inclined to equalize everybody's income. Hirschman and Rothschild (1973) proposed an influential theory called the "tunnel effect," whereby the support for redistribution may not be high among the poor to the extent that people expect to become rich in the future. Ravallion and Lokshin (2000) found that, in the Russian Federation, not only was support for redistribution the lowest among those who had been on an increasing consumption path, even among the poor,

FIGURE 4.3

Perceived Inequality, by Income Quintile, in the Middle East and North Africa, Selected Countries, 2012

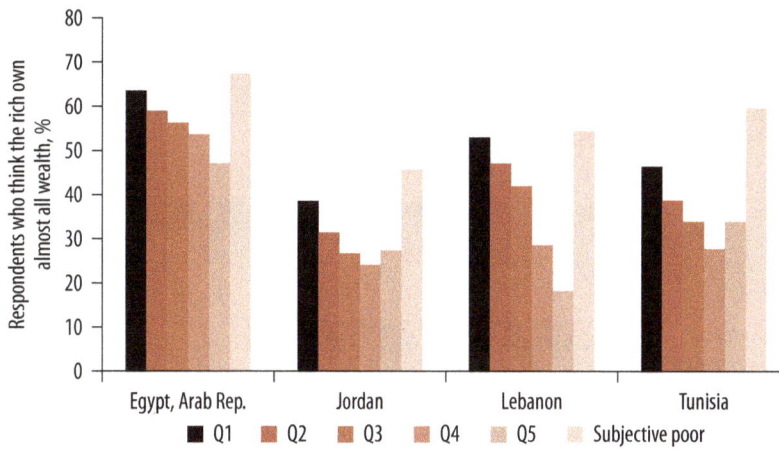

Source: Authors' calculations based on MENA SPEAKS Survey 2012.

Note: This graph depicts the percentage of MENA SPEAKS respondents who think the rich own almost all the wealth, as opposed to the percentage who think the rich hold more than half, about half, or less than half of the total wealth held by individuals. "Subjective poor" = individuals who perceive themselves as poor but whose income is not in the bottom quintile. Q = income quintile (1 = lowest, 5 = highest).

but also that rich individuals on a downward path expressed a greater demand for redistribution.

And data from Jordan Gives indicate that perceptions about upward mobility are skewed according to social classes. In Jordan, the upper-middle class is much more likely than those in the lower-middle class to believe that hard work is the cause of professional success, as opposed to luck and connections (see figure 4.4). As shown in chapter 3, the employment outcomes of the poor are lower than those of the rich, and these data suggest that the poor tend to be much more disgruntled about opportunities and more aware of the role of privilege in determining such outcomes.

Those who think their living standard is improving are less likely to think that (a) the rich own almost all of the total wealth in the country, and (b) the government has primary responsibility for helping the poor (see figure 4.5, panel a). In Egypt, Jordan, and Tunisia, they are also more likely to think the government is very or somewhat effective in providing SSNs to the poor (see figure 4.5, panel b). However, this group tends to be composed of nonpoor individuals (see figure 4.6).

FIGURE 4.4

Opinions on Causes of Success among the Jordanian Middle Class, by Subjective Income Level, 2012

What is in your opinion the main cause of professional success?

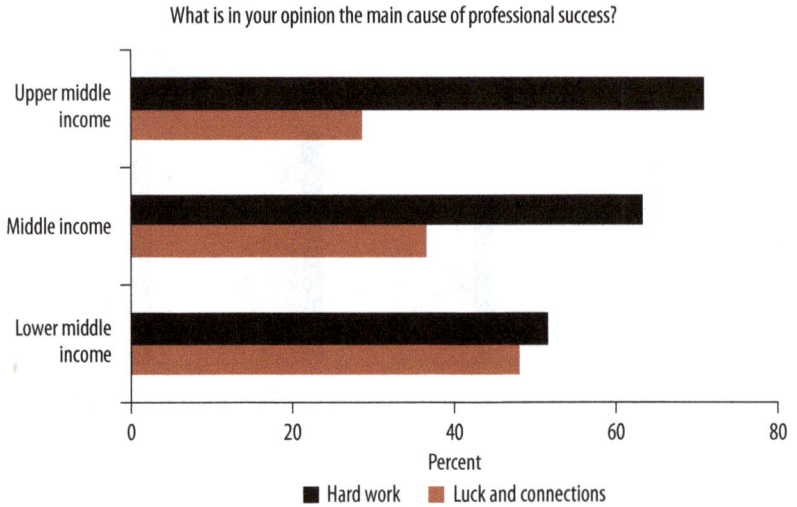

Source: Authors' calculations based on Jordan Gives 2012.
Note: Results based on data.

FIGURE 4.5

Support for Government SSN Provision, by Prospective Living Standard, Middle East and North Africa, Selected Countries, 2012

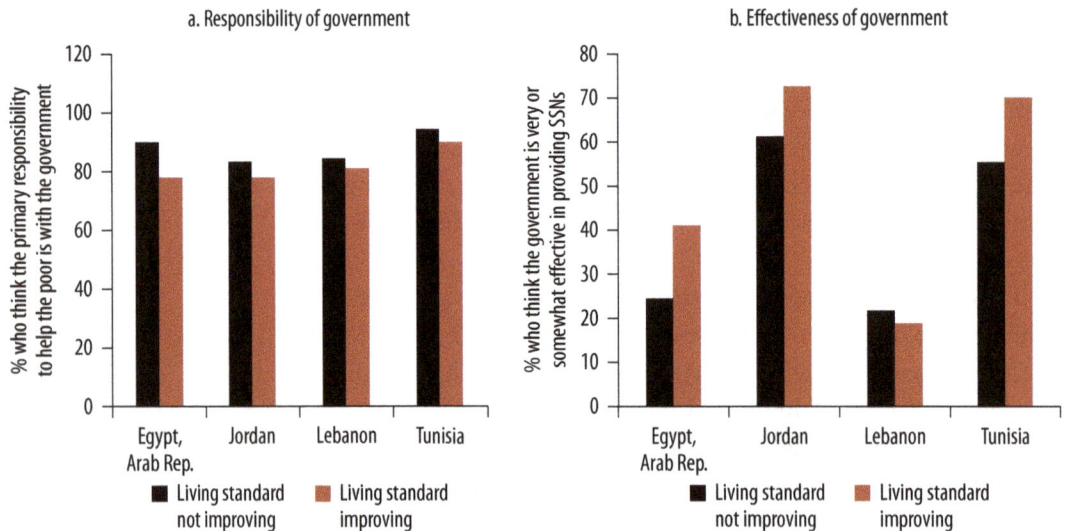

Source: Authors' calculations based on MENA SPEAKS Survey 2012.
Note: SSN = social safety net.

FIGURE 4.6

Perception of Improving Living Standards, by Wealth Quintile, in the Middle East and North Africa, Selected Countries, 2012

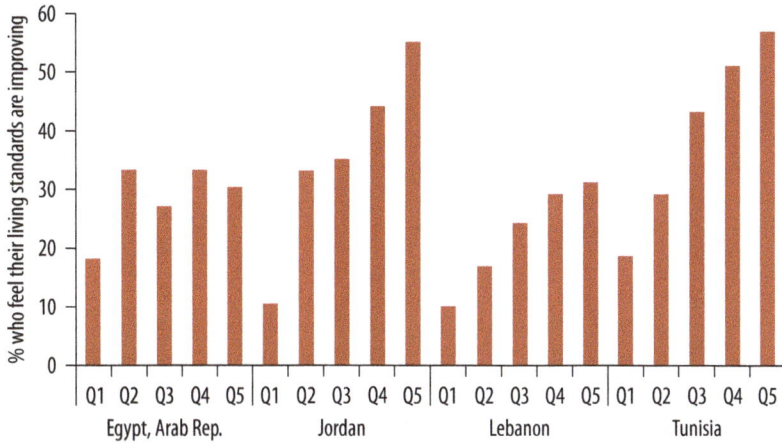

Source: Authors' calculations based on MENA SPEAKS Survey 2012.

Note: Q = wealth quintile (1 = lowest, 5 = highest).

Citizens' Regard for Existing SSN Systems

Satisfaction with Existing SSN Programs

Almost all citizens interviewed in the four countries saw government as the main actor responsible for addressing poverty. An equally large majority agreed with the statement that their government should provide SSNs to the poor, as figure 4.7 shows. Thus, on a general level, citizens' demand for SSNs—and the expectation that governments should intervene in providing them safety—appears to be high.

However, large percentages of the population, particularly in Egypt and Lebanon, do not find their governments to be effective in providing SSNs. Figure 4.8 shows that less than 30 percent of all Egyptians and Lebanese think that their governments provide SSNs effectively. Jordanians and Tunisians appear to be more satisfied, even though satisfaction in these countries is significantly higher among the upper classes than among the poor and vulnerable. Satisfaction with government effectiveness in providing SSNs is generally higher and more income-related in Jordan and Tunisia than in Egypt and Lebanon, where the low levels of satisfaction are fairly similar across income groups. The positive assessment of Jordan's SSNs by most citizens tends to be in line with findings in chapter 3 that SSNs perform relatively well in Jordan compared with the rest of the region.

FIGURE 4.7

Opinions about Responsibility for SSNs in the Middle East and North Africa, Selected Countries, 2012

a. Who should be most responsible for the poor in your country?

b. Should the government provide social assistance to the poor?

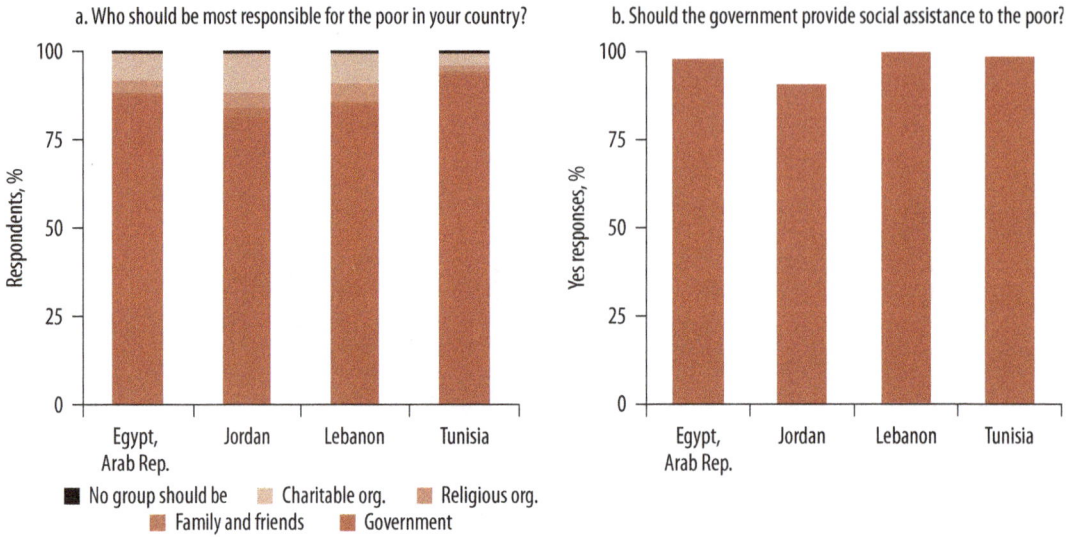

■ No group should be   ▨ Charitable org.   ■ Religious org.
▨ Family and friends   ■ Government

Source: Authors' calculations based on MENA SPEAKS Survey 2012.
Note: SSN = social safety net.

FIGURE 4.8

Opinions of SSN Effectiveness in the Middle East and North Africa, Selected Countries, 2012

How effective is social assistance in your country?

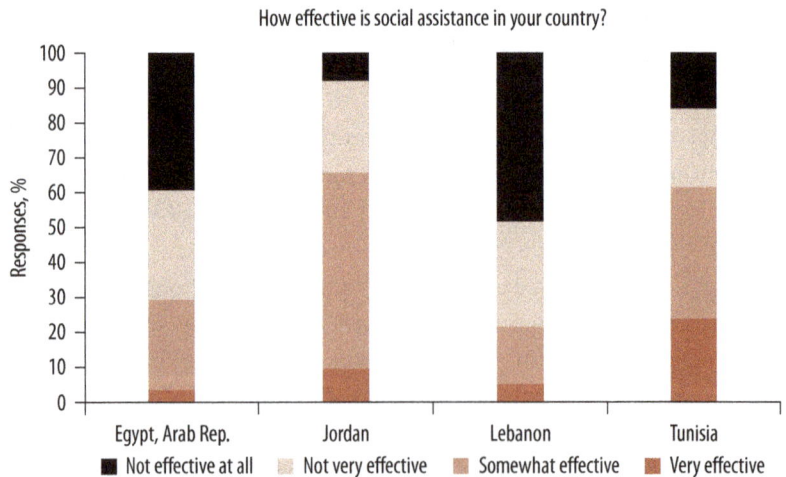

■ Not effective at all   ▨ Not very effective   ■ Somewhat effective   ■ Very effective

Source: Authors' calculations based on MENA SPEAKS Survey 2012.
Note: SSN = social safety net.

Both the economic poor and the subjective poor—those who felt likely to need safety nets in the future—were much more critical of the existing system than other people. Dissatisfaction was highest among the subjective poor in Egypt, Jordan, and Lebanon, possibly because they felt more in need but were less eligible for assistance (see figure 4.9). Another evidence of the link between vulnerability and perceptions of the effectiveness of SSNs comes from the regression (see annex 4F). In Egypt, Jordan, and Lebanon, individuals who perceived the economy to be deteriorating tended to see SSNs as less effective. Similarly, in Egypt and Jordan, those who found inequality to be higher were more dissatisfied with the effectiveness of SSNs.

Across all countries, citizens' perceptions of government corruption also strongly predict their assessment of SSN effectiveness, according to regression analysis on the MENA SPEAKS survey (annex 4F), controlling for actual income levels and other demographic characteristics. A media study on SSNs in Brazil has shown that corruption cases can immediately taint the popularity of programs (Lindert and Vicensini 2010).

However, the Jordan Gives experiment provides evidence that enhancing transparency of delivery can increase support for redistribution among citizens who have low trust in the existing system. The experiment allowed, through random selection of participants into control and treat-

FIGURE 4.9

Perceptions of Government Effectiveness in Providing SSNs, by Income Quintile, in the Middle East and North Africa, Selected Countries, 2012

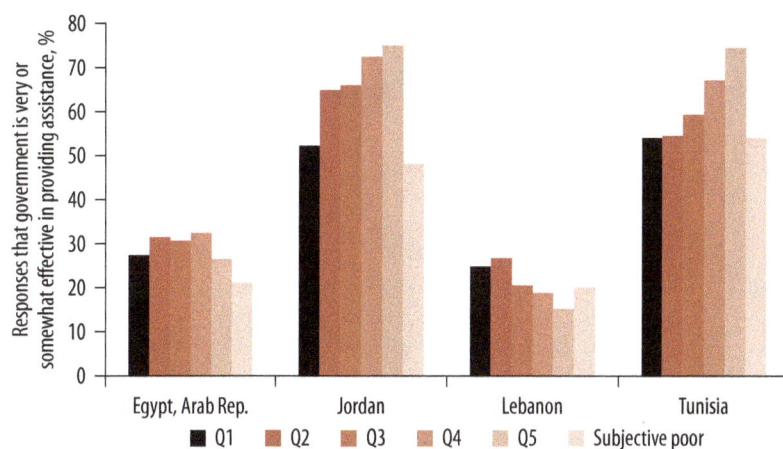

Source: Authors' calculations based on MENA SPEAKS Survey 2012.

Note: SSN = social safety net; "Subjective poor" = individuals who say they feel poor but whose income is not in the bottom quintile; Q = income quintile (1 = lowest, 5 = highest).

ment groups, evaluation of the impact of several design features meant to enhance participants' confidence that their donations would reach only poor people. Responses to the survey questions conducted as part of Jordan Gives indicate that nearly 50% of the middle class have little confidence in the way beneficiaries are selected for social assistance programs in their country (figure 4.10a). Qualitative evidence from focus group discussions supports this finding and highlights that many participants believe connections and favoritism play an important role in the assignment of benefits. Because targeting in Jordan tends to be more accurate than in most other countries in the region (as discussed in chapter 3), it is likely that confidence in the targeting of SSNs in the other countries is even lower.

The Jordan Gives experiment showed that those with low trust in the accuracy of the existing targeting of Jordanian SSNs also displayed an overall lower tendency to donate their fuel vouchers, which was particularly evident in the three cash-based SSN designs. However, this tendency was countered in treatment groups by the transparency-enhancing feature, which allowed participants to verify in person the delivery of the benefit at the end of the experiment (figure 4.10b).

The evidence from this experiment suggests that there is scope for governments to improve individuals' support for SSNs, even from low levels of confidence, through transparency enhancement measures. In Brazil, for instance, the list of beneficiaries of the cash transfer program *Bolsa Familia* is published online. Some programs in Sub-Saharan Africa

FIGURE 4.10

Jordan Gives Experiment Results Regarding Trust in SSN Institutions

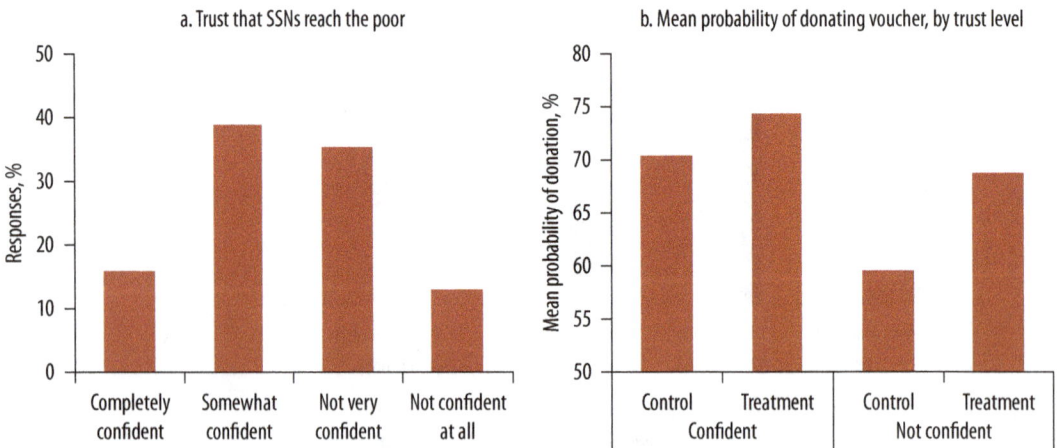

a. Trust that SSNs reach the poor

b. Mean probability of donating voucher, by trust level

Source: Authors' calculations based on Jordan Gives 2012.

Note: Results based on data. SSN = social safety net.

adopt community-level vetting of social assistance program beneficiary lists (for instance, the cash transfer program in Rwanda). Another way to improve oversight is to publish financial flows for social assistance programs up to the local level. When designing these measures, it is important to be mindful of the social and power structures in place and the degree of accountability of civil society groups at the local level, as well as social norms about confidentiality and the eventual stigma attached to receiving social assistance.

SSN Programs' Recognition and Outreach

Awareness of SSN Programs

Some countries are much better than others at raising awareness of the SSN programs available in their countries. The MENA SPEAKS survey included two questions evaluating respondents' awareness of SSNs.[2] Figure 4.11 shows that awareness (defined as either mentioning the program or acknowledging its existence when prompted) differed dramatically by country. In Lebanon, a quarter of the respondents knew about three out of five programs on the list of major programs in the country; in Jordan, respondents knew about three to four out of six programs. Tunisians had the highest awareness of SSN programs, with about 30 percent of respondents having heard about five out of six programs. Egyptians had the lowest awareness, with 23 percent of respondents having never heard about a single SSN program, even after being prompted with program names; 30 percent acknowledged only one such program (see annex 4C).

By definition, SSN programs deliver income support or goods and services to the poor and vulnerable. However, it appears that in the Middle East and North Africa, knowledge about the existence of these programs is skewed toward wealthier groups. Figure 4.12 shows that awareness in all four countries rises with income. In Egypt, the richest quintile knew about twice as many SSN programs as the poorest quintile. This implies that awareness-raising campaigns are not reaching their target audiences, undermining the government's efforts to improve coverage and reduce poverty.

Knowledge of SSN Program Beneficiaries

The MENA SPEAKS survey may provide indirect information about the targeting of programs, even if the results should be treated with caution. Data regarding personal knowledge of someone who is an SSN beneficiary could be a proxy for the accuracy of targeting in some major programs. When people displayed awareness of a particular SSN program, MENA SPEAKS asked them if they personally knew someone who had received assistance from this program.

FIGURE 4.11

Awareness of SSN Programs in the Middle East and North Africa, Selected Countries, 2012

percentage of population

a. Egypt, Arab Rep.: Number of programs known by the population

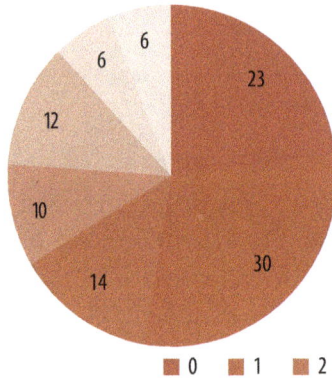

b. Jordan: Number of programs known by the population

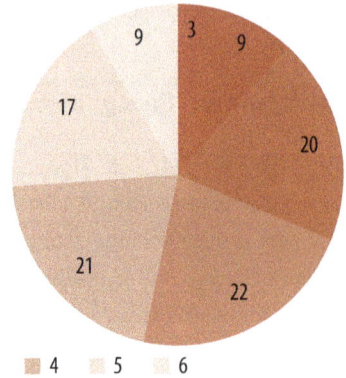

c. Lebanon: Number of programs known by the population

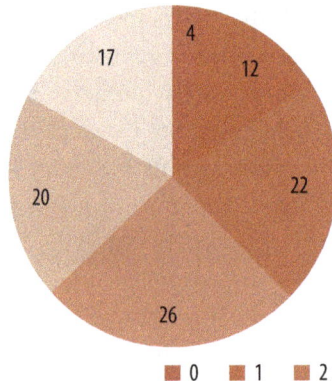

d. Tunisia: Number of programs known by the population

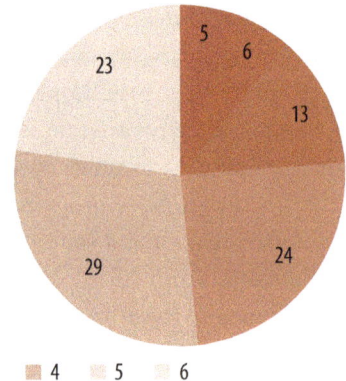

Source: Authors' calculations based on MENA SPEAKS Survey 2012.
Note: SSN = social safety net.

Plotted against income quintiles, this information is revealing and can potentially provide insights into programs' targeting accuracy. However, interpretation of the results has to be predicated on two assumptions about social networks in the Middle East and North Africa: (a) that the density of social networks is fairly similar across income quintiles, and (b) that the probability of knowing someone outside one's own income group can be somehow estimated. In reality, the poor tend to have sparser social networks (so one would expect the rich to simply know more people, including more poor people, than the poor would know). In addition,

FIGURE 4.12

Awareness of SSNs, by Income Quintile, in the Middle East and North Africa, Selected Countries, 2012

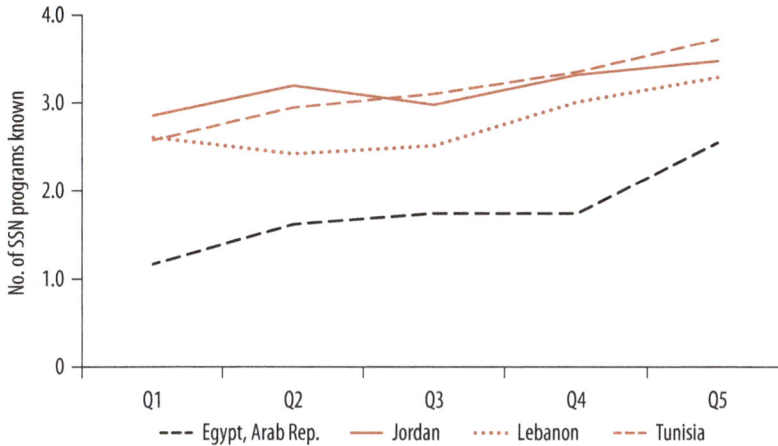

Source: Authors' calculations based on MENA SPEAKS Survey 2012.
Note: SSN = social safety net; Q = income quintile (1 = lowest, 5 = highest).

the rich tend to know many more poor people by being their potential employers; the poor, on the other hand, do not generally have a comparable way of becoming known to the rich.

Figure 4.13 shows that people in Jordan and Lebanon are more likely than people in Egypt and Tunisia to know someone who receives assistance from SSNs. In part, this finding could be driven by the larger area and population size of the latter countries; holding nationwide coverage of a program constant, a person in a small country such as Lebanon is more likely to know someone who is participating than a person in a large country such as Egypt.

The most striking result from the figure, however, comes from the within-country comparisons:

- In Jordan, the average number of SSN programs for which a respondent knew an assistance beneficiary was 1.4 for those in the bottom quintile and less than 1.1 for the top quintile. With the caveats mentioned above, this is in line with the observation that SSNs in Jordan are targeted to the poor and vulnerable.

- In Tunisia, on the other hand, the pattern is surprising: in the bottom quintile, the average number of programs for which respondents knew a beneficiary was very low, at 0.3. Although most of those in the wealthiest quintile didn't know even one person participating in an SSN program, their probability of knowing an SSN beneficiary was

FIGURE 4.13

Average Number of SSN Programs of Which Respondents Know a Beneficiary, by Income Quintile, in the Middle East and North Africa, Selected Countries, 2012

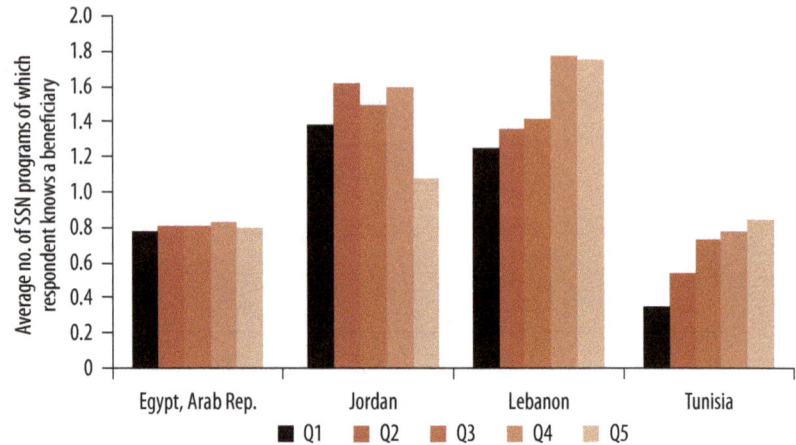

Source: Authors' calculations based on MENA SPEAKS Survey 2012.
Note: SSN = social safety net. Q = income quintile (1 = lowest, 5 = highest).

2.4 times that of people in the bottom quintile. Indeed, the probability of knowing someone who received SSN assistance rose fairly steeply between the bottom and the middle-income quintiles.

- In Lebanon, those in the top two quintiles knew an SSN beneficiary of, on average, 1.8 SSN programs, while the corresponding figure for the bottom quintile was only 1.2.

- In Egypt, the probability of knowing someone in an SSN program appeared to be relatively uncorrelated with income.

Therefore, under this indirect measure of targeting, SSNs in Tunisia and, to a lesser extent, in Lebanon appear to have high rates of leakage.

Coverage and Targeting of SSN Programs

Around 60 percent of the bottom quintile in the respective countries know someone who participates in Egypt's Sadat Pension, Jordan's National Aid Fund and school nutrition program, and Lebanon's hospital fee waivers, as figure 4.14 illustrates. This finding implies that these programs probably have the best in-country reach to the bottom quintile.

In terms of targeting accuracy, most programs in Jordan had the expected downward slope, which conforms well to the SSN performance assessment based on the household survey analysis in chapter 3. There-

FIGURE 4.14

Knowledge of Specific SSN Program Beneficiaries, by Income Quintile, in the Middle East and North Africa, Selected Countries, 2012

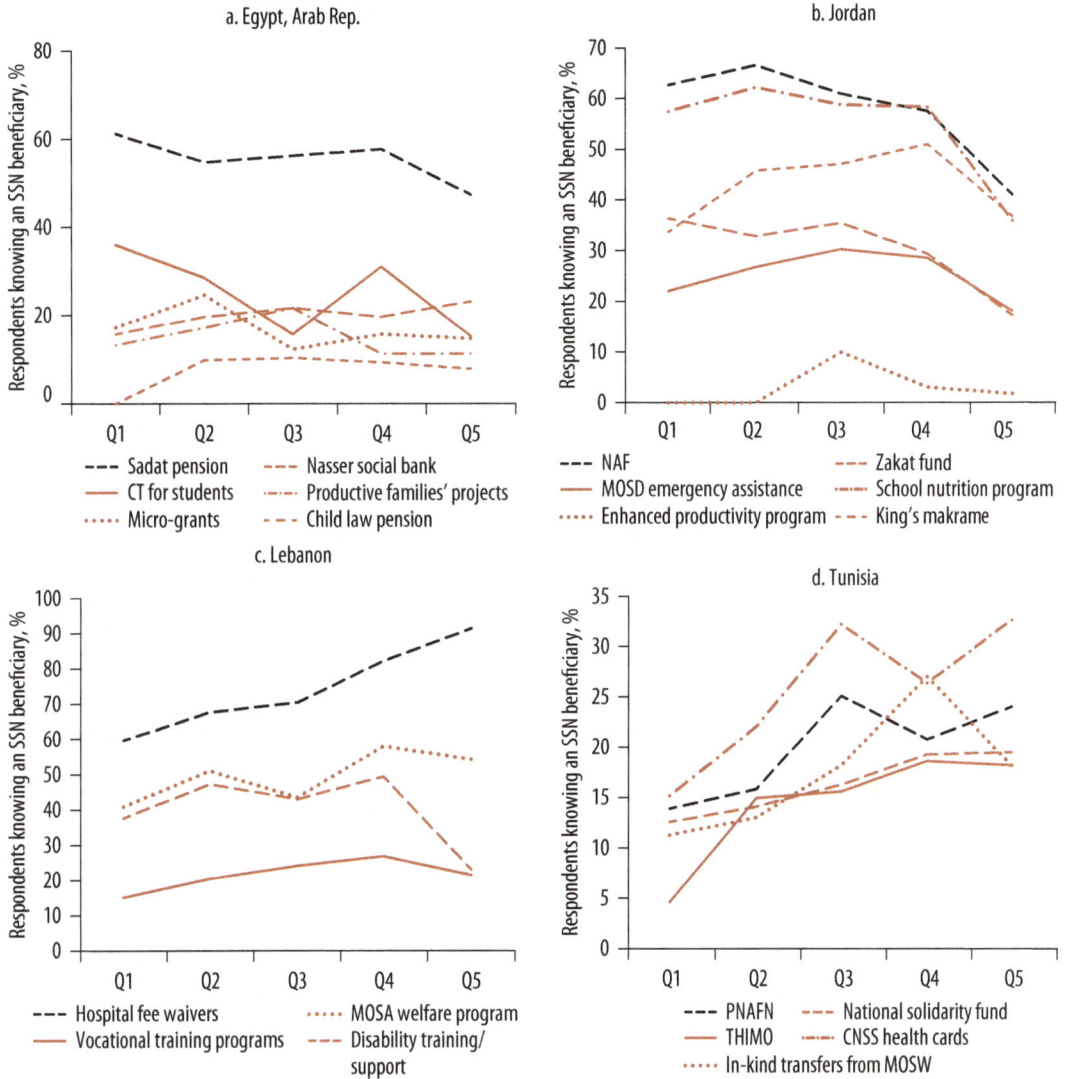

a. Egypt, Arab Rep.

Legend (a. Egypt):
- Sadat pension
- CT for students
- Micro-grants
- Nasser social bank
- Productive families' projects
- Child law pension

b. Jordan

Legend (b. Jordan):
- NAF
- MOSD emergency assistance
- Enhanced productivity program
- Zakat fund
- School nutrition program
- King's makrame

c. Lebanon

Legend (c. Lebanon):
- Hospital fee waivers
- Vocational training programs
- MOSA welfare program
- Disability training/support

d. Tunisia

Legend (d. Tunisia):
- PNAFN
- THIMO
- In-kind transfers from MOSW
- National solidarity fund
- CNSS health cards

Source: Authors' calculations based on MENA SPEAKS Survey 2012.

Note: CNSS = Caisse Nationale de Sécurité Sociale; CT = cash transfer; MOSA = Ministry of Social Affairs; MOSD = Ministry of Social Development; MOSW = Ministry of Social Welfare; NAF = National Aid Fund; PNAFN = Program of Assistance for Needy Families (*Programme National d'Aide aux Familles Nécessiteuses*); Q = income quintile (1 = lowest, 5 = highest); SSN = social safety net; THIMO = Public Works (*Travaux à Haute Intensite de Main d'œuvre*).

fore, among the specific SSN programs, Jordan's NAF and school nutrition programs appear to perform well on the implicit measures of both coverage and targeting of the poorest quintile.

In Egypt, the Sadat Pension seemed to be the best-targeted program (and was mildly progressive), followed by micro-grants; for other programs, the propensity to know someone receiving assistance fluctuated across quintiles (for example, regarding cash transfers for students and Productive Families' projects) or was mildly regressive (as in assistance from the Nasser Social Bank and Child Law Pension).

For all but one SSN program in Lebanon and for all SSN programs in Tunisia, those in the wealthiest quintile were more likely to know someone receiving assistance than those in the poorest quintile. For example, more than 90 percent of respondents from the richest quintile knew someone who used hospital fee waivers, while only 60 percent of respondents from the poorest quintile could say the same. In Tunisia, most SSN participants had friends or family in the middle or top quintile; for virtually all programs, respondents in the bottom quintile were about 10–15 percent more likely to know an SSN program participant; for the middle quintile, that figure was 25 and 32 percent for the Program of Assistance to Needy Families (*Programme National d'Aide aux Familles Nécessiteuses*; PNAFN) and *Caisse Nationale de Sécurité Sociale* (CNSS) health cards, respectively.

A diverse literature discusses whether public support for redistribution can best be obtained through loose or universal targeting, rather than through a narrow targeting of the most needy. Some researchers argue that targets are difficult to identify and that targeting is administratively difficult; for this reason, they predicate that loose targeting would be best for public support or even that a program should have both a universal and a targeted component for it to be politically sustainable (Gelbach and Pritchett 2002; Pritchett 2005; Sen 1995).

However, earlier sections have shown that the nonpoor may also be ready to support redistribution—for instance, when they find inequality to be excessive—without expecting a direct individual gain. In other words, considerations beyond self-interest may influence public opinion in support of narrow targeting. One of them is the concern that public funds be used efficiently. For instance, De Janvry et al. (2005) showed that the expansion of Brazil's *Bolsa Escola* program among the poor at the municipal level predicted positively mayors' reelection, while high leakage to the nonpoor had the opposite effects. Therefore, the accuracy and level of targeting of existing programs matter not only for program effectiveness but also for programs' political support.

SSN Design Features that Rally Support

MENA SPEAKS collected data on respondents' preferences related to design features of a hypothetical nonsubsidy SSN program. Specifically, the survey asked respondents (a) whether, in their opinion, this SSN program should support the poor or support specific groups of people; (b) whether the assistance should be provided in cash or in-kind; and (c) whether any conditions should be attached to continued support (and, if so, the preferences on specific conditions). Policy makers can use this wealth of information to gauge potential public support when designing new SSN programs or when reforming existing ones.

Categorical Targeting versus Targeting the Poor

When asked whether they thought SSNs should focus mainly on serving the poor or specific groups of people (such as widows, orphans, the sick, and the elderly—whether or not members of those groups are poor), respondents in all four Middle Eastern and North African countries unequivocally supported targeting the poor, as shown in figure 4.15. The share of people who preferred categorical targeting ranged between 8 percent in Egypt and 16 percent in Lebanon.

People who felt poor (based on the MENA SPEAKS subjective income question) were more likely to prefer SSNs targeted to the poor. In Egypt, for example, 96 percent of those who felt poor wanted SSNs to target the poor, as opposed to 87 percent of those who put themselves in the top two income categories. Interestingly, subjective income predicts preference on this question better than the more objective income quintiles: for example, although preference for targeting decreased monotonically with subjective income groups in Egypt, Jordan, and Lebanon, when plotted against objective income quintiles, the lowest preference for targeting SSNs to the poor was in the middle quintiles for these countries.

Cash versus In-Kind Benefits

Based on the MENA SPEAKS survey, most people prefer SSN programs to provide cash rather than goods (in-kind transfers). More than two-thirds of respondents in each of the four countries under study expressed a preference for cash-based SSNs (from 68 percent in Lebanon to 85 percent in Jordan), as shown in figure 4.16, panel a. The relatively low preference for cash in Lebanon can probably be explained by its politicization, given that many political parties use cash to garner electoral support. In Egypt and Lebanon, the poor had a much stronger preference for cash-based SSNs than the self-identified upper-middle and wealthy groups; this can perhaps be attributed to a paternalistic view of the poor as being unable to spend cash wisely. Interestingly, in Jordan, those who categorized themselves as lower middle class had the highest preference for cash in SSNs, providing a potential support group for the government if it were to reform price subsidies or cash out its in-kind Food Security Program.

FIGURE 4.15

SSN Targeting Preferences in the Middle East and North Africa, Selected Countries, 2012

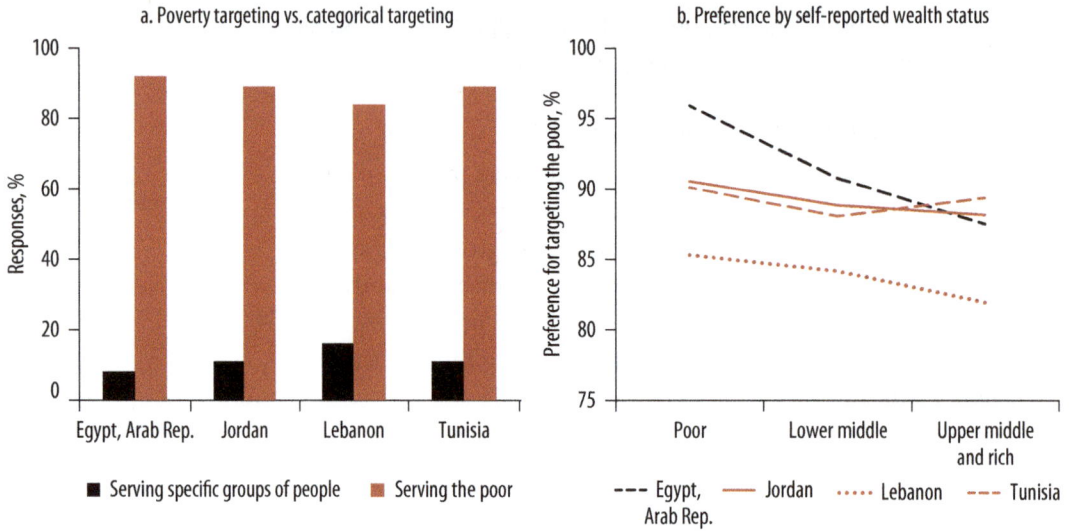

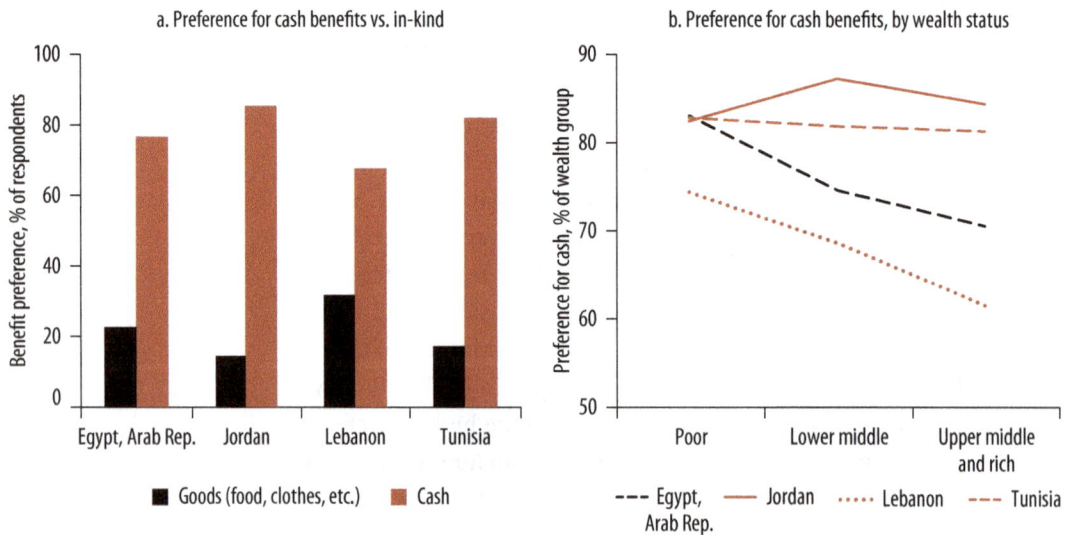

a. Poverty targeting vs. categorical targeting

b. Preference by self-reported wealth status

■ Serving specific groups of people   ■ Serving the poor

–––– Egypt,   —— Jordan   ········ Lebanon   – – – Tunisia
Arab Rep.

Source: Authors' calculations based on MENA SPEAKS Survey 2012.
Note: SSN = social safety net.

FIGURE 4.16

SSN Design Preferences in the Middle East and North Africa, Selected Countries, 2012

a. Preference for cash benefits vs. in-kind

b. Preference for cash benefits, by wealth status

■ Goods (food, clothes, etc.)   ■ Cash

–––– Egypt,   —— Jordan   ········ Lebanon   – – – Tunisia
Arab Rep.

Source: Authors' calculations based on MENA SPEAKS Survey 2012.
Note: SSN = social safety net.

Conditional versus Unconditional Benefits

The MENA SPEAKS survey tested respondents' preferences for conditioning SSN transfers on recipient behavior, as is done in some highly successful SSN programs in Latin America, such as Mexico's *Oportunidades* program and Brazil's *Bolsa Familia*. The survey respondents were told that "in some countries, recipients of government SSNs are required to do something in exchange for monthly assistance. For example, they could be required to have their children attend school regularly. If their children stop attending school, the assistance would no longer be provided." Respondents were then asked if they thought recipients of SSN programs should be required to do something in exchange for the assistance or whether there should be no requirements.

Unlike Latin America and the Caribbean, where conditionality of cash transfers increased support for SSNs, most respondents in the Middle East and North Africa were not ready to impose requirements on safety net recipients, as shown in figure 4.17, panel a. About two-thirds of respondents in Egypt and Lebanon and three-fourths of respondents in Jordan and Tunisia rejected the idea of conditioning SSN transfers. Interestingly, in Egypt, the self-identified poor were much more open to the idea of conditionality (with 45 percent supporting it) than the middle class and the wealthy (about 30 percent). In Lebanon and Tunisia, the middle class and the wealthy were more supportive of conditionality,

FIGURE 4.17

Preferences for Conditionality of SSN Programs in the Middle East and North Africa, Selected Countries, 2012

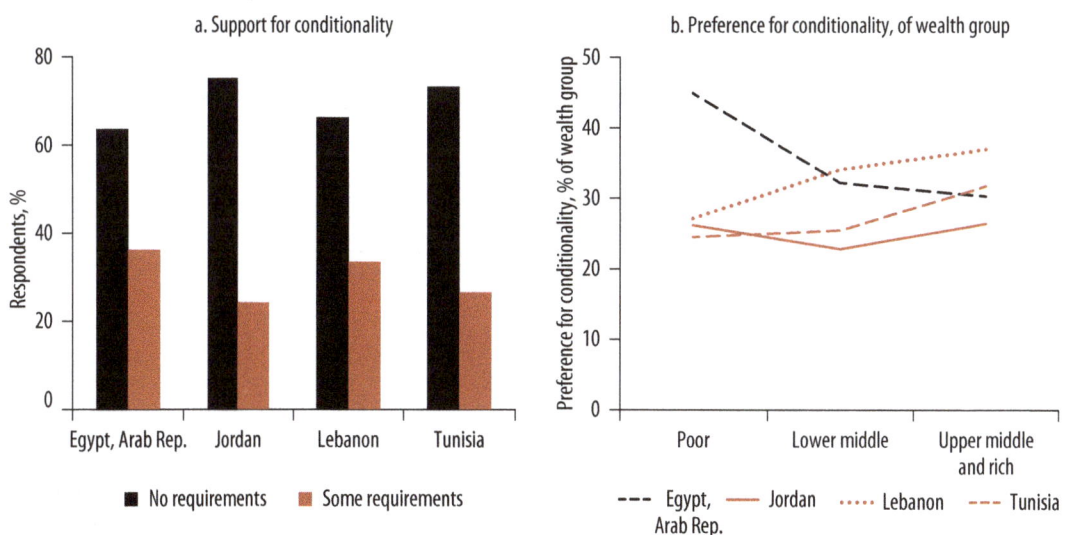

Source: Authors' calculations based on MENA SPEAKS Survey 2012.

Note: SSN = social safety net.

while in Jordan, the preference was relatively flat across self-identified income groups.

There are several possible interpretations for the apparent limited support for conditionality. Although in Latin America conditionality became a key factor to secure the buy-in of middle classes toward redistributive programs, it is possible that citizens do not find it fair to condition aid on recipients' behavior, given the historical legacy of universal targeting of many public transfers through subsidies. It is also possible that Middle Eastern and North African citizens do not want beneficiaries to depend on public services to receive aid because they are aware that many of the poor have little access to them (as shown in chapter 2), or even that they do not consider it right to reward individuals to comply with what should otherwise be considered a duty (such as sending children to school). Regardless of the reason, this finding calls for further qualitative research to understand the main motives for these preferences. If conditionality is to be introduced in a program, a well-designed communication campaign to explain the rationale and benefits is warranted.

Respondents who thought that there should be some conditionality for SSN assistance were asked follow-up questions related to specific conditions used around the world in conditional cash transfer programs. The most popular conditions in the Middle East and North Africa were related to recipients (a) ensuring that children attend school regularly and (b) actively searching for work, as shown in figure 4.18. The lowest ac-

FIGURE 4.18

Types of SSN Conditions Preferred in the Middle East and North Africa, Selected Countries, 2012

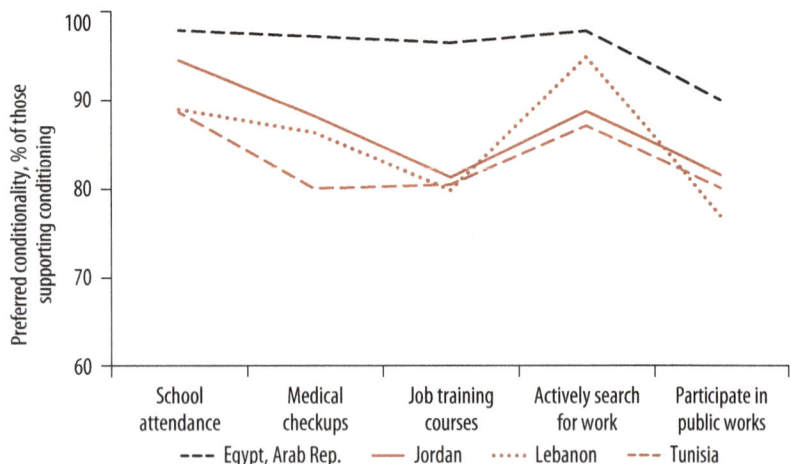

Source: Authors' calculations based on MENA SPEAKS Survey 2012.

Note: SSN = social safety net.

ceptance rates were for attendance at job training courses and for accepting work provided by the program in exchange for the assistance (that is, participating in a public works program). The reluctance to condition SSN transfers implies that if a government were to establish such a program, an effective information and communication strategy would be essential to convince the public of the benefits of the program and its proven effectiveness in other regions.

The Jordan Gives behavioral experiment provides empirical evidence on some of the characteristics that drove preferences for particular methods of redistribution. Participants in the experiment were offered the possibility to give up a gasoline voucher in exchange for helping the poor under different scenarios (see box 4.1 and annex 4B for details). In each scenario, participants could choose to give up their vouchers in exchange for one of the following methods of assistance:

- Unconditional in-kind transfer to poor families, in the form of food

- Unconditional cash transfer to poor families

- Unconditional cash transfer that would go half to a local school, half to poor families

- Cash transfer to poor families who complete a training course increasing their employability.

In addition, the experiment enabled the evaluation, through a randomized controlled trial, of the impact of introducing additional information meant to enhance the participants' confidence that the transfers would reach the intended target (see figure 4.19). Overall, individuals in the treatment group tended to donate more than those in the control group (though this difference is not statistically significant). The treatment, however, significantly increased donation rates among two large groups of participants: young people, and those who had low trust in the accuracy of the existing targeting of national SSN programs.

An important consequence of enhancing transparency was that while in the control group the SSN design that achieved the highest rate of fuel voucher donations was unconditional in-kind transfer, in the treatment group the most popular decision was unconditional cash transfers, which may be perceived as more prone to elite capture in spite of being more beneficial for the welfare of the poor.

The econometric analysis of participants' behavior (see table 4.3) highlights some individual characteristics that predict the decisions to donate in different forms:

- Overall, individuals who defined themselves as belonging to the lower-middle-income group showed a higher propensity to donate their fuel

FIGURE 4.19

Propensity to Donate Vouchers by SSN Design and Treatment Group in Jordan, 2012

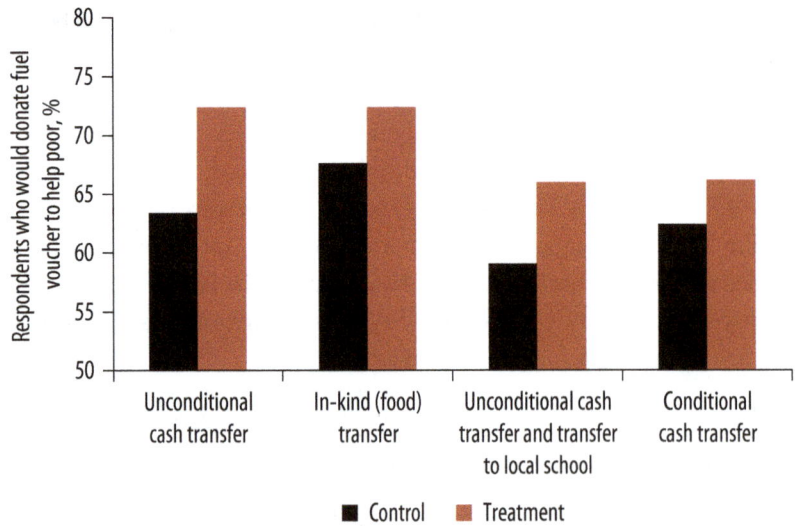

Source: Authors' calculations based on Jordan Gives 2012.

Note: SSN = social safety net. Results based on data.

TABLE 4.3

Jordan Gives Experiment: Significant Correlates of Decision to Donate Voucher under Different Social Assistance Scenarios

Participant characteristics	Cash	Food basket	Cash + school donation	Cash conditional on training
Adults (base = youth)	0.357***	—	0.375***	0.325**
Elder (base = youth)	—	—	0.671*	—
Subjective income: medium (base = low)	0.292**	0.509***	0.475**	—
Subjective income: high (base = low)	—	—	—	—
Perceived ineffectiveness of existing social assistance programs	0.210**	0.229**	—	—
Low confidence that public SSNs reach intended beneficiaries	−0.181**	—	−0.173*	—
Success comes from hard work	0.335***	0.413***	0.305**	0.253**
Poverty caused by laziness (base = "social injustice or bad luck")	—	—	−0.287**	—

Source: Authors' calculations based on Jordan Gives 2012.

Note: SSN = social safety net. — = not significant. Preliminary Results. Include controls for education, gender, employment status, number of cars in the household, and participation in treatment group. Results represent marginal effects of probit regressions significant at * = 10%, ** = 5%, and *** = 1% levels—that is, the added probability of donating for a given option, compared with being in the baseline situation.

vouchers than those who defined themselves as being in the poor or upper-income groups. Although it is understandable that lower-income people may value the voucher relatively more, this finding is more surprising for upper-income individuals who may actually be less inclined to donate. Only cash donations conditional on training found similar acceptance across groups.

- Finally, individual opinions about the social order mattered: those who believed that poverty is caused by laziness rather than an unjust society or bad luck chose less often to donate to the school, while, surprisingly, those who thought that career success comes from hard work (as opposed to luck and connections) were more likely to donate to the poor in all options.

Subsidy Reforms: Acceptance and Options

Public Awareness of Subsidies

The MENA SPEAKS survey collected information on public awareness of subsidies like it did for awareness of nonsubsidy SSN programs.[3] The extent of general awareness of governments' efforts to subsidize product prices varies by country and by the type of product being subsidized, as shown in figure 4.20. Egyptians and Tunisians were more likely to know about price subsidies in their countries than were Jordanians and Lebanese. Two goods subsidized in all four countries are diesel fuel and bread or flour. The recognition of the diesel subsidy ranged from 25 percent in Jordan to 47 percent in Tunisia. The awareness of the bread subsidy ranged from 47 percent in Lebanon to 87 percent in Egypt.

Notably, public awareness of food subsidies was much higher than awareness of fuel subsidies. In Egypt, for example, the awareness of fuel subsidies for liquefied petroleum gas (LPG), diesel, and gasoline was around 40 percent, while more than 80 percent of Egyptians recognize that their cooking oil, sugar, and *baladi* bread are sold at subsidized prices. This is an important finding since chapter 3 showed that Egypt spends much more on fuel subsidies (6.9 percent of gross domestic product [GDP] in 2009) than on food subsidies (1.8 percent of GDP). Similar differences in awareness of food and fuel subsidies exist in the other three countries under study. The results in figure 4.20 suggest that the political economy of fuel subsidy reform should be relatively easier than food subsidy reform, given the higher recognition of the latter.

Knowledge about subsidies improves with income, especially for fuel subsidies. The gradient for awareness of fuel subsidies is typically much steeper than for food subsidies (see figure 4.21). In Egypt, the awareness of sugar, cooking oil, and *baladi* bread subsidies is fairly stable across quintiles, while the recognition of gasoline, diesel, and LPG subsidies rises by 15–20 percentage points between the third and fourth quintiles. In Tuni-

FIGURE 4.20

Awareness of Specific Subsidies in the Middle East and North Africa, Selected Countries, 2012

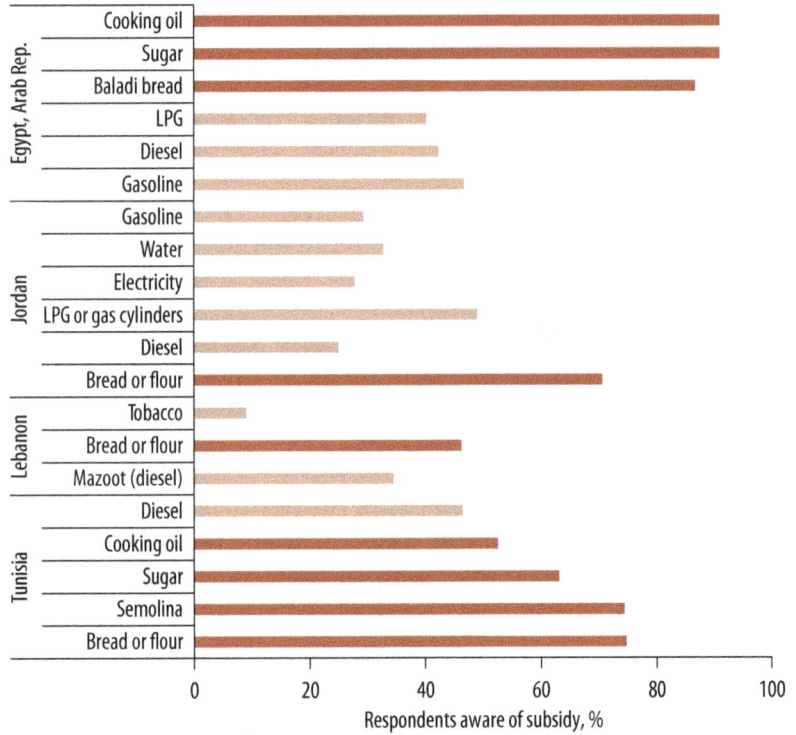

Source: Authors' calculations based on MENA SPEAKS Survey 2012.

Note: LPG = liquefied petroleum gas.

sia, the awareness of food subsidies by the richest quintile is 1.3 times that of the poorest quintile when it comes to bread and semolina subsidies, while the corresponding ratio for diesel is 2.6. If the wealthy are much more likely to know about some subsidies than the poor, this could imply that they are much more likely to benefit from them, a hypothesis supported by the information presented in chapter 3 on the regressiveness of fuel subsidies.

Public Acceptance of Subsidy Reform

Acceptance of subsidy reform is very country-specific: people in Lebanon and Tunisia appear more tolerant of debate on this topic than people in Egypt and Jordan. MENA SPEAKS asked respondents in all four countries the following two questions: "If the government could not afford to subsidize all of the following products, which product's price would you

FIGURE 4.21

Knowledge of Subsidies, by Income Quintile, in the Middle East and North Africa, Selected Countries, 2012

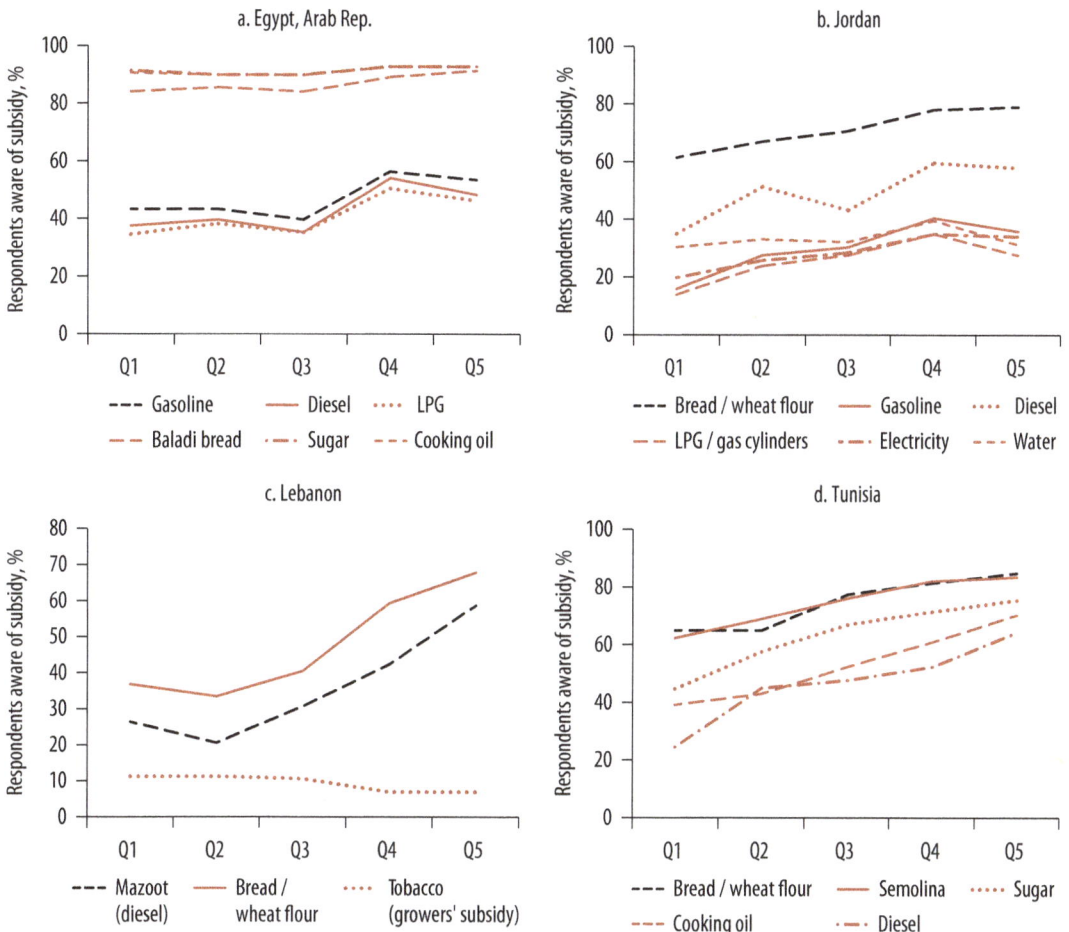

Source: Authors' calculations based on MENA SPEAKS Survey 2012.
Note: LPG = liquefied petroleum gas; Q = income quintile (1 = lowest, 5 = highest).

want the government to stop subsidizing?" And what would be your second choice?" The general acceptance of subsidy reform varied by country: 59 percent of Egyptians, 56 percent of Jordanians, 11 percent of Lebanese, and 37 percent of Tunisians refused to accept subsidy reform of any one product on the list, implying strong aversion to this reform, as shown in figure 4.22.

One important finding is that, in all countries, the lower-middle-income group is slightly less likely to be opposed to subsidy reform than the upper-middle and wealthy group. And in all countries except Lebanon, the lower-middle-income group is more willing to consider subsidy

FIGURE 4.22

Opposition to Subsidy Reform on Any Product, by Self-Reported Income Group, in the Middle East and North Africa, Selected Countries, 2012

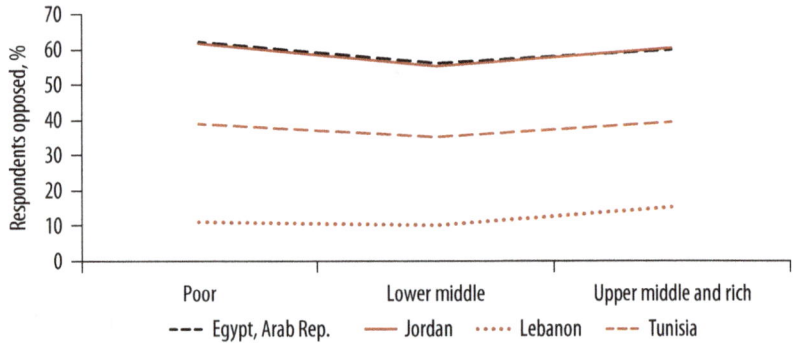

Source: Authors' calculations based on MENA SPEAKS Survey 2012.

reform than the self-reported poor. One hypothesis explaining this could be that those of lower middle income do not depend on subsidies as much as the poor, but they also do not consume most of the subsidy benefits, as do those of upper-middle income and the rich. Governments can use this information in building a pro-reform coalition when discussing the reform agenda with the public.

Figure 4.23 illustrates the relative tolerance of subsidy reform for specific products. This response, of course, was only available for people who were willing to consider subsidy reform of at least one product. It also combines the first- and the second-choice answers.

This comparison reveals that, in the Middle East and North Africa, people are much more tolerant of fuel subsidy reform than of food subsidy reform, as follows:

- In Egypt, out of those willing to consider subsidy reform, only 6–17 percent of respondents named a food subsidy as their first or second choice to reform, while 31–53 percent were willing to consider removing the subsidy on diesel, LPG, or gasoline.

- In Jordan, out of those willing to consider subsidy reform, the most popular candidate for reform was diesel (picked by 50 percent), but it was followed by the bread subsidy. (The electricity and LPG subsidies in Jordan appear to be very politically sensitive.)

- In Lebanon, bread was the most sensitive subsidy, which only 7 percent of respondents were willing to consider reforming. However, 20 percent were willing to sacrifice the mazoot (diesel) subsidy, and 97 percent were perfectly willing to get rid of the tobacco subsidy (which

FIGURE 4.23

Preferred Product for Subsidy Removal (Assuming Reform Is Inevitable) in the Middle East and North Africa, Selected Countries, 2012

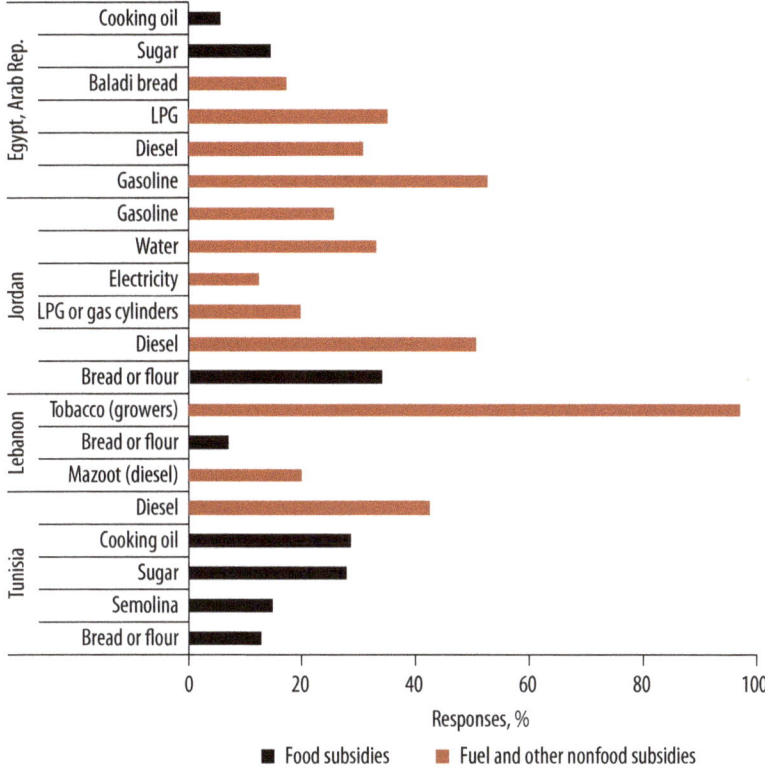

Source: Authors' calculations based on MENA SPEAKS Survey 2012.
Note: LPG = liquefied petroleum gas.

is a producer subsidy to tobacco farmers and considered part of the country's SSN).

- In Tunisia, 13–15 percent offered bread and semolina as the most preferred goods for subsidy reform, 28 percent suggested sugar or cooking oil, and more than 40 percent preferred to let go of the subsidy on diesel. Given that fuel subsidies are notoriously expensive and regressive, it appears that their removal would face less opposition than reform of any food subsidies.

Policy Options for Subsidy Reform

Figure 4.24 plots the share of respondents in each self-identified income group mentioning a certain product as their most preferred or second-

FIGURE 4.24

Preferred Product for Subsidy Removal, by Self-Reported Income Group, in the Middle East and North Africa, Selected Countries, 2012

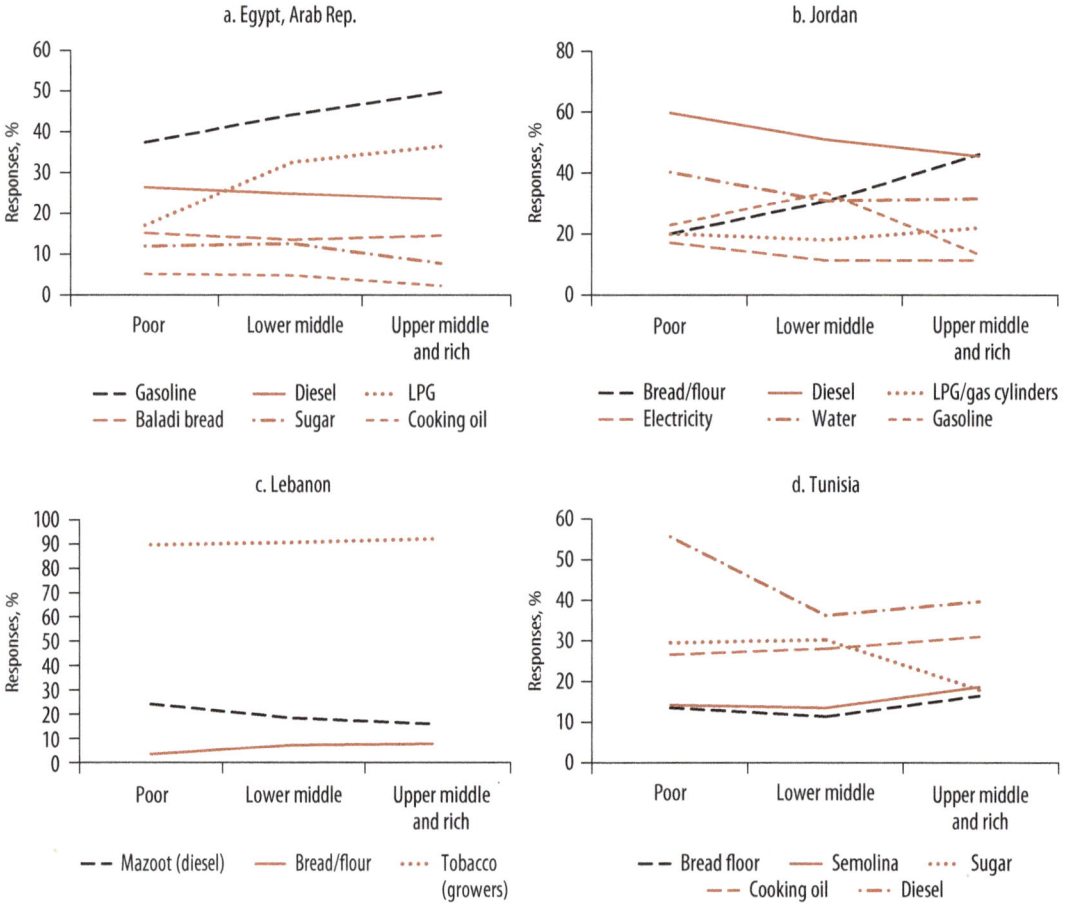

Source: Authors' calculations based on MENA SPEAKS Survey 2012.

Note: LPG = liquefied petroleum gas.

most preferred candidate for subsidy reform. Such disaggregation allows for the analysis of potential subsidy reform coalitions that governments can draw on for support of specific reforms, as follows:

- In Egypt, the middle class prefers to sacrifice the gasoline and LPG subsidy more than the poor. If the poor can be compensated for the loss of the subsidy with a targeted SSN cash transfer, the government could save significant fiscal resources and invest in other priority social sectors.

- In Jordan, a coalition of the middle class and the wealthy appears to be possible for subsidy reform of bread, LPG, and diesel. Because the poor are very averse to subsidy reform of these products, they would have to be adequately compensated to avoid immiseration and potential unrest.

• In Lebanon, everyone appears to support elimination of the tobacco growers' subsidy, which should be relatively easy for the government to do, given the detrimental effect of tobacco on health. A portion of the savings from this subsidy should be used, at least in part, to compensate tobacco farmers who would be the losers from the removal of this subsidy.

• In Tunisia, the lower middle class appears to be more tolerant of the removal of the sugar subsidy, while the poor are more willing to consider the removal of the subsidy on diesel.

MENA SPEAKS respondents who were willing to consider subsidy reform for at least one product were asked the following question: "Instead of spending money on subsidizing the price of [the good you were most willing for the government to stop subsidizing], the government could spend that money on something else." The respondent was then asked to choose among the following four options: (a) distribute that money to the poor; (b) distribute that money to all families except the wealthy; (c) distribute that money to all families including the wealthy; or (d) distribute a portion of that money to the poor and spend the rest on health care and educational programs for all.

As shown in figure 4.25, the option of distributing the money to the poor was the top choice in Egypt, Jordan, and Tunisia, while distributing a portion of the money to the poor and spending the rest on health and education was preferred by most Lebanese respondents. However, it is important to read these results in light of the fact that a broader spectrum of the population defined themselves as poor than those belonging to the bottom consumption quintile, and it is likely that these individuals would also feel entitled to the compensation as "poor."

Disaggregating subsidy reform preferences by self-identified income group sheds light on the preferred reform options for different groups of people in the country. In all countries except Lebanon, the poor are the most likely to want distribution of all savings from subsidy reform to the poor, as shown in figure 4.26. This is not surprising, as they expect to get the highest private gain from this reform option. In addition, in all countries except Lebanon, the preference for investing in health and education for all rises with self-identified income group. In Egypt and Tunisia, the upper middle class and the wealthy are the most likely to support the option of giving some money to the poor in addition to investing in health and education for all.

Usually, governments worry about the middle class demanding compensation for subsidy reform; this is usually the justification for loose targeting. As figure 4.26 illustrates, only a small minority of the self-iden-

FIGURE 4.25

Preferred Destination of Savings from Subsidy Reform in the Middle East and North Africa, Selected Countries, 2012

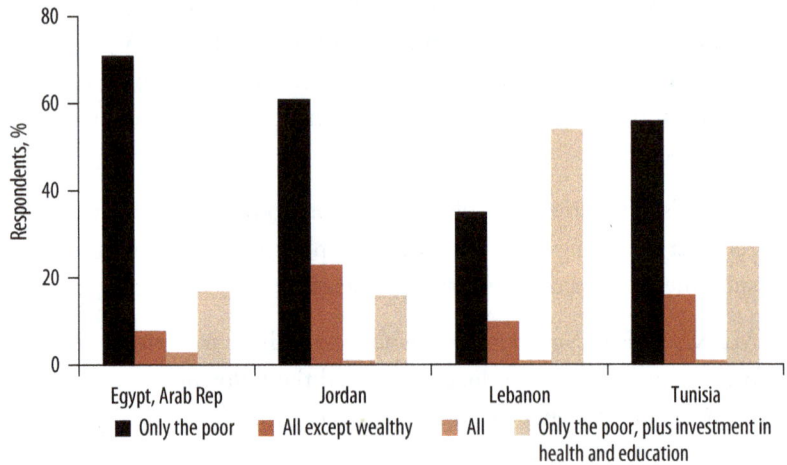

Source: Authors' calculations based on MENA SPEAKS Survey 2012.

tified middle class prefers this option to the option of paying cash compensation only to the poor: among the middle class, 8–10 percent of Egyptians, 15–30 percent of Jordanians, 10–15 percent of Lebanese, and 15–18 percent of Tunisians chose cash transfers to the poor as their most preferred compensation for subsidy reform. Individuals from the Jordanian middle class who participated in the Jordan Gives experiment confirmed the patterns from MENA SPEAKS: redistribution to the poor and to public goods was strictly preferred among the simulation participants, but this preference was weaker among those who self-reported a lower income, as shown in figure 4.27.

What Works? International Experience of SSN Reforms that Increased Acceptability

Assessing and building public opinion are the first steps toward building a broader consensus and getting wider support for policy reforms. However, an even bigger challenge is to navigate the complex world of politics to actually change existing policies. A vast literature discusses the strategies that have enabled the successful implementation of reforms. This section reviews such literature and illustrates specific country examples from around the world to highlight which strategies could also facilitate SSN reform in the Middle East and North Africa—particularly the transition from universal subsidies to better-targeted interventions.

FIGURE 4.26

Preferred Compensation for Subsidy Reform, by Self-Reported Income Group, in the Middle East and North Africa, Selected Countries, 2012

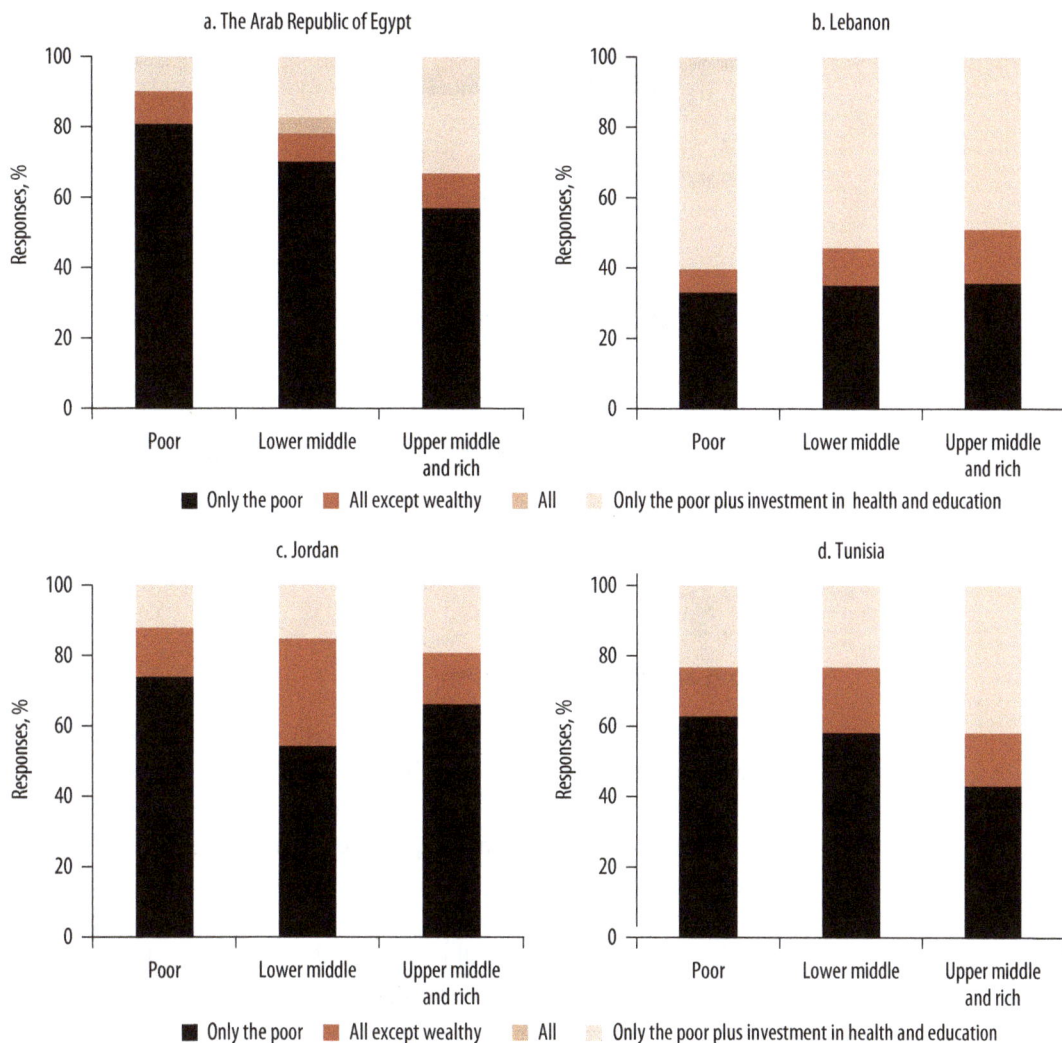

Source: Authors' calculations based on MENA SPEAKS Survey 2012.

Four major aspects emerge from the existing literature on successful reforms:

- Timing and pacing of the reform

- Appropriate communication strategy

- Broad coalitions of support and compensation to short-run losers

- Technical capacity, leadership, and commitment.

FIGURE 4.27

Preferred Compensation for Subsidy Reform within the Jordanian Middle Class, by Self-Reported Income Group, 2012

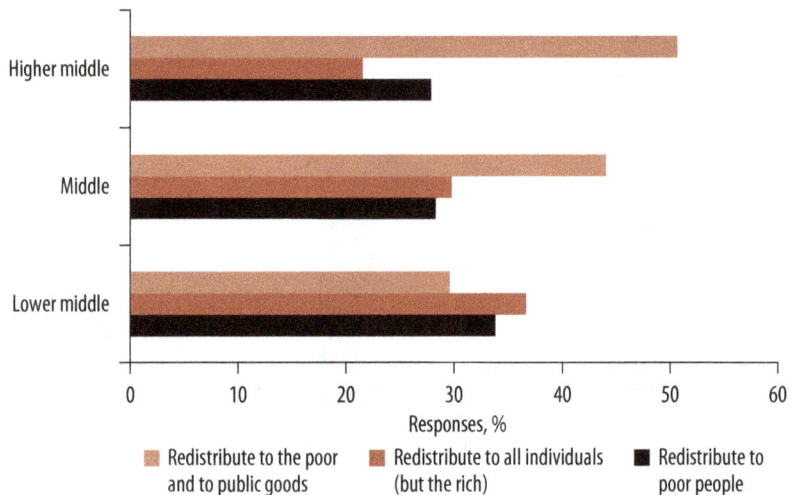

Source: Authors' calculations based on Jordan Gives 2012.
Note: Results based on data.

Timing and Pacing of Reform

The existing literature highlights the importance of crisis while implementing a reform. Grindle and Thomas (1989) distinguish between "crisis-ridden" reforms and "politics-as-usual" reforms. Crisis-ridden reforms are forced on policy makers, and decision making in these reforms tends to be dominated by concerns about major issues of political stability. In particular, crisis moments can facilitate consensus building among opposing coalitions because all parties involved are aware that noncooperation would be overly costly. Graham et al. (1999) suggest that acting early on in a government's mandate, immediately after a crisis, usually is the best time for these reforms: rice subsidy reform in Indonesia and the social security reforms in Peru in 1992 took place during such periods (see boxes 4.2 and 4.3). During crises, external pressure from international creditors can also play a major role, as was the case in Egypt (see box 4.4). However, there is a limit to what crisis politics can achieve, and an effort to reform labor law in Argentina serves as a good example (see box 4.5).

Reforms are also possible under noncrisis circumstances, when policy makers have the freedom to choose the reform and have much greater autonomy in pushing the necessary institutional change (Grindle and Thomas 1989). The main risk associated with these politics-as-usual reforms is that they tend to be dominated by bureaucratic and micropolitical concerns.

BOX 4.2

Indonesia: Rice Subsidy Reform during the Asian Crisis

Indonesian policy makers have historically defined food security in terms of the nation's ability to provide itself with adequate supplies of rice at an affordable price. Subsidies through BULOG (the National Food Logistics Agency) had ensured stable prices in the 1980s and 1990s. However, because of the currency crisis, the food security system had been badly compromised. The government reacted by imposing sweeping controls on trade and marketing of food grains to hold down food prices. Food price subsidies, which were budgeted to be Rp 4 trillion, eventually reached Rp 12 trillion in 1999.

In addition, as the gap between domestic and international prices widened, large quantities of rice and other food grains were smuggled out of the country. As supplies became scarce, there was almost panic in urban markets, and the government was forced to reform its existing subsidy policy. It introduced Special Market Operation (*Operasi Pasar Khusus*; OPK) to protect the food security of poor households. BULOG was confined to domestic procurement activities and disposed of its nonrice food stocks. These reforms were possible only because of the ongoing currency crisis, and they show the importance of circumstances in implementing reforms.

Source: Tabor and Sawit 2001.

BOX 4.3

Peru: National Debate and Reforms

Peru successfully reformed the pension system in 1993–94 by running an effective publicity campaign during the economic crisis. President Alberto Fujimori struggled to overhaul the health and education sector but better succeeded in reforming the pension system because it was directly linked to the crisis. The link between successful adjustment of the pension system and alleviation of fiscal pressure formed the basis of a high-profile publicity campaign that helped garner public support. The press campaign for privatization of the pension system highlighted efficiency and ownership of contributions rather than loss of benefits. After the law was reformed, most new workers opted for the new private system. Support from the new stakeholders in the financial sector and labor market has sustained the reforms. The Peru case highlights the role of the media in enlisting allies.

Source: Graham et al. 1999.

Egypt: Reduction of Subsidy Burden

Egypt's successful policy reform can be attributed to external pressure, an effective information campaign, and gradual changes. The country tried to reduce its subsidy burden in 1977, but major food riots prevented any meaningful change. As Egypt's external debt started increasing, it was forced to sign standby agreements with the International Monetary Fund to reduce its subsidy burden in 1977 and 1987. Hence, the government was forced to use various strategies to reduce the subsidy burden in the early 1980s (Ali and Adams 1996).

Earlier, in 1977, the government had failed to prepare the public for the abolition of subsidies. However, in the 1980s, it started to compare the cost of subsidies with the revenues from the Suez Canal to highlight the magnitude of the subsidy cost upon the population. Furthermore, it reduced the overall costs of subsidies by gradually changing unit costs as well as the number of products it subsidizes (Alderman 2002). For instance, when the government implemented the first set of subsidy reforms, it kept the main bread of Egypt (*baladi*) heavily subsidized (Adams 2000), but it stopped subsidizing the high-quality bread (*fino*)

Source: Authors, using Adams 2000 and Ali and Adams 1996.

Apart from timing, adopting an appropriate pace for reform is also an important factor, specifically when reforming subsidies. There is evidence to support both slow and rapid reform strategies: Egypt gradually phased out its subsidies in the 1980s after a failed attempt in 1977. However, Indonesia and Zimbabwe (see box 4.9) used the economic crisis to carry out rapid subsidy reforms.

Communications Strategy

Policy makers need to explain reforms to the public, create a clear consensus on their direction, and build central-level commitment (Graham 2002). The effectiveness of a communication campaign depends on the leader's ability to assess the prevailing environment (Graham et al. 1999). The right communications strategy should depend on the circumstances around the reform and on the sophistication of the public debate in that area (Graham et al. 1999). For instance, in situations where the press's technical competence is low, a low-profile strategy will prevent the debate from being captured by political opposition to the reform. However, in the case of social security and other complex reforms, information campaigns become important to the success of the reform strategy. Fur-

---

BOX 4.5

Argentina: The Limits of Crisis Politics

The Argentine government successfully passed several reforms during the economic crises in the late 1980s and early 1990s, but as the crisis-related urgency subsided, the pace of reform slowed down. The Carlos Menem government, elected during a severe economic crisis in 1989, used the crisis to convince people to bear the short-term costs of reforms. This need for quick action increased the pressure for building coalitions. Menem also attracted support from the disgruntled public by successfully privatizing a telecom company, and he chose reform leaders to please all sides of the coalition. However, as the crisis faded into the past, Menem had to negotiate with the Congress to overhaul the social security system.

Eventually the technical and political capability of the finance minister enabled the Menem government to partially reform the social security system. However, the government's efforts to reform the labor law were not at all successful because there was no urgency and the administration did not create visible winners to replace the support of the losers from the reform. The Argentine case tells us that there are limitations to crisis politics and that coalitions formed during a crisis can also disband quickly.

Source: Graham et al. 1999.

---

thermore, D. Romer's (2003) model of misconceptions suggests that efforts to improve officials' and voters' understanding of policy reforms can systematically change outcomes.

Particularly in the case of subsidy reform, informing the public of the cost of the current system is fundamental. In illustrating strategies that have worked in successful subsidy reforms, Alderman (2002) points out, among other things, the importance of publicity regarding the reform. The broad public—including the poor and the illiterate—need to be informed of its rationale at an early stage of the reform. For example, the government could publicize that subsidy reforms will create fiscal savings for other programs such as education. Egypt used this strategy effectively by comparing the cost of subsidies with the revenues from the Suez Canal, which highlighted the high cost of subsidies. In general, the relatively low degree of public awareness of subsidies shown by MENA SPEAKS (particularly awareness of the most regressive subsidies) suggests that there is more scope for information to influence public opinion in Middle Eastern and North African countries and to build consensus on the need for reform.

A key reason for a communication strategy is that the media are likely to spontaneously cover changes in major welfare reforms. A study by Lindert and Vicensini (2010) on the media coverage of Brazil's *Bolsa Fa-*

milia program (a conditional cash transfer program) exceptionally captured the behavior of the media in this respect. This study showed the following:

- Large welfare programs can receive high attention and scrutiny because of their scale and direct impact on the general public. This holds true even if there is general endorsement of the objectives of the program within society.

- Scaling up the program can be perceived either negatively or positively. Media coverage is highly dependent on the maturity and implementation quality of the institution implementing the program.

- There is technical interplay between the press and the government. The government tends to react to press coverage about inadequacies of the program, and reportage often becomes favorable when the government improves the welfare program. This implies a "virtuous cycle" for accountability between the government and the press, which helps strengthen the program.

- The program falls under higher scrutiny during election time.

Compensation to Short-Term Losers

Every reform will create winners and losers, and compensating the politically relevant losers will be critical to the success of a reform. The fiscal constraints can sometimes make it difficult to give direct monetary benefits. In this case, innovative ways of reconfiguring the stakeholders or creating new stakeholders (Graham et al. 1999) can be a successful strategy.

New stakeholders will change the balance of power and can be extremely useful in broadening the support base. For instance, in Peru and Bolivia, new stakeholders created by social sector reforms (private pension funds) became long-term political supporters. However, in Uruguay, the government struggled to reform health care as it confronted a major interest group (see box 4.6). Furthermore, gradual reforms diffused the major political opposition groups in Bangladesh (see box 4.7).

Several strategies can be used to compensate for loss in purchasing power while reducing subsidy expenditures. Individuals may strongly prefer to avoid immediate losses than reap greater future gains (Kahneman and Tversky 1979). Thus, even if subsidy removal may be beneficial collectively in the medium term, reducing the scope for short-term discontent is politically essential because it is essential to protect the purchasing power of the poor. Putting in place credible compensation policies for subsidy removal is thus crucial to building coalitions, particularly among poor people who could become net winners from the reform. These com

BOX 4.6

Uruguay: Avoid Antagonizing Powerful Interest Groups

Sometimes major reforms cannot be passed because they face opposition from a powerful interest group. Uruguay's struggle with health care reform is a good example. The country successfully reformed its social security system under President Julio Maria Sanguinetti, even though the background for reforms did not seem auspicious: no economic crisis, power abundantly distributed among the various branches, low party loyalty, and continual citizen votes for increased social spending.

Sanguinetti was still successful for three reasons: new pressures for coalition building, timing of reforms with respect to the election cycle, and political knowledge gained from the previous reforms. In addi-

tion, a high-profile publicity campaign was instrumental in building a coalition of winners. However, the Minister of Health Alfredo Solari struggled with the same strategies when trying to achieve health care reform. The health reform directly confronted the powerful, well-organized medical establishment (the medical profession-al's union, Federación Médica del Interior [FEMI]), while the winners (health consumers) were diffused. Even bundling the reform with the budget bill did not work. Subsequently, the passed reform did not confront FEMI. Uruguay shows us that clear losers and diffused winners are difficult conditions for reforms, even in a successful administration.

Source: Graham et al. 1999.

pensation policies can be cash transfers or direct compensation, but they should be designed to provide net fiscal savings after the subsidy reform. Furthermore, the presence of an effective SSN program during the reform will boost government credibility and enhance public support.

In this context, gradual targeting (such as that used in Indonesia) may be politically effective because, in the short term, most individuals will receive benefits to adjust for price increases, while eventually only the poor would continue to benefit (see box 4.2). A more radical case is the recent subsidy reform in the Islamic Republic of Iran, where the entire population received undifferentiated cash compensation to meet the ensuing loss of purchasing power (see Guillaume, Zytek, and Reza Farzin 2011). A successful way to increase targeting and reduce spending is to introduce self-targeting in the system by differentiating certain products more consumed by the poor in terms of "time costs, stigma and quality" (Tuck and Lindert 1996). Many case studies prove that self-targeting can be a useful political economy strategy—for example, in Egypt, Bangladesh (see box 4.7), Pakistan (see box 4.8), and Tunisia (as discussed in chapter 3, box 3.4). This strategy is useful especially when governments' capacity to identify the poor is limited.

BOX 4.7

Bangladesh: Politics of Food Subsidy Reforms

Bangladesh's food subsidy reforms provide valuable lessons in gradual speed of reforms, diffusion of major political opposition groups, enlisting allies, and self-targeting. The Bangladesh Public Food Distribution System (PFDS) dispensed food grains through ration channels to consumers at varying rates of subsidization and procured grains from farmers. It faced two competing policy objectives: increase farm productivity by maintaining high prices and improve food access to the poor by subsidies. It tried to achieve this dual objective by providing price support to farmers through domestic procurement and distributing subsidized food grains to different groups of consumers through various ration channels. However, this policy did not achieve any of the set objectives.

Because of rent-seeking lobbies (mill owners and the military and police) and rent-seeking bureaucrats, the system failed to benefit the poor. Even after setting up a rural rationing channel in the 1970s, the program had 69.4 percent leakage (Ahmed 1992). On the procurement side, mill owners and Ministry of Food officials "split" the difference between market price and procurement prices (Adams 1998). Apart from organized rent seekers, the government reforms would have also potentially faced opposition from the 15 million ration-card holders.

In the early 1980s, when the government started its reform process, it decided to adopt a gradual reform process instead of a quick shock treatment because it faced too many vested interest groups. First, it lifted the off-take price from the ration channels by linking it to the procurement price, thus reducing the subsidy in ration channels. This helped in enlisting the support of the powerful Ministry of Agriculture and the Planning Commission, whose top priority was to increase the food grain production. It also slowly eroded the incentives for card holders to draw rations and for ration dealers and food officials to reroute them (Ahmed, Haggblade, and Chowdhury 2000). The off-take from PFDS decreased from 2.5 million tons in the late 1980s to 1.6 million tons in 1998. This averted possible opposition from urban ration recipients and diffused a major opposition group.

The government in Bangladesh was also effective in enlisting the support of external and internal allies. External allies, particularly the World Bank, the U.S. Agency for International Development, and Canada, helped in executing reforms by placing conditions on food and lending programs. The donors also diverted some of the "political heat" to themselves from the internal reform advocates (Ahmed, Haggblade, and Chowdhury 2000). Internally, enlisting interministerial allies was also critical because the Ministry of Agriculture was eager in increasing procurement price to benefit the farmers and pushed the reforms.

Bangladesh also instituted a Food-For-Works (FFW) program, which reduced rent seeking and leakages. The FFW program offered wheat wages to the rural poor, who were willing to work in construction jobs. Wheat has a negative income elastic-

BOX 4.7 *Continued*

ity of demand in Bangladesh. According to the humanitarian organization CARE, the FFW leakages were as low as 30–35 percent, compared with about 70 percent in the earlier programs. FFW was successful for three reasons (Adams 1998): First, it focused on inferior food, which was not highly valued by nonpoor people, further reducing the incentives for rent seekers. Second, because FFW demanded work in exchange for wheat, only the poor and the needy participated. Finally, it reduced the need for government bureaucrats because it relied on self-targeting. Del Ninno and Dorosh (2002) also conclude that in-kind transfers, such as the FFW program, lead to greater wheat consumption than would result from an equivalent increase in cash income. The results of these reforms have been impressive. Overall, the government has saved more than US$75 million in costs since 1992.

In spite of coalitions of public support, small interest groups that face large losses are among the main opponents of subsidy reform and should not be ignored. Small groups united by important interests have a great incentive to organize, while large groups may find it more difficult to coalesce around a common interest because the incentives to bear the cost of collective action are attenuated (Olson 1965). Each country has several groups whose survival may depend on the existing subsidy system and for whom adjustment could be particularly costly. These include subsidized producers (such as mills, bakeries, and refineries); retailers (such as special shops for subsidized food); industries that consume subsidized input intensively; and organized rent seekers (see box 4.7). For instance, energy-intensive industries in Egypt in 2007 directly consumed more than 50 percent of energy subsidies in the country (Abouleinein, El-Laithy, and Kheir-El-Din 2009).

Hence, it is important that policy makers recognize the repercussions of these strong interest groups and devise a concrete compensation strategy for the losers of the subsidy reforms. In Pakistan, retail shops received loans to restock and sell different products. In Egypt's case, losers can be compensated through credit and technical assistance to facilitate a transition to more energy-efficient production. Another potential strategy is to change institutional arrangements such that economic rents received by these small groups are passed on to the general public even if there are no immediate savings. This would be helpful in two ways: First, the reforms would garner larger public support because of the added benefits. Second, interest groups that were benefiting from the status quo would be weakened.

BOX 4.8

Pakistan: Derationing of Flour Subsidies in the 1980s

Pakistan's derationing of subsidies is a good example to see the importance of compensating the losers of the policy reforms, enlisting allies through incentives, and choosing the right timing for the reform. The Pakistani government decided to implement comprehensive derationing reforms following a marked decline in the number of households relying on ration shops. The flour subsidy had declined from a high of 2.2 percent of GDP in 1974 to 0.6 percent of GDP in 1986. Pakistan's flour subsidy was already self-targeting to a large extent. As incomes increased, families started purchasing flour from the open market, which was perceived to be of higher quality. Surveys had estimated that 69 percent of the subsidized wheat was not drawn by consumers but leaked through the system. In light of this, the government anticipated opposition from three major interest groups: ration depot shoppers, ration depot employees, and public sector employees who benefited the most from this subsidy.

To win the support of all the different interest groups, the government devised a compensation strategy for each of the los-ers. First, it created a transitional price, which lowered the price of flour for the majority and avoided a sudden change to the unsubsidized open market price for the ration shoppers. Second, it did not dismantle the administration of the ration shops, even though their jobs were redundant; the shops received loans of up to PRs 25,000 to assist in transition to a fair-price shop. Last, low-paid government employees received a raise at the same time as derationing and even additional compensation for the expected change in flour prices. These measures helped the Pakistani government gain new supporters and mute potential opposition.

The Pakistani government also paid special attention to the timing of the reforms. The derationing reforms were announced to be effective in April, which coincided with the beginning of the wheat harvest. The salary increase of employees was announced at the same time as the derationing reform. The government also used the media to emphasize the inefficiency of the ration system, even though this was an indirect admission of its own inefficiency.

Source: Alderman 1988.

Technical Capacity, Leadership, and Commitment

Finally, technical and committed leadership is key in shaping reforms (Graham et al. 1999; Grindle and Thomas 1989). Leaders need to have a sound understanding of the institutional structure of the country and society, and their technical and ideological coherence is needed to overcome political opposition and administrative obstacles.

BOX 4.9

Zimbabwe: Reforms during a Crisis

Zimbabwe reformed its subsidy system under donor pressure after a fiscal crisis in the 1980s. After gaining independence, Zimbabwe expanded the state procurement infrastructure to control maize supplies and pricing. Though the system initially served the objective of boosting maize production, several problems emerged: First, marketing costs escalated, making the existing system unaffordable. Second, the state infrastructure became increasingly unreliable for both consumers and producers. Third, farmers started to switch to other crops.

Last, the instability of maize sales dependent on less reliable rainfall further strained the fiscal health.

The fiscal crisis in the 1980s and the failure of partial reforms led donors to lose patience. Because the state infrastructure was beneficial only to a dominant elite composed of bureaucrats, urban consumers, and industry, the reforms were met with little opposition. The donor pressure and the fiscal situation left the government with no choice but to reduce marketing subsidies and allow private trading of grains.

Source: Jayne and Jones 1997.

Technical analysis and advisors have been crucial in shaping outcomes in Indonesia (Grindle and Thomas 1989), the Republic of Korea, and Turkey (Önis and Webb 1992). A study by Lee, Moretti, and Butler (2004) further highlights the role of policy makers in reforms. The empirical analysis in the study shows that there is little evidence that members of the U.S. Congress change their position on policies in response to a large exogenous change in voter preference. The finding suggests that the public doesn't affect policies, it just elects them.

Annex 4A

MENA SPEAKS Questionnaire

Egypt

1. Each stack of coins on this card represents a different income group in this country. In which income group is your household? **(Show card)**

   1   Group 1

   2   Group 2

   3   Group 3

   4   Group 4

   5   (DK)

   6   (Refused)

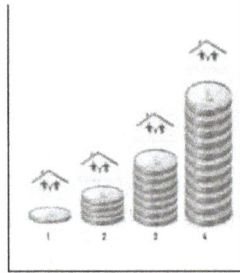

2. Now please think about the total wealth held by individuals in **Egypt**. What portion of this total wealth do you think is held by the rich in **Egypt? (Read 1–4)**

   1   The rich hold almost all of the total wealth held by individuals.

   2   The rich hold more than half of the total wealth held by individuals.

   3   The rich hold about half of the total wealth held by individuals.

   4   The rich hold less than half of the total wealth held by individuals.

   5   (DK)

   6   (Refused)

3. Which one of the following groups do you think should be most responsible for helping the poor in this country, if any? **(Read 1–5)** **(Allow ONE response)**

    1 The government

    2 Family and friends

    3 Religious organizations

    4 Charitable organizations

    5 No group should be responsible

    6 (DK)

    7 (Refused)

4. How effective is the government in providing SSN for the poor in this country? **(Read 1–4)**

    1 Very effective

    2 Somewhat effective

    3 Not very effective

    4 Not effective at all

    5 (DK)

    6 (Refused)

    (If code 1 in Q86/WP13275, Skip to Q89/WP13278;
    Otherwise, Continue)

5. How much responsibility should the government take for helping the poor in this country? **(Read 1–4)**

1 A great deal	**(Skip to Q90/WP13279)**
2 Some	**(Skip to Q90/WP13279)**
3 Not very much	**(Continue)**
4 None at all	**(Continue)**
5 (DK)	**(Continue)**
6 (Refused)	**(Continue)**

6. An SSN project is a government project in which money or other goods and services are provided to the poor. Do you think the government should provide SSN to people in this country who are poor, or not?

1   Yes   **(Continue)**

2   No   **(Skip to Q91/WP13280)**

3   (DK)   **(Continue)**

4   (Refused)   **(Continue)**

7. Ideally, do you think that an SSN project should focus mainly on serving the poor OR mainly on serving specific groups of people, such as widows, orphans, the sick, and the elderly, whether or not they are poor?
(If respondent says "both," read:) Please tell me which group you think the project should focus on.

1   Serving the poor

2   Serving specific groups of people, whether or not they are poor

3   (DK)

4   (Refused)

8. Do you think it would be better for recipients of government SSN to receive assistance in the form of cash OR to receive assistance in the form of goods, such as food or clothes? **(Allow ONE response) (If respondent says "both," read:)** Which do you think is better for them to receive?

1   Cash

2   Goods (food, clothes, etc.)

3   (Neither) **(Do NOT read)**

4   (DK)

5   (Refused)

9. In some countries, recipients of government SSN are required to do something in exchange for monthly assistance. For example, they could be required to have their children attend school regularly. If their children stop attending school, the assistance would no longer be provided. Do you think recipients of SSN should be required to do something in exchange for the assistance, or should there be no requirements?

1 Yes, there should be some requirements	**(Continue)**
2 No, there should not be any requirements	**(Skip to Q94/Text before WP13317)**
3 (DK)	**(Continue)**
4 (Refused)	**(Continue)**

10. Please indicate whether each of the following should be required in order to receive government SSN on a regular basis. **(Read A–E)**

	Yes	*No*	*(DK)*	*(Refused)*
A. Recipients must ensure their children regularly attend school.	1	2	3	4
B. Recipients must get medical checkups for children and expecting mothers.	1	2	3	4
C. Recipients must attend job training courses.	1	2	3	4
D. Recipients must actively search for work.	1	2	3	4
E. Recipients must accept the work provided by the program in exchange for the assistance.	1	2	3	4

11. Please name any government SSN projects in this country that you know about. **(Do NOT read A–F) (Open ended and code)**

	Mentioned	Not mentioned
A. Social Solidarity pension (Sadat Pension)	1	2
B. Child Law pension (Child Cash Assistance)	1	2
C. Cash transfers for students in school (children in families benefiting from the SS program)	1	2
D. Grants for Micro projects	1	2
E. Assistance from Social Nasser Bank	1	2
F. Productive Families' projects	1	2

12. Please tell me whether or not you have heard of the following government SSN projects. **(Read A–F, as appropriate) (INTERVIEWER: Read all programs listed below that were NOT mentioned in Q94)**

	Yes	No	(DK)	(Refused)
A. Social Solidarity pension (Sadat Pension)	1	2	3	4
B. Child Law pension (Child Cash Assistance)	1	2	3	4
C. Cash transfers for students in school (children in families benefiting from the SS program)	1	2	3	4
D. Grants for Micro projects	1	2	3	4
E. Assistance from Social Nasser Bank	1	2	3	4
F. Productive Families' projects	1	2	3	4

(If code 1 to ANY in Q94 A–F or code 1 to ANY in Q95 A–F, Continue; Otherwise, Skip to Q97/Text before WP13335)

13. Do you personally know anyone who has received assistance from any of these projects? **(Read A–F, as appropriate) (INTER-VIEWER: Read all programs listed below that were mentioned in Q94 or were code 1 in Q95)**

		Yes	No	(DK)	(Refused)
[WP13329]	A. Social Solidarity pension (Sadat Pension)	1	2	3	4
[WP13330]	B. Child Law pension (Child Cash Assistance)	1	2	3	4
[WP13331]	C. Cash transfers for students in school (children in families benefiting from the SS program)	1	2	3	4
[WP13332]	D. Grants for Micro projects	1	2	3	4
[WP13333]	E. Assistance from Social Nasser Bank	1	2	3	4
[WP13334]	F. Productive Families' projects	1	2	3	4

14. In some countries, governments subsidize the prices of certain products by keeping their prices fixed or at least preventing their prices from rising too fast. Which products do you think the government of your country is subsidizing? **(Do NOT read A–F) (Open ended and code)**

		Mentioned	Not mentioned
[WP13335]	A. Gasoline	1	2
[WP13336]	B. Diesel—fuel for vehicles	1	2
[WP13337]	C. LPG—fuel for heating	1	2
[WP13338]	D. Baladi bread and flour	1	2
[WP13339]	E. Sugar	1	2
[WP13340]	F. Cooking oil	1	2

15. Do you think the government of **Egypt** is subsidizing the price of any of the following products? **(Read A–F, as appropriate) (INTERVIEWER: Read all programs listed below that were NOT mentioned in Q97)**

		Yes	No	(DK)	(Refused)
[WP13341]	A. Gasoline	1	2	3	4
[WP13342]	B. Diesel—fuel for vehicles	1	2	3	4
[WP13343]	C. LPG—fuel for heating	1	2	3	4
[WP13344]	D. Baladi bread and flour	1	2	3	4
[WP13345]	E. Sugar	1	2	3	4
[WP13346]	F. Cooking oil	1	2	3	4

16. If the government could not afford to subsidize all of the following products, which product's price would you want the government to stop subsidizing? **(Read 1–6) (Prompt for second response:) What would be your second choice? (Allow TWO responses) (If respondent says "None" or "Don't know," read:)** If you had to pick one product, which one would it be?

    1 Gasoline

    2 Diesel—fuel for vehicles

    3 LPG—fuel for heating

    4 Baladi bread and flour

    5 Sugar

    6 Cooking oil

    7 (None)

    8 (DK)

    9 (Refused)

[WP13347] A. (First response) _____

[WP13348] B. (Second response) _____

(If code 7, 8, or 9 in Q99A/WP13347, Skip to Q101/WP12213; Otherwise, Continue)

[WP13316]

17. Instead of spending money on subsidizing the price of **(response in Q99A/WP13347)**, the government could spend that money on something else. Should the government **(read 1–4)? (Show card)**

    1 Distribute that money to the poor

    2 Distribute that money to all families except the wealthy

    3 Distribute that money to all families including the wealthy

    4 Distribute a portion of that money to the poor and spend the rest on health care and educational programs for all

    5 (DK)

    6 (Refused)

Annex 4B

Methodology of MENA SPEAKS Surveys and Jordan Gives Experiment

Because the literature on SSN support is largely based on high-income countries or on a few Middle East and North Africa-specific qualitative studies, two data collection projects were conducted as part of this regional study. The findings presented in this report represent an unprecedented attempt to shed light on the specificities of the political economy of SSNs in the region through nationally representative data. These data are also unique in their application of behavioral economics to study the preferences for SSNs in the Middle East and North Africa.

MENA SPEAKS: MENA Social Protection Evaluation of Attitudes, Knowledge, and Support (SPEAKS)

MENA SPEAKS surveys are four nationally representative surveys conducted as part of the Spring 2012 wave of Gallup's World Poll in Egypt, Jordan, Lebanon, and Tunisia. The surveys collected data from 1,000 randomly selected households in each country about their subjective income; perceptions on existing inequality; the role of the state as the main provider of SSNs; knowledge of existing SSN programs; preferences on SSN design features (cash versus in-kind, categorical versus poverty targeting, conditional versus unconditional transfers, and acceptability of different types of conditionality); knowledge of existing subsidies; and preferences regarding subsidy removal and different compensation packages. For an example of a MENA SPEAKS questionnaire (Egypt), see annex 4A.

Jordan Gives: Jordan Behavioral Experiment on Redistribution Preferences

Jordan Gives is a behavioral game that collected information on people's preferences and support for several redistribution alternatives. The value added of the game through a simple survey is that participants tend to think more deeply about trade-offs when the consequences of their choices translate into concrete monetary costs and benefits. Thus, the information elicited through their decisions should be a more reliable measure of their true preferences for redistribution.

The game was carried out in Jordan with 42 groups of 10 citizens each by the Center for Strategic Studies at the University of Jordan. The sampling units were drawn from a sample of the Jordanian middle class (explained further below). In each randomly selected primary sampling unit (PSU), two groups (treatment and control) played simultaneously in separate rooms, with participants randomly assigned to one of the groups. At the beginning of the game, each participant received fuel vouchers issued by Jordan Petroleum Refinery: a JD 5 (Jordanian dinars) voucher as a show-up fee and a JD 10 voucher to play the game. The magnitude of the voucher for the game (JD 10) is essentially equivalent to the minimum daily wage (the mandated minimum wage in Jordan in 2012 was JD 190 per month). Participants were offered four independent proposals, as listed below, and for each proposal they had to decide whether to accept it (implying willingness to give up the JD 10 voucher to have the proposal implemented) or to reject it (implying a preference to keep the JD 10 voucher instead of implementing the proposal).

Each redistribution proposal had a total value of JD 100 (corresponding to the sum of the vouchers of the 10 participants in the room). The proposals, which portrayed as closely as possible different SSN designs, were the following:

- [Cash transfer] You give up your JD 10 voucher. Our team gives JD 20 cash per family to five poor families in this community. Do you accept or reject the proposal?

- [In-kind transfer] You give up your JD 10 voucher. Our team gives a food basket worth JD 20 per family to five poor families in this community.

- [Conditional cash transfer] You give up your JD 10 voucher. Our team gives JD 20 cash per family to five poor families in this community conditional on their completion of a free training program on work-related skills.

- [Cash transfer and money to the local school] You give up your JD 10 voucher. Our team gives JD 20 cash per family to two poor families in this community, and JD 60 cash will go to the local school.

After participants marked the decision on each proposal on a decision card, they were also asked to pick their most preferred and second-most preferred proposal out of the four proposals. All cards were then collected and placed in a glass bowl. Another glass bowl contained numbers 1 through 4 corresponding to proposal numbers. Facilitators proceeded to draw one decision card from the first bowl and one number from the second bowl. The decision on the selected decision card for the selected proposal number was implemented on the whole group. If the selected decision was "accept," then the JD 10 voucher was collected from each participant and the selected proposal was implemented in that local community.

The difference in acceptance rates between the presented alternatives can be attributed to the differences in preferences for particular proposal features (cash versus in-kind, conditional versus unconditional, private goods only versus private and public). The difference in the game played in the treatment groups as opposed to the control groups consisted of additional information provided only to the treatment groups. This information appealed to the Arab values of solidarity and listed the potential "shopping cart" a poor family could buy with JD 20 (including, for example, enough essential supplies to allow a poor family to get by for several weeks or two bottles of gas that would provide either supplies for cooking for two months or for a gas heater for three weeks). Moreover, treatment groups were offered the option to accompany the facilitator after the game to witness the implementation of the proposal if the selected decision was "accept." Thus, the first part of the treatment appealed to the cultural norms for redistribution, the second sensitized middle-class participants to the value of JD 20 for a poor family, and the third increased transparency of implementation. These treatments were chosen as a result of a focus group on the perceived barriers to redistribution as well as consultations with Jordanian experts and experimental game practitioners.

This activity was complemented by evidence collected through a questionnaire implemented after each participant recorded his or her decisions and cards were collected but before the final decision was selected and before focus group discussions at the end were framed by a more concrete sense of redistribution options.

The sample was nationally representative of the middle class to represent the median voter, who was expected to have lower self-interest in increasing redistribution and to be more likely to actively oppose SSN reform. The sample adopted the definition of "middle class" developed by the government of Jordan's study of the middle class (ESC 2008), which comprised those individuals between twice and four times the poverty line. This corresponded to the population between the fourth and the eighth income deciles according to the 2004 Jordanian census data. Income deciles were estimated by applying a proxy-means-testing formula to the census data, which included the following variables: average household size, owning a fixed phone, owning a computer, having an Internet connection, having central heating, owning a microwave, home ownership, and having at least one family member with a university education.

Because of the national scale of the experiment and to ensure homogeneity of implementation across groups, a video in the local language was used in all groups. This video provided detailed instructions to the participants and projected each of the proposals on the screen. The role of the facilitator was to stop the video to distribute or collect items and allow participants to make decisions, to answer questions according to a predeveloped answer script, and to lead the focus group discussion that followed the game. The order of the proposals was randomized for each PSU to distinguish preferences for each proposal from anchoring on preceding proposals; for within-PSU comparability, the order of the proposals in the control and treatment groups was always the same.

Annex 4C

Public Awareness of SSN Programs and Subsidies

Awareness of Nonsubsidy SSNs

Egypt

Awareness of the Social Pension (formerly known as the Sadat Pension) is very high and fairly uniform across income quintiles. The program has very high association with a safety net, since 25–32 percent of Egyptians mentioned it as a safety net program without being prompted. The second-highest association for an SSN is the Social Nasser Bank (with 11 percent of the middle and top quintiles mentioning it as an SSN program), but awareness of this program increases with income (from 26 percent in the bottom quintile to 53 percent in the top quintile). The Child Law Pension has the lowest recognition, especially among the poor.

Jordan

Awareness about National Aid Fund Assistance is very high and fairly uniform across income quintiles. This program also has a very high association with being a safety net, since 38–53 percent of Jordanians mentioned it as a safety net program without being prompted. The second-highest association for an SSN is Zakat Assistance (with 68 percent of the middle quintile and 62 percent of the top quintile mentioning it as an SSN program). The Enhanced Productivity Program has the lowest recognition, especially among the poor.

Lebanon

Awareness about SSN programs seems to be high in Lebanon across income quintiles. The hospital fee waivers program has the largest awareness among the programs surveyed. It also has a high association with a safety net, since 21–59 percent of Lebanese mentioned it without being prompted. The second-highest association for an SSN is with the Welfare Program. The awareness about this program is also high across quintiles (over 80 percent in the highest quintile). Vocational training programs have the lowest recall, but awareness increases with income.

Tunisia

Awareness about SSN programs seems to be high in Tunisia and increases with income for all programs. The National Solidarity Fund has the highest awareness among the programs surveyed. It also has a very high association with being a safety net, since 33–58 percent of Tunisian respon-

Public Awareness of Nonsubsidy SSNs in the Arab Republic of Egypt, 2012

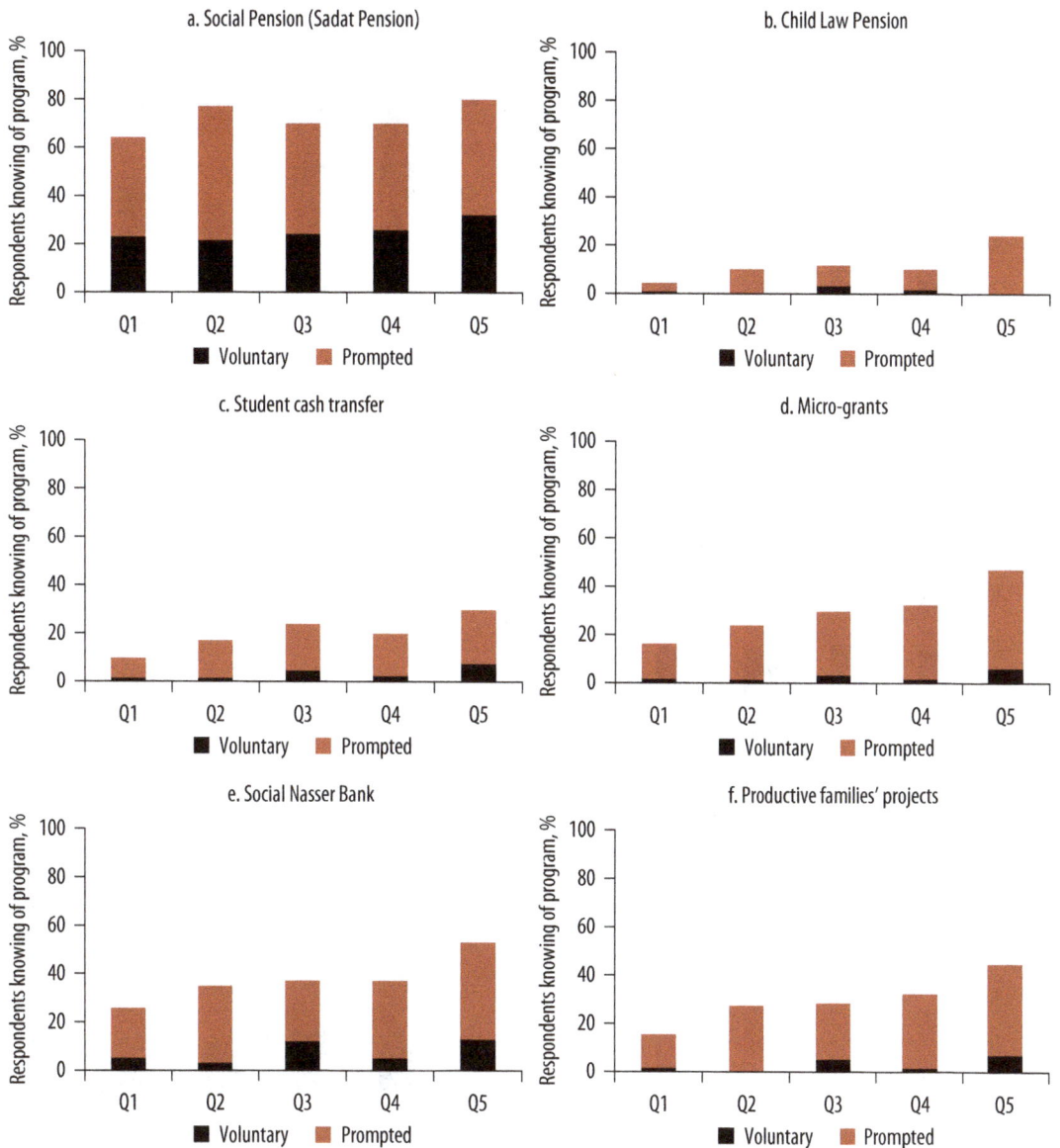

a. Social Pension (Sadat Pension)

b. Child Law Pension

c. Student cash transfer

d. Micro-grants

e. Social Nasser Bank

f. Productive families' projects

Source: Authors' calculations based on MENA SPEAKS Survey 2012.

Note: SSN = social safety net; Q = income quintile (1 = lowest, 5 = highest).

dents mentioned it without being prompted. The second-highest association for an SSN is with the Health Insurance Card from CNSS (Assurance Santé CNSS). The awareness about this program also increases with income (over 90 percent in the highest quintile). Awareness about in-kind transfers is relatively low relative to other SSN programs in Tunisia.

FIGURE 4C.2

Public Awareness of Nonsubsidy SSNs in Jordan, 2012

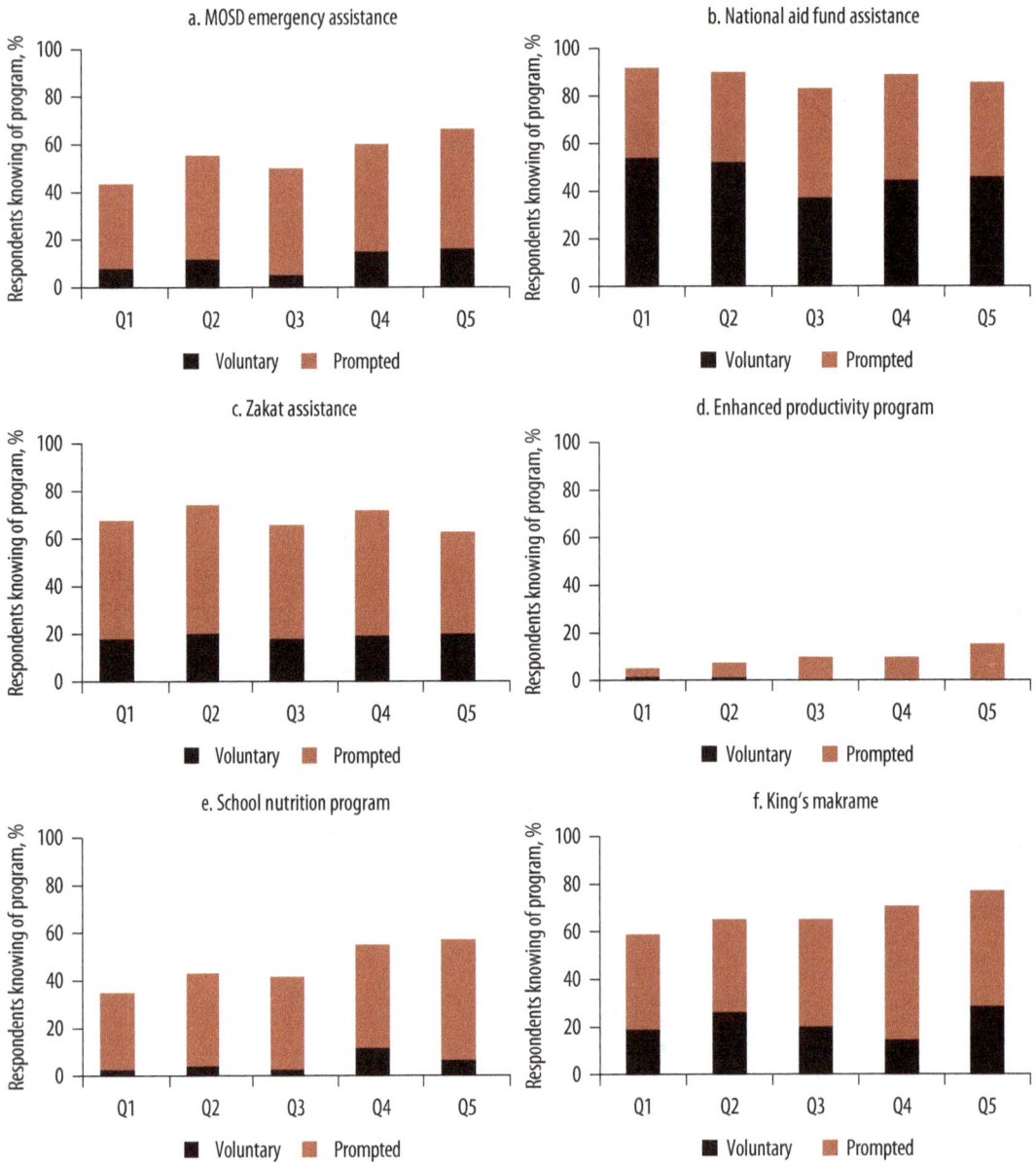

a. MOSD emergency assistance

b. National aid fund assistance

c. Zakat assistance

d. Enhanced productivity program

e. School nutrition program

f. King's makrame

Source: Authors' calculations based on MENA SPEAKS Survey 2012.

Note: MOSD = Ministry of Social Development; SSN = social safety net; Q = income quintile (1 = lowest, 5 = highest).

FIGURE 4C.3

Public Awareness of Nonsubsidy SSNs in Lebanon, 2012

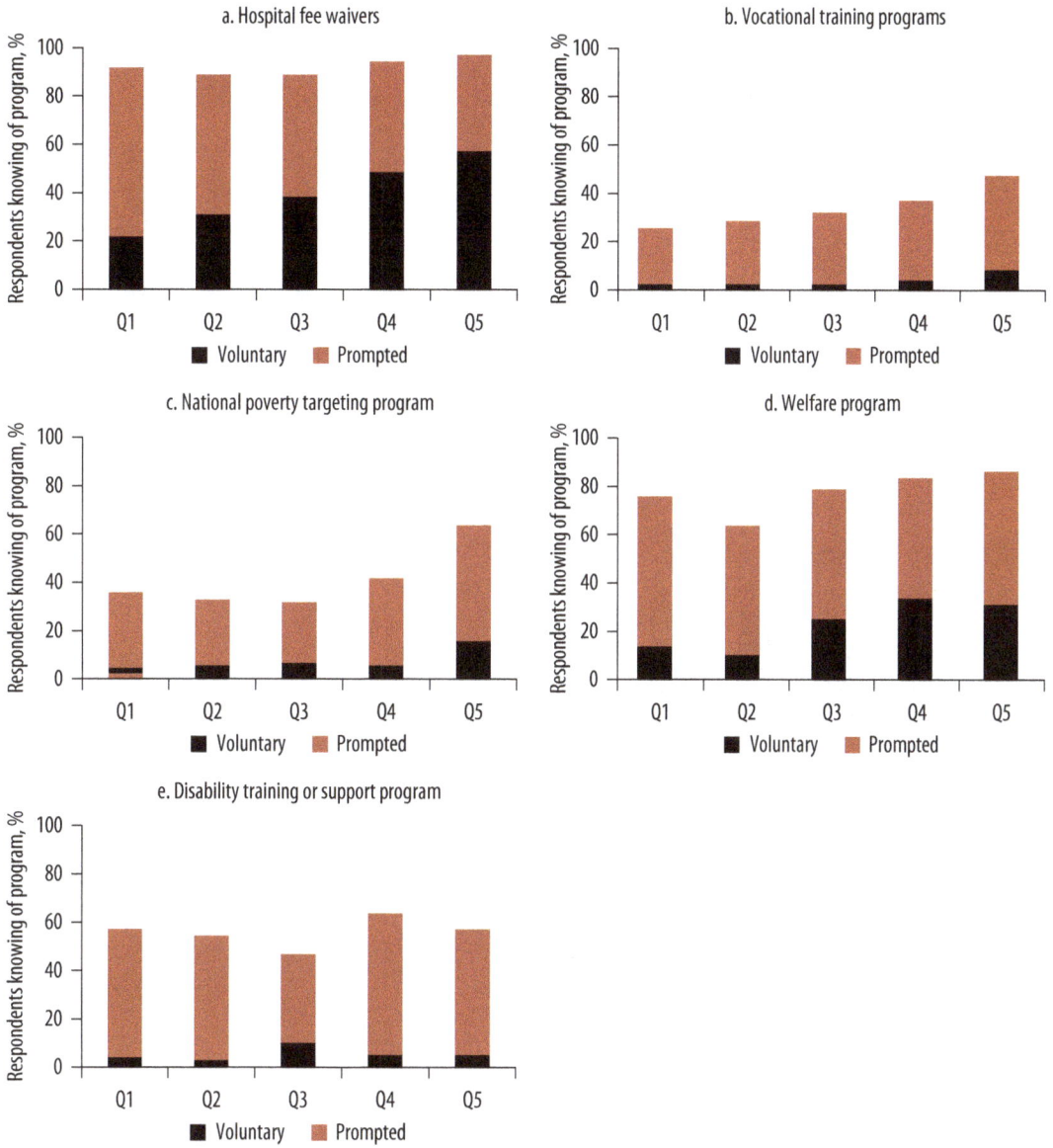

a. Hospital fee waivers

b. Vocational training programs

c. National poverty targeting program

d. Welfare program

e. Disability training or support program

Source: Authors' calculations based on MENA SPEAKS Survey 2012.

Note: SSN = social safety net; Q = income quintile (1 = lowest, 5 = highest).

FIGURE 4C.4

Public Awareness of Nonsubsidy SSNs in Tunisia, 2012

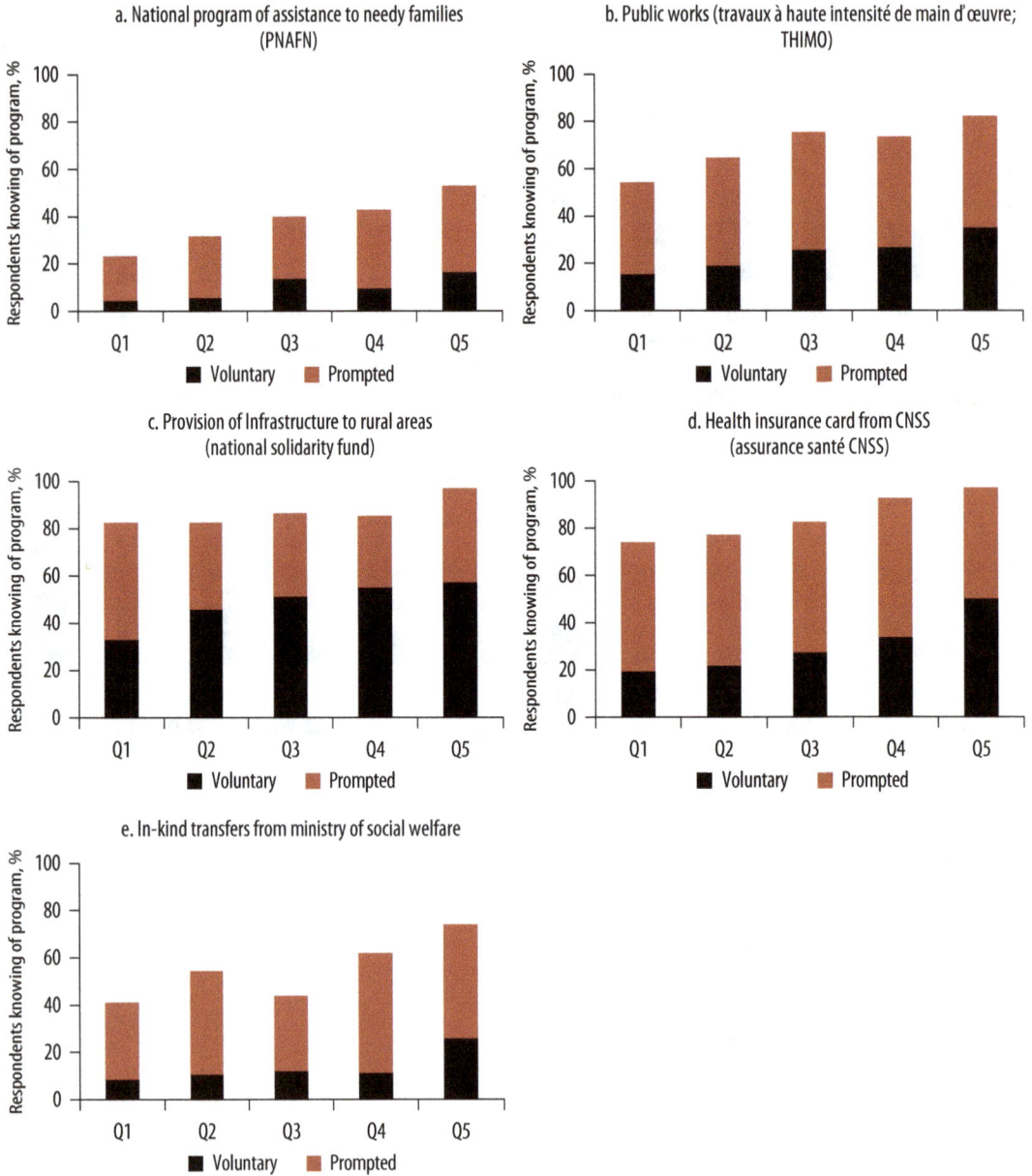

a. National program of assistance to needy families (PNAFN)

b. Public works (travaux à haute intensité de main d'œuvre; THIMO)

c. Provision of Infrastructure to rural areas (national solidarity fund)

d. Health insurance card from CNSS (assurance santé CNSS)

e. In-kind transfers from ministry of social welfare

Source: Authors' calculations based on MENA SPEAKS Survey 2012.

Note: CNSS = Caisse Nationale de Sécurité Sociale; SSN = social safety net; Q = income quintile (1 = lowest, 5 = highest).

Awareness of Subsidies

Egypt

Awareness about food subsidies is much higher than awareness of fuel subsidies in Egypt across income quintiles. Most Egyptians volunteered being aware of food subsidies (more than a 50 percent response across quintiles in all programs). Contrarily, fuel subsidies have a very low recall; most people responded only after being prompted (less than 10 percent voluntary recall in most quintiles in all programs).

Jordan

Awareness of the bread and wheat flour subsidies is very high and fairly uniform across income quintiles. These subsidies also have a very high voluntary recall: 44–64 percent of Jordanians mentioned them without being prompted. There is also high awareness about the LPG subsidy (with 31 percent of the middle quintile and 32 percent of the top quintile mentioning it voluntarily). All other fuel subsidies have very low awareness, especially among the poor.

Lebanon

Awareness about bread, wheat, and flour subsidies seems to be highest among the people surveyed in Lebanon; 16–39 percent of Lebanese mentioned them without being prompted. The second-highest awareness is of fuel subsidies (with 32 percent of the top quintile mentioning it voluntarily); it increases with income (from 27 percent in the bottom quintile to 59 percent in the top quintile). The tobacco subsidy has the lowest recognition, across income levels.

Tunisia

Awareness about the bread and flour subsidy seems to be highest among the people surveyed in Tunisia. It also has a high voluntary recall, since 29–51 percent of Tunisians mentioned it without being prompted. Awareness about the semolina subsidy is also very high (with 45 percent of the top quintile mentioning it voluntarily), and it increases with income (from 62 percent in the bottom quintile to 84 percent in the top quintile). The diesel subsidy has the lowest recognition, especially among the poor.

FIGURE 4C.5

Public Awareness of SSN Subsidies in the Arab Republic of Egypt, 2012

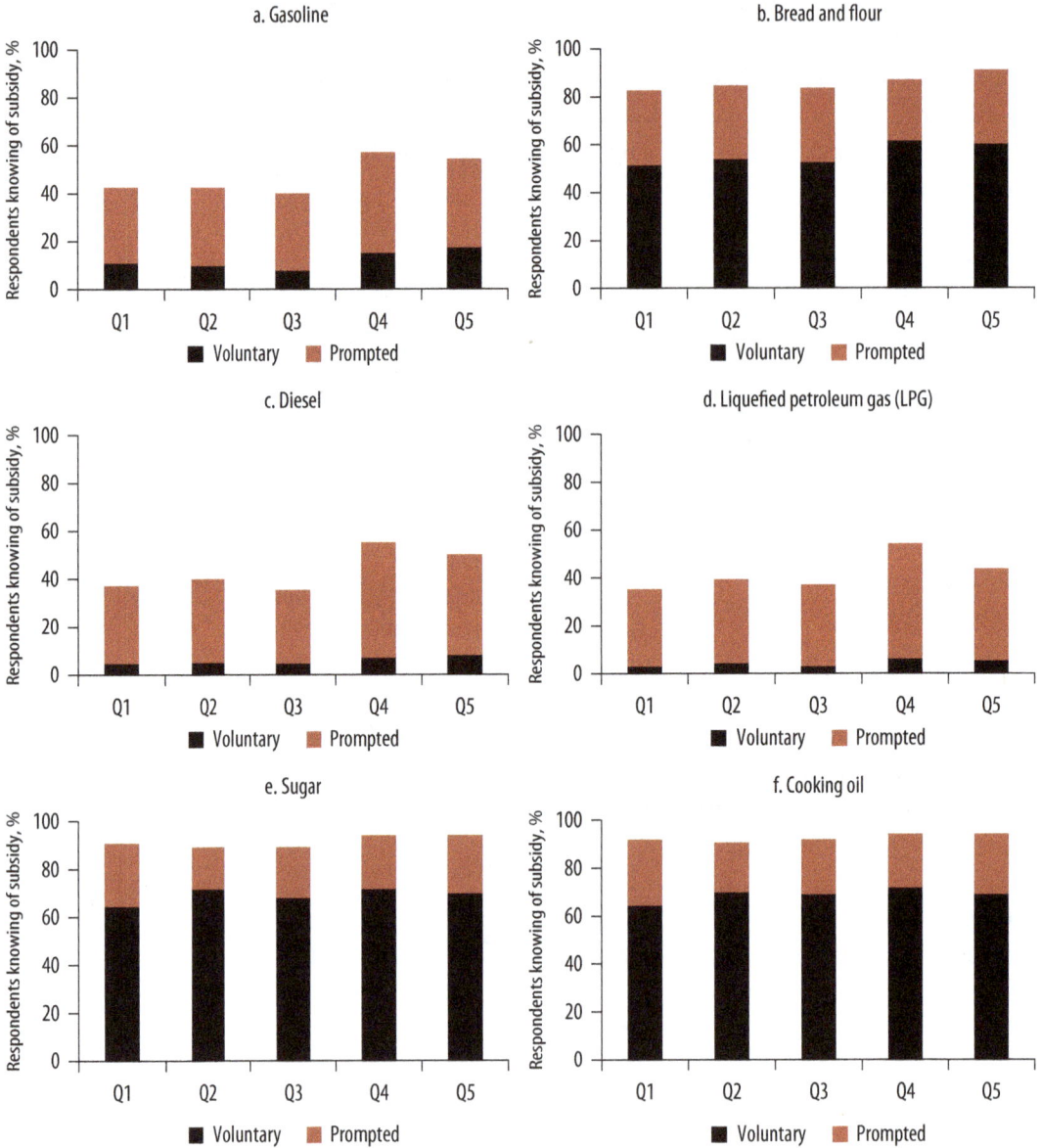

a. Gasoline

b. Bread and flour

c. Diesel

d. Liquefied petroleum gas (LPG)

e. Sugar

f. Cooking oil

Source: Authors' calculations based on MENA SPEAKS Survey 2012.

Note: SSN = social safety net; Q = income quintile (1 = lowest, 5 = highest).

FIGURE 4C.6

Public Awareness of SSN Subsidies in Jordan, 2012

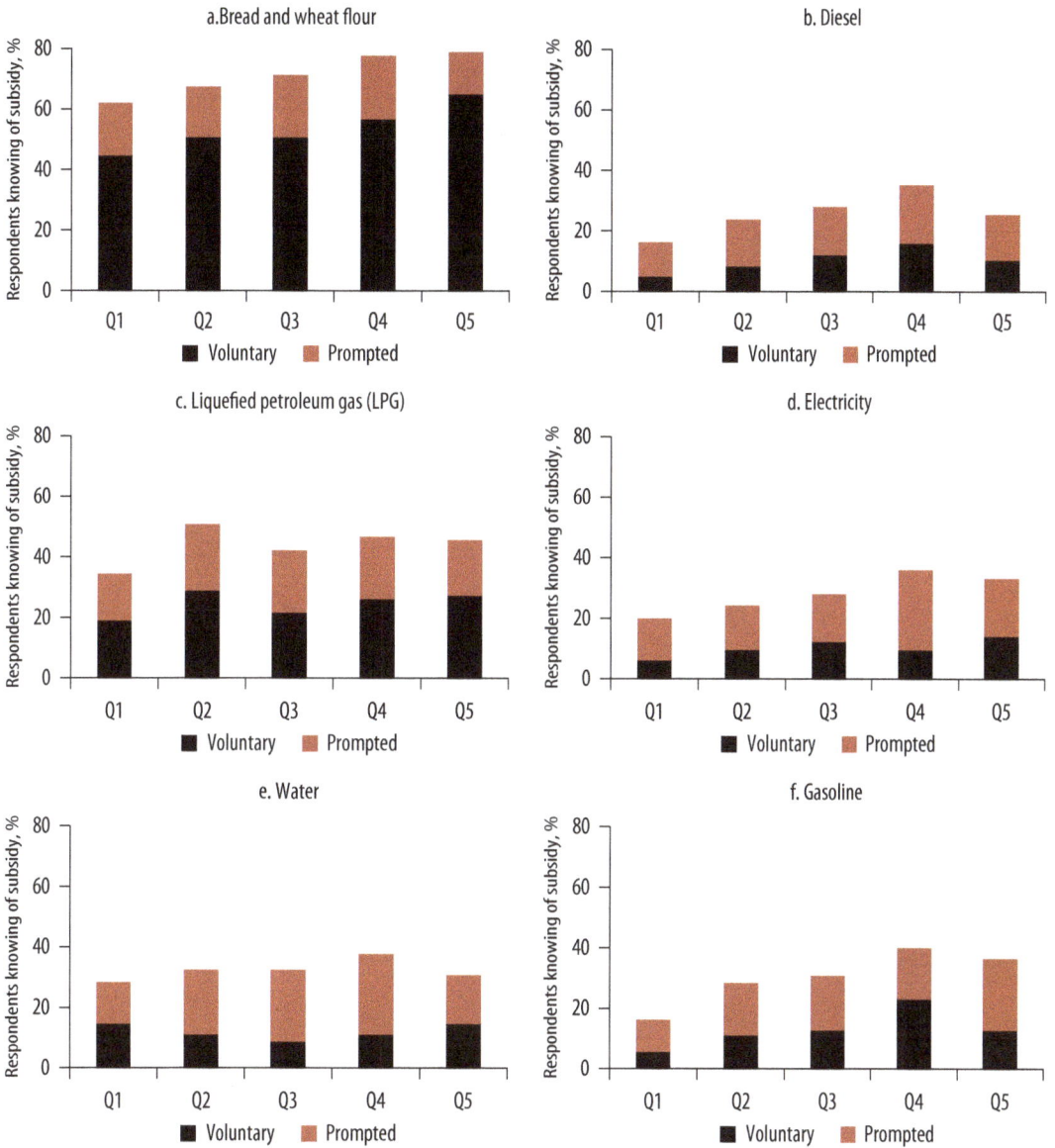

Source: Authors' calculations based on MENA SPEAKS Survey 2012.

Note: SSN = social safety net; Q = income quintile (1 = lowest, 5 = highest).

Public Awareness of SSN Subsidies in Lebanon

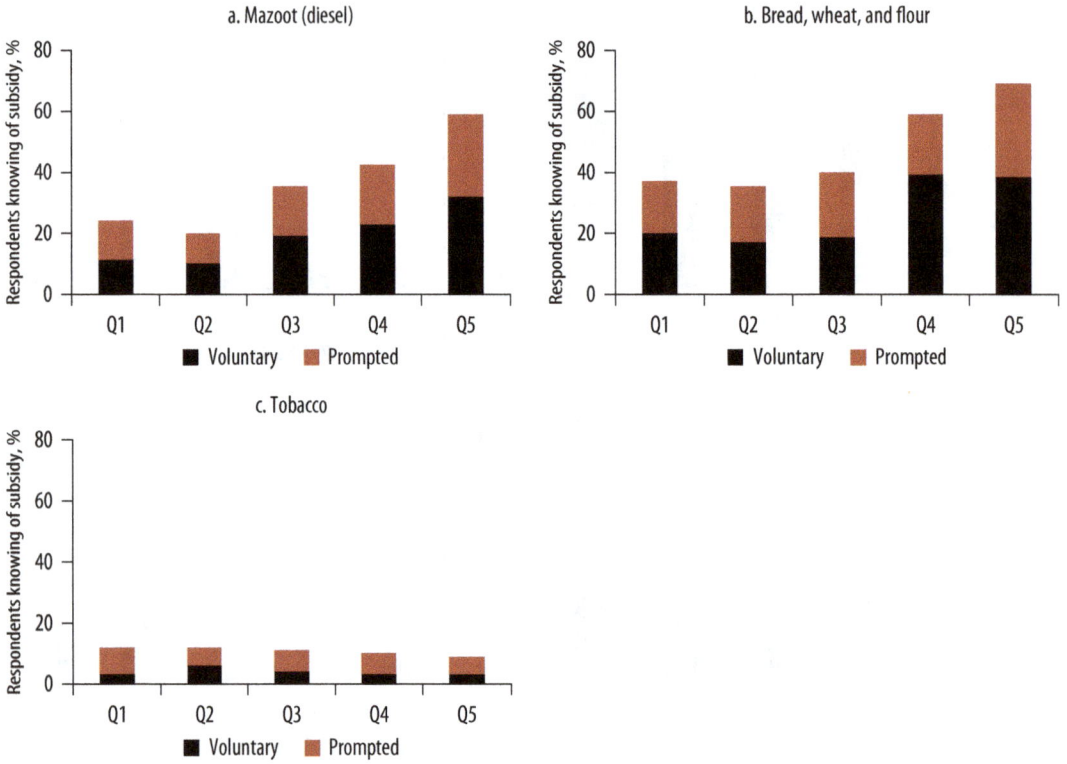

a. Mazoot (diesel)

b. Bread, wheat, and flour

c. Tobacco

Source: Authors' calculations based on MENA SPEAKS Survey 2012.

Note: SSN = social safety net; Q = income quintile (1 = lowest, 5 = highest).

Public Awareness of SSN Subsidies in Tunisia, 2012

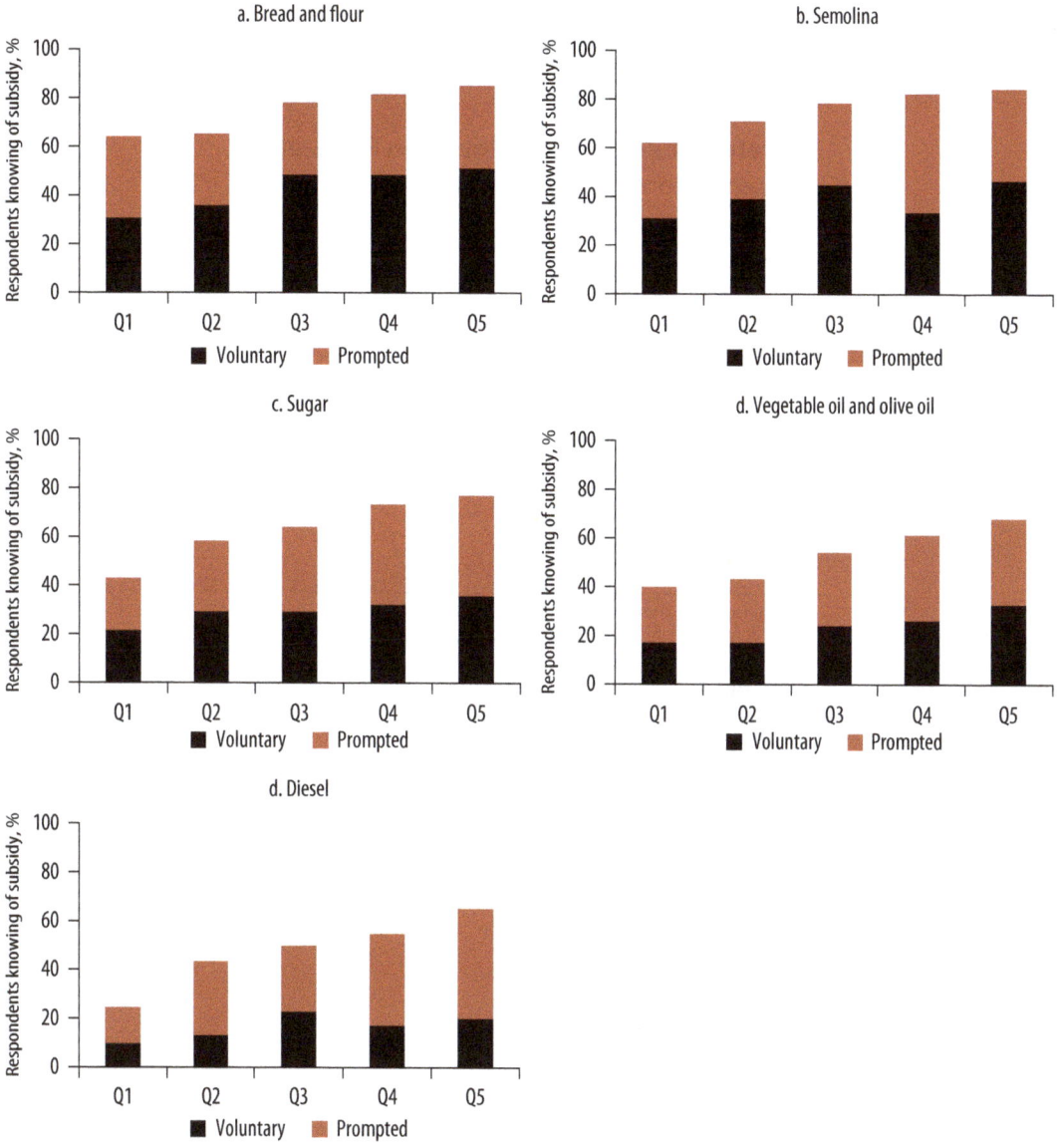

Source: Authors' calculations based on MENA SPEAKS Survey 2012.

Note: SSN = social safety net; Q = income quintile (1 = lowest, 5 = highest).

Annex 4D

Determinants of Redistribution Preferences among Jordan's Middle Class

TABLE 4D.1

Determinants of Redistribution Preferences among Jordan's Middle Class, 2012

Ordered probit	Disapproves redistribution
Subjective income: middle	0.312
	(2.45)*
Subjective income: upper	0.476
	(2.31)*
Can rely on informal safety net	−0.354
	(−2.63)**
Thinks poor are lazy	0.298
	(3.75)***
Worried to lose job or income	0.103
	(1.40)
Observations	395

Source: Authors' calculations based on Jordan Gives 2012.

Note: z statistics in parentheses. Controls for gender, education, and employment. Baseline subjective income: lower middle class. "Subjective income" = self-reported perceived income level.

*p < .1   **p < .05   ***p <.01

Annex 4E

Determinants of Perceiving High Inequality

TABLE 4E.1

Determinants of Perceiving High Inequality in the Middle East and North Africa, Selected Countries, 2012

Variables	Perceives high inequality.			
	Egypt, Arab Rep.	Jordan	Lebanon	Tunisia
Living standard getting better	−0.0921**	−0.116***	0.00504	−0.113***
	(0.0408)	(0.0374)	(0.0504)	(0.0411)
Income q2	−0.0249	−0.0612	−0.0372	−0.0486
	(0.0557)	(0.0516)	(0.0589)	(0.0594)
Income q3	−0.0524	−0.118**	−0.0682	−0.0659
	(0.0609)	(0.0508)	(0.0632)	(0.0591)
Income q4	−0.0884	−0.148***	−0.172***	−0.120*
	(0.0592)	(0.0484)	(0.0578)	(0.0648)
Income q5	−0.159***	−0.120**	−0.279***	−0.0262
	(0.0606)	(0.0543)	(0.0543)	(0.0744)
Observations	1,003	883	960	737
r2_p	0.0263	0.0511	0.0757	0.0393

Source: Authors' calculations based on MENA SPEAKS Survey 2012.

Note: q = income quintile (1 = lowest, 5 = highest). Robust standard errors in parentheses. Controls for gender, age, education, work status, and household assets.

*p < .1   **p < .05   ***p <.01

Annex 4F

Effects of Perceptions about Corruption, Inequality, and Deteriorating Economic Situation on the Evaluation of SSN Effectiveness

TABLE 4F.1

Effects of Selected Perceptions on Evaluation of SSN Effectiveness in the Middle East and North Africa, Selected Countries, 2012

Find social assistance effective	Egypt, Arab Rep.	Jordan	Lebanon	Tunisia
Income quintile 2	0.04	0.23	−0.03	−0.07
Income quintile 3	0.07	0.01	−0.23	0.07
Income quintile 4	−0.10	0.36	−0.39	0.28
Income quintile 5	−0.10	0.24	−0.44*	0.38
Economic worsening	−0.17	0.01	−0.50***	0.18
Gov. corrupt	−0.60***	−0.76***	−0.57***	−0.93***
Low inequality	0.14*	0.15*	−0.13	0.04
Donated	0.16	−0.11	−0.34	−0.74**
Feels poor	−0.39**	−0.44**	−0.15	−0.14
_cons	−0.34	0.65	2.51***	2.41**
pseudo R-sq	0.086	0.145	0.084	0.133
N	992	794	925	663

Source: Authors' calculations based on MENA SPEAKS Survey 2012.

Note: SSN = social safety net. Dependent variable is equal to 1 if the individual responded that SSN in his country is effective or very effective, and equal to 0 otherwise. The coefficients are probit marginal effects. Results control for gender, age squared, education, work status, and household size.

*$p < .1$ **$p < .05$ ***$p < .01$

Notes

1. To the authors' knowledge, no study had previously examined attitudes toward SSNs or redistribution in the Middle East and North Africa. Several studies that conducted experiments on trust with university students in Gulf countries (Kuwait, Oman, Saudi Arabia, and the United Arab Emirates) and two Western countries (Switzerland and the United States) found a lower level of trust in the Gulf states than in the West, as well as lower responsiveness to changes in the payoffs associated with giving trust to unknown individuals (Bohnet et al. 2010; Bohnet, Herrmann, and Zeckhauser 2010).
2. The first question explained what an SSN program is and then asked the respondents to name any government SSN projects in their country that they knew about. Programs were defined as "a government project in which money or other goods and services are provided to the poor." The interviewer checked off programs on a preset list of five or six existing programs (obtained from the MENA SSN Inventory and validated by Gallup's country experts). If a program on the list was not mentioned, the interviewer followed up by asking whether the respondent had heard about it. See annex 4A for the full questionnaire.
3. After defining what a price subsidy is ("in some countries, governments subsidize the prices of certain products by keeping their prices fixed or at least preventing their prices from rising too fast"), the interviewer asked respondents whether they thought their governments were subsidizing any products and checked the mentioned items off a preset list (obtained from a desk review of World Bank publications and cross-checked with Gallup country experts). If a product on the list was not mentioned, respondents were asked whether they thought that their countries' governments subsidized the price of this specific good.

References

Abouleinein, S., H. El-Laithy, and H. Kheir-El-Din. 2009. "The Impact of Phasing Out Subsidies of Petroleum Energy Products in Egypt." Working Paper 145, Egyptian Center for Economic Studies, Cairo.

Adams, R. H., Jr. 1998. "The Political Economy of the Food Subsidy System in Bangladesh." *Journal of Development Studies* 35 (1): 66–88.

———. 2000. "Self-Targeted Subsidies: The Political and Distributional Impact of the Egyptian Food Subsidy System." *Economic Development and Cultural Change* 49 (1): 115–36.

Ahmed, A. U. 1992. "Operational Performance of the Rural Rationing Program in Bangladesh." Project Papers and Notes, International Food Policy Research Institute, Washington, DC.

Ahmed, R., S. Haggblade, and T. Chowdhury, eds. 2000. *Out of the Shadow of Famine: Evolving Food Markets and Food Policy in Bangladesh*. Baltimore, MD: Johns Hopkins University Press.

Alderman, H. 1988. "The Twilight of Flour Rationing in Pakistan." *Food Policy* 13 (3): 245–56.

————. 2002. "Subsidies as a Social Safety Net: Effectiveness and Challenges." Social Safety Net Primer Series Discussion Paper 224, World Bank, Washington, DC.

Alesina, A., and G.-M. Angeletos. 2005. "Fairness and Redistribution." *American Economic Review* 95 (4): 960–80.

Alesina, A. F., and P. Giuliano. 2009. "Preferences for Redistribution." Working Paper 14825, National Bureau of Economic Research, Cambridge, MA.

Alesina, A. F., and E. La Ferrara. 2005. "Preferences for Redistribution in the Land of Opportunities." *Journal of Public Economics* 89 (5): 897–931.

Ali, S. M., and R. H. Adams. 1996. "The Egyptian Food Subsidy System: Operation and Effects on Income Distribution." *World Development* 24 (11): 1777–91.

Bénabou, R., and E. A. Ok. 2001. "Social Mobility and the Demand for Redistribution: The Poum Hypothesis." *The Quarterly Journal of Economics* 116 (2): 447–87.

Bénabou, R., and J. Tirole. 2006. "Incentives and Prosocial Behavior." *American Economic Review* 96 (5): 1652–78.

Bohnet, I., B. Herrmann, M. Al-Ississ, A. Robbett, K. Al-Yahia, and R. J. Zeckhauser. 2010. "The Elasticity of Trust: How to Promote Trust in the Arab Middle East and the United States." Working Paper RWP10-031, Harvard Kennedy School, Cambridge, MA.

Bohnet, I., B. Herrmann, and R. Zeckhauser. 2010. "The Requirements for Trust in Gulf and Western Countries." *Quarterly Journal of Economics* CXXV (2): 811–28.

Cruces, G., R. P. Truglia, and M. Tetaz. 2011. "Biased Perceptions of Income Distribution and Preferences for Redistribution: Evidence from a Survey Experiment." Discussion Paper 5699, Institute for the Study of Labor (IZA), Bonn.

De Janvry, A., F. Finan, E. Sadoulet, D. Nelson, K. Lindert, B. de la Brière, and P. Lanjouw. 2005. "Brazil's *Bolsa Escola* Program: The Role of Local Governance in Decentralized Implementation." Social Protection Discussion Paper 542, World Bank, Washington, DC.

Del Ninno, C., and P. A. Dorosh. 2002. "In-Kind Transfers and Household Food Consumption: Implications for Targeted Food Programs in Bangladesh." Discussion Paper 134, Food Consumption and Nutrition Division, International Food Policy Research Institute, Washington, DC.

ESC (Economic and Social Council). 2008. "Assessing the Middle Class in Jordan." Policy Paper, Amman.

Fong, C. 2001. "Social Preferences, Self-Interest, and the Demand for Redistribution." *Journal of Public Economics* 82 (2): 225–46.

Gelbach, J. B., and L. Pritchett. 2002. "Is More for the Poor Less for the Poor? The Politics of Means-Tested Targeting." *Topics in Economic Analysis and Policy* 2 (1): 1–26.

Graham, C. 2002. "Public Attitudes Matter: A Conceptual Frame for Accounting for Political Economy in Safety Nets and Social Assistance Policies." Social Protection Discussion Paper 233, World Bank, Washington, DC.

Graham, C., M. Grindle, E. Lora, and J. Seddon. 1999. *Improving the Odds: Political Strategies for Institutional Reform in Latin America*. Monograph. Washington, DC: Inter-American Development Bank.

Grindle, M. S., and J. W. Thomas. 1989. "Policy Makers, Policy Choices, and Policy Outcomes: The Political Economy of Reform in Developing Countries." *Policy Sciences* 22 (3): 213–48.

Grosh, M., C. Del Ninno, E. Tesliuc, and A. Ouerghi. 2008. *For Protection & Promotion: The Design and Implementation of Effective Safety Nets*. Washington, DC: World Bank.

Guillaume, D., R. Zytek, and M. Reza Farzin. 2011. "Iran—The Chronicles of the Subsidy Reform." Working Paper 11/167, International Monetary Fund, Washington, DC.

Hirschman, A. O., and M. Rothschild. 1973. "The Changing Tolerance for Income Inequality in the Course of Economic Development." *The Quarterly Journal of Economics* 87 (4): 544–66.

Jayne, T. S., and S. Jones. 1997. "Food Marketing and Pricing Policy in Eastern and Southern Africa: A Survey." *World Development* 25 (9): 1505–27.

Kahneman, D., and A. Tversky. 1979. "Prospect Theory: An Analysis of Decision under Risk." *Econometrica: Journal of the Econometric Society* 47 (2): 263–91.

Lee, D. S., E. Moretti, and M. J. Butler. 2004. "Do Voters Affect or Elect Policies? Evidence from the U.S. House." *The Quarterly Journal of Economics* 119 (3): 807–59.

Lindert, K., and V. Vincensini. 2010. "Brazil—Social Policy, Perceptions and the Press: An Analysis of the Media's Treatment of Conditional Cash Transfers in Brazil." Social Protection Discussion Paper 70613, World Bank, Washington, DC.

Meltzer, A. H., and S. F. Richard. 1981. "A Rational Theory of the Size of Government." *The Journal of Political Economy* 89 (5): 914–27.

Olson, M. 1965. *The Logic of Collective Action: Public Goods and the Theory of Groups*. Cambridge, MA: Harvard University Press.

Önis, Z., and S. B. Webb. 1992. "Political Economy of Policy Reform in Turkey in the 1980s." Policy Research Working Paper 1059, World Bank, Washington, DC.

Pritchett, L. 2005. "The Political Economy of Targeted Safety Nets." Social Protection Discussion Paper 31498, World Bank, Washington, DC.

Ravallion, M., and M. Lokshin. 2000. "Who Wants to Redistribute? The Tunnel Effect in 1990s Russia." *Journal of Public Economics* 76 (1): 87–104.

Romer, D. 2003. "Misconceptions and Political Outcomes." *The Economic Journal* 113 (484): 1–20.

Romer, T. 1975. "Individual Welfare, Majority Voting, and the Properties of a Linear Income Tax." *Journal of Public Economics* 4 (2): 163–85.

Sen, A. 1995. "The Political Economy of Targeting." In *Public Spending and the Poor: Theory and Evidence*, edited by D. Van de Walle and K. Nead, 11–24. Baltimore, MD : Johns Hopkins University Press.

Tabor, S. R., and M. H. Sawit. 2001. "Social Protection via Rice: The OPK Rice Subsidy Program in Indonesia." *The Developing Economies* 39 (3): 267–94.

Tuck, L., and K. Lindert. 1996. "From Universal Food Subsidies to a Self-Targeted Program: A Case Study in Tunisian Reform." Discussion Paper 351, World Bank, Washington, DC.

WVS (World Values Survey) (database). n.d. World Values Survey Association, Stockholm. http://www.worldvaluessurvey.org.

The Way Forward: How to Make Safety Nets in the Middle East and North Africa More Effective and Innovative

Introduction

This report has made a case for putting in place more effective social safety net (SSN) programs in the Middle East and North Africa. As described in the framework for SSN reform (chapter 1, figure 1.4), SSNs can be a powerful instrument to promote

- *Social inclusion*, by enabling investment in human capital (such as supporting school attendance or better nutrition for children);

- *Livelihood*, by protecting against destitution; and

- *Resilience to crises*, by helping households navigate the effects of shocks.

Achieving these outcomes requires a focus on the following goals:

- Enhance the emphasis on the poor and vulnerable

- Empower individuals with tools to improve their lives

- Ensure ready and rapid temporary support in response to crises to better promote resilience

- Give citizens a greater voice to promote civic engagement and policy ownership.

To fulfill these goals, SSNs need to be carefully designed and implemented in ways that ensure they are reaching the most vulnerable since 2009, through improved administrative and governance systems. Currently, 80 percent of developing countries have plans to initiate or strengthen their safety nets, according to World Bank assessments (World Bank 2012).

Continued growth and poverty reduction, as well as a growing middle class in the Middle East and North Africa, often go hand in hand with increasing inequality and economic volatility that have created pockets of poverty and exclusion, as well as high vulnerability to shocks. Against this background, current SSN systems feature a program mix highly dependent on fuel and food subsidies; have low coverage and high fragmentation of nonsubsidy SSN programs; inadequately target most cash transfers, relying mostly on categorical or geographical methods; and provide limited opportunities for either activation or graduation (previously covered in chapter 3).

These human development and institutional challenges call for cost-effective SSNs that promote social inclusion and productivity. The emerging safety net agenda emphasizes that (a) well-designed SSN programs work and can be both efficient and affordable; (b) SSNs are needed at all times, and having them in place *before* a crisis increases effectiveness of coping with the consequences; (c) SSNs should reduce poverty as well as promote growth; and (d) SSNs should be conceived as part of a broader social protection system.

This chapter addresses the main points discussed during extensive consultations in the region, followed up with online discussions. Consultations in the context of this report included two main types of activities:

1. *Three regional consultation workshops* were jointly organized with the team developing the World Bank Social Protection Strategy for the Middle East and North Africa. Workshop components included a presentation of the preliminary results from the regional report, expert cafés or roundtables on key challenges and options for reform in each country, showcases of best SSN practices in the region and internationally (with posters and a quiz with prizes), and focus group discussions using a modified version of the Jordan Gives game. (See box 5.1 for an overview of the main issues discussed in the consultation workshops.)

2. *In-depth national consultations* in Jordan, Lebanon, and Tunisia sought feedback on the draft report.

The proposals presented in this chapter are based on these extensive consultations as well as international experience (success stories and key practical steps on how to get there). The evidence presented in the preceding chapters—such as rigorous analysis of the needs of the region's poor and vulnerable (chapter 2), the performance assessment of existing SSN systems (chapter 3), and citizens' SSN preferences (chapter 4)—lays the foundation for moving forward. This chapter builds on this evidence base, proposes a reform agenda (aligned with the SSN objectives discussed in chapter 1), and translates its key items into practical suggestions for how to proceed.

BOX 5.1

Main Issues Discussed at SSN Consultation Workshops

Extensive consultations on SSN reform were held in the Middle East and North Africa, including three regional workshops—in Beirut (January 13–14, 2012), Tunis (January 16–17, 2012), and Muscat (April 16–17, 2012)—jointly organized with the World Bank's MENA (Middle East and North Africa) Social Protection Strategy team. There were more than 80 participants in each workshop, including representatives from government, academia, civil society, nongovernmental organizations (NGOs), community-based organizations, and donors in the region (including the International Labour Organization and the United Nations Economic and Social Commission for Western Asia). Representatives from Algeria, Bahrain, Iraq, Jordan, Kuwait, Lebanon, Morocco, Oman, Saudi Arabia, Tunisia, the United Arab Emirates, and West Bank and Gaza identified the main issues and challenges in designing SSNs. Workshop participants raised the following questions, among others:

- *How can countries ensure that the temporary income support given by the SSN programs has long-lasting results for beneficiaries?* Participants felt that just giving income to families may not have long-term effects. The consensus was that income support should be temporary, targeted to those in need, and associated with enhancing beneficiaries' livelihoods and increasing their employment possibilities through better access to social services such as education, health, and employment services.

- *How can benefits best be targeted to the truly needy?* Most delegations wanted details on how to target various programs. Participants acknowledged that each existing program uses a different targeting mechanism to reach its beneficiaries. A consensus seemed to emerge on the need to target the poor, and questions were centered on the best way to do so in each country. There was significant interest in international experience on proxy means tests (PMT). The advantages and disadvantages of alternative targeting methods were discussed.

- *What is the role of NGOs and civil society organizations (CSOs) in SSNs?* The consultation process witnessed CSOs demanding greater involvement, not only in the context of SSN design and implementation but also more broadly in social, political, and economic issues. There was a lot of interest in how NGO and CSO participation in service provision and social accountability can be enhanced, and when such participation adds the most value.

- *In practice, how have subsidy reforms been implemented, and how has the compensation package been designed?* A lot of concern surrounded increasing fiscal spending on subsidies as well as political economy issues; therefore, there was substantial interest in the practical implementation and sustainability of subsidy reforms, such as the features of the compensation package.

(box continued on next page)

BOX 5.1 *Continued*

- *How can countries best balance limited resources and widespread needs?* Participants acknowledged that significant amounts are spent on SSN systems with limited impacts on poverty and inequality. The consensus was that it is important to make programs more cost-effective and results-oriented. Participants were interested in achievements of cost-effective SSN programs around the world.

- *How can social programs avoid dependency?* Beneficiaries of some unconditional cash transfer (UCT) programs in the region were perceived to treat the cash they receive as their "salary." Although this situation may reflect the fact that many beneficiaries comprise categories of disabled and elderly persons or others unable to work, there was a consensus that it is important to move from perceiving programs as an entitlement to perceiving them as an opportunity—as an investment in people rather than as a handout. Governments in the region

were struggling to curtail dependency, especially when programs switch from categorical to poverty-based targeting. Strategies used around the world to avoid dependency were discussed, including targeting on correlates of poverty rather than labor income; conditioning transfers on behaviors that enhance human capital; requiring regular recertification; and channeling the assistance to women.

- *How can SSNs be seen in a broader context?* The main concerns raised were (a) how to ensure that SSNs adequately serve all the poor, given their different circumstances and needs (for example, the disabled, the elderly, and young couples without children); and (b) how to make SSNs true insurance mechanisms, given that insurance is currently largely missing. The consensus was to focus on a few large-scale programs with different windows and use a common targeting database as the anchor.

A Path toward Effective and Innovative SSNs

SSNs in the Middle East and North Africa are ripe for reform. As chapter 3 showed, the region relies heavily on inefficient and pro-rich price subsidies and ration cards. Subsidies aside, SSNs in the region are small and fragmented. Most of the poor and vulnerable fall through the cracks of nonsubsidy SSNs because of low coverage. Moreover, poor targeting practices lead to inefficient use of resources. Although subsidies are often pro-rich and ineffective relative to other SSN interventions, many people depend on them for their livelihoods. Thus, moving from the status quo toward more effective, reliable, and equitable SSNs requires careful thinking about technical aspects as well as the political economy of reform.

SSNs in the region can better promote inclusion, livelihood, and resilience, and citizens expect them to do so. Because of their politically sensitive nature, SSN reforms require consensus building, the grounds for which already appear to exist: The MENA SPEAKS survey and Jordan Gives experiment have revealed that people hold the government responsible as the main provider of SSNs, and many are not satisfied with the effectiveness of current SSN policies and programs. In fact, the kinds of programs preferred by citizens in several Middle Eastern and North African countries are in line with the best practices in SSN design. Thus, governments have an enabling environment that can be rallied behind SSN reform. Moreover, several economies in the region have already implemented successful reforms that have attained significant positive results (see box 5.2).

While there are no single solutions, the path toward more effective and innovative SSNs calls for action on four agenda items: improving the impact of SSN programs; enhancing the reliability and flexibility of SSN

BOX 5.2

Emerging SSN Best Practices in the Middle East and North Africa

Djibouti: Making a Workfare Program Work for Women and Children

At the time of the 2008 food and fuel crisis, the country did not have SSNs in place that could be scaled up. Following the crisis, the government implemented a "workfare plus" program. The innovative SSN program provides short-term employment opportunities in community-based, labor-intensive works and supports the improvement of nutrition practices among participating households, focusing on preschool children and pregnant or lactating women. This combination of a workfare program with a nutrition intervention is designed to have a multigenerational impact by leveraging, through transfer of knowledge on nutrition, the use of additional income to improve a family's health status. It promotes a holistic, community-driven approach, providing employment opportunities for both men and women.

Lebanon: Establishing a Targeting System Using Modern Technology

Lebanon recently launched the National Poverty Targeting Program (NPTP), which establishes a central targeting database for social safety nets. The program automates data entry of applications and relies on local Social Development Centers to conduct household visits and outreach.

Morocco: Launching a CCT Program to Boost School Attendance

Morocco's conditional cash transfer (CCT) program has had a significant positive impact, as demonstrated through impact evaluation. To reduce school dropouts in rural areas, especially of girls, the government launched a cash transfer conditional on primary school attendance. The impact evaluation of the pilot demonstrated that dropout rates decreased by 57 percent and the rate of dropouts' returning to school increased by

(box continued on next page)

BOX 5.2 *Continued*

37 percent. Recently, program coverage increased from a pilot of 80,000 students in 2009 to 690,000 children in 406,000 households in 2011–12. The total budget rose from US$10 to US$62 million.

West Bank and Gaza: Reducing Fragmentation and Building Administrative Capacity

West Bank and Gaza has a fully fledged unconditional cash transfer (UCT) program in place, which resulted from a merger of the two largest donor-funded cash transfer programs. The program uses PMT targeting methodology and a unified registry of beneficiaries that enabled it to provide assistance to more than 93,000 of the poorest households in the country in 2011. Moreover, to respond to crisis conditions in 2010, the system was quickly scaled up by 25,000 additional households.

The Republic of Yemen: Having a Working Safety Net for Rapid Crisis Response

The existing cash assistance and workfare programs provided instruments for a rapid response to the 2008 food and fuel crisis. They consisted of (a) temporary cash assistance (US$15–20 per month for 12 months) to poor households, and (b) scaling up the workfare program, which provided temporary job opportunities to 16,824 households. The vast majority of beneficiary households (95 percent) used the funds to bridge a consumption gap. The workfare program also created community assets by rehabilitating water harvesting systems, clearing up land for agricultural activities, rehabilitating terraces from erosion, and fixing feeder roads, among other activities.

infrastructure for better crisis preparedness, achieving cost-effectiveness through consolidation; and rebalancing SSN financing and priorities. Engaging citizens and other stakeholders in this agenda can improve feasibility and facilitate success:

- *Improving the impact of SSN programs.* Currently, most nonsubsidy SSN programs in the Middle East and North Africa have a limited impact on poverty and inequality because of a combination of low coverage, inefficient targeting practices, and inadequate or nonexistent monitoring and evaluation (M&E) systems. Hence, the way forward could entail

  o Prioritizing interventions that promote investment in human capital;

  o Enhancing programs' targeting toward the poor and vulnerable;

  o Improving the focus on results through M&E and social accountability; and

○ Reaching out to other stakeholders, including citizens, NGOs, CSOs, the private sector, and nonprofits.

• *Enhancing reliability and flexibility of SSN infrastructure for better crisis preparedness.* An effective SSN system can help citizens navigate the effects of both idiosyncratic and systemic shocks. The recent global economic crisis underscored the weak capacity of existing SSN systems in the Middle East and North Africa to serve this function. Promoting households' resilience to shocks through SSNs requires a strong administrative infrastructure. Having this infrastructure in place *ahead* of a crisis allows for quicker and more efficient development of remedial and mitigation actions, such as scaling up of benefits for the most vulnerable or expanding coverage, thus enhancing resilience. Specifically, strengthening the administrative SSN infrastructure could entail

○ Creating unified registries of beneficiaries; and

○ Using effective service delivery mechanisms.

• *Consolidating fragmented SSN systems.* In the Middle East and North Africa, direct transfer programs (cash-based or in-kind) are often small and highly fragmented. International experience suggests that having a few comprehensive programs, specifically designed to reach different segments of the poor and vulnerable, can address current vulnerabilities and social protection gaps by increasing both coverage (currently below 20 percent of the poor in most countries) and benefits (currently at about 5–10 percent of consumption of the poor). Parts of the region (for example, Morocco and West Bank and Gaza) have already started reforming their SSNs in this direction.

• *Rebalancing SSN financing and priorities.* Effective reforms include focusing on targeted programs rather than on subsidies. Middle Eastern and North African countries spend the lion's share of SSN expenditure, in terms of GDP, on energy subsidies and a small share on targeted safety nets. Reducing costly and regressive general fuel and food price subsidies would decrease fiscal imbalances and free up resources for safety net programs. In particular, this effort could entail

○ Increasing spending on and improving coverage of nonsubsidy SSNs to protect against destitution; and

○ Reforming price subsidies through wholesale and internal reforms.

In what follows, the chapter will follow the agenda outlined above to provide key practical steps using best practices from the Middle East and

North Africa and elsewhere to enable the region's SSNs to better promote inclusion, livelihood, and resilience.

Improving the Impact of SSN Programs

Prioritizing Interventions that Promote Investment in Human Capital

Middle Eastern and North African countries differ in their human development challenges. To better promote social inclusion, the prioritization of SSN programs should reflect this diversity. For example, in countries where the key challenge is high malnutrition (such as in Djibouti), programs can be geared toward the prevention of this problem. In other countries, where low educational outcomes are the most pressing social issue (such as in Morocco), providing incentives for school enrollment and attendance is crucial. In many countries around the world—including some in the Middle East and North Africa—these concerns have been tackled by scaling up existing successful CCT and workfare programs; tweaking program design to make them work better for children, youth, and women; creating new interventions to fill the gaps based on best practices around the world; and collaborating with supply-side providers and involved agencies.

Scaling Up a Successful Program. Morocco's Tayssir program, which started out as a pilot, was based on solid empirical evidence of high dropout rates in rural areas (especially among girls) and higher absenteeism of teachers in rural areas. The CCT intervention targeted pockets with higher dropout rates and poverty (Benhassine et al., forthcoming). The Tayssir program has been shown to decrease dropout rates, especially for girls, and to improve learning outcomes for boys. Since 2009, the program has expanded in coverage and budget. Success stories such as these can be scaled up further to promote human capital investment nationwide. To scale up a program, governments need to assess supply-side availability (for example, the presence of schools and teachers in the area) as well as to evaluate the administrative capacity to provide transfers to a greater number of recipients.

Tweaking Program Design for Greater Effectiveness. Improving the reach of existing SSN programs can help them work better for subgroups of recipients while also strengthening their impact on education, nutrition, and job skills. Some UCTs can be transformed into CCTs by introducing conditions linked to the main human development challenges in the country, such as by complementing cash transfers with training vouchers for disadvantaged youth, early childhood development interventions, or conditions linked to nutrition. However, findings from the MENA

SPEAKS survey and the Jordan Gives experiment suggest that the use of conditionality as a mechanism to promote human capital accumulation—which would be largely new to the Middle East and North Africa—remains little endorsed (or understood) in the four surveyed countries.

Thus, qualitative research to understand the reasons for these views (or the factors behind the success of existing pilots in the region in spite of these perceptions), together with piloting and communication campaigns, are all important elements to consider when planning to introduce such an innovative program design. Moreover, including gender-sensitive activities in workfare programs could promote women's participation, which might have positive externalities on their children. In tweaking the design of UCTs, governments need to be careful to protect the income support function of SSNs for groups that cannot comply with the selected conditions (such as the elderly and the disabled).

Creating New Interventions Using Global Best Practices. In countries where programs that promote inclusion are absent, new programs can be designed with the existing global best practice in mind. Djibouti provides a good example of program creation to tackle a country's most pressing problems. Rigorous analytical work indicated that unemployment and malnutrition were priority challenges in Djibouti (World Bank 2009). Unfortunately, in 2009, no SSN programs attempted to address those challenges directly. The government has since developed a workfare program that also provides a nutrition intervention, aiming to leverage the effect of the additional income on the families' nutritional status through behavioral change. The design of the nutrition component was inspired by the international best practice of Madagascar's Expanded Food Security and Nutrition program (*Sécurité alimentaire et nutrition élargie*; SECALINE). Unlike existing programs, newly created interventions have more flexibility to choose the target group that maximizes the intervention's impact because they do not take away benefits from any particular group.

Collaborating with Supply-Side Providers and Involved Agencies. Use of health and education services depends on both demand and supply factors. As discussed above, effective SSNs can increase demand for schooling or preventive care, but the desired impacts can be achieved only in the presence of effective supply of such services. In scaling up, tweaking, or designing new SSN interventions, governments need to assess the supply-side capacity to absorb the extra demand that CCTs or workfare programs would stimulate. Close collaboration with involved agencies such as the Ministries of Education, Health, and Labor can facilitate the right sequencing of supply and demand interventions, thus helping to ensure success.

Enhancing Targeting toward the Poor and Vulnerable

Poverty-based targeting is important for three main reasons: (a) it contains costs and ensures that money is spent on those who have the greatest needs and for whom funds will deliver the highest returns; (b) it ensures equity; and (c) it allows SSNs to act as true insurance (state-contingent transfers), which is still missing in most Middle Eastern and North African countries. Strategic policies and programs that define, identify, and reach the intended beneficiaries through targeting can deliver more resources to the poorest groups of the population—ensuring that all who are eligible to receive benefits are included, that those who are no longer eligible are systematically removed, and that new or newly poor households can access safety nets in a crisis. Countries using targeting have increased the amount of assistance for each targeted beneficiary, enhancing program impact and containing the system's total cost through overall savings.[1] However, although the importance of targeting is recognized in the Middle East and North Africa, there is no consensus yet on which combination of methods fits each country's situation best.

Two decisions frame the targeting strategy. The first decision is whether to use poverty-based targeting. Chapter 3 shows that in the region, many SSN programs are targeted categorically (that is, to single mothers, widows, orphans, and the disabled, irrespective of their poverty level). When poverty is not concentrated in these groups, this targeting method often leads to leakage of program resources to the non-needy as well as undercoverage of the poor who do not fit these categories. Categorical targeting also limits programs' ability to scale up when governments try to reach beneficiaries who do not fit any of the predefined categories. Finally, categorical targeting may negatively associate a program with charity, thus stigmatizing SSN beneficiaries.

The second decision revolves around the selection of the specific poverty-based targeting method. Other than categorical and geographical, the main targeting methods used in the Middle East and North Africa are (unverified) means tests, PMT, community targeting, and self-targeting. Often different methods are combined for higher effectiveness, as illustrated below.

Poverty-Based Targeting Methods. The main methods, their advantages and disadvantages, and strategies for making them work are as follows:

- *Means tests.* This method relies on information about households' income or wealth. A *verified means test* verifies the information provided by applicants against independent sources, while an *unverified means test* relies only on self-reported information.

    o *Verified means tests* are more accurate but can be costly and can lead to exclusion of people who meet the eligibility criteria but lack proof of income (for example, those who have informal jobs). Verified means tests are most common in countries where the government's information systems allow for cross-linking of registries and where interagency cooperation and data sharing are in place. When this is not possible, households may be asked to submit copies of records of transactions, such as pay stubs, utility bills, or tax payments.

    o *Unverified means tests* are easier to administer but are less accurate, are subject to underreporting by applicants, and have high leakage due to inclusion of ineligible beneficiaries. Few countries use this method; Brazil is an exception, but its program management runs a PMT on household welfare information to check its plausibility (and mandates a household visit if the PMT and the self-declaration do not match), publishes the list of beneficiaries in a local newspaper and on the Internet, and has established a complaint mechanism.[2]

- *Proxy means tests.* PMTs generate a score for each applicant household based on observable characteristics such as education, household size, location, quality of dwelling, and ownership of durable goods. The information provided by the applicant at registration is usually verified either by a home visit from a program official or by having the applicant bring written verification of part of the information to a program office. Eligibility is determined by comparing the household's score against a predetermined cutoff. This method is fairly accurate in identifying the poor, can be quickly implemented, and is suitable for national-scale programs. PMTs are a good alternative to means tests in contexts where there are many informal workers or where few data are available for cross-checks across tax records, pay stubs, and pension systems.[3]

- *Community-based targeting.* This method uses a group of community members not associated with the programs to decide who in the community should benefit. Usually, special committees composed of community members, or a mix of community members and local officers, are formed to determine eligibility for a program. Often the central government or the program's implementation agency provides a list of

characteristics that beneficiaries should have based on the main correlates of poverty from a national household survey (no job, education
below a certain level, no land or business, and so on). Community
members rank eligible households by poverty and vulnerability level.
Community lists are then periodically updated and used in combination with discussions at community meetings. This method can be
highly acceptable by communities but often can be captured by the
elite. It is a good alternative for countries with high community
participation.

- *Self-targeting.* Self-targeted programs are technically open to all but
  are designed in such a way that take-up is expected to be much higher
  among the poor than the nonpoor. Most workfare programs define eligibility based on geographical targeting (by which only people who
  live in designated areas are eligible). Wages are set at a level at which
  less-poor households will not be interested in participating because
  they will be able to command higher wages elsewhere.

Key Lessons for Targeting-Related Reforms. Eight key lessons (and steps)
drawn from these and other experiences could be useful for Middle Eastern and North African countries when undertaking targeting reforms (see
box 5.3 for examples of such reforms in the region):

- *Gather information on poverty and estimate costs for different benefit amounts
  and coverage levels.* Using a new household survey or existing data, estimate the share of the population in poverty and their main characteristics (individual characteristics such as education and employment as
  well as possession of assets, such as the material used in walls or floors
  of the dwelling or number of cars). Using this information, simulate
  the total cost of the program under different scenarios for the amount
  of the transfer and the desired number of beneficiaries or coverage of
  the poor.

- *Build political consensus.* Changing the targeting method of programs
  can cause some current beneficiaries to become ineligible and lose access to SSN programs. Thus, this reform requires political will, support from the highest level of government, and a broad-based consensus on poverty reduction. As shown in chapter 4, MENA SPEAKS
  respondents generally had a strong preference for poverty-based targeting of SSN programs (as opposed to provision of transfers to specific groups). Given government commitment to the targeting reforms
  and effective communication campaigns that explain their objective,

---

BOX 5.3

Examples of Enhancing Targeting in the Middle East and North Africa

West Bank and Gaza: Improving UCT Targeting

The Cash Transfer Program underwent a major targeting reform in 2010. An effective, unique PMT mechanism and central registry were established, which facilitated the merger of the two largest cash transfer programs into a Palestinian Authority-administered cash transfer program. The reform improved targeting (confirmed by independent consulting firms) and increased donor trust, which has resulted in greater flows of funds into the system.

The Republic of Yemen: Increasing Coverage of the Poorest

The Social Welfare Fund (SWF) administers Yemen's cash transfer program. Al-

though its budget grew from US$4 million in 1996 to US$200 million in 2008/09, the program suffered from a combination of low benefits, poor targeting, and chronically low coverage of the poorest, resulting in negligible poverty impact. Based on the findings of the 2007 Yemen Poverty Assessment (Government of Yemen, World Bank, and UNDP 2007), the government implemented a program of fundamental reforms to the SWF to improve poverty targeting (with a PMT formula), strengthen capacity for service delivery, and implement a new legal and policy framework. As a result, the SWF is now an increasingly effective mechanism for reaching the poor; during the recent global economic crisis, it reached 1.5 million poor households.

---

the findings from MENA SPEAKS imply that governments can proceed with confidence in their citizens' support.

- *Ensure administrative capacity for getting accurate information and verifying eligibility.* When administrative capacity is limited, a mix of targeting methods often works best. For example, in a developed-country context, means tests and PMTs can be implemented based on available data. In many middle-income countries, PMTs can provide a good starting point, balancing between information needs and administrative capacity. In a data-constrained context, a mix of geographic and community-based methods may be used, particularly to reach more remote settings.

- *Avoid targeting criteria that carry stigmas, which might affect people's decision to participate.* In many countries, poverty is associated with shame, and this can lower program take-up. Locally based registration processes and payment of benefits through smart cards can mitigate this effect.

- *Link the targeting method to a specific benefit.* Targeting is an instrument, not an objective in itself. If the poor and vulnerable do not understand the advantage of registering, they are not likely to do so, and the program targeting based on this registry will suffer from large exclusion errors.

- *Reach out to the extremely poor.* Complementing mobilization campaigns aired on television with campaigns on the radio and those aimed at the level of community committees has achieved high coverage of the intended beneficiaries. Alternatively, governments can consider conducting a census of the poor to reach the pockets of greatest need.[4]

- *Develop strategies that minimize applicants' program registration costs.* Costs include the time and cost of traveling, queuing for registration, and complying with any conditions. Strategies for lowering these costs include setting up registration points near the targeted communities, applying simplified verification procedures (for example, verification documents that can be mailed rather than presented in person, simplifying the requirements for obtaining identification documents), and providing staff to help households fill out simple registration questionnaires.

- *Within eligible households, consider transferring benefits to women.* Literature and experience around the world suggest that intrahousehold allocation of resources matters for spending priorities (Haddad, Hoddinott, and Alderman 1997; Quisumbing and Maluccio 2000). In general, SSN benefits received by women are as likely (but frequently much more likely) to be invested in children's welfare than benefits received by men. Existing CCT programs already use this finding by delivering benefits explicitly to mothers or their proxies (Grosh et al. 2008). For example, the CCT benefits in *Oportunidades* in Mexico, *Bolsa Familia* in Brazil, and *Familias en Acción* in Colombia are all delivered into the hands of women in eligible households. In the context of the Middle East and North Africa, transferring SSN benefits to women instead of men can also increase women's decision-making power within households and promote social inclusion.

Improving the Focus on Results through M&E and Social Accountability

Importance of M&E and Accountability. M&E can help allocate budget resources between programs, monitor day-to-day operations, and track results of interventions. It has been particularly effective when the evaluation results and empirical data produced are used to inform budgetary decisions and reshape programs.[5] This was the case in West Bank and Gaza and the Republic of Yemen, for example. Moreover, introducing well-functioning social control systems can improve efficiency and accountability while combating corruption.

A central M&E system would define strategic outcomes as well as specific indicators and track their progress and results. To implement such a system, data requirements (type and frequency of information) and transmission methods from each agency to the central government need to be defined. Successful information technology (IT) systems establish a harmonized set of core indicators, standardized tables, and updating schedules. Indicators are normally linked with the SSN strategy defined by the line ministry. In countries where a unified registry of the poor and vulnerable exists and payment of benefits is linked to this registry, automatic reports on the number of beneficiaries (disaggregated by gender as well as other characteristics of particular concern) and main outcomes can be produced. Program administrators can use such reports to assess whether the system is functioning well or whether any adjustments need to be made. In the Middle East and North Africa, enhanced M&E for SSNs at the central level could help governments better allocate budget resources among programs and track results of their investment in fighting poverty. Beyond simply tracking outcomes, an M&E system creates a commitment to accountability that enhances the overall efficiency of the system.

To monitor progress in reaching the poor, core indicators at the central level are the total number of beneficiaries, the budget or number of SSN programs, and the percentage of the poor receiving assistance (aggregated coverage of the poor across programs). It is also important to have an inventory of programs by type of benefit provided and the number of beneficiaries and expenditures across different programs by benefit type (for example, beneficiaries of UCTs, CCTs, social pensions, other cash transfers, in-kind transfers, cash-for-work, food-for-work, school feeding programs, and other SSN programs). These data are normally available from program or project administrative records, but their accuracy should be verified. In addition, it is important to track the impact of the overall SSN system through indicators across programs, such as the number of person-days of work or the number of employment opportunities generated (for workfare programs), or the increase in school attendance or visits to clinics among participating households (for CCTs). Using a common identification across programs also enables the government to know which households are receiving more than one program and helps to focus a bundle of interventions according to household needs.

Central M&E systems can become a platform for sharing knowledge and experience. Meeting to discuss the global outcomes of programs can be a good opportunity to bring practitioners together to share best practices and lessons learned and to establish an effective community of SSN experts. In addition, the better management resulting from M&E systems tends to increase donor and private sector trust and funding.

M&E and Accountability Trends. A new wave of results-oriented programs in the Middle East and North Africa use integrated M&E systems. Cash transfer programs (such as in Morocco, West Bank and Gaza, and the Republic of Yemen), and workfare programs (for example, in the Republic of Yemen) have generated robust evidence that the programs work, and when they are well implemented they are achieving the intended results. In addition, pilot programs in Djibouti and Tunisia include rigorous impact evaluations in their design. This trend in the region is new and promising.

Another emerging trend is the development of integrated *program* monitoring systems. Economies like Djibouti, West Bank and Gaza, and the Republic of Yemen developed (computer-based) integrated management information systems (MIS) that became the backbone of the program operation cycle. These systems set up (a) the institutional channels through which the data required to process program transactions circulate, and (b) the modules from which the data can be accessed. An MIS also establishes procedures for data collection and processing, as well as for access control and database management to provide end users with analytical information for everyday implementation, control, and supervision. In particular, these systems create and automate business transactions under the program, allow for easy control of funds for program administration needs, and systematize information for targeted provision of benefits.

Beyond learning how well a program achieves its expected outcomes, it may also be important to determine whether a program meets its objectives, whether the program's benefits outweigh the costs, and what the program's estimated net impact is. Impact evaluations often involve external entities such as universities, NGOs, think tanks, and international organizations to guarantee impartiality and credibility.[6] In the Mexico CCT, *Oportunidades*, for example, credible impact evaluations demonstrated that the program had sustainable impacts on education, health, nutrition, and diet, which enabled the program to prevail even after a change in government.[7] Following Mexico's pioneering of impact evaluation, most CCT programs in Latin America and elsewhere now incorporate robust monitoring and impact evaluation studies done by independent third parties, usually local universities and international research centers. In the Middle East and North Africa, a few countries are starting to promote impact evaluations of programs, but these are still a minority.

Traditionally SSN budgets have been approved based on historical allocations, regardless of programs' outputs or results, but many countries are changing this practice. For instance, CSOs, media organizations, and academia have been active in reviewing the policies, operational rules, and procedures of the Philippines' CCT program Pantawid Pamilyang Pilipino Program (4Ps), leading to significant improvements in addressing exclusion, payments, updates, and grievances (see box 5.4). In El Salvador, NGOs actively help mothers and families meet the conditions of the *Red Solidaria* CCT program and link them with other social programs. So although SSN programs have not often been subject to open scrutiny by the public or CSOs or to rigorous M&E, these new, well-functioning social accountability systems could provide the scrutiny necessary to keep the programs' focus on results.

Reaching Out to Other Stakeholders (Citizens, NGOs, CSOs, Private Sector, and Nonprofits)

Currently, awareness about existing SSN programs is low and skewed toward the wealthy. Chapter 4 highlighted the low level of name recognition of some SSN programs in the Middle East and North Africa (for example, in the Arab Republic of Egypt, 23 percent of the MENA SPEAKS survey respondents did not know a single SSN program in the country).

For programs with on-demand registration, awareness about the existence of the program, eligibility criteria, and application procedures is essential. Comprehensive communication campaigns are needed to inform poor and vulnerable citizens of the safety net that is available to them. Moreover, engaging a broader spectrum of stakeholders (such as NGOs, CSOs, and nonprofits) in financing and implementing SSN programs could leverage their existing financial and human resources.

The private sector can also participate in financing and implementing SSNs. In countries such as the United States, a significant part of SSN financing comes from individual citizens' or private corporations' donations. NGOs and CSOs run many of the programs. In addition, government funds can finance other operators to implement specific programs. For example, in the city of New York, nonfederal SSN programs are designed by the mayor's office, which publishes a call for implementation proposals from NGOs and CSOs. After interested CSOs and NGOs send financial and technical proposals, a transparent competition selects the best proposal. A performance-based contract—agreeing to pay a provider for the achievement of an outcome—is then signed with the selected provider. The role of the government then shifts from implementation to funding and regulation, which allows for more efficient use of scarce administrative capacity.

BOX 5.4

Social Accountability and the Role of Civil Society Organizations

Introducing social control mechanisms is becoming common practice in safety net systems. Academia, media organizations, and CSOs have become key players in improving efficiency and accountability and combating corruption. Two examples—one from Latin America and one from Asia—illustrate how CSO participation and oversight have been critical in improving budget execution and program results.

Colombia: Bogotá Cómo Vamos (Bogotá, How Are We Doing?)

In 1997, civil society developed an innovative model for social control, *Bogotá Cómo Vamos*, to monitor and evaluate the delivery of government services in the capital city and to strengthen public participation in the supervision of government services. The program was developed and funded by the Bogotá Chamber of Commerce, the daily newspaper *El Tiempo*, and Fundación Corona, a private foundation, and had two objectives: (a) to build a set of indicators to track the performance of government services most important to the citizens of Bogotá, and (b) to disseminate information about the indicators and promote debate to improve the quality of services.

A group of experts defines the relevant result indicators and collects information on them. The program also investigates citizens' perceptions about the coverage and quality of public services through open forums, town hall meetings, and opinion surveys. All information is regularly published in *El Tiempo* and aired on Bogotá's television stations. The program has increased scrutiny of the city's budget and development plans over several administrations in the past 15 years, and similar models being used in other Latin American cities include Rio Como Vamos and São Paulo Como Vamos in Brazil.

The Philippines: Pantawid Pamilyang Pilipino Program (4Ps)

CSOs, the media, and academic organizations participate in the review of the Philippines' CCT program's policy and program operation manuals and procedures. They also help with validation procedures to improve targeting and address complaints and grievances. CSOs and the media actively participate in ensuring that people voice their concerns and inquire about the program and that managers respond in a timely fashion. Finally, CSOs are involved in linking mothers to other social programs, including health insurance, early child development programs, and reproductive health information.

Social Innovation Funds can be a good entry point for public-private partnerships. In 2009, the U.S. government developed such a fund—a program of the Corporation for National and Community Service—to pilot and evaluate innovative SSN programs that could be replicable as a public-private investment. Approximately US$100 million was awarded to 16 intermediary organizations nationwide over two years, matched 3 to 1 by private funds. New York City's Social Innovation Fund had five key partners, including NGOs, philanthropists, the city government, and the governments of partner cities where the program was being piloted.[8] Programs being piloted nationwide through the Social Innovation Fund include a CCT (Family Rewards, with conditions on children's education, family preventive health care, and parents' work and training); an education-conditioned internship; a community-based workfare program for public housing residents; a sector-focused training and advancement program; and a savings program for the poor linked to tax refunds.

Enhancing Reliability and Flexibility of SSN Infrastructure for Better Crisis Preparedness

An effective SSN system can help citizens navigate the effects of both idiosyncratic and systemic shocks. The recent global economic crisis underscored the weak capacity of existing SSN systems in the Middle East and North Africa to serve this function. Promoting households' resilience to shocks through SSNs requires a strong administrative infrastructure. Having this infrastructure in place *ahead* of a crisis allows for quicker and more efficient deployment of remedial and mitigation actions, such as scaling up of benefits for the most vulnerable or expanding coverage, thus enhancing resilience.

Two key systems need to be in place, both for smooth functioning of SSNs in good times and for rapid response during systemic shocks (such as the recent food, fuel, and financial crises as well as the ongoing challenge posed by climate change): (a) a unified registry system and (b) an effective service delivery mechanism.

Unified Registry Systems

In normal times, unified registry systems can reduce costs (because each agency does not need its own registry system) and facilitate coherence and convergence (because all agencies work with the same database [registry]). Unified registries also typically result in increased benefits to beneficiaries of complementary and synergetic programs by improving the impact and adequacy of safety nets. In times of crisis, unified registries can be used to quickly disburse additional benefits to the target population or to promptly expand coverage by adjusting eligibility criteria.

There are issues to consider when introducing a unified registry system:

- It requires (a) building administrative and operational capacity; (b) securing a budget; and (c) introducing quality controls, a grievance redress system, and M&E (see box 5.5 for more detailed steps).

BOX 5.5

Building Unified Registry Systems

Unified targeting and registry systems were pioneered by Chile in the 1980s and Colombia in the early 1990s. Aided by advances in technology and renewed attention to safety nets and social protection programs, these registries are regaining popularity in many countries. Most registries include poverty criteria as a way to rank or select beneficiaries. The following are steps to consider when building such systems:

- *Select the responsible agency.* This agency will develop procedures, assemble the database, and share it with other agencies. In some countries, this is the National Planning Agency (for example, in Chile and Colombia); in others, it is the Social Ministry (in Brazil and the Philippines).

- *Decide on welfare (poverty) assessment methods and procedures.* Options include verified income and wealth tests (common in Organisation for Economic Cooperation and Development [OECD] countries), unverified means tests, and PMTs. PMTs using income or expenditures or multidimensional poverty indicators are common in middle- and low-income countries with high informality and a lack of property, tax, or other asset or income databases (in Chile, Colombia, Indonesia, Mexico, the Philippines, and Turkey, among others).

- *Decide on updating, recertification, and complaints resolution systems.* In OECD countries, beneficiaries reapply for so-cial benefits every year. In most other countries, reapplication for benefits is less frequent (for example, two years in Brazil, or three years or more when PMT systems are used). Registries are generally open to applicants at any time, and grievance systems are in place.

- *Mandate use of the unified registry system.* Existing program administrators are generally resistant to using the new system for fear of having to delist noneligible households or facing questions about the reliability, objectivity, and accuracy of the system. To overcome these concerns, registry systems must develop quality controls and be able to withstand scrutiny by all stakeholders, including academia, CSOs, and the public. Uses of the registry for government programs can also be mandated by decree (as Brazil does for its registry, *Cadastro Único*) or other legal mandates.

- *Ensure IT and communications support.* Registries involve management of large databases that grow rapidly—sometimes exponentially, with recertifications, complaints, grievances, and the required feedback from user programs. Sufficient IT and database capacity is the key to having a functional system. Modern registries now share data or subregistries through the Internet or governments' secure private networks. Inadequate staff capacity to develop and support systems over time is often a major constraint.

BOX 5.5 *Continued*

- *Support M&E.* Registry systems need to be supported by sound M&E systems. Monitoring is critical for controlling data quality, assessing inclusion and exclusion errors, and dealing with complaints and grievances. Evaluation can examine the incentives to game the system (through the impact on labor effort and informality) and the targeting outcomes (the extent to which benefits reach the poor and vulnerable population).

- There is a risk that some of the poor will be excluded and thus have no access to benefits.

The latter concern can be mitigated through comprehensive outreach campaigns and regular updating of the registry. In addition, methods like the aforementioned census of the poor could be used to increase the coverage of the poor in the registry.

During crises, the usefulness of the information collected in the unified registry depends, in large part, on the nature of the crisis and the selected assessment method. For instance, although PMT has a well-established track record in identifying chronic poverty, it performs less well in spotting transitory poverty, which is usually tied to changes in income rather than assets.

Service Delivery Mechanisms

In normal times, effective use of modern technologies in benefit delivery systems is important to reduce administrative costs, leakage to nonbeneficiaries, and corruption. The ideal system is one that delivers cash or other benefits directly to beneficiaries without passing through intermediaries such as local public officials. During a crisis, modern technology makes cash a much more flexible instrument for rapid response than in-kind transfers.

Fortunately for the Middle East and North Africa, citizens seem to be in favor of cash-based SSN transfers, as demonstrated in the MENA SPEAKS surveys (detailed in chapter 4). Use of smart cards, mobile payments, and over-the-counter payments in bank branches also facilitate an effective response during a crisis when benefits need to reach the targeted population quickly. Smart cards can be used to withdraw money at automatic teller machines (ATMs) at any time. However, in some countries, ATM networks might not cover rural or periurban areas, calling for alternative methods. These alternative modalities include over-the-counter payments in bank branches and mobile payments using direct cell phone transfers or cell phone companies' points of service or correspondents (local stores, pawn shops, or others). The best choice depends on existing infrastructure, cost, and the preferences of beneficiary families. In Brazil, for instance, the 12 million beneficiary families of the CCT *Bolsa Família* program use cash cards.

Crisis Preparedness

The preparation of the SSN system can facilitate action when a crisis hits (World Bank 2012). Food price crises, natural disasters, and financial crises affect different groups and thus call for different SSN responses. Changing the eligibility criteria, thresholds, or benefit levels and duration can be effective for some SSN instruments such as cash transfers and workfare programs. For such adjustments to happen rapidly in a crisis situation, increased funding should be made available quickly with the expectation that it will be scaled down after the crisis. Preestablished rules that define triggers for scaling SSN programs up and down also help to save time during the crisis and to manage entitlement expectations. Finally, continuous open enrollment for SSN programs can improve their effectiveness during crises, while regular recertification can aid the scaling-down process afterward.

As mentioned above, SSNs can help poor and near-poor people adapt to changing livelihood and climatic conditions or support them when adaptation fails. Heltberg, Jorgensen, and Siegel (2008) note the need to balance institutional development, infrastructure sectors, productive natural resource sectors, and social policy (including SSNs) as part of an adaptive response to climate change. Most attention to date has focused on policy and infrastructure responses, however, and far less on forward-looking analyses of how SSNs themselves will need to adapt to help beneficiaries respond to climate change. Some relevant but still-open questions include the following: How, and by how much, will SSN beneficiary groups change in urban low-lying coastal areas (for example, ports) versus rural low-lying coastal areas? Can SSN program size and disbursements be made scalable with weather indexes in the short term? Can public workfare programs be integrated in micro-watershed rehabilitation efforts?

Consolidating Fragmented SSN Systems

In the Middle East and North Africa, direct transfer programs (cash-based or in-kind) are often small and highly fragmented. The region's countries rely on a multiplicity of low-coverage, low-benefit SSN programs that have different targeting criteria often confined to certain categories of the population (for example, as found in Jordan, Lebanon, Morocco, and Tunisia, further discussed in chapter 3). To effectively fill coverage gaps, there must be a robust and flexible SSN system consisting of only a few programs that governments can coordinate and run more efficiently and at lower administrative cost.

International experience suggests that consolidating many small programs into a few comprehensive programs, specifically designed to reach different segments of the poor and vulnerable, can help to address current vulnerabilities and social protection gaps. For example, simpler and fewer programs were key reforms in Brazil and the Philippines. In particular, by merging four food and cash transfer programs in 2003, Brazil created its flagship SSN program, *Bolsa Família*, which provides cash benefits of over 15 percent of average poor households' consumption and covers nearly 30 percent of the population. The program costs no more than 0.5 percent of Brazil's GDP because of cost savings and better administration. A few parts of the Middle East and North Africa (for example, Morocco and West Bank and Gaza) have already started reforming their SSNs in this direction.

Consolidation of SSNs does not have many prerequisites; thus, Middle Eastern and North African countries can move forward on this agenda item by following three key steps:

1. *Identify the different risks faced by the poor and vulnerable, the programs available to help families address these risks, and the existing gaps.* Chapter 2 identified several groups that face the most difficult challenges in the Middle East and North Africa (including children in poor households and people living in rural or lagging urban areas), and chapter 3 showed that the region's SSNs leave many of these groups uncovered or inadequately covered. Besides coverage or generosity gaps, other gaps can be in terms of program design: for instance, nutrition programs that focus only on food assistance but neither provide nutrition education nor promote behavioral change to improve children's nutrition, or insurance packages that do not adequately finance expensive hospital care or medicines.

2. *Based on the nature and extent of risks, identify a small number of programs that could be expanded or effectively consolidated.* Options to consider include (a) early-childhood development programs (to address malnutrition and promote early child stimulation and development); (b) CCTs that link cash assistance to undertaking basic health care activities (such as growth monitoring, vaccinations, and maternal care); and (c) enrollment in schools (as done in Brazil, Chile, Colombia, Mexico, and Turkey). Other programs include public, on-the-job training for youth with NGOs (for example, the *Trabajar* and *Jefes* programs in Argentina) and private sector participation (for example, *Jóvenes en Acción* in Chile and Colombia), as well as community-driven development funds (such as projects in the Republic of Yemen and under

preparation in Lebanon with World Bank support). In addition, reforming the labor code to waive or reduce temporarily or permanently some payroll contributions (as in Colombia's 2002 labor reform law and later 2011 adjustment) would encourage firms to hire youth in apprenticeship programs.

3. *Develop a strategy for implementation of the reform and set up a national database for targeting.* A single registry system (as addressed in box 5.5) has effectively been the main instrument of coordination and convergence of programs because it allows administrators to quickly assess needs and to target and monitor poor and vulnerable households.

Rebalancing Financing and Priorities of SSN Systems

Increasing Spending and Improving Coverage of Nonsubsidy SSNs to Protect against Destitution

Successful reforms of subsidies around the world have shown the importance of gaining citizens' trust in their government's capacity to deliver fair and reliable compensation. Chapter 2 highlighted the multifaceted challenges faced by the region's poor and socially excluded groups. Thus, the important gaps in coverage identified in chapter 3 call for urgent action on the part of the government. Also, in light of the evidence provided by the MENA SPEAKS survey and Jordan Gives experiment (covered in chapter 4), demonstrating readiness to deliver effective and inclusive SSN programs would be an essential step on the path toward comprehensive subsidy reform. This could be achieved without overloading the available fiscal space by creating new affordable programs or increasing the cost-effectiveness of the existing SSN system. Expansion of nonsubsidy safety nets should be an integral part of subsidy reform.

Targeted SSN programs can reach a large share of the poor and vulnerable at a low cost. The largest CCT programs in the world (*Bolsa Familia* in Brazil and *Oportunidades* in Mexico) reach about 30 percent of the population and cost about 0.5 percent of GDP (Fiszbein and Schady 2009). Similarly, the largest workfare programs in the world (the Productive Safety Net Program in Ethiopia and the Mahatma Gandhi National Rural Employment Guarantee Act [MNREGA] in India, reaching more than 7 and 20 million people, respectively) each cost about 0.5 percent of GDP (IEG 2011). Well-targeted UCT programs can also be affordable: Georgia's targeted SSN program provides benefits to about 10 percent of the population at a cost of 0.6 percent of GDP.

To achieve cost-effectiveness, funds can be allocated more efficiently among different SSN programs based on the number of beneficiaries and the coverage goals. In addition, developing effective payment methods is crucial. Four key steps drawn from global experience are to

- Ensure that the funding provided is commensurate with the needs of the number of people who meet the eligibility criteria;

- Allocate funds to jurisdictions based on explicit, transparent, and complete criteria to minimize arbitrariness at the local level;

- Keep eligibility criteria and benefit formulas as simple as possible; and

- Use payment mechanisms that operate through financial agencies and that pay beneficiaries directly.

Reforming Price Subsidies through Wholesale or Internal Reforms

Reducing general subsidies in Middle Eastern and North African countries can result in large fiscal savings, some of which can be devoted to increasing SSN funding—as countries in other regions have also demonstrated. In Indonesia, for instance, fuel price subsidy reform in 2005 resulted in savings of about 2 percent of GDP, which allowed the government to spend about 0.7 percent of GDP on a compensatory cash transfer for 19 million poor households and to increase spending on education and health insurance (see box 5.6). Similarly, Mexico in 1995/96 instituted gradual elimination of general food price subsidies that had benefited urban dwellers at the expense of rural areas. This reform led to savings, part of which was redirected toward the introduction of the country's well-known and successful targeted CCT program, *Oportunidades*.[9] In Turkey, reforms to reduce untargeted agricultural support subsidies not only eliminated their distortionary effects on local prices but also resulted in large fiscal savings that allowed the government to finance a direct income support program for farmers in 2002/03.

Sequencing of sensitive reforms, such as those to reduce or eliminate universal price subsidies, is crucial for their success. To gain credibility, a government could start with internal reforms, such as improving subsidy targeting. This could be achieved through differentiated marketing and packaging, which led to self-targeting in Tunisia (as discussed in chapter 3, box 3.4). It could also be accomplished by narrowing subsidy coverage—for example, by introducing lifeline electricity tariffs rather than providing a universal subsidy for electricity. Finally, better monitoring of the distribution chain for subsidized products can potentially reduce expensive leakages.

Another way to initiate subsidy reform is by identifying the subsidies that people value the most and focusing reform instead on the most regressive ones. According to the MENA SPEAKS survey, the least-preferred product for subsidy reform was cooking oil in Egypt, bread in Lebanon and Tunisia, and electricity in Jordan. These subsidies could be subject to reform only when governments have already demonstrated their success at reforming less-sensitive subsidies. Given that fuel subsidy

BOX 5.6

Indonesia's Fuel Subsidy Reform and SSN System

Increasing international prices in 2005 put increasing fiscal pressure on the Indonesian government's subsidization of fuel. Combined with the regressive nature of the subsidy, this pressure led the government of Indonesia to sharply reduce subsidies. In March 2005, fuel prices increased by a weighted 29 percent, and by another 114 percent in October 2005, with kerosene prices tripling. To mitigate the impact of price increases on poor and near-poor households, the government introduced three SSN programs, also in 2005: a UCT program (*Bantuan Langsung Tunai* or BLT); a health insurance program (*Asuransi Kesehatan Masyarakat Miskin* or Askeskin); and an education subsidy program, Operational Aid to Schools. Later, in 2007, the poorest households were enrolled into a CCT pilot program (*Programme Keluarga Harapan* or PKH). The following is a brief description of the BLT and the PKH, which provided immediate and medium-term responses to the effects of the fuel subsidy reform.

The BLT, under the Ministry of Social Affairs, ran for 12 months, from late 2005 to 2006. This UCT program reached approximately 19 million poor and near-poor households, giving a flat rate benefit representing about 15 percent of the poverty line. The 2006 cost of the program was about 0.7 percent of GDP, or about 25 percent of the savings from the subsidy reductions. The poor and near-poor were the target populations, representing the bottom third of the national consumption dis-

tribution and defined as households with consumption below 1.5 times the poverty line. Targeting and selection of recipients was developed using PMT, with a set of household indicators that are highly correlated with poverty and easily verifiable, such as floor, wall, and roofing materials; source of drinking water; access to electricity; and asset ownership.

Funds were disbursed directly to beneficiaries through the post office system. The BLT was always intended as a temporary one-off assistance during a time of inflationary pressures on the poverty basket, and it ended in late 2006 as fuel prices declined. The broadly targeted nature of the BLT made the program one of the key response options available to Indonesia when the food price crisis hit in 2007/08. In 2008, with food and fuel prices increasing sharply, the government responded by initiating a new round of BLT. As with the first BLT, poor and near-poor households, or the bottom 30 percent of the consumption distribution, were the intended recipients. Targeting was based on an updated list from the first round of the program, resulting in 18.5 million households receiving benefits at a cost of about 0.3 percent of GDP.

The PKH started in 2007 as a CCT pilot program and transferred cash to about 1 million poor households in 2010. Households receive the equivalent of about US$150 annually for up to six years, conditional on children attending school and obtaining preventive basic health and nutrition services, similar to Mexico's *Opor-*

BOX 5.6 *Continued*

tunidades. The program targets poor households with children up to 15 years of age and pregnant women, again using PMT methods to determine household economic status.

PKH is a long-term assistance program and is designed to provide considerable financial support while also encouraging changes in household health and education behaviors, which lead households out of poverty in the longer term. The PKH initially suffered from poor MIS and operational difficulties, including supply-side readiness issues, but these have been overcome recently and, based on positive results from impact evaluation studies, expansion is planned to reach a target of 3 million households by 2014. The total cost of PKH in 2007 was less than 0.1 percent of GDP. However, this is expected to increase significantly as PKH is expanded.

spending is more than three times the spending on food subsidies, it appears that nonfood subsidy reform is the lower-hanging fruit. In MENA SPEAKS, citizens indicated that if they had to pick one subsidized product for reform, this product would be tobacco in Lebanon, gasoline in Egypt, and diesel in Jordan and Tunisia.

Compensation packages tailored to citizens' preferences combined with comprehensive information and communication campaigns can increase the tolerance for subsidy reform. Governments can use the findings from the MENA SPEAKS surveys to engage citizens early on in a dialogue on preferred compensation packages in their countries. The evidence so far shows that people in the Middle East and North Africa prefer to target cash-based compensation for subsidy reform to the poor alone (in Egypt, Jordan, and Tunisia) or to combine such targeted cash transfers with investment of the savings in education and health (in Lebanon). As pointed out in chapter 4 (the "What Works?" section), formulating the right communication strategy and promoting awareness through information campaigns are crucial to the success of such sensitive reform.

Four key lessons (and steps) drawn from subsidy reforms around the world could be useful for the region's countries when undertaking such reforms:

- *Identify potential winners and losers of reforms.* By using household income and expenditure surveys (available in most Middle Eastern and North African countries), winners and losers can be identified by income, expenditure, or wealth index quintiles. Work has already been done in some countries with World Bank support, as illustrated in this report. Additional studies on the extent of economic distortion and waste caused by fuel and food price subsidies will augment the case for (and public discussion of) policy reform.

- *Prepare an action plan for reform, including compensation programs.* Adequate compensation is needed to protect the poor and vulnerable from the effects of policy reform and complementary interventions for the lower middle class. As mentioned in chapter 3, many in the Middle East and North Africa depend on subsidies to stay out of poverty. MENA SPEAKS revealed that when asked to choose among different compensation packages for subsidy reform, citizens prefer cash-based transfers targeted to the poor (in the case of Lebanon, combined with investment in health and education). Such a targeted cash transfer program can compensate for the inevitable price shock, and targeting it to the poor will absorb only a fraction of the subsidy's cost.

- *Determine basic program parameters for a compensation package.* These parameters include the target population, benefit levels, institutional arrangements, payment modalities, and M&E systems, including social accountability. All parameters and program costs can be estimated and simulated using household surveys, along with the likely impacts on headcount poverty, the poverty gap, and the severity of poverty. One of the most difficult and time-consuming activities is designing a registry of potential beneficiaries in countries that have limited experience with national targeting systems (see box 5.6 on Indonesia's experience).

- *Prepare a registry and a payment system.* The purpose of the registry is to capture the population to be targeted by the compensation scheme, and an appropriate payment mechanism should be in place before the subsidy reform is launched. For instance, in the Islamic Republic of Iran, subsidy removal was preceded by establishing a fund, with the government opening bank accounts for all Iranians who registered to receive compensatory payments. The first compensation transfer into these accounts was made on the day of the first subsidy reduction (see Guillaume, Zytek, and Reza Farzin 2011).

The Way Forward

This section brings together findings from the previous chapters to analyze, in a country-by-country setting, key challenges and possible ways forward for SSNs in the Middle East and North Africa. It summarizes the main poverty and vulnerability challenges facing citizens in the region (chapter 2); institutional challenges in existing systems that decrease their performance (chapter 3); citizens' knowledge, attitudes, and support for different reforms (chapter 4); and different possibilities for progress using the agenda discussed earlier in this chapter (improving SSN program impact; enhancing reliability and flexibility of SSN infrastructure for better crisis preparedness; consolidating fragmented SSN systems; and rebalancing financing and priorities).

As established in chapter 2, most Middle Eastern and North African countries lag behind their development peers on human development outcomes. Indeed, with the exception of Jordan and West Bank and Gaza, most of the region's economies have human development outcomes (as proxied by the United Nations Development Programme's [UNDP] Human Development Index [HDI] ranks) that are significantly lower than their gross national income (GNI) per capita ranks, even when compared with countries at similar levels of development. This demonstrates the scope for improvements in human development outcomes. SSNs can be an important instrument in this process, but while some Middle Eastern and North African countries have well-established SSNs that can be enhanced and expanded, others have limited experience with implementing SSNs. Hence, in some countries the reform of the existing systems can be the crucial first step forward, building the foundation for deeper reforms, while in others the creation of new programs and systems is the priority agenda item. The region's countries also vary in how much their SSN spending tilts toward subsides, and thus in the fiscal pressures associated with subsidization, which might make subsidy reform a more immediate priority.

General Strategies

In each country, an SSN reform strategy would involve short- and medium-run interventions with complementary and mutually reinforcing objectives. In the short run, Middle Eastern and North African countries can start demonstrating better results from existing SSN systems by

- Scaling up programs targeted to the poor and vulnerable and adding new components to cash transfer or workfare programs that make them work better for women and children;

- In countries where existing SSNs are still nascent, designing and rapidly implementing interventions to protect the poor and vulnerable (for example, starting with piloting programs) and establishing an SSN infrastructure to pave the way for the next generation of reforms; and

- In countries under increasing fiscal pressure from subsidies, implementing internal reforms in this system or wholesale reforms focused on less-sensitive products, gradually introducing these changes while building credibility.

In the medium run, the focus can shift to reforms that require more preexisting capacity, such as refining the SSN infrastructure and comprehensive subsidy reform. This second-generation set of reforms can entail

- Sharpening the focus on results in SSN programs through M&E and social accountability, reaching out to other stakeholders in financing and implementation, and strengthening administrative capacity among relevant institutions;

- Consolidating existing fragmented safety net programs for more effectiveness and results, thereby reducing overlaps and bridging coverage gaps; and

- Launching wholesale subsidy reforms.

Country-by-Country Summary and Strategies

Countries in the Middle East and North Africa find themselves at different stages of progress on human development outcomes and SSN reforms. Table 5.1 presents an overview of the achievements in the region,

TABLE 5.1

Progress on Human Development Outcomes and SSN Reform, by Stage, in the Middle East and North Africa, 2011

HDI level	SSN reform		
	Advanced stage	Intermediate stage	Early stage
Low HDI	Yemen, Rep.	Djibouti	
Medium HDI	West Bank and Gaza	Jordan	Algeria
		Morocco	Egypt, Arab Rep.
			Iraq
			Syrian Arab Republic
High to very high HDI		Bahrain	Kuwait
		Lebanon	Oman
			Qatar
			Saudi Arabia
			Tunisia
			United Arab Emirates

Source: Authors using UNDP 2011 data for HDI.

Note: Libya and the Islamic Republic of Iran are not included due to insufficient data. HDI = Human Development Index (of the United Nations Development Programme); SSN = social safety net.

both on human development outcomes (using the UNDP HDI as an aggregate proxy) and their stage of progress to date on SSN reform (early, intermediate, or advanced). Table 5.2 presents a country-by-country summary of human development challenges, SSN system challenges, on-going SSN initiatives, and possible strategies going forward.

Low-HDI Countries

Djibouti and the Republic of Yemen still have low human development outcomes according to HDI. Their particular challenges (as listed in table 5.2) are chronically high poverty and malnutrition rates, which are among the world's highest. The Republic of Yemen's progress on SSN reform has been highlighted throughout the report, especially the targeting reforms of the SWF as well as the rapid crisis response using a public works program that protected consumption of the poor and vulnerable and built community assets of the poor. While facing similar challenges, Djibouti's advancement on SSN reform is more recent, but substantial improvements have already taken place with the creation of the "workfare plus nutrition" program that addresses child malnutrition in a holistic way. The way forward for these two countries is to build on successful experiences, leverage the SSN infrastructure that is already in place, and track closely the results attributable to existing interventions on human development indicators.

Medium-HDI Countries

Seven middle-income countries in the Middle East and North Africa have achieved medium human development outcomes according to HDI. Within this group, these economies face varying challenges. In both Iraq and West Bank and Gaza, for example, recent conflicts have negatively affected livelihoods; however, they have attained different degrees of progress on SSN reform. West Bank and Gaza is the region's pioneer in consolidating its many programs into a single Cash Transfer Program (CTP) and creating a unified registry of beneficiaries that allows for targeting transfers across multiple programs; future directions include careful management of the rapid expansion of the CTP and strengthening its financial sustainability. For Iraq's part, while preparing for a move away from ration cards (the Public Distribution System or PDS) toward more targeted SSNs, the country has just started on the path for reform, with the road map including proposals for creating SSNs that promote human capital, improving targeting, and enhancing administrative capacity in the SSN program to build credibility for PDS reform.

Jordan and Morocco, despite their large numbers of SSN programs, both have deep pockets of poverty in rural and lagging regions as well as high child poverty and malnutrition among the poor. The progress to

TABLE 5.2

Challenges for SSN Systems and Possible Ways Forward in the Middle East and North Africa, Selected Countries, 2012

	Human development challenges	SSN system challenges	Main ongoing SSN initiatives	Possible way forward
Djibouti	High poverty (40% live with less than $2/day). High malnutrition (33% of all children 0–5 years old and 45% in the poorest quintile stunted). High unemployment (55%).	Nonsubsidy SSNs have low coverage of the poor (3%) and are highly fragmented. Lack of experience. Strong focus on capacity building.	Implementing a "workfare plus" program, viewed as a model for the region. High in-country visibility and ownership. Prepared SSN strategy.	Set up a unified registry of beneficiaries of social assistance. Scale up "workfare plus" program. Use ongoing initiatives as platform for support. Engage new stakeholders.
Egypt, Arab Rep.	High child poverty (29%). High vulnerability (17% live with $2–2.5/day). High malnutrition (29%). Spatial pockets of poverty (rural).	Nonsubsidy SSNs have low impact on poverty, linked to low coverage of the poor (14%), low targeting accuracy, and low size transfer provided. They are highly fragmented. Increasing fiscal pressure from subsidy system.	Workfare program under preparation.	Rebalance SSN away from subsidies. Create new, cost-effective, and flexible targeted SSN. Consolidate fragmented SSNs.
Tunisia	Spatial pockets of poverty (rural). High unemployment and discouragement among the poor. Higher levels of school dropout and maternal mortality among poor.	Weak M&E systems at the central, regional, and program levels. Leakages to nonpoor for direct SSNs (unconditional cash transfers and health cards). Increasing fiscal pressure due to universal subsidies.	Implementing pilots: (a) workfare project, and (b) skills development in community-driven rural development and service delivery project. Improving information systems and creating a unified registry of beneficiaries. Evaluating national cash transfer and health card program and building social accountability systems.	Enhance targeting. Rebalance SSNs by focusing on targeted programs rather than subsidies. Strengthen SSNs that promote human capital and assets of the poor and vulnerable. Establish SSN infrastructure and, in particular, develop a unified registry of beneficiaries. Consolidate SSN programs across different programs and agencies or ministries.
Iraq	High child poverty (27%). High vulnerability (16% live with $2–2.5/day). Spatial pockets of poverty (rural). Postconflict environment.	Nonsubsidy SSNs have low impact on poverty, linked to low coverage of poor (6%) and high leakages. Low transfer size. SSN consisting mostly of subsidies, are under increasing fiscal pressure. Food ration system has high leakages.	Enhancing targeting of cash transfer program. Developed strategy for subsidy reform.	Create SSNs that promote human capital and assets of the poor. Enhance targeting. Enhance administrative capacity.
Jordan	High child poverty (20%) and malnutrition rates among the poor (15% of children 0–5 years old in poorest quintile are stunted). Pockets of poverty in lagging areas (Al-Mafraq). Large poor-rich divide in human development indicators.	Nonsubsidy SSNs have small poverty impact linked to low coverage of the poor (23%), fragmentation and low transfer size. Increasing fiscal pressure from subsidy system.	Developing targeting and poverty reduction strategy. Preparing a unified registry of beneficiaries.	Prioritize interventions focused on children and that help build human capital. Rebalance SSNs away from subsidies. Establish administrative systems. Consolidate fragmented SSNs.

Country				
Lebanon	Regional inequities in access to basic infrastructure and social services. Relative deprivation in lagging areas (Akkar, Dinniyeh).	Due to limited experience in implementing SSNs, the focus has been on capacity building, mainly on targeting.	Developing first national targeting database (NPTP).	Expand the coverage of the targeting database through outreach. Institutionalize NPTP systems and business processes. Rationalize and improve the targeting of existing SSN programs. Improve the evidence base for policy making through regular household survey data collection.
Morocco	High child poverty and malnutrition rates among the poor (29% of children 0–5 years old in the poorest quintile are stunted). High vulnerability (11% live with $2–2.5/day). Spatial pockets of poverty (rural). High inequality in access to basic services between poor and rich, urban and rural residents. High unemployment and discouragement among the poor.	Nonsubsidy SSNs have low coverage of the poor (17%) Scope to improve targeting. Weak coordination between institutions implementing SSN and fragmentation. Increasing fiscal pressure from subsidy system.	Developed social protection strategy. Implementing CCT on education.	Prioritize interventions focused on children and that help build human capital (e.g., scaling up the education CCT). Rebalance SSNs by focusing on targeted programs rather than subsidies. Consolidate fragmented SSN.
Yemen, Rep.	High poverty rate (35% live with less than $2/day). High malnutrition rates (almost 60% of all children 0–5 years old are stunted). Spatial pockets of poverty (rural).	Limited coverage of the poor (29%, which is below world average). Scope to improve targeting. Increasing fiscal pressures from fuel subsidy system.	Implementing a workfare program, a cash assistance program, and a community-driven development program. Capacity building for cash transfer program to scale up during future crises. Has expanded coverage of the poor. Currently, cash transfer reaches over 1 million households.	Build on successful workfare and cash transfer program and existing administrative systems. Link SSNs to interventions that build human capital. Strengthen sustainability and coordination of implementing agencies.
West Bank and Gaza	Conflict has negatively affected people's livelihoods and access to food, health, and education.	Lack of graduation strategies to divert less-poor households to other programs. Despite overall good targeting, there are concerns about inclusion and exclusion errors.	Expanded coverage of cash transfer program. Created unified registry of beneficiaries. Enhanced targeting. Invested in enhancing targeting and data collection.	Manage the rapid expansion of the program. Strengthen sustainability and coordination.
Bahrain	High vulnerability.	Nonsubsidy SSN system has fragmentation. High leakages to nonpoor. Heavy reliance on costly universal subsidies.	Evaluating and benchmarking existing SSNs.	Establish targeted SSN. Develop administrative systems. Simplify eligibility criteria.

(table continued on next page)

TABLE 5.2

Continued

	Human development challenges	SSN system challenges	Main ongoing SSN initiatives	Possible way forward
Saudi Arabia	High population growth, increasing cost of living, and inadequate social services in some areas. High vulnerability. High rates of disability (15–20% of population).	Main types of SSNs are subsidies and transfers from government, families, private and charitable organizations. Limited program coordination targeting methods, case management, and M&E.	Evaluating efficiency and sustainability of existing SSN. Reviewing global experience on the implementation and results of community-driven approaches.	Establish targeted SSN. Develop administrative systems.
Kuwait	Increasing cost of living. Low female labor market participation (45% of women participate in the labor market relative to 83% of men) and high female-male income disparity (with a female-to-male earned income ratio of about 36 percent).	Main types of SSNs are subsidies and transfers from government, families, private and charitable organizations. Limited administrative capacity. Limited program coordination targeting methods, case management, and M&E.	Evaluating and benchmarking existing SSN programs.	Develop an SSN strategic framework. Establish targeted SSN. Develop administrative systems.
Libya	Postconflict reintegration of youth at risk (including ex-combatants). High unemployment (notably youth). Weak integration of poor migrants.	Increasing fiscal pressure from subsidy system (food, fuel, electricity). Lack of clear eligibility criteria for postconflict cash transfer programs. Weak M&E systems at central and regional levels.	Assessment of postconflict priorities for integrating unemployed populations and youth at risk. Coordination with international agencies on developing work programs and support to migrant populations.	Establish M&E systems. Strengthen SSN programs, coordinated with labor and skills development programs that promote human capital and assets of the poor, vulnerable, and women.

Note: Dollar ($) amounts are in U.S. dollars. CCT = conditional cash transfer; M&E = monitoring and evaluation; SSN = social safety net.

date on SSN reform has had observable achievements in Jordan (where the National Aid Fund has the best targeting accuracy in the region) and Morocco (where a CCT pilot, Tayssir, has been promoting rural children's school attendance, with positive results). Moving forward, although poverty pockets can in theory call for geographic targeting, lower leakage and greater coverage can be achieved through poverty-based targeting methods, such as the PMT, combined with massive outreach in these pockets (through a census of the poor) and on-demand application in the rest of the country. The short-run agenda for Jordan and Morocco is prioritizing interventions focused on children and increasing the cost-effectiveness of their SSN systems through consolidation of existing programs.

High vulnerability and child poverty in Egypt stand in stark contrast to the near-absence of SSN instruments; the road ahead for the most populous country in the region is to start creating SSN interventions that promote human capital and to initiate internal subsidy reforms that improve SSNs' internal efficiency.

High-HDI Countries

Finally, two upper-middle-income countries (Lebanon and Tunisia) and six high-income Gulf Cooperation Council (GCC) countries (Bahrain, Kuwait, Oman, Qatar, Saudi Arabia, and the United Arab Emirates) already have high or very high performance on human development outcomes. Despite these achievements, the performance of these countries relative to their level of development leaves scope for improvement. Indeed, for all these countries except Tunisia, HDI ranks are much worse than GNI per capita ranks because of lower life expectancy and educational attainment compared with respective development peers.

The main challenge in Lebanon, according to table 5.2, lies in regional disparities in terms of access to services and infrastructure, leading to relative deprivation in pockets of poverty. Until recently, SSN provision in Lebanon was very decentralized, with many poor people falling through the cracks of the system. In 2011, Lebanon moved toward building SSN capacity at the national level by developing the first national targeting database (NPTP), which uses a PMT. The forward-looking agenda is to institutionalize NPTP as the database used by multiple SSN programs across ministries, improve the implementation capacity of the Ministry of Social Affairs, and establish a coherent and sustainable SSN financing mechanism.

The challenge for Bahrain is high vulnerability to shocks. The country's heavy reliance on subsidies as an SSN does not allow for an effective crisis response, and the multitude of fragmented and categorically targeted cash transfer programs do not provide a reliable safety net for the vulnerable population. Bahrain has started the reform process by evaluating and benchmarking existing SSN programs; the road ahead includes establishing targeted SSNs with simple eligibility criteria and developing the SSN infrastructure. Apart from Bahrain, GCC countries currently are at an early stage of SSN reform, with many countries contemplating action on this agenda. Tunisia, facing the particular challenges of spatial disparities and high unemployment, has begun a pilot workfare program and a cash transfer program evaluation, but progress is yet to be made on creating SSNs that promote human capital and assets of the poor, establishing an SSN infrastructure, and enhancing the targeting of cash transfer programs.

Notes

1. For more information on the rationale for targeting and international experiences, see Grosh et al. (2008).
2. In Brazil, several verification systems are in place at the community level. Brazil establishes a budget for each community based on poverty measures. Potential beneficiaries are identified based on their reported income, and a cutoff level for the highest income that can be supported is established. The list of beneficiaries is published in the local newspaper for public review. Potential errors (inclusion and exclusion) are investigated and a new list is produced. Recertification is easily done on a regular basis.
3. See Castañeda et al. (2006) for a detailed description of how to implement a PMT targeting method.
4. A census of the poor is an alternative to on-demand application, whereby poverty maps are used to identify geographic areas with high poverty incidence, and applications in these areas are done in a census-like way (that is, by going door to door and filling out applications for potential beneficiaries).
5. For more information on the rationale for M&E and its foundation for a results-based culture in SSNs, see Rawlings (2010).
6. For more information on how to develop and implement impact evaluations, see Khandker, Koolwal, and Hussain (2010).
7. For more information on the results of evaluations of the Mexico CCT, see Levy (2006), and for other CCTs, see Fiszbein and Schady (2009).
8. For more information about New York's Social Innovation Fund, see http://www.nyc.gov/html/ceo/html/sif/sif.shtml. For more information about the U.S. federal program, see http://www.whitehouse.gov/administration/eop/sicp/initiatives/social-innovation-fund.
9. For more details on the creation of Mexico's CCT to promote the transition out of subsidies, see Levy and Rodriguez (2004) and Parker (2003).

References

Benhassine, N., F. Devoto, E. Duflo, P. Dupas, and V. Pouliquen. Forthcoming. "Unpacking the Effects of Conditional Cash Transfer Programs on Educational Investments: Experimental Evidence from Morocco on the Roles of Mothers and Conditions."

Castañeda, C., K. Lindert, B. de la Brière, L. Fernandez, C. Hubert, O. Larrafaga, M. Orozco, and R. Viquez. 2006. "Designing and Implementing Household Targeting Systems: Lessons from Latin America and the United States." World Bank Social Protection Discussion Paper 526, World Bank, Washington, DC.

Fiszbein, A., and N. Schady. 2009. *Conditional Cash Transfers: Reducing Present and Future Poverty*. World Bank Policy Research Report, World Bank, Washington, DC.

Government of Yemen, World Bank, and UNDP (United Nations Development Programme). 2007. *Yemen Poverty Assessment*. Report 53076, World Bank, Washington, DC.

Grosh, M., C. del Ninno, E. Tesluic, and A. Ouerghi. 2008. *For Protection & Promotion: The Design and Implementation of Effective Safety Nets*. Washington, DC: World Bank.

Guillaume, D., R. Zytek, and M. Reza Farzin. 2011. "Iran: The Chronicles of the Subsidy Reform." Working Paper 11/167, International Monetary Fund, Washington, DC.

Haddad, L., J. Hoddinott, and H. Alderman. 1997. *Intrahousehold Resource Allocation in Developing Countries: Models, Methods, and Policy*. Baltimore, MD: Johns Hopkins University Press.

Heltberg, R., S. L. Jorgensen, and P. B. Siegel. 2008. "Climate Change, Human Vulnerability, and Social Risk Management." Paper prepared for the Workshop on Social Aspects of Climate Change, World Bank, Washington, DC, March 5–6.

IEG (Independent Evaluation Group). 2011. *Social Safety Nets: An Evaluation of the World Bank Support, 2010–2011*. Washington, DC: World Bank.

Khandker, S., G. Koolwal, and A. Hussain. 2010. *Handbook on Impact Evaluation: Quantitative Methods and Practices*. Washington DC: World Bank.

Levy, S. 2006. *Progress against Poverty: Sustaining Mexico's Progresa-Oportunidades Program*. Washington, DC: Brookings Institution Press.

Levy, S., and E. Rodriguez. 2004. *Economic Crisis, Political Transition and Poverty Policy Reform: Mexico's Progresa-Oportunidades Program*. Poverty Dialogue Series. Washington, DC: Inter-American Development Bank.

Parker, S. 2003. "Mexico's Oportunidades Program." Case study summary, Shanghai Poverty Conference, World Bank, Washington, DC.

Quisumbing, A. R., and J. A. Maluccio. 2000. "Intrahousehold Allocation and Gender Relations: New Empirical Evidence from Four Developing Countries." Food Consumption and Nutrition Division Discussion Paper 84, International Food Policy Research Institute, Washington, DC.

Rawlings, L. 2010. "Monitoring and Evaluation: The Foundations for Results." Safety Nets Core Course presentation, World Bank, Washington, DC.

UNDP (United Nations Development Programme). 2011. *Sustainability and Equity: A Better Future for All*. Human Development Report 2011. New York, NY: UNDP.

World Bank. 2009. "Republic of Djibouti: Social Assistance Options to Combat Malnutrition." Unpublished Policy Note, Washington, DC.

———. 2012. *Safety Nets Work: During Crisis and Prosperity*. Report prepared for the Development Committee Meeting, Washington, DC, April 21.

Description of the Data Used for the Micro-Analysis

Country	Survey	Year	Description
Egypt, Arab. Rep.	Labor Market Panel Surveys (ELMPS)	2006	ELMPS was conducted by the Population Council and the Central Agency for Public Mobilization and Statistics (CAPMAS) with support of USAID (U.S. Agency for International Development), Egypt, and Ford Foundation.
	Household Income, Expenditures and Consumption Surveys (HIECS)	2005 and 2008/09	HIECS are carried out by CAPMAS.
.	Survey of Young People in Egypt (SYPE)	2009	The Population Council conducted SYPE in collaboration with the Egyptian Cabinet, Information and Decision Support Center.
Iraq	Iraq Household Socio-economic Survey (IHSES)	2006–07	The Ministry of Planning and Development Corporation and the Central Organization for Statistics and Information Technology undertook IHSES with the support of the World Bank.
Jordan	Demographic and Health Survey (DHS)	2009	The Jordan Population and Family Health Survey (JPFHS) was carried out by the Department of Statistics (DOS).
	Household Income and Expenditure Survey (HIES)	2010	The Jordan HIES is carried out by the Jordanian DOS.
	Jordan Labor Market Panel Survey (JLMPS)	2010	The JLMPS was carried out by the Economic Research Forum in cooperation with the National Center for Human Resource Development (NCHRD) and the Jordanian DOS.
	Jordan Gives Behavioral Experiment	2012	Behavioral experiment designed by the World Bank for this study, and conducted by the Center for Strategic Studies, University of Jordan, on a representative sample of the Jordanian middle class.
Lebanon	National Survey of Household Living Conditions (NHS)	2004	The NHS was conducted by the Ministry of Social Affairs, the Central Administration for Statistics and the United Nations Development Programme (UNDP) in 2004.
Morocco	The Morocco Household and Youth Survey (MHYS)	2010	The MHYS 2009–10 collected information from a nationally representative sample of 2,000 households across the country.
Syrian Arab Republic	Household Income and Expenditure Survey (HIES)	2004	The Syrian HIES 2003–04 was conducted by the Central Bureau for Statistics (CBS), Syria's official statistical agency.
Yemen, Rep.	Household Budget Survey (HBS)	2005–06	The HBS 2005–06 was conducted by the Central Statistical Organization of Yemen.

(table continued on next page)

Country	Survey	Year	Description
Multiple countries	Multiple Indicator Cluster Survey (MICS)	2006	The MICS is an initiative conducted by the United Nations Children's Fund (UNICEF) to assist countries in collecting and analyzing data to fill data gaps for monitoring the situation of children and women.
	MENA SPEAKS Survey	2012	New dataset designed for this study by the World Bank and Gallup Inc., and fielded as part of the Gallup World Poll Survey on nationally representative samples of the population of Egypt, Lebanon, Jordan, and Tunisia.
	MENA SSN Inventory	2008–11	New database of administrative SSN data, created for this study. A standard questionnaire template was formulated to obtain detailed information on SSN programs, including the number of beneficiaries and budgetary costs. The template was completed by triangulating desk reviews of relevant documents complemented by information obtained from government websites. This data collection was followed up by extensive consultations with World Bank focal points in the region and/or key informants in respective governments, including participants of the consultation workshops held in Beirut, Tunis, and Muscat. It is important to note that the data collected in the Inventory can differ from the latest official estimates. The World Bank envisions this Inventory as a continuing data collection effort to stimulate ongoing monitoring of SSNs in the region, and encourages submission of updated information to the authors.

Nonsubsidy SSN Programs Included in Household Survey Assessment

TABLE B.1

Nonsubsidy SSN Programs in Household Survey Assessment of Selected Middle Eastern and North African Countries, c. 2002–10

Type of transfer	Program name
Djibouti—Djibouti Household Survey (EDAM) 2002	
Cash transfers	Micro-credit from the government
	Micro-credit from the FSD
	Assistance for demobilized from ADETIP
	Assistance for demobilized from FSD
	Assistance for demobilized from the government
	Other direct assistance from FSD
	Other direct assistance from the government
Social assistance from religious organizations or NGOs	Micro-credit from United Nations
	Micro-credit from PRAC
	Assistance for demobilized from United Nations
	Assistance for demobilized from PRAC
	Disability assistance from other NGOs
	Other assistance from PRAC and United Nations
Egypt, Arab Rep.—Household Income, Expenditure, and Consumption Survey (HIECS) 2009	
Cash transfers	Government cash transfers
Social assistance from religious organizations or NGOs	Zakat assistance
	Other NGO assistance
Social pensions	Monthly Social Pension (Sadat Pension)
Iraq—Iraq Household Socio-Economic Survey (IHSES) 2007	
Cash transfers	In-kind assistance from the government
	Income from Social Protection network donations
	Income from gifts, donations, and compensation from the government
	Cash assistance from government sources
Fee waivers and vouchers for education	Education scholarships
Social assistance from religious organizations or NGOs	Income support from Zakat funds
Allowances	Vocational training allocations

(table continued on next page)

TABLE B.1

Continued

Type of transfer	Program name
Jordan—Household Income and Expenditure Survey (HIES) 2010	
Cash transfers	Transfers from National Aid Fund (NAF)
	Zakat transfers
Social assistance from religious organizations or NGOs	Cash transfers from NGOs
	Other transfers
Morocco—Morocco Household and Youth Survey (MHYS) 2010	
Cash transfers	Government assistance for weather shocks
	Government assistance for unexpected increase in commodity prices or fall in demand
	Government assistance for reduction in employment
	Government assistance for unexpected increase in input prices
	Government assistance for the loss of assets
	Government assistance for a cutoff in remittances
	Government assistance for the death of the main earner or other family members
	Government assistance for serious injury
	Government assistance for a big amount of dowry
	Government assistance for divorce or abandonment by husband
Housing subsidies	Villes sans bidonvilles
	Lodging for old people in Entraide Nationale and INDH
Micro-finance programs	Micro-finance programs in Mokawalati: ANAPEC and INDH
Fee waivers and vouchers for education	Dar Attalib
	Transport scolaire
	Cités universitaires & internats de l'enseignement supérieur
	Bourses de licence
	Bourses de 3e cycle
	Jardin d'enfant
	Pre-scholaire
	Cantines
	Second chance education program
	Literacy Program
	Other scholarships and housing assistance for students
Social assistance from religious organizations or NGOs	Disability assistance from NGO Association
	NGO assistance for an unexpected increase in commodity prices or fall in demand
	Old people housing assistance from NGOs
	NGO assistance for reduction in employment or loss of job
	NGO assistance for an unexpected increase in input prices
	NGO assistance for the loss of assets
	NGO assistance for a cutoff in remittances
	NGO assistance for the death of the main earner or other family members
	NGO assistance for serious injury
	NGO assistance for a big amount of dowry
	NGO assistance for divorce or abandonment by husband
	NGO assistance for weather shocks

TABLE B.1

Continued

Type of transfer	Program name
West Bank and Gaza—Expenditure and Consumption Survey (ECS) 2009	
Cash transfers	Cash assistance from Social Affairs
	Cash assistance from other Palestinian Authority foundations
	Cash assistance from political parties
	Cash assistance from international organizations
	Cash assistance from UNRWA
	Cash assistance from other Arab countries
Social assistance from religious organizations or NGOs	Zakat assistance
	Assistance from charities
	Assistance from labor unions
	Assistance from national banks
	Assistance from the local committee
	Other NGO aid
Yemen, Rep.—Household Budget Survey (HBS) 2005/06	
Cash transfers	Transfers from the Social Security Fund
	Transfers from the Social Welfare Fund
	Transfers from the General Authority for the care of Martyrs' families
	Transfers from the fund of promotion of agriculture and fishing
	Transfers from Tribes Authority Affairs
	Medicine funds for disabled
	Transfers from other international and local programs
Social assistance from religious organizations or NGOs	Assistance received from charity organizations

Note: ADETIP = Djiboutian Agency for the Implementation of Public Works (*Agence Djiboutienne d'Exécution de Travaux d'Intérêt Public*); ANAPEC = National Agency for the Promotion of Employment and Competences (*Agence nationale de promotion de l'emploi et des competences*); EDAM = Djibouti Household Survey (*Enquete Djiboutienne Auprès des Ménages*); FSD = Social Development Fund (*Fonds Social de Développement*); INDH = National initiative for human development (*L'initiative nationale pour le développement humain*); NGO = nongovernmental organization; PRAC = Reinsertion program for demobilized personnel; SSN = social safety net; UNRWA = United Nations Relief and Works Agency for Palestine Refugees in the Near East.

SSN Programs in MENA SSN Inventory

TABLE C.1

Middle East and North Africa SSN Inventory, c. 2008–11

Country	Program name	Program type	Targeting method	Number of beneficiaries (individuals)[a]	Expenditure (LCUs, millions)[b]	Year
Bahrain	Food, water, electricity, and oil and gas subsidies	Price subsidies and ration cards	Universal	—	868.4	2011[c]
Djibouti	Cash transfers (Zakat)	Cash transfers	Categorical	n.a.	n.a.	n.a.
	Food distribution program	Food and other in-kind transfers	Geographical	n.a.	n.a.	n.a.
	Scholarships for education	Fee waivers, education, and health benefits	Categorical	n.a.	n.a.	n.a.
	School feeding program	Food and other in-kind transfers	Geographical	n.a.	n.a.	n.a.
Egypt, Arab. Rep.	*Baladi* bread subsidy	Price subsidies and ration cards	Universal	—	n.a.	2010
	Child cash assistance	Cash transfers	Categorical	43,562	49.4	2010
	Cooking oil ration card	Price subsidies and ration cards	Universal	—	n.a.	2010
	Education grant	Fee waivers, education, and health benefits	Categorical	624,996	189.7	2010[d]
	Emergency assistance for former public employees	Cash transfers	Categorical	5,927	2.1	2010
	Fuel subsidy (gasoline, diesel, LPG, kerosene, natural gas)	Price subsidies and ration cards	Universal	—	n.a.	2010
	Martyr's family cash assistance	Cash transfers	Categorical	n.a.	n.a.	n.a.
	Micro grants	Cash transfers	Categorical	19,899	40.0	2010
	Military family assistance	Cash transfers	Categorical	n.a.	n.a.	n.a.
	Rice ration card	Price subsidies and ration cards	Universal	—	n.a.	2010
	Monthly assistance from social security to poor families	Cash transfers	Categorical	105,533	135.0	2010
	Shock assistance	Cash transfers	Categorical	60,328	68.4	2010
	Monthly social pension (Sadat Pension)	Cash transfers	Categorical	1,180,000	1,570.0	2010
	Sugar ration card	Price subsidies and ration cards	Universal	—	n.a.	2010
	Temporary circumstantial assistance	Cash transfers	Categorical	132,877	36.6	2010

(table continued on next page)

TABLE C.1

Continued

Country	Program name	Program type	Targeting method	Number of beneficiaries (individuals)[a]	Expenditure (LCUs, millions)[b]	Year
Iraq	Ration cards	Price subsidies and ration cards	Universal	—	5,810,000.0	2009
	Social Safety Net (Social Protection Network)	Cash transfers	Categorical	900,000	929,600.0	2009
Jordan	Bread or wheat flour subsidy	Price subsidies and ration cards	Universal	—	92.3	2009
	Community projects	Others	Geographical	n.a.	n.a.	n.a.
	Electricity subsidy	Price subsidies and ration cards	Universal	—	49.2	2009
	Emergency assistance	Cash transfers	Categorical	7,290	0.2	2009
	Enhanced Productivity Program	Micro-credit and income-generating activities	Geographical	950	62.9	2009
	Food Security Program	Food and other in-kind transfers	Means tested	n.a.	n.a.	n.a.
	Health insurance for poor	Fee waivers, education, and health benefits	Means tested	n.a.	n.a.	n.a.
	Housing for the poor	Housing	Means tested	n.a.	2.4	2009
	Micro-credit	Micro-credit and income-generating activities	Geographical	n.a.	n.a.	n.a.
	Micro-credit	Micro-credit and income-generating activities	Geographical	n.a.	n.a.	n.a.
	Micro-credit	Micro-credit and income-generating activities	Self-targeting	n.a.	n.a.	n.a.
	Micro-credit	Micro-credit and income-generating activities	Self-targeting	n.a.	n.a.	n.a.
	Micro-credit	Micro-credit and income-generating activities	Means tested	n.a.	n.a.	n.a.
	Micro-credit	Micro-credit and income-generating activities	Self-targeting	n.a.	n.a.	n.a.
	National Aid Fund assistance	Cash transfers	Means tested	441,126	83.7	2009
	National Company for Employment and Training	Training	Self-targeting	4,000	20.0	2009
	Petroleum subsidy	Price subsidies and ration cards	Universal	—	41.0	2009
	School nutrition	Food and other in-kind transfers	Geographical	530,000	18.6	2009
	Student Support Program	Fee waivers, education, and health benefits	Means tested	n.a.	1.0	2009
	Vocational Training Center	Training	Self-targeting	10,000	13.2	2009
	Water subsidy	Price subsidies and ration cards	Universal	—	108.7	2009
	Zakat assistance	Cash transfers	Means tested	70,800	10.7	2009
Lebanon	Agricultural exports subsidy ("Export Plus")	Price subsidies and ration cards	Categorical	n.a.	31,650.0	2010
	Bread subsidy (consumer)	Price subsidies and ration cards	Universal	—	42,000.0	2010
	Disability Training or Support Program	Fee waivers, education, and health benefits	Categorical	30,147	9,143.0	2010[d]
	Education: scholarships	Fee waivers, education, and health benefits	Categorical	200,000	450.0	2009[c]

Country	Program	Benefit type	Targeting		Amount	Year
	Education allowance	Fee waivers, education, and health benefits	Categorical	n.a.	154,500.0	2010
	Health Fee Waivers in Public and Private Hospitals (through Ministry of Public Health)	Fee waivers, education, and health benefits	Categorical	2,113,500	322,500.0	2010[e]
	Mazout diesel subsidy	Price subsidies and ration cards	Universal	—	45,000.0	2010
	National Poverty Targeting Program (NPTP)	Fee waivers, education, and health benefits	PMT	n.a.	1,315.0	2010
	Population and development program	Training	Geographical	100	202.5	2010
	Tobacco subsidy	Price subsidies and ration cards	Universal	—	45,000.0	2008
	Transfer to Electricité du Liban (EdL)	Price subsidies and ration cards	Not specified	n.a.	1,800.0	2010
	Vocational training programs	Training	Geographical	50	206.0	2010
	Welfare program	Not specified	Not specified	n.a.	100,500.0	2010
	Wheat subsidy (producers)	Price subsidies and ration cards	Categorical	n.a.	18,000.0	2010
Morocco	Alphabetization of Adults (illiteracy programs)	Fee waivers, education, and health benefits	Categorical	394,000	144.0	2008[f]
	Flour subsidy	Price subsidies and ration cards	Geographical	n.a.	4,886.0	2008
	Fuel subsidy	Price subsidies and ration cards	Universal	—	27,014.0	2008
	Housing of Entraide Nationale	Fee waivers, education, and health benefits	Categorical	59,000	12.0	2008
	Idmaj	Price subsidies and ration cards	Categorical	46,000	149.0	2008
	Income-generating activities of Agence de Developpment Sociale	Micro-credit and income-generating activities	Geographical	6,000	n.a.	2008
	INDH: Program against poverty in rural areas	Others	Geographical	3,800,000	611.0	2008
	INDH: Program against social exclusion in urban areas	Others	Geographical	2,500,000	1,094.0	2008
	INDH: Program for Fighting Precariousness	Others	Categorical	50,000	583.0	2008
	INDH: Transversal Program	Others	Geographical	n.a.	816.0	2008
	Promotion Nationale	Workfare programs	Self-targeting	45,000	1,000.0	2009
	RAMED: Regime d'Assistance Medicale	Fee waivers, education, and health benefits	PMT	151,000	138.0	2009[g]
	School feeding program "canteens" and housing	Food and other in-kind transfers	Self-targeting	1,039,100	815.0	2008
	School supplies program	Food and other in-kind transfers	Categorical	1,273,800	437.0	2008
	Sugar subsidy	Price subsidies and ration cards	Universal	—	2,854.0	2008
	Tayssir	Cash transfers	Geographical	80,000	149.0	2009
	Villes Sans Bidonvilles (Cities without Slums)	Housing	Geographical	136,000	220.0	2009[g]
Syrian Arab Republic	Food and fuel subsidies	Price subsidies and ration cards	Universal	—	386,766.0	2010
	Public works program	Cash transfers	Categorical	n.a.	13,813.1	2010
	Social Welfare Fund	Cash transfers	Categorical	n.a.	13,813.1	2010

(table continued on next page)

TABLE C.1

Continued

Country	Program name	Program type	Targeting method	Number of beneficiaries (individuals)[a]	Expenditure (LCUs, millions)[b]	Year
Tunisia	Subsidized health card program	Fee waivers, education, and health benefits	Does Not specify	2,312,000	70.0	2011
	Program allocation of handicap card	Others	Categorical	181,000	12.0	2011
	Defense program and social integration	Training	Categorical	n.a.	1.0	2011
	Programme National d'Aide aux Familles Nécessiteuses (PNAFN): Cash transfers	Cash transfers	Means tested	940,000	292.0	2011
	Programme National d'Aide aux Familles Nécessiteuses (PNAFN): health cards	Fee waivers, education, and health benefits	Means tested	940,000	39.0	2011
	Social counseling, child care, and adult education programs	Fee waivers, education, and health benefits	Categorical	n.a.	9.0	2011
West Bank and Gaza	Cash Transfer Program (CTP)	Cash transfers	PMT	365,466	239.0	2010
	Economic Empowerment Program (DEEP)	Micro-credit and income-generating activities	PMT	12,642	6.8	2010
	Emergency Assistance program	Cash transfers	Categorical	14,502	10.4	2010
	Food Parcels Program (WFP)	Food and other in-kind transfers	PMT	211,510	140.7	2010
	Orphans Sponsorship Program	Cash transfers	Categorical	15,318	10.3	2010
	The Disabled Rehabilitation Fund	Cash transfers	Categorical	858	2.5	2010
Yemen, Rep.	Fund for Productive Families	Micro-credit and income-generating activities	Categorical	n.a.	n.a.	n.a.
	Agricultural and Fish Production Promotion Fund	Micro-credit and income-generating activities	Geographical	n.a.	n.a.	n.a.
	Disability Fund	Fee waivers, education, and health benefits	Categorical	n.a.	2,700.0	2009
	Petroleum subsidies	Price subsidies and ration cards	Universal	—	327,000.0	2009
	Public Works Project	Workfare programs	Geographical	6,584,000	19.1	2009[e]
	Social Fund for Development	Workfare programs	Geographical	6,472,402	30,008.6	2009[e]
	Social Welfare Fund	Cash transfers	PMT	7,911,585	40,829.0	2009[e]

Note: INDH = National initiative for human development (*L'Initiative nationale pour le développement humain*); LCU = local currency unit. Nonsubsidy SSN data for Bahrain, Kuwait, and Saudi Arabia are not presented in this table for confidentiality reasons; LPG = liquefied petroleum gas; PMT = proxy means testing; RAMED = *Regime d'Assistance Medicale*; SSN = social safety net; — = not available; n.a. = not applicable.

a. Household figures have been converted into individuals using the latest household survey data.

b. US$ figures were converted into LCUs using the exchange rate on May 30, 2012.

c. Beneficiaries year is 2010.

d. Beneficiaries year is 2009.

e. Beneficiaries year is 2011.

f. Beneficiaries year is 2007.

g. Beneficiaries year is 2008.

www.ingramcontent.com/pod-product-compliance
Lightning Source LLC
Chambersburg PA
CBHW080230270326
41926CB00020B/4199